Islamic Extremism in Kuwait

This book is the first to provide a complete overview of Islamic extremism in Kuwait. It traces the development of Islamist fundamentalist groups in Kuwait, both Shi'ite and Sunni, from the beginning of the twentieth century. It outlines the nature and origins of the many different groups, considers their ideology and organization, shows how their activities are intertwined with the wider economy, society and politics to the extent that they are now a strong part of society, and discusses their armed activities, including terrorist activities. Although focusing on Kuwait, it includes coverage of the activities of Islamist groups in other Gulf States. It also discusses the relationship between ruling families and Islamist political groups, thereby demonstrating that the intertwining of Islamic ideology and armed activities with politics is not a new development in the region.

Falah Abdullah al-Mdaires is Professor in the Department of Political Science at Kuwait University.

Durham Modern Middle East and Islamic World Series
Series Editor: Anoushiravan Ehteshami
University of Durham

Islamic Extremism in Kuwait

From the Muslim Brotherhood to
al-Qaeda and other Islamist
political groups

Falah Abdullah al-Mdaires

Routledge
Taylor & Francis Group

LONDON AND NEW YORK

First published 2010
by Routledge
2 Park Square, Milton Park, Abingdon, Oxfordshire OX14 4RN

Simultaneously published in the USA and Canada
by Routledge
711 Third Avenue, New York, NY 10017

First issued in paperback 2014

*Routledge is an imprint of the Taylor & Francis Group,
an informa business*

Typeset in Times by
RefineCatch Limited, Bungay, Suffolk

British Library Cataloguing in Publication Data
A catalogue record for this book is available
from the British Library

Library of Congress Cataloging-in-Publication Data
Almdaires, Falah Abdullah.
Islamist extremism in Kuwait : from the Muslim Brotherhood to
Al-Qaeda and other Islamist political groups / Falah Abdullah
Almdaires.
p. cm.—(Durham modern Middle East and Islamic world series ; 17)
Includes bibliographical references and index.
1. Islamic fundamentalism—Kuwait—History. 2. Jama'at al-Ikhwan
al-Muslimin (Kuwait) 3. Qaida (Organization)
4. Islam—Kuwait—History—20th century.
5. Islam—Kuwait—History—21st century. I. Title.
BP63.K9A46 2010
322'.1095367—dc22

2009041676

ISBN 13: 978-1-138-86299-9 (pbk)
ISBN 13: 978-0-415-56719-0 (hbk)

To my best friend
'Abdul-Rahman al-Na'aimi, the historical leader of the Popular Front in
Bahrain, who struggled against oppression and fought for freedom
throughout his life, and a true brother who backed me up throughout my
life. He is still fighting in a different way – this illness which we all hope he
will defeat quickly.

Contents

Acknowledgements

First of all my great thanks to my wife, Fotouh, my daughter Haya and my son 'Abdullah who supported and encouraged me to finish this book.

I am also grateful to Professor Ahmad al-Bagdadi, whose remarks were of great importance for this work. I also thank my friend Hamza Alyan from al-Qabas Information Center for his co-operation, Professor Qanim al-Najjar and Dr. 'Abdulwahab al-Musalam for their help.

Abbreviations

AAIA	Aden Abyan Islamic Army
AM	Adherence Movement
ANM	Arab Nationalist Movement
AUB	American University of Beirut
BIFM	Bahrain Islamic Freedom Movement
CIA	Central Intelligence Agency
CIRM	Clearing the Islamic Ranks Movement
CNY	Constitutional National Youth
CSG	Consultative Supporters Group
CSM	Committee for Serving al-Mahdi
DJM	Democracy and Justice Movement
DNPG	Defending the Nation's Principles Gathering
DRO	Dawn Revolutionary Organization
FKC	Free Kuwaiti Center
FKPV	Free Kuwaiti People Voice
FSM	Freedom Supporters Movement
GCC	Gulf Cooperation Council
GEC	Group of Ethical Control
HMC	Hussein Martyrs Committees
ICM	Islamic Constitutional Movement
ICP	Islamic Call Party
IFLB	Islamic Front for the Liberation of Bahrain
IGPC	Islamic Group for Preaching and Combat
IGS	Islamic Guidance Society
IHRS	Islamic Heritage Revival Society
IJG	Islamic Jihad Group
IPG	Islamic Popular Gathering
INC	Islamic National Coalition
INCM	Islamic National Consensus Movement
IROAP	Islamic Revolution Organization in the Arabian Peninsula
ISCGK	Islamic Shi'ite Clerics Gathering in Kuwait
ISMG	Imam al-Sadiq Mosque Group
JPG	Justice and Peace Gathering

KDF	Kuwaiti Democratic Forum
KIL	Kuwaiti Islamic League
KNG	Kuwaiti Nationalist Gathering
KPDM	Kuwaiti Progressive Democratic Movement
LP	Liberation Party
MBG	Muslim Brotherhood Group
MP	Member of Parliament
MVM	Missionaries Vanguard Movement
NCG	National Charter Gathering
NDA	National Democratic Alliance
NG	Notification Group
NGC	National Groups Coalition
NHMG	National Humanitarian Message Gathering
NIA	National Islamic Alliance
NIC	National Islamic Coalition
NIGLL	National Independent Gathering for Love and Life
NP	Nation Party
NUKS	National Union of Kuwait Students
PF	Popular Front
PGB	Party of God – Bahrain
PGCP	People's General Congress Party
PGH	Party of God – Hijaz
PGK	Party of God – Kuwait
SCIRIKO	Supreme Council for Islamic Revolution in Iraq – Kuwait Organization
SCS	Social Culture Society
SG	Salafiah Group
SIG	Salafi Islamic Gathering
SM	Salafiah Movement
SPG	Shi'ites Principles Gathering
SRS	Social Reform Society
SSG	Sayyed Shirazi Group
SSM	Scientific Salafiah Movement
SYC	Salafiah Youth Call
VG	Virtue Gathering
YFG	Youth Forum Group
YRG	Yemen Reform Group
YSP	Yemen Socialist Party
ZHG	Zhara House Gathering

Introduction

The history of the Islamist political groups extends from the late 1920s until now. It is a scattered history that is limited to particular groups. Most people know general information about the Muslim Brotherhood in Egypt, but what about the other groups? What about the Shi'ite groups, which have an almost unknown history and information? What about their social and political role in the Gulf region? How were they founded? How did they work in the past? How do they work today at the political, social and organizational level? How do they recruit followers? How do they operate within communities and political systems? What types of terrorist operation are carried out by the Shi'ite, Sunni and other groups, and why? These are just a few questions that we will try to answer in this study about the Islamist political groups in Kuwait since the 1950s.

This study tries to shed some light on the nature of intellectual organizational activity of both Shi'ite and Sunni groups operating in Kuwait, on their origins and nature, on the newspapers and magazines that carry their ideologies, and how they have evolved to become a strong part of society. Which groups have armed wings in the organizational structure, and why? And what was the fate of each of these groups? Some of them have political agendas and strong popular support throughout the Kuwaiti governorates, such as the Muslim Brotherhood Group, Salafiah Group, Shirazi Group, Salafiah Movement, Islamic Popular Gathering and Islamic National Coalition. Others have no political agenda, official documentation or even permanent headquarters, while a few others are a single-family organization. These mini-groups command limited membership, such as Shi'ites Principles Gathering, Freedom Supporters Movement, Clearing the Islamic Ranks Movement, Consultative Supporters Group, and Democracy and Justice Movement. It is natural for the Muslim society of Kuwait, being dominated by conservative tribal traditions, to find fertile ground among the religious public segments and support and backing of the regime, which has exploited the religious right to its advantage in order to clamp down on its leftist and liberal foes. There is no doubt enlightenment has to be shed on the terrorist side, which few people know about, not only because of the lack of information, but also because most of this information is either difficult to access or it is scattered in multiple references that are not easily accessible by the reader. This study tries as much as possible to gather such information and present it in a scientific way, as far as possible, so that even the ordinary reader can follow and identify the nature of the groups belonging to different ideologies, their role in society and the practices carried out by some that are terrorist groups and some that are not, and why, when and how. Moreover, without going into the details of traditional information, what is the value of any study that does not give the reader new information? What is new? This is a question that can be raised by any reader, while at the same time the Arab arena is filled with books on these Islamic religious groups. Simply, the answer lies in the armed side of these groups. This new side is unfamiliar to the Gulf communities, which did not use any type of weapons in domestic disputes, both on the social level or in relation to the political system. Yes, there are armed conflicts within the ruling families, but it is rare, and these conflicts have mostly stopped since the ruling families received constitutional backing and have become legitimate, but we never heard or read that Gulf states solved their conflicts by the use of religious Takfir (excommunication). What is not known for these societies and political systems in the Gulf region is the way Islam has been intertwined with all social, economic and political arenas and has been used as an ideology instead of a religion. The harsh Wahhabi movement's methods of long ago, for the most part, have ceased, and the armed fundamentalist religious groups are trying to turn the society backwards. Unfortunately, they have succeeded in achieving their objectives to a large extent, at least for the time being. However, there are equally powerful Islamic groups that do not promote violence.

The social and political conflicts are features of communities, particularly those that are not afraid of struggle. Today, in the age of globalization, 'terrorism' has also become global. The struggle is comprehensive not only between political regimes and terrorist groups, but also between the community and these groups. Can we say that it is the conflict of survival and existence? The answer is definitely yes.

Briefly, the study provides detailed information about the Islamist political groups and some that have terrorist roles in the Arab states of the Gulf. The study does not provide solutions to solve this problem, which is close to becoming a tragedy, but it is a gateway that provides the necessary information of the intellectual roots of the crisis that has swept Gulf society. It is hoped that it might be a gateway to other studies, which may help to shed light on more information and submit proposals for solutions to the current 'terrorist' crisis that is sweeping not only the Gulf area, but also the entire world.

1 The roots of the Islamist political groups

Kuwait witnessed both extremist and tolerant religious movements in the beginning of the last century, before the emergence of the Islamist political groups such as Jam'at al-Ikhwan al-Muslimin (the Muslim Brotherhood Group (MBG)), Hizb al-Tahrir (The Liberation Party (LP)), al-Jama'ah al-Salafiah (The Salafiah Group (SG)), and the Shi'ite groups in the political arena of Kuwait. The supporters of the tolerant religious movement contributed significantly to the development of Kuwaiti society socially, economically and politically. Among these were scholars and merchants who have been affected by Arab religious reformers, such as Jamal al-Din al-Afagani, Mohammad 'Abduh, 'Abdul-Rahman al-Kawakiby, and Rashid Rida.[1] The Sheikh 'Abdul-'Aziz al-Rashaid,[2] Sheikh Yousef Bin 'Isa al-Qina'i,[3] Farhan al-Khalid, Yasin al-Tabtabae, Khalid al-'Adsani, Sheikh Ahmad Khamis al-Khalaf, and others, were the Kuwaiti reformers who were impressed by the Arab reformers movement in the Arab countries, and have sought to try to achieve those same reforms in Kuwaiti society.

The Kuwaitis were lucky because, between 1910 and 1927, a number of Arab reformers came to Kuwait; among them were Rashid Rida, 'Abdul-'Aziz al-Tha 'aliby, Mohammad al-Shanqiti and Hafiz Wahba. These particular reformers played a substantial role in preparing the Kuwaitis' minds for the reform movements that followed slowly afterwards,[4] through their speeches in the mosques and their visits to places where the Kuwaitis used to gather every day to exchange ideas. The Kuwaitis were affected by these reformers to a great extent. Al-Rashaid tells us about those events by saying:

> The free ideas and the precious advice which has been spread in Kuwait by those well educated foreigners had a very strong impact on the Kuwaitis, by criticizing the conservative people and preaching their modern ideas.[5]

As a result, in 1913, the first charitable society was founded by Farhan al-Khalid, who was not content with the inadequate provision of education and health systems in Kuwait. In the statement that was distributed inviting the notables to join the society, the objectives of the charity were: to send students to the Islamic societies in the modern Arab countries and to pay their expenses; to request an Islamic instructor to speak to the public and advise them; to request a doctor and a chemist to treat the poor people free of charge; and to distribute water, the most important necessity in the lives of the people.[6]

From these targets we notice that the members of the charitable society realized the country's backwardness, which prevented participation of the citizens. Therefore, a priority was to send students abroad to continue their higher education while at the same time retaining their Islamic and Arabic culture, and then return home carrying new ideas for the benefit of their country. Another of its public aims was to provide for the health of the people. According to 'Abdullah al-Nuri, one of its unpublished aims was to resist the missionary movement in Kuwait and the Gulf states.[7] The people were strongly opposed to the presence of the American mission in Kuwait because of their fears of the ideas that this mission could spread.

The job of teaching in this society was given to Mohammad al-Shanqiti, but this structured society did not last long because the ruler Sheikh Mubarak al-Sabah suspected that the teachers had leanings towards the Ottoman Empire, so he closed the society, silencing the teachers' voices.[8]

Rashid Rida, the owner of *Majallat al-Manar* (*al-Manar Journal*), had a particularly strong influence on the Kuwaitis, who started to show a desire to study modern science (previously forbidden). The number of Kuwaitis subscribing to Majallat al-Manar increased from a handful to a significant number.[9]

Besides the Egyptian, Iraqi and Syrian press, al-Rashaid published the first journal in Kuwait history in 1928, naming it *Majallat al-Kuwait* (*Kuwait Journal*) to spread his reformative ideas. He sent for Arab writers who were engaged in the reform movement in the Arab region to participate by writing articles in the journal. Some articles were published by Shakib Arslan, Rashid Rida, Mohammad al-Alusy, 'Abdul-Qadir al-Maghribi, 'Abdul-'Aziz al-Tha 'aliby, and others amongst the famous Arab men of letters. His vision for the unity of thought had led him to the belief in the necessity of filling the gap between the ideological development in some Arab countries and the cultural stagnation in Kuwait at that time.[10] This journal continued for several years, although the conservatives provoked the public against it, claiming that its owner did not believe in God. One of their religious men, 'Abdul-'Aziz al-'Alajy, announced that:

> The killing of three Kuwaiti people is the price for entering heaven without any questions.[11]

Al-Rashaid was one of these. In fact, the most important difficulties which faced *Majallat al-Kuwait* was the opposition of those people who saw the journal as a danger to the Islamic religion and society.[12] Kuwait was living in social inertia and the people were asking whether it was right to learn foreign languages, read newspapers and magazines or not. For example, al-Rashaid entered into an argument with the conservatives over whether the earth was a sphere or not; conservatives at that time thought that whoever believed that the earth was a sphere was a Kafir (unbeliever).[13]

From this it is apparent that conflict was likely to occur between Kuwaitis because of the dissemination of newspapers and magazines.[14] Some people tried to kill Rashid Rida in his visit to Kuwait.[15] These reformers had adopted the ideas of the Arabic awakening and they wanted it to spread among their people, but they faced so many difficulties from the conservatives who stood against them without any knowledge of their own religion. So *Majallat al-Kuwait* stopped for a while and Kuwait remained without a local press until the end of 1946.

The Kuwaiti reformers called for the establishment of schools and the education of modern science. Prior to World War I, there were no secular schools in either Kuwait or its neighbors, the Arabian Gulf sheikhdoms, and no modern education as it is now known. The majority of the Kuwaiti population was uneducated and unable to read or write, with the exception of a very small portion, who were from wealthy families and had the chance of acquiring some rudiments of learning sufficient to meet the needs of government, trade or diving business. The majority of the people did not have time to join the Kuttab where they could learn how to read and write because most of them were the children of divers who would follow their fathers to go diving to learn the job, which was their only way to earn a living. A diver who spent almost all the year at sea could not send his children to Kuttab.[16]

In the Kuttab, students learned how to read the Quran and had some instruction in the Arabic language and mathematics.[17] Madrasat Mula Marshad (Mula Marshad School), one of the famous Kuttab at which many Kuwaitis finished their studies, was closed in the late 1950s, thus bringing to an end old-fashioned education and making way for a modern one.

After World War I and at the beginning of the modern Arab awakening, the first public school in Kuwait was created – Madrasat al-Mubarakia (al-Mubarakia School). Behind the establishment of this school was Yasin al-Tabtabae, who was one of the pioneers of modernization in Kuwait. He took advantage of the celebration of the Prophet Mohammad's birthday in 1911 to speak to the public about education in Islam, explaining how the Prophet Mohammad encouraged it, and arguing that we have to follow our prophet's example by opening new schools to save the nation from backwardness. Hence, Islam was in favor of education, not against it. At the end of the speech, the public was very impressed.[18]

Some Arab reformers had their first experience of teaching in the al-Mubarakia school, including Hafiz Wahba and Mohammad al-Shanqiti. Some of the reformers worked as teachers in al-Mubarakia and al-Ahmadia schools. Hence, many Kuwaitis graduating from there were influenced by the reform movement.

The Kuwaiti reformers started to build more schools in addition to the al-Mubarakia school; this experiment in the organization of education was totally public.[19] The Kuwaiti reformers faced many problems in modernizing education in their country against the opposition of conservatives. The reformers, in trying to develop education in the al-Mubarakia school, wanted to bring teachers from the Egyptian institutes and include English language and geography in the educational program, exacerbating the conflict with the conservatives. At the head of the conservative group was the religious Sheikh Ahmad Noor al-Farasi and Sheikh 'Abdul-'Aziz al-'Alajy, who said that education should be conducted by religious sheikhs, such as Sheikh 'Abdullah Khalaf and Sheikh Mahmud, the teacher of the Quran.[20] Sheikh 'Abdul-'Aziz al-'Alajy expressed very reactionary ideas and thought that the new understanding of religion could be dangerous and should be prevented.

Finally, the reformers succeeded in their attempt by leaving the al-Mubarakia school to the conservatives and establishing a new school, called Madrasat al-Ahmadiya lil Nash'a al-Wataniya (al-Ahmadia School for the National Youth). It was a free school where no one could interfere in its affairs. They introduced a new system for the school, which was modern to some extent. Particularly, they recruited Egyptian teachers who were highly educated and included geography and any science that would be useful for the society.[21]

The reformers also built a third school, named Madrasat al-Sa'ada (The Happiness School), for the poor people. It was established in 1924 by Shamlan bin 'Ali, who was a wealthy pearl merchant.[22] These schools were not recognized by the opposition of the extremist religious movement; they even described the schools as Christian schools.[23] Being faced by major opposition, supporters of the extremist religious movement of Sheikh al-'Alajy and Sheikh al-Farisi and others – who considered modern education such as foreign languages and geography to be against Islam and that education must be limited to keeping the Quran only with writing and reading – caused provocation of the Kuwaiti people against the reformers.[24]

In 1920, the reformers continued the struggle for a better society. They established al-Nadi al-Adabi (the Literary Club), which became the ideal place for poets and men of letters to read magazines and newspapers and hold seminars and lectures. From the first years of the establishment of this club, a cultural movement took place among the young. About 100 people were members of this club. A selection of scientific and literary lectures were held that had a very strong influence on Kuwaiti society.[25] Two years later al-Nadi al-Adabi was converted into a political club under the impact of the ideological and political movement in Egypt. The members of the club were influenced by the attitudes of the Egyptian parties, such as Hizb al-Wafd (al-Wafd Party) and al-Hizb al-Watani (the Nationalist Party), and Egyptian leaders, such as Mustafa Kamil and Sa'd Zaghlul through the Egyptian press, such as al-Ahram, al-Balagh and al-Seyassah al-'Usbu 'iya.[26]

The appeal of Qasim Amin, Huda Sha 'rawi and Safiya Zaghlul in Egypt for the freedom of women was also present in the minds of the Kuwaiti reformers. The members of the Literary Club spread the revolutionary ideas that had been announced by the Women's Liberation Movement in Egypt.[27] The members of the club also expressed their opinions during discussions of public problems.

Al-Nadi al-Adabi did not last long; after a few years it was closed by the ruling authority when it became obvious how dangerous it was in developing political and cultural consciousness in the country. In spite of this, the reformers were back in 1923 and formed al-Maktaba al-Ahliya (the Public Library) to be a meeting place for educating people. It was run by the people who donated most of the books and magazines and subscribed to al-Ahram and al-Muqatam newspapers.[28]

These cultural tribunes did not last long because they were usually suppressed, either by the authorities or by conservatives who looked on the reading of modern books and newspapers as the devil's work. However, the reformers did not give up; they used the Diwan for meetings every night. The Diwan is a room attached to the house where men who know each other's social position usually meet. This acts as a social institution with a deep effectiveness on the Kuwaiti society as they discuss political, social and economic issues of the day. The Diwan in Kuwait is an intricate part of Kuwaiti life, almost like a club, as it is the social center for the elite, and it still plays the same role today. Some of the owners of the Diwan used to be men of letters, so that books were read and lectures and seminars were held in their Diwans. Some of these Diwans contain an enormous number of books on different subjects: literature, politics, religion and science, so much so that many Arab reformers used to attend the Diwans on their visits to Kuwait.

As the Kuwaiti reformers belonging to the tolerant religious stream played a significant role in the intellectual and cultural development of Kuwaiti society, they also contributed to the political life in Kuwait by participating in the membership of the first Consultative Council, founded in 1921 during the reign of Sheikh Ahmad al-Jaber al-Sabah. Sheikh Yousef Bin 'Isa al-Qina'i and Sheikh 'Abdul-'Aziz al-Rashaid were the most prominent members belonging to this movement, thus they became part of the council. The tolerant religious reformers played a major role in the political reformation movement of 1938, which led to the foundation of the Legislative Council, which is the first, not only in Kuwait but also in the whole Arabian Peninsula and Gulf region. Sheikh al-Qina'i and Sheikh Ahmad Khamis al-Khalaf were members of this council.[29]

The reformers of the tolerant religious movement did not limit their activities to the political reforms in Kuwait; they also supported Arab issues. In 1933, they sent a letter signed in the name of al-Shabiba al-Kuwaitiyah (the Kuwaiti Youth) to the political agent in Kuwait, saying:

> We on behalf of all our old men and young men and on behalf of our gentle women folk, beg to lay before your Excellency, our sharp protest

against His Majesty's Government's methods towards our brothers, the Arabs of Palestine, which no nation could take any sort of pride in as your government does. Indeed, such treatment may also estrange the world from entering under your protection, which we wish to be strong and worthy. Be very sure that such unjust treatment will cause seventy million Arabs, and three hundred and fifty million of Mohammedans . . . await the hour of vengeance, for, verily everything has an end, and time will inevitably turn against the cruel. We, . . . shall thank you to refer our protest to Your High Government.[30]

In the mid-1930s, there were rebellions in Palestine, the most famous one being in 1936, which generated a very strong, enthusiastic reaction among Kuwaitis. For this reason, they formed Lajnat October (October Committee) in 1933 with the co-operation of the youth from the merchant class, who were greatly concerned with the events taking place in Palestine. This was the first committee formed in Kuwait to support the Palestinian people and Sheikh al-Qina'i was one of its prominent members. The committee succeeded in collecting 7,500 rupees as donations and called for a meeting of solidarity with the Palestinian people, which was attended by 150 citizens. Some religious figures from the tolerant movement, such as Sheikh 'Abdul-'Aziz Hamada, the judge of Kuwait, and Sheikh Ahmad Khamis al-Khalaf, made impressive speeches, bringing most of the audience to tears.[31]

When the Peel Committee Report was published, proposing the division of Palestine, the Kuwaiti reformers expressed their anger towards it by a meeting of a group of 12 people who called themselves Lijnat Shabab al-Kuwait (The Kuwaiti Youth Committee). After long discussions they decided to send protest telegrams to the League of Nations, the House of Commons and the Colonial Secretary. This action obliged Sheikh Ahmad al-Jabir al-Sabah to send a telegram to the Colonial Secretary in London requesting the British Government to pay attention to the dangers of the division, and that justice must be done in Palestine.[32]

Despite British opposition, Kuwaiti reformers supported the Palestinian national movement, not only by collecting money but also with some of the reformers volunteering to supply the latter with weapons, which were sent to Palestine through the desert. The religious movement in general was not represented in a form of religious organizations of a political nature, but its role in society was the guidance of people because of the following factors:

1   Kuwaiti society is an Islamic society by nature, and thus there would be an effective presence of the religious orientations of both conservative and tolerant movements.
2   The lack of communication between Kuwait and the rest of the world.
3   The emergence of the Wahhabi movement founded by Mohammed bin 'Abdul-Wahab in a neighboring country, which had common borders

with Kuwait, where the Wahabis tried to expand their religious influence over the societies of the Arabian Peninsula and the Gulf region.

These factors helped to keep the Arab societies, whether in Kuwait or in the rest of the Arabian Peninsula and the Arabian Gulf countries, in a state of weakness for a long period of time because of the impact of the Salafiah movement. In addition, British colonialism – which dominated the area, including Kuwait – sought to keep its communities in a state of ignorance.

2 Sunni Islamist political groups

Kuwaitis faced political and social difficulties in the 1940s, which witnessed the fall of the democratic Majlis al-Umah al-Tashre'i (the National Legislative Council) in 1938. The council issued the first constitution of the country containing advanced articles, in comparison with the Constitution of 1962, which was passed by al-Majlis al-Tasisi (the Constituent Council). The National Legislative Council experiment ended following the conflict between its supporters belonging to al-Kutlah al-Wataniya (the National Bloc) in alliance with Kutlat al-Shabab al-Watani (the National Youth Bloc), and the Kuwaiti regime.[1] This confrontation affected Kuwaiti society and was immediately followed by the outbreak of the Second World War. In addition, it was affected by the large amount of time Kuwaitis had to spend on their daily lives, as a result of the difficulty of obtaining material supplies.[2] It was natural in such circumstances that talking about political issues was ignored and the concentration of power was in the hands of the ruler. This situation lasted until the death of Sheikh Ahmad al-Jaber al-Sabah (1921–50), the ruler of Kuwait, and the recognition of his cousin Sheikh 'Abdullah al-Salem al-Sabah as the new ruler (1950–65). It is known that Sheikh 'Abdullah al-Salem al-Sabah was one of the supporters of the National Legislative Council of 1938 – as he took the presidency of this Council – and that he was known for his liberal policy. In light of this political climate established by Sheikh 'Abdullah al-Salem al-Sabah, Kuwait witnessed during his reign democratic breakthroughs, which led to the emergence of clubs, cultural ties and political trends represented by various political groups and movements in the eastern Arab region of the world. Thus, political parties began their underground activities in Kuwait.[3]

This coincided with the Palestinian Disaster in 1948 and the establishment of the Zionist state, which led to the expulsion of the Palestinians from their homeland to several Arab countries – Kuwait was one of the countries that received Palestinian refugees. After the flow of oil wealth, Kuwait witnessed a massive immigration from other Arab countries, such as Syria, Lebanon, Egypt and Iraq, because of the need for laborers to work in the different sectors of education, health and construction. These Arabs carried their own organizational experience with them to Kuwait. In this regard,

Sheikh Ahmad al-Shirbasi recalls in his book, *Aiam al-Kuwait* (*Days of Kuwait*):

> There are four currents in Kuwait ... the Islamic current, the Arab nationalist current, the current of regional interest, and the current of humanism.[4]

The Egyptian writer Ahmad Baha al-Deen says in an article issued in *Majllat Sabah al-Khair* (*Good Morning Journal*) under the title 'A Week in Kuwait':

> During my visit to Kuwait in 1959, and from the first moment of my arrival at the Guest House, Kuwaiti visitors started coming to me and I admit that I was surprised when I found that all the political currents and all forms of consciousness existed in this small country: Those that are Arab Nationalists, those that are Ba'thists, those that are Communists, Socialists, those that are Muslim Brothers, those that belong to the Islamic Liberation Party, and those who belong to the Syrian Social National Party ... All the political currents known by the Arab region have their representatives and those who believe in them ... but through my observations of the audience attending my lectures ... the major political issue there is the Arab nationalism.[5]

On this basis, secret branches of various political parties and movements in the eastern Arab countries emerged in the late 1940s and early 1950s, such as Harakat al-Qawmiyin al-'Arab (the Arab Nationalist Movement (ANM)), Hizb al-Ba'th al-'Arabi al-Ishtriaky (the Arab Socialist Baath Party), movements with Marxist orientations represented by al-Lajan al-Wataniya li Ansar al-Salam (the National Committee of Partisans of Peace in Kuwait) and al-'Usba al-Dimuqratiya al-Kuwaitiya (the Kuwaiti Democratic League).[6] The Muslim Brotherhood Group was among those secret parties and movements.

The Muslim Brotherhood Group (MBG)
Jama'at al-IKhwan al-Muslimin

The activity of the MBG emerged in Kuwait in 1947, when 'Abdul-'Aziz 'Ali al-Mutawa' was introduced to Hassan al-Banna, al-Murshid al-'Amm (the supreme guide) of the MBG, in Mecca, and he formed the first cell for the MBG in Kuwait. It was regarded as the first Islamist political group in Kuwait since the late 1940s and the beginning of the 1950s. Al-Mutawa' became its first al-Muraqib al-'Amm (general observer) in Kuwait. The activity of the MBG in Kuwait was linked to the MBG in Egypt, and on the recommendation of al-Banna, al-Mutawa' became a member of Maktab al-Irshad al-'Amm (the General Guidance Office) of the MBG in Egypt.[7]

Al-Mutawa' attended meetings for the establishment of the international organization for the MBG in Egypt, which included all general observers in the Arab countries and were represented by Mustafa al-Siba'i of Syria, Mohammad Mahmoud al-Suaf of Iraq, 'Ali Talab Allah of Sudan, 'Abdut Rahman Mohammad Khalifa of Jordan, and representatives of the MBG in Lebanon, Morocco, Palestine and Djibouti.[8]

Al-Ma'had al-Deeni (Religious Institute) was the center of recruitment for the new members of the MBG, especially since most of the teachers administrating the Institute graduated from al Azhar and belonged to the MBG in Egypt. In 1952, the MBG in Egypt sent some of its members to Kuwait to contribute to the organizational activity of the group. In this regard, 'Abdullah 'Ali al-Mutawa',[9] one of the symbols of the MBG in Kuwait, explained the reasons behind the establishment of the first Islamic political organization in Kuwait by saying:

> Our Islamic movement began since the early fifties with the fierce western attack not only against Kuwait, but also against the Arab region and the entire Islamic world. They proposed to us secular ideas and principles, like Arab nationalism whose source is the American University in Beirut, and the Ba'th party whose originator is Michel Aflaq who is supported by the west, socialism and modernization, and all of them keep the nation away from its religion and creed, so we the people of Kuwait decided to create an Islamic political group to deal with this vicious attack.[10]

'Abdullah al-'Atiqi, one of the leaders of the MBG in Kuwait, mentioned that when the number of citizens belonging to the MBG became adequate, it was decided to find a society as a front for the group. Several preparatory meetings were held. The first one was in the Diwan of 'Abdullah Sultan al-Kulaib in 1952. This meeting was followed by other meetings in the house of 'Abdul-'Aziz 'Ali al-Mutawa' and 'Abdul-'Aziz al-Muzaini. A delegation from the MBG in Egypt participated in some of these meetings, which resulted in an agreement to establish an Islamic society.[11]

The founders of the MBG in Kuwait faced two obstacles. Firstly, that Kuwait had a bitter experience with Wahabism, who had fought against Kuwait in the al-Jahara Battle.[12] Secondly, that the Kuwaitis were notoriously sensitive towards the word 'party' and this caused the founder to suggest calling it by another name, to which al-Banna agreed.[13]

In 1952, they called their organization Jam 'iyat al-Irshad al-Islamiya (the Islamic Guidance Society (IGS)). In this regard, al-Banna said:

> It is not compulsory to advocate on behalf of the Muslim Brotherhood Association, our only purpose is to repair the ruined lives and souls, let it be al-Nsar schools, Hira institutes and social clubs . . . then groups are formed.[14]

The IGS in Kuwait was not something new for the MBG, as the MBG in Syria had taken different names such as Dar al-Arkam (al-Arkam House) and Jam'iyat al-Makarim (al-Makarim Society) at the beginning of the establishment of the organization. It also took different names in Bahrain, such as Nadi al-Talabah (Students Club) and Jam'iyat al-Aslah (Reform Society).[15] 'Abdul-Aziz 'Ali al-Mutawa' was its general supervisor, while Sheikh Yousef bin 'Isa al-Qinai', who belonged to the founding family, became its chairman. The objectives of the IGS, according to its internal rules, were to:

- spread Islamic culture among the new generation and animate the religion in the nation
- direct the nation according to its religion and its glorious history by establishing correct beliefs and pure intentions with righteous work
- show Islam as a creed and way of life.[16]

The IGS recruited people through its formal committees, such as the Call Committee, the Sports Committee, the Press Committee, and the Righteousness and Social Services Committee.[17]

Although the internal rules of IGS called for non-interference with the political affairs on the basis that it was a religious society,[18] it could be argued that the IGS was a social and religious front through which the members of the MBG in Kuwait could practice their political activity, similar to other clubs and associations licensed by the Department of Social Affairs at that time. Ahmad al-Shirbasi, one of the MBG members of the al-Azhar mission in Kuwait, who came to Kuwait in the early 1950s, justifies the purpose of establishing the IGS in Kuwait by saying:

> One can see similarities between IGS and other Islamic movements at that time. For example, the call for Islam is religion and state, worship and leadership, holy text and sword, and Mosque and school is shared between the IGS and the MBG. Therefore, when we talk about the IGS, we mean, in actual fact, the MBG in Kuwait.[19]

The establishment of the IGS was associated with the arrival of members of the MBG from Egypt and other branches in the eastern Arab countries and the Islamic world to work in Kuwait in the educational sector or others. As the membership of the clubs and associations was not limited to Kuwaiti people but was open to other Arab nationalities as well, the MBG took the opportunity and pushed some of its members to join the IGS, among whom were Zuhdi Abu Al'iz and Sheikh 'Abdul-'Aziz al-Sisi and other members of the MBG in Egypt, who fled to Kuwait after being chased by the Nasserite regime. Those Egyptian members had a big role in the IGS, on both the educational and organizational levels.[20]

During the period 1952–59, which was marked with liberalism in Kuwait, the MBG exploited its social front. The IGS hid its true ideology to gain more members. To achieve its objective, the IGS divided Kuwait City into three sectors: al-Murgab, al-Qibla (western) and al-Sharq (eastern). These sectors had the highest population in Kuwait in the 1950s. The majority of the population lived in Kuwait City, which was made up mostly of urban people. However, other areas that were mostly populated by Bedouins were not shown any interest by the IGS until the late 1970s.[21] Three sections were allocated to be run with the organizational activity of the MBG in the city of Kuwait by the IGS:

> First: The students section would be responsible for recruiting students in the student organization of the MBG.
> Second: The laborer section would be responsible for recruiting workers in the laborer organization of the MBG.
> Third: The merchants section would be responsible for recruiting merchants to the MBG ranks. This sector was very important to the MBG because of its social, economic and political weight within Kuwaiti society.[22]

The educational program of the MBG depended on teaching books written by Hassan al-Banna, Sayyed Qutb, Abu al-A'la al-Mawdudi, the Emir of al-Jamma'ah al-Slamiyah (Islamic Group) in Pakistan, Abu Hassan al-Nadawi, Said Sabag, Yousef al-Qaradawi and Mustafa al Siba'i. The internal rules of the MBG adopted three principles: selectivity in the choice, gradual promotion, and discipline and obedience in a way similar to the military concept of proceed then discuss. This organizational structure was similar to that of the MBG in Egypt, according to its internal rules, which depended on an iron structure where the General Guide was the ruler who had the final say in all issues related to the organization. For this reason, the rest of the organizational ranks were linked to him; Maktab al-Irshad al-'Amm (the General Guidance Council) and al-Haya al-Tasisiyya (the Consultative Assembly) were next in the organizational structure, where the first consisted of 12–20 members and the second consisted of 100–150 members, and from both of them the Majlis al-Shura al-'Amm (the General Consultative Council) was formed. At the base of the organizational structure was the Shu'ba (Section) followed by region in hierarchy, then the administrative office was responsible for the state or province, then came families, which comprised five members. By the end of the 1930s – and because of the differences that had occurred over the history of the organization – the Supreme Guide, Hassan al-Banna, formed a parallel organization, giving it the name of a secret organization, which was the armed wing and military power of the organization. It was an armed militia whose members were subject to secret military training sessions, which nobody knew except the Supreme Guide.[23]

The student section or, as it is called by the MBG Kuwaiti branch, al-Katab al-'Almia (the Scientific Phalanges),[24] was one of the most active sections, which played a significant role in the process of recruiting new members, whether Kuwaitis or Arab and Islamic immigrants. It played a big role in the organization of members through Madrasat al-Irsahd al-Islamiya (the Islamic Guidance School), founded by the MBG in the early 1950s and also taken by the MBG front organization for the dissemination of educational ideological group. The number of Quranic centers reached 47, with 23 centers for men and 24 centers for women. The number of students in Madrasat al-Irsahd al-Islamiya reached 400 and a number of MBG members were among its graduates. The admission policy followed in the Maadrest al-Irsahd al-Islamiya allowed Arab and non-Arab Muslims to join the school regardless of their nationality.[25]

The activity of the MBG exceeded Madrasat al-Irsahd al-Islamiya to colleges and public schools, especially al-M'ahad al-Dini, which became another educational front for the group, knowing that the majority of the teachers were from the al-Azhar mission who belonged to the MBG in Egypt. The activity of the group was more visible in al-Shuwaikh Secondary School, which was the scene of activity for all political groups in the Kuwaiti arena. The groups represented in the schools were the Arab nationalists, Ba'athists and communists, with the MBG being the most prominent political group because of its good organisation.[26] The MBG had been successful in attracting a number of Kuwaiti students and their publications were distributed in classrooms.[27] The MBG started forming cells through the student section, which was the responsibility of Ahmad al-Di'aij at that time. The student section was the backbone of the IGS, which was responsible for organizing the rallies and camps in order to form the cells or families. They succeeded in attracting the students because these families were distributed throughout all the schools in Kuwait. In the late 1950s, after Ahmad al-Da'aij left the MBG, 'Isa Majed al-Shaheen and 'Abdul-Rahman al-Sa'idan emerged at the top of the student section for the MBG. Through the Firkat al-Yarmouk (the rover troops) in the al-Shuwaikh Secondary School, they managed to attract a number of students to join the ranks of the MBG.[28]

The MBG in Kuwait tried to expand to the ranks of the working class. For this purpose, they established a special division for the recruitment of workers. However, this was unsuccessful. Ahmad al-Di'aij justified this failure by claiming that there was no real working class in Kuwait at that time.[29] The truth is that what the MBG failed to achieve was met with some success by the ANM, which succeeded through al-Nadi al-Thaqafi al-Qawmi (the National Cultural Club) and Nadi al-'Ummal (Workers Club) in recruiting Kuwaiti workers, such as Hussein Saqer, Hassan Falah al-'Ajmi and Husein al-Youha, who formed the nucleus of the labor movement in Kuwait. By these, the trade unions in Kuwait and the General Union of Workers of Kuwait were established.[30] The success of the latter groups proved the incorrectness of the justification made by Ahmad al-Di'aij.

The MBG also sought to expand throughout the ranks of the merchants, but most of the merchants were not enthusiastic towards this invitation and this attempt faced the same fate as that when seeking to penetrate the ranks of the workers.[31] While the ANM achieved a stronger response from the merchants who joined the movement, the Souq al-Tujar (merchants market) was transformed to a major center for the activity of the ANM, as well as the use of al-Rabitah al-Kuwaitiya (the Kuwaiti League), which led the national activity at that time. This, in turn, demonstrated the growing sense of nationalism among the Kuwaiti people in general, in addition to the control of the national movement over the Kuwaiti arena at that time.

The MBG sent many of its representatives to Syria, Jordan, Iraq, Lebanon and Egypt to join the camps for party education and military training.[32] In return, Maktab al-Irshad al-'Amm of the MBG (the highest hierarchy) in Egypt sent some guides, such as the Algerian al-Fdil al-Wartlani, who played a significant role in organizing the MBG in Yemen in 1947.[33] Another organizer of the MBG in Egypt who played a great part in Kuwait was Najib Jewaifil, who was sentenced to death by the Egyptian authorities during Nasser's rule and who worked in Kuwait under the pseudonym of 'Abdul-'Aziz al-Salem. Both al-Wartlani and Jewaifil worked to organize the MBG in Kuwait through the committees of the IGS, such as Lajnat al-D'awa (Call Committee).[34] Yousef Hashem al-Rifa'i, former Minister of State, and Khalid al-'Isa al-Saleh, former Minister of Public Works, were responsible for this committee. Al-Wartlani together with many members of the MBG came to Kuwait while Abu Hassan al-Nadawi held weekly educational lectures.[35] The monthly *Majallat al-Irshad* (*Guidance Journal*), published in 1952, was the mouthpiece of the MBG and contributed to spreading its ideology. It was headed by 'Abdul-'Aziz 'Ali al-Mutawa', the founder of the MBG in Kuwait and the General Supervisor of the IGS. Then it was headed by the new General Supervisor of IGS, 'Abdul-Razzak al-Saleh. Many leaders of the MBG wrote articles in *Majallat al-Irshad*, such as Abu al-A'la al-Mawdudi, the Emir of al-Jamm'h al-Islamiya (Islamic Group) in Pakistan, Abu Hassan al-Nadawi, Mohamed Yousef al-Najjar, Shakar al-Natshe of Palestine, Mustafa al-Seba'i, the General Supervisor of the MBG in Syria, Sayyed Qutb, Mohammad Qutb, Mohammad Abozahrah, Ahmad al-Shirbasi, 'Ali 'Abdalmn'm, 'Ali al-Bolaqi, the Head of the al-Azhar Mission and others.[36]

The IGS held weekly lectures for its members and members of the Egyptian al-Azhar Educational Mission in Kuwait. They used the mosques as places to spread their propaganda. The MBG was able to use the Kuwait Broadcasting Station for their own programs. The Kuwaiti clubs, representing the nationalist movement, protested and demanded the same facilities. As a result, the authorities decided not to allow any organization to broadcast any program.[37]

Its distinguishing public activity was the petition sent to the Ruler of Kuwait, Sheikh 'Abdullah al-Salem al-Sabah, criticizing the system of education such as teaching music, dancing and acting in Kuwait schools and protesting against sending girls to educational missions or to universities outside Kuwait. They demanded the prohibition of alcoholic drinks and movies. They then demanded that the Ruler should establish a committee for al-Amr bi al-Ma'ruf wa al-Nahi 'an al-Munkar (the promotion of virtue and the prohibition of vice).[38]

Despite good organization, which was a characteristic of the MBG, the mass deployment of the MBG in Kuwait had been limited due to the strength of the ANM compared with the MBG in this area and the fact that all sports and cultural clubs came under the control of the ANM branch in Kuwait, especially after the emergence of Lajnt al-Andiya al-Kuwaitiya (the Kuwaiti Committee clubs), Ettihad al-Andiya al-Kuwaiti (the Union of Kuwaiti clubs) and al-Rabitah al-Kuwaiti (the Kuwaiti League). The ANM in Kuwait was the backbone for those associations, which led the popular national struggle in the 1950s in Kuwait. All societies and leagues joined these unions except the IGS.[39]

Despite the differences between the MBG and the ANM, the former participated in the campaign to aid Egypt during the Anglo–French–Israeli aggression in 1956. It issued a statement congratulating Egypt in its defeat of this aggression, reading:

> We advocate Arab unity because the Arabs are the first bearers of Islam and we advocate the Islamic union according to the Prophet's orders.[40]

In another pamphlet, the IGS backed the struggle of the Egyptians.[41] The MBG also participated in the campaign supporting the Algerian Revolution and wrote a letter to the Kuwaiti Government showing its support for the Algerians and its readiness to collect donations to back their Revolution.[42]

As for local issues, the MBG participated in the 1958 elections of representatives to the boards of government departments, which supervised the activity of the government departments.[43] The results of the elections show the weakness of the MBG when compared with the national trend composed of the Nasserites and the ANM, which won most of the seats. The most dynamic elements of those who were elected representing the ANM were: Jassim al-Qatami with 325 votes, Dr. Ahmad al-Khatib with 251 votes, and 'Abdul-Razzaq al-Khalid with 204 votes. The supporters of the ANM, which were the merchants, also achieved significant results, such as: 'Abdul-'Aziz Hamad al-Saqer with 370 votes, Bader al-Salem with 368 votes, Hamoud Zaid al-Khalid with 352 votes, Sulaiman al-Mosallam with 328 votes, Maisa'n al-Khadir with 326 votes, Yousef Ibrahim al-Ghanim with 311 votes, Khalid al-'Adsani with 392 votes and 'Abdul-Atif al-Ghanim with 239 votes. Those who were supporting the religious movement represented in the MBG were: Subeih Barrak al-Subeih, who received 226 votes, 'Abdul-'Aziz al-Qotaivi with 165 votes and Mohammad al-'Adsani with 108 votes. 'Abdullah 'Ali al-Mutawa', who was a leading member of the MBG in Kuwait, got only 119 votes.[44]

The MBG witnessed the emergence of two opposing movements among its ranks in the 1950s. Firstly, the moderate movement headed by the General Supervisor of the IGS, 'Abdul-'Aziz 'Ali al Mutawa'. Secondly, the hard line movement represented by the student section led by Mohammad al-'Adsani, 'Abdul-Rahman al-'Atiqi, and Ahmad al-Di'aij.[45] Najib Jewaifil played a big role in increasing the differences between the two movements.[46] The reason behind these differences was the issue of arresting the leaders of the MBG in Egypt. The extremist movement supported the adoption of a clear position towards the Egyptian regime, while the supporters of the moderate movement, who represented the majority, were in favor of neutrality. This may have been due to the mutual interests between this majority and the Kuwaiti regime and that taking a firm attitude towards the Nasserite regime threatened those interests because of the relations between Kuwait and Egypt, especially in the field of education and other areas of public services. This dispute led a large number of the IGS leading members to desert the organization's activity. For this reason, 'Abdul-'Aziz 'Ali al-Mutawa' resigned from his position as a General Supervisor of the IGS and was then replaced with 'Abdul-Razzaq al-Saleh. This division had a clear impact on the group, both at the organizational and activity levels.[47]

In February 1959, the Kuwaiti regime closed all sports and cultural clubs for political reasons. This situation continued until 1961 when Kuwait gained its independence from Britain as a result of the termination of the 1899 treaty, with the exception of the IGS. The IGS was not included in the resolution issued by Sheikh 'Abdullah al-Mubarak al-Sabah, the Vice Prince at that time, on the basis that it was a religious society and not a political society. The real purpose of the resolution was to weaken the pro-President Jamal 'Abdel Nasser nationalist movement, which became more popular and more dominant in the Kuwaiti arena. The MBG took advantage of this resolution and continued its activities.[48]

However, the MBG lost support in Kuwait for many reasons. The attempted assassination of President Nasser and the subsequent trial and imprisonment of Egyptian members of the Brotherhood discredited them. Meanwhile, the popularity of the Nasserite nationalism was increasing generally in the Arab region, particularly in the Peninsula and the Arabian Gulf; the MBG was unable to resist the tide of nationalism.

After Kuwait's independence, Kuwaiti society witnessed a kind of political relaxation and a return to a liberal policy adopted by Sheikh 'Abdullah al-Salem al-Sabah after his inauguration as the Ruler of Kuwait in 1950, which marked the return to the climate of democratic political activity. Therefore, the first step taken by Sheikh 'Abdullah al-Salem al-Sabah was approval to reopen the sports and cultural clubs to practice their usual activities. This political climate coincided with the arrival of some members and leaders of the MBG in Iraq, especially from the area of al-Zubair, following the coup led by 'Abdul-Karim Qassem. He was loyal to the Soviet Union at that time and suppressed the group's activity in Iraq. The relationships between the MBG in Iraq and the MBG in Kuwait dated back to the 1940s, when Sheikh Mohammad Mahmoud al-Swaf, the General Supervisor of the MBG in Iraq, made several visits to Kuwait where he met the General Supervisor of

Kuwait, 'Abdul-'Aziz 'Ali al-Mutawa' and his brother 'Abdullah 'Ali al-Mutawa'.
Majallat al-liwa al-Islamiya (*Islamic Brigade Journal*), the mouthpiece of the
MBG in Iraq, was read in Kuwait regularly, and Sheikh al-Sawaf participated
in founding the IGS in Kuwait.[49]

After Kuwait's independence, the IGS was dissolved. Thus, 30 members
of the MBG in Kuwait and their supporters met in the Diwan of Fahed al-
Khalid and decided to establish Jamiyat al-Islah al-Ijtima'i (the Social Reform
Society (SRS)). This society was just an extension of the IGS. The first
chairman for the SRS was Yousef al-Nafeesi, followed by Yousef al-Haji, the
former Minister of Awqaf and the current chairman of al-Munadhama al-
Islamiya al-Khayriya al-'Alamia (the International Islamic Charitable Organization), then 'Abdullah 'Ali al Mutawa', the General Supervisor of the MBG
in Kuwait and a member of the Executive Office of the international organization for the MBG.[50] After the death of al-Mutawa' in 2006, Hamoud
al-Rumi became chairman of the SRS. The number of the official registered
members of the SRS is 1,138 as of 2007.[51] Its announced objectives do not
differ from those of the IGS.[52] In this regard, 'Abdullah 'Ali al-Mutawa' says:

> When the IGS was founded, Kuwait was under the British protection.
> During the reign of Sheikh 'Abdullah al-Salem al-Sabah, the State minis-
> tries, including the Ministry of Social Affairs, requested the re-registration
> of the existing institutions, but the IGS decided to change its name,
> based on the vision and consultation among its members, by establishing
> the Social Reform Society in the early sixties which had the same goals
> and principles as the IGS. Changing the name does not mean a change in
> our strategic visions.[53]

One of the most important committees that emerged from the SRS was the
Cultural Committee. Through this committee, the ideology of the MBG was
spread among Kuwaiti society. It held social activities such as a week of
Ramadan, a week of pilgrimage, a week of the Quran, a week of the application of Shari'a law, a week of 'our Shari'a protects our Kuwait', and a week
of al-Aqsa. All these activities were officially sponsored by the Kuwaiti
Government. Furthermore, the Cultural Committee held rallies of solidarity
with the mujahedeen (fighters for a religious cause) that took part in the
conflicts in Afghanistan and Chechnya.[54]

In 1968, the first center for the education of the Quran was opened with
88 students enrolled. By 1990, the number of these centers reached 317 for
men and 79 for women, with a total number of 82,627 students.[55] It is thought
that these centers were turned into undeclared headquarters for the MBG in
Kuwait through which new members were recruited. It is worth mentioning
that these centers were based in the mosques, which are scattered throughout
Kuwait and the religious centers. *Majallat al-Mujtama'* (*Society Journal*),
which replaced *Majallat al-Irshad*, also reflected the ideology of the MBG in
Kuwait. This was in addition to brochures, publications, cassettes and video

tapes issued by the SRS and publishing firms that belonged to the MBG, in which some of them were calling for jihad. The SRS also held Islamic book fairs and formed other committees, such as Marakez al-Nash'a (Young Centers), Marakez al-Shabab (Youth Centers), Lijan al-'Amal al-Ijtama'i (social work committee), Lajnat al-Worood (the Roses Committee) for middle school girls, and Markaz al-Muruj Center for secondary school girls.[56] All of the above contributed to the spread of the ideology of the MBG in Kuwait.

Representatives of the MBG in Kuwait and their supporters from the religious movement participated in the first parliamentary elections in Kuwait for a general election of the first Constituent Assembly in Kuwait in 1962. The fundamental task of the Assembly was to create a constitution of Kuwait. The results of these elections showed the weakness of the MBG in particular, and the religious movement in general, and the superiority of the ANM and the representatives of other national groups in the parliamentary elections. Sayyed Yousef Hashim al-Rifa'i, a supporter of the MBG, failed, while the candidates of the ANM and its supporters from the merchant class achieved significant results.[57] These results indicated the strong belief of the Kuwaiti people in the idea of Arab nationalism.

In the elections of the National Assembly in 1963, the MBG faced a major defeat, where only al-Rifa'i from the First Constituency, al-Sharq, which is the stronghold of Shi'ites in Kuwait, won a seat. This gives us an indication that the success of al-Rifa'i was not due to the strength of the Sunni Islamist political groups in that constituency but due to the mutual interests between al-Rifa'i and the Shi'ite sect. None of the MBG candidates won in other constituencies, such as 'Abdul-'Aziz al-Qatifi, 'Abdul-Rahman al'Omar, 'Abdullah Sultan al-Kulaib, 'Abdullah 'Ali al-Mutawa' and Ahmad Bazi' al-Yasin.[58]

The 1970s and even the beginning of the 1980s were considered to be the greatest time where the ideology and activity of the MBG in Kuwait spread. It was especially noted after the decrease in the activity of the MBG in Egypt since its clash with the leadership of 'Abdel Nasser in the 1950s and until the decline of the leftist and nationalist tide in the late 1960s and early 1970s. This period witnessed the retreat of the nationalist and leftist forces in favor of the growing religious movement in general and the MBG in particular and its relation with the Kuwaiti regime. Both the MBG and the Kuwaiti regime benefited from this relation, where the first extended its domination over the popular action institutes and the second got rid of the leftists and nationalists who had benefited from such institutions as pressing groups to go against the inclinations of the Kuwaiti regime.

In the elections of the National Assembly in 1981, most of the left and nationalist candidates belonging to al-Tajamu' al-Dimuqrati (the Democratic Gathering) and al-Tajamu' al-Watani (the National Gathering) failed, while many candidates of the Islamist political groups won, such as Hamoud al-Rumi and 'Isa Majed al-Shaheen, representing the MBG. The MBG slogan during the electoral battle was amending Article II of the Constitution and the Islamization of laws. The group succeeded in passing some resolutions, such as:

- a law that forbids drinking and selling alcohol in the foreign embassies in Kuwait
- a law that Kuwaiti nationality is granted to Muslims only.[59]

The MBG in Kuwait participated in the elections of the National Assembly in 1985 and won three seats, but this Assembly did not last long because the political authorities dissolved it unconstitutionally and suspended some articles of the Constitution.

After the dissolution of the National Assembly, an atmosphere of oppression dominated the country and state security was supervising the deputies of the dissolved Assembly as well as popular students' unions and organizations.[60] In such a climate, the MBG joined the political opposition, which included leftists and Arab nationalists, and issued a statement condemning the dissolution, which was ratified by four political groups: the National Gathering, the Democratic Gathering, the Nationalist Gathering and the Islamic Coalition.[61]

In 1989, the MBG participated in establishing al-Haraka al-Dusturiya (the Constitutional Movement (CM)), which brought together all political groups. It defined itself in its constitutional statement as being a popular Kuwaiti movement that included in its ranks all Kuwaiti citizens who believed that the Kuwaiti Constitution was the legal system of governance and legislation.[62] Although the MBG had contributed to the founding of the CM, it did not encourage its members to have effective participation in the popular gatherings and rallies.[63] It was cautious towards these gatherings because it felt that the crowds had gone far beyond its narrow objectives. It is worth mentioning that afterwards, the Sunni Islamist political groups found themselves isolated from the popular movements, which were getting bigger with the participation of all classes of society. The MBG began feeling isolated from the people; they knew the importance of the people so they began to catch up. However, even this participation was small, in which they only participated in signing memos or statements. They didn't participate in the rallies or the protests that the popular movements led. The reason behind this minimal participation was that the MBG was afraid that taking a stand against the government would take away the advantages the government gave them.[64]

During the Iraqi occupation of Kuwait, the MBG members were engaged in the civil resistance and played a role in the supervision of the co-operatives and urged the citizens to stand firm. It also co-operated with other political forces to ensure material supply to citizens. The MBG leaders, who fled Kuwait during the occupation, participated in Moatamer Jeddah al-Sha'bi (Jadah Popular Congress), which was held in Jeddah in October 1990.

After the liberation of Kuwait by the coalition forces from Iraqi occupation, the MBG established al-Haraka al-Dusturiya al-Islamiya (the Islamic

Constitutional Movement ((ICM)) as an extension of the MBG in Kuwait, which is still active in the community and the political arena. The movement's alliance with the Kuwaiti regime is a significant factor that led to its growth.

The Liberation Party (LP)
Hizb al-Tahrir

The second religious political group formed in Kuwait was the Liberation Party (LP), which started its activity in Kuwait in 1953. Before dealing with the LP in Kuwait, we have to tackle its central organization in the eastern Arab countries, since they all carry the same ideology.

The LP was founded by Taqi al-Deen al-Nabhani in Jerusalem in 1952 as a reaction to the occupation of Palestine and the establishment of the Zionist State. Al-Nabhani was born in 1909 in the Ajzam village in Haifa in Palestine. He received his primary education in the village's school and learned the Quran and Islamic jurisprudence at the hands of his father, Sheikh Ibrahim al-Nabhani. He left for Egypt for a higher education at al-Azhar and returned to Palestine to work as a teacher in the schools of Haifa and AlKhalil. After leaving the teaching profession, he joined the judiciary system and was appointed as a judge in a number of Palestinian cities. After the Palestinian Disaster in 1948, he left Palestine with convoys of Palestinian refugees to Beirut and settled there with his family until 1950, when he left for the West Bank – which was under the rule of the Royal Jordanian regime – and became a member of the Court of Appeal in Jerusalem. Shortly after, he resigned from the judiciary and joined the Islamic College in Amman as a teacher.[65] He resigned in 1952 and founded the LP, which presented the idea of seizing power in one of the Arab countries to be the base emirate under which the rest of the emirates would be under the Caliph leadership. Jordan was his dream for that base emirate and, therefore, he was expelled from Jordan and then moved between Syria and Lebanon until his death in Beirut in 1977.[66]

In the beginning of al-Nabhani's political life and before the founding of the LP, he joined Kutlat al-Qawmiyeen al-Arab (the Arab Nationalists Block), which was founded in Haifa in 1947. He was influenced by the national thought adopted by the Ba'ath Party. This can be seen clearly in the three publications issued by him before the establishment of the LP: *Nedham al-Mujtama'* (*The Community System*), *Ingathe Palestine* (*Saving Palestine*) and *Resalat al'Arab* (*The Arabs' Message*), in which he expressed his adoption of the idea of nationalism. He did not print second copies of any of his publications issued before founding the LP.[67] On the contrary, those were issued after the foundation of the party.[68] He also had a good relationship with the MBG before founding the LP, where he gave lectures in their meetings admiring their ideology and their founder, Hassan al-Banna. In spite of this relationship, however, al-Nabhani insisted on the establishment of an Islamic party independent of the MBG. The MBG made many attempts to deter him from the founding of his party on the basis that the Islamic scene cannot bear two parties that have the same ideology. For this reason, Sayyed Qutb met with al-Nabhani during his visit to Jerusalem to convince him to refrain from this idea, but the latter insisted on his position. This was the starting point of differences between the two groups, especially since the LP became a strong competitor for the MBG in Jordan, Palestine and Syria and started to attract more Muslim youth to join its ranks. One criticism the LP addressed to the MBG was that they occupied themselves with tasks that the Islamic state is responsible for, such as charities, building hospitals, orphanages and social securities. The LP saw this as something that kept people away from demanding the establishment of the Islamic state headed by the Caliph. The MBG considered the LP as one of its strongest competitors to the degree that if any of its members communicated with the LP, they would be dismissed from the party.[69]

Following the death of al-Nabhani, Sheikh 'Abdul-Qadim Zaloom became the leader of the LP. He is the author of the book *Hakatha Hadimat Alkilafah* (*This Way the Caliphate was Demolished*). Zaloom led the party for 26 years until he died on 29 April 2003. He was born in the city of Alkhalil in Palestine in 1924; he finished his secondary education there and joined al-Azhar University in Egypt. He returned to Palestine to work as a teacher at the Hussein Ben 'Ali secondary school. Zaloom participated in the parliamentary elections in 1956, but did not succeed; the party accused the Jordanian Government of forging the election results and, subsequently, Zaloom was arrested. Zaloom was the right arm of the party founder Sheikh al-Nabhani, where he assisted him in the formulation of the party's ideology. Following his death, 'Ata Abu Arashta succeeded him in the leadership of the LP. Abu Arashta was born in Palestine in 1943 into a religious family; he left with his family to the AlKhalil city in 1948, where he completed his high school studies. He joined the ranks of the LP when he was a student in the elementary school. He joined the Faculty of Engineering at the University of Cairo in 1961 to get a degree in civil engineering in 1966 and worked in a number of Arab countries as an engineer. Abu Arashta was arrested in 1999 charged with distributing leaflets for an unlicensed association and belonging to a banned party, but King Abdullah II ordered his release at the end of March of the same year. He became well known after delivering the party's speech in Pakistan in 2003, which led to a conflict with the authorities there and was banned. In statements made by him, he claimed that the party had armed militias operating under his orders, although it is not directly part of the party structure. Before being elected as the emir of the party, Abu Arashta was the official spokesman of the party in Jordan.[70]

The LP depends on the writings of its founder, Sheikh al-Nabhani, to build its concept and ideology, such as: Nedham al-Islam (system of Islam), al-Nedham al-Eqtisadi (economic system), Nedham al-Hukm fi al-Islam (system of government in Islam), al-Nedham al-Ajtami' fi al-Islam (social system in Islam), al-Dawlah al-Islamiya (the Islamic state), Asas al-Nahdah (the foundations of the Renaissance), al-Shakhsia al-Islamiya (islamic personality), al-Takatul al-Hizbi (Block Party), al-Khilafah (the Caliphate) and al-Tafkeer (thinking). There are also some books issued by the LP without reference to the author of the book, such as: *Mafaheem Hizb Altahreer* (*The Concepts of the Liberation Party*), *Mafahim Seyasai li Hizb al-Tahreer* (*Political Concepts of the Liberation Party*), *al-Fikr al-Islamiya* (*Islamic Thought*). The LP sent some of these publications to some leaders of the Arab and Islamic nations, such as the King of Jordan, the Libyan President Muammar al-Gaddafi, Ayatollah Khomeini and the Yemeni President ʿAli ʿAbdullah Saleh as an expression of its ideology: creating an Islamic state represented in Dawlat al-Khalifa (the Caliphate State). It worked very hard to establish this state. The LP declares that its aim is to resume the Islamic way of life and convey the Islamic call to the world. According to the LP, before the establishment of the Caliphate State, the party must pass through three stages:[71]

- the stage of working underground through recruiting new members who believe in the party's ideology, and educating them
- the stage of working in public where the party interacts with the nation
- the stage of operation, in which the party establishes the Islamic state after overthrowing the existing regimes, which is totally compliant with Islamic rules.

To achieve this purpose, the LP prepared a draft of the constitution of the Caliphate State, which consists of 186 articles based on creed, political, economic and social articles. These articles concentrated on the following points:[72]

1   Islamic creed is the foundation of the state and all rules running all aspects of life have to be built upon it.
2   The centralization of government and decentralization of administration.
3   The economic system must be based on three bases: individual ownership, public ownership and state ownership.
4   Allowing the establishment of political parties based on Islamic creed, and that the establishment of any Islamic party does not need any license, while any party not based on Islam is prohibited.
5   Women can be appointed at the state administrations and can participate in the parliamentary elections through both nomination and voting. They can also participate in the elections of the Caliph. The party's constitution prohibits women from being at the top of the government or the judiciary, or the emir of jihad.
6   The constitution divided countries into two parts: countries that have to be fought, which include Israel, the USA, the United Kingdom, France and Russia, and countries that are linked with the Islamic state through financial, commercial and cultural treaties and, therefore, are friendly countries.

7   Boycotting international organizations not based on Islam, such as the United Nations, the International Court of Justice, the International Monetary Fund, the World Bank and national organizations such as the League of Arab States because the LP does not believe in nationalism and consider it inhuman, causing discrimination between people, and see it as nationalist in trying to impose control over others. Moreover, it regarded nationalism as an emotional bond arising from the survival instinct.[73]

The LP considered advocating for nationalism as an act against Islam and a great sin.[74] The idea of nationalism was created by infidel states in the Muslim countries to prevent the application of the Shari'a and the return of the Islamic Caliphate state.[75] The LP prohibited joining these nationalist parties because they work to steer Muslims away from their religion and away from their creed.[76] The LP believes that colonialism encouraged the nationalist movements and gathered them in the First Arab Conference, which was held in Paris in 1913, to fight against the Ottoman state and to demand the independence of the Arab countries.[77] This is why the LP believed that al-Thawrah al-'Arabia al-Kobrah (the Great Arab Revolution) led by Sharif Husein, who fought the Ottoman state, was made by colonialism that aimed to eliminate the Ottoman state with the help of the 'greatest traitor Sharif Husein and his children traitors Faisal and Abdullah,'[78] and that the League of Arab States was created by colonialism to prevent the foundation of an Islamic state.[79]

The LP was regarded as one of the Islamic parties whose movements worked underground, so it is difficult to know the precise organizational construction of the party, although it worked in public at some intervals. The organizational structure of the party was like a pyramid: the top was represented by the leadership committee headed by the chairman of the party's central leadership. In this regard, it resembles the nationalist leadership of the Arab Baa'th Socialist Party and the Executive Committee for the ANM. The committee was headed by al-Nabhani, the founder of the party, who believed in absolute leadership and explained the meaning of the word Khalifa as a succession of the Prophet Mohammad, which allowed him to adopt policies and make decisions without referring to the committee leadership. This strategy imposed by al-Nabhani caused the desertion of a number of party members.[80] Second in the hierarchy was Lajnat al-Wilaya (province committee), which was formed in each country where the party was active, such as Pakistan, Iraq, Lebanon and Kuwait. Each state was headed by an emir who was primarily responsible for running the party's affairs in each province. The party members in each country elected between five and eight representatives to the committee of each state under the supervision of the base committees of the party. The province committee was responsible for the task of political communication with the politicians in the country in which it was active. The secret leadership committee planned the party's strategy and issued orders to the committees in the Arab, Islamic and European countries. The third in the organizational hierarchy was the al-Lajna al-Mahaliyya (the local committee), which was responsible for the educational sector, such as schools and universities. Its task was to follow up with the members' affairs within its area of operation, to recruit new members and educate them regarding the party's culture.[81] The membership of the LP was open to all men and women, regardless of their ethnic, national or religious origins; however, the party demanded all Muslims to adopt Islamic regulations, which was different from the MBG, which was restricted to Sunni Muslims only. The charter of the LP prevented any member from expressing any view or activity different from the party's, otherwise they may be expelled from the party. Members were also prohibited from writing books or articles or participating in any debate contrary to the views of the party, otherwise appropriate action would be taken.[82] Each member would take the oath of loyalty to the party, which states:

> I swear to Almighty God that I will be an honest guardian of Islam, sponsor views of the Liberation Party and its Constitution and be confident in its leadership, implement its resolutions, even if they contradict with my opinion, spend every effort to achieve its objective as long as I am a member and God is a witness to all of what I say.[83]

The LP is one of the religious parties that has been active in Kuwait since 1953. The party is spread in Kuwait between Arab communities coming from Palestine, Syria, Jordan and Lebanon. Khalid al-Hassan, a member of the Central Committee of the National Palestinian Liberation Movement (Fatah), was one of the most prominent party leaders in Kuwait. He was one of the founders of the LP, the right arm of Sheikh al-Nabhani before he joined the Fatah movement.[84] Evidence of the early activity of the LP in Kuwait was the constituent statement, which was published in *Majallat al-Raed (The Pioneer Journal)* issued by Nadi al-Mo'alamin (the Teachers Club) in 1952.[85]

The LP tried to spread its ideas among Kuwaiti society and to exert authority over members of its party. However, the ANM – through its mass media – played an effective role in alerting people about the ideas and concepts of the LP and demanded the expulsion of LP members from governmental work.[86]

There has been no report of the success of the LP in attracting Kuwaitis to join the party in recent times. Despite the fact that the MBG was a political Islamic group, which was founded in Kuwait at the same time as LP, the MBG was able to penetrate Kuwaiti society and attract a number of Kuwaiti citizens much sooner than the LP.[87] In general, the LP's appearance in Kuwait and until the Iraqi occupation was limited to the Arab communities and some Kuwaiti citizens who did not dare openly declare their membership of this party.

After Kuwait gained independence from Britain on 19 June 1961, Kuwait became a constitutional state. For the first time the people participated in the elections of the Constitutional Assembly, which put together the first constitution of Kuwait. In 1963, Kuwait also witnessed the election of the first National Assembly. All the political groups participated in these elections, including religious groups represented by the MBG, and their supporters from the religious movement, with the exception of the LP, which refused to participate because it believes that democracy contradicts Islam. In their view, democracy is manmade, while Islam is God's system carried out by his messenger Mohammad. The LP also believes that democracy means sovereignty of the people, while in the Islamic regime sovereignty is for Shari'a and not for the nation, and God is the only legislator.[88]

The LP in Kuwait sets a group of legitimate conditions to be qualified for the nomination for the parliamentary elections, mainly:[89]

1   A candidate has to announce in public his rejection of the Western capitalist system and all the infidels.
2   A candidate has to announce that he worked to change the regulations of infidelity and replace them with Islam.
3   A candidate has to follow the Quran and Sunna in his political program.
4   A candidate has to use his seat in the Parliament as a platform to advocate for Islam.

The LP stressed that the work of the member of the parliament is a legitimate act. Furthermore, they stated that Muslims should participate in the elections if the conditions mentioned above are fulfilled and that the Parliament should be used as a platform to demolish the infidels' existing constitution and laws, to alert the people of their danger in that the mere existence of such governments is munkar (a reprehensible act) and must be replaced with the Caliphate State.[90] It is noted that the LP contradicts itself in that when some of its members were arrested in the countries in which it was active, the party members quickly asked for the help of the parliamentary councils and civil society institutions and urged them to intervene with the ruling authorities in these countries for the release of the arrested party members. The best example of that is the appeal made by the LP–Yemen branch to the Yemeni parliament and the institutions of civil society to assist in the release of the party's detainees.[91]

Despite the opposition of the LP to the Iraqi Ba'ath rulership, it regarded the Iraqi occupation of Kuwait simply as Iraqi forces entering Kuwait. It used the major mosques in the Jordanian capital, Amman, to mobilize its supporters against the international coalition forces.[92] It also issued a publication in which it appealed to Muslims to fight the coalition forces that were attacking Islam and Muslims and condemned the American intervention, which aims to attack Iraq militarily and impose American domination on the Arabian Peninsula and the Arabian Gulf. The party also condemned

Majlas al-Ta'awan al-Khalijy (the Gulf Cooperation Council (GCC)) for allowing the presence of foreign troops on their lands and demanded the expulsion of these troops. The statement neither mentioned the Iraqi occupation nor condemned it.[93] The party members in Kuwait did not take part in the civilian and military resistance against the Iraqi occupying forces, contrary to all other different political groups that confronted the invading forces and made dozens of martyrs in defense of the sovereignty of the homeland. Instead of defending the sovereignty of Kuwait, the LP indulged itself in finding a religious justification for the occupation of Kuwait.[94]

The LP condemned the security treaty held between the governments of the United States and Kuwait after the liberation by saying that it is forbidden by the Islamic Shari'a, which prohibits such agreements that allow the infidels to control the destiny of Muslims. It held the Kuwaiti Government responsible for waiving its sovereignty and wealth to the infidel enemy and considered these treaties as political suicide, as the protector will dominate all aspects of the protected state. Moreover, it stated that the security of Kuwait, the Gulf and the Arabian Peninsula can only be achieved through the foundation of the Caliphate State, which is based on the doctrine of the nation as it applies Islamic law and unifies Muslim countries against the influence of infidel systems.[95]

When the American and the British air forces raided Iraq on 17 December 1998, the LP issued a statement supporting the Saddam Hussein regime saying that the countries from which the aggressive raids were launched, such as Kuwait, Saudi Arabia, Bahrain, Qatar and Oman, are partners of America and Britain in this aggression against the Iraqi people. It urged the Islamic states that did not participate in this aggression to take the initiative to break off diplomatic and economic relations by closing the embassies with the expulsion of their nationals from Islamic lands instead of keeping silent.[96]

The LP criticized the statements made by the former US Secretary of State Colin Powell in which the United States considered Kuwait as a major ally outside NATO. The party considered these statements and the use of Kuwait as an American military base that supported the American troops as a munkar kabaier (great reprehensible act). It urged the Kuwaiti regime to refuse the alliance with the United States and they promoted the abolishment of the security and defense treaty, thus ending the American military presence. The statement also demanded from every Muslim, whether a member of parliament, a preacher, an imam or a government official, to stand against the United States and to establish a unified country under the banner of the Muslim Caliph and to expel the infidel Americans and others from Muslim countries.[97] The party accused the Kuwaiti regime of being behind the hostile feelings of the people of Kuwait towards the Iraqi people.[98] The party alleged that the Kuwaiti regime played a role in 'the infidel strategy to achieve the nation's disintegration and weakening.'[99] The LP issued a statement on the occasion of the visit of US President George W. Bush to Kuwait on 11 January 2008, showing its objection to this visit. The statement urged the

Kuwaiti Government not to welcome him and warned from responding to any proposal made by the US president that will increase the American influence and domination over the country.[100]

On 24 October 2001, state security forces in Kuwait arrested one of the members of the LP while distributing publications inside the Kuwaiti National Assembly that urged the Kuwaiti people to demand their government cancel the security arrangements with the United States and fight the American forces stationed inside and outside Kuwait territory; the battle is between the infidels and Islam, and that America has taken the subject of fighting terrorism as an excuse to achieve its objectives that serve its interests since it has limited terrorism to Islam and the Muslims.[101]

After the liberation of Kuwait by the international coalition forces, the political arena in Kuwait witnessed an important development where seven political groups, representing different political orientations in the country, announced their political, economic and social programs publicly through press conferences. These groups were: al-Manber al-Demoqrati al-Kuwaiti (Kuwaiti Democratic Forum (KDF)), Takattul al-Nuwab (the Parliamentary Bloc), the ICM, the Popular Islamic Gathering, the Islamic National Coalition, al-Tajammu' al-Dostoory (the Constitutional Gathering), Tajammu' al-Mustaquileen (the Independent Gathering).[102] In this atmosphere, which seemed to have encouraged the LP to announce itself and work in public, the party members of the Kuwaiti youth started to attend and participate in symposiums and lectures, introducing their names and allegiances, trying to expose the political regime and describing democracy and the state's constitution as an infidel, and urged the establishment of the Caliphate State. Moreover, the LP members started to write articles in the local press introducing the concepts and ideas of the party and calling for the establishment of the Caliphate State.

In 1995, Mohammad al-Faraj, one of the LP members, published a book entitled *Anthemat al-khilafah al-Islamiya fi 'Asrena al-Hader* (*Systems of Islamic Caliphate in the Present Time*), which contains political and religious programs of the party.[103] For the first time, he participated in the meeting called for by the ICM, and attended by the political groups, as a representative of the LP. This meeting was boycotted by the liberal political groups such as the KDF and al-Tahalf al-al-Watani al-Daimiqrati (the National Democratic Alliance (NDA)). Mohammad al-Faraj criticized the ICM, which called for the implementation of Islamic Shari'a and at the same time believed in the constitution, while according to the LP application of Shari'a it meant undermining the constitution. Al-Faraj refused to count the LP within the political groups working in Kuwait and had no ambition to be one of them because the party was working worldwide.[104]

On 10 October 2004, the LP took an unprecedented step when it organized a public lecture in the al-'Adan district under the name al-Hamlah al-Amrikiah 'Alah al-Islam (The American Campaign against Islam), attended by around 400 people.[105] The number of the audience reflected the popularity of the party in Kuwait, where no seminar or lecture held by the major political groups in Kuwait was ever attended by such a large number of people. Special forces and state security forces arrested a number of the organizers of the lecture, who were released after being interrogated.[106] Two members of the party, 'Abdullah al-Rashed and Mohammad al-'Otaibi, criticized this act on the basis that it was an intellectual lecture that discussed the conflicts between civilizations and democracy, which the party does not believe in.[106] They also criticized the interference of the American Embassy in the lives of Kuwaitis.[107] They added that the party rejects the use of violence and depends on logic and that the members will continue their struggle until they achieve their goal, which is the establishment of a Caliphate State in Kuwait and all Arab and Islamic countries.[108] As a result, the security forces detained a number of non-Kuwaiti party members who were involved in a secret organization calling for ending the American presence in Kuwait.[109] After a period of time, paid advertisements in the local newspapers, such as *al-Qabas* and *al-Seyassah*, started to appear for the first time, signed by the name Shabab Hisb al-Tahrir–al-Maktab al-I'lamy (Youth Liberation Party–Kuwait Media Bureau) expressing the party's condolence on the death of the leader of the MBG in Kuwait 'Abdullah 'Ali al-Mutawa', as well as the occasion of the Ramadan month. For the first time, one of the party leaders, Hassan al-Dhahi, who was at the same time the chairman of the media bureau of the LP in Kuwait, showed himself through an interview conducted by the *al-Watan* newspaper in which he made a violent criticism to the political regime in Kuwait, saying that Kuwait had become an American thorn that hits more than one place. He strongly rejected the opening of the northern borders of Kuwait for the American forces and regarded the presence of American bases in Kuwait as being directly against the interests of Muslims, stressing that the presence of infidel military forces in Muslim countries is not acceptable and that Kuwait, as well as the rest of the Arab Gulf states, are occupied by the United States. He also considered the democratic system as kufr (infidel) and that it is forbidden to engage in parliamentary work and deal with embassies.[110]

In August 2007, the Turkish Embassy made a complaint to the Kuwaiti Ministry of Foreign Affairs that it received a threat against its interests. Accordingly, the state security forces arrested some of the leaders of the LP, including Hassan al-Dhahi. These arrests were followed by public activities for the party through making visits to the Diwans of Kuwait and the institutions of civil society and distributing publications that advocated the ending of the security treaty with the United States. The general prosecutor accused them of trying to overthrow the regime and trying to form a Caliphate State. They confessed before the prosecutor to sending a letter to the Turkish Embassy inviting them to apply the Islamic Shari'a, which was based on the system of succession and the abolition of the secular system. They also admitted their belonging to the LP and that they saw that the best way to survive is to stay away from America, the country of the infidels. They also said that there must be one ruler governing the Islamic nation, who is the Khalifa, and that the most appropriate one is 'Ata Abu Arashta, the leader of the LP. They confirmed that Abu Arashta met the seven requirements to be a Caliph: a male, free, Muslim, mature, responsible, just and capable of carrying the responsibilities of the Caliphate. They stressed that they are doing the right and proper thing and that they are against the existence of the National Assembly. They demanded the National Assembly to be replaced with a Shura Council in accordance with Islamic law and urged the Kuwaiti people to implement the Islamic Shari'a using peaceful methods with this advocacy. They rejected the existing economic, social and political laws because they do not comply with Islamic law and that their ideas will not change until the expulsion of the Americans occur. After a period of investigations, four of the party members were released after paying bail of 1,000 Kuwaiti dinars and three of them were prevented from leaving the country.[111]

There are several factors that led to the failure of the LP in forming a popular base among the Kuwaiti society:

1   The ideology of the LP refused to support the existing regime and called for its removal on the basis that it is a non-Muslim entity, and to create the establishment of the Caliphate State.[112] It is known that the Kuwaiti people rejected these extremist arguments. Since the first political movement in Kuwait, which was the National Bloc that emerged in 1938, and the one which led to the reform movement in that period, ended in an armed clash with the authority, the demand of the political groups was not to replace the ruling family, but rather to establish a civil constitutional system based on the principle of separation of powers. This contradicted the ideology of the LP, and that is why Kuwaiti society did not respond to their call.[113]

2   The absence of influential public Kuwaiti figures, such as 'Abdullah al-Saqer, and 'Abdul-Latif Thenian al-'Ghanim, and others in the National Bloc, and Ahmad al-Khataib, Jassim al-Qatami and Sami al-Munayyis in the ANM, and 'Abdul-'Aziz 'Ali al-Mutawa' in the MBG.

3   The popularity of President Jamal 'Abdel Nasser as a charismatic leader during the 1950s and 1960s in Kuwait and the Arab region due to his solid Arab-nationalist attitudes towards suspicious Western alliances, such as the Hilf Baghdad (Baghdad Pact), the al-Itihad al-'Arabi (the Arab Union), the al-Helf al-Islamiya (Islamic Pact), as well as events that dominated the Arab region, such as the tripartite aggression on Egypt, and the nationalization of the Egyptian Suez Canal, and the establishment of the first Arab federal state in 1958, declaring the state of union between Egypt and Syria. In addition was Nasser's emergence as a world political leader during the Bandung Conference held in April 1955 in Indonesia. All these circumstances led to a growing belief among members of Kuwaiti society in the idea of Arab nationalism and lack of support for the idea of Islamic Khalifate raised by the LP, which is an

expansion of the absolute rule of the Ottoman state that is opposite to the idea of Arab nationalism and was resisted by the Arab people.[114]

4   The experiment of the Kuwaiti people with the Wahhabi movement, which started from the Arabian Peninsula when it tried to extend its influence to Kuwait through the attempt to invade Kuwait in 1919 during the al-Jahra battle. This attempt created a reaction against religious extremism, especially when the Wahabis accused the ruler and the people of Kuwait of not being pious Muslims.

5   The weakness of the religious groups in general and the LP in particular. Also due to the strength of the national movement in general and the ANM in particular. The LP did not find a place to practice its activity in the 1950s, 1960s or 1970s, and its influence was limited despite the fact that the LP was present in Kuwait since the early 1950s. At the same time, the nationalist movements, represented in the ANM, continued to expand and gain control in the political arena in Kuwait during the 1950s. After Kuwait's independence, the ANM dominated the civil society institutions.[115]

6   The conflicts between the LP and the MBG since the foundation of the earlier in Jordan – the MBG later regarded the LP as its strongest competitor to the extent that it would expel any member who had connections with the LP, fearing that it may extract the leadership of the Islamic Movement from them.[116] Especially since the LP considers other religious groups as a threat to the Muslim community because they don't believe that they have a clear Islamic ideology in society. It is not unlikely that the MBG in Kuwait provoked against the ideas of the LP.

7   The party does not enjoy a press influence such as the ANM and the MBG, which had many newspapers and magazines. The LP restricts its published activity in underground leaflets and pamphlets in order not to be prosecuted.

8   The party refused to participate through the institutions of any civil society, such as al-Itihad al-ʾAm li ʿUmmal al-Kuwait (the General Union of Kuwait Workers), al-Itihad al-Watani li Talabat al-Kuwait (the National Union of Kuwait Students (NUKS)), the Teachers Association, the Journalists Association and others, depriving the party from having religious, cultural and social channels through which it communicates with people.

9   The party did not believe in democracy and popular participation and it fought all democratic institutions, regarding them as infidels and creations of colonial powers.

10   The absence of the LP from the active social sectors, which had a great influence on the society, such as the merchants sector – this was contrary to other political groups, such as the ANM, which succeeded in mobilizing these sectors.

The Salafiah Group (SG)
Al-jama'ah al-Salafiah

This organization is considered an extension of the Wahhabi movement, which emerged in the Arabian Peninsula almost 100 years ago. Its first appearance in Kuwait was in the mid-1960s in the form of cells, focusing initially on the al-Faiha, Kaifan and al-Qadisiyah Districts. The SG member could be distinguished from the MBG member by shorter clothing, longer beards and by adopting the mosque as a place for his religious practice, such as the mosques of al-'Abdul-Jalil and Ahmad Bin Hanbel in the al-Faiha District and the al-'Alban mosque in the Kaifan District. Some of the most prominent figures that emerged at that time were Nashmi al-Nashmi, Mosaa'd al-'Abdul-Jader, Khalid al Khadir, 'Abdul-Wahab al-Asnien and Salim al-Salim.[117]

The SG activity concentrated on the establishment of religious activities explaining Ahadeeth al-rassoal (the Prophet sayings), as well as making trips every Friday night to the al-Mangaf shore, where weekly organizational sessions were held. Then their activities developed after the founding of al-Dar al-Slafiyah (Slafiyah House), which is located in Kuwait City. The main activity of the SG members was collecting Zakat (compulsory almsgiving) from the citizens; later new members who had the funds joined the group, such as Khalid al-Sultan, a prominent economist and a graduate of American universities who belonged to a wealthy family. Before joining the SG, al-Sultan was a liberal and chairman of the Kuwaiti Graduates Society, which adopted nationalist and liberal ideals.

Arab immigrant members contributed to the process of incorporation and organization of the SG in Kuwait, such as sheikhs Sheikh 'Abdul-Rahman 'Abdul-Khaliq – a Palestinian in origin who holds Egyptian nationality and arrived from Saudi Arabia to strengthen the SG cells in Kuwait, thus becoming the official spiritual leader of SG – Sheikh 'Abdullah al-Sabt and 'Omar al-Ashqar and others.[118] The main reason behind the emergence of the SG in Kuwait lies in the ambition to be a rival of other religious groups that began to emerge in Kuwait after 1947, such as the MBG, the LP and Jama'at al-Tableegh (Notification Group).[119] The SG criticized the MBG and Jama'at al-Tableegh for not serving the creed properly and for having narrow goals.[120] The SG also accused the MBG of following Ashariate[121] and of deviating in their interpretations of the names and attributes of God.[122] Jassim al-'Oun, a leader in the SG, expressed the differences between them and the MBG in Kuwait by saying that they differ with the MBG in ideologies and methods, where the latter's ideology was based on the MBG leaders' writings, such as Hassan al-Banna and Sayyed Qotb, which had produced Jama'at al-Takfir wa al-Hijra (Denouncement and Holy Flight Society).[123] The religious differences between the two groups had gone further to a dishonest competition, where each group took the opportunity to hold a lecture or seminar in which it tried to erase the significance of the other. Organized and trained members who had the ability of speech in all aspects of religion, culture and economics were employed. The committees of the two groups were active in Ramadan every year in order to mobilize people. The walls were covered with newspapers in the mosques in which they expressed the group's ideologies. In one incident, a member of the MBG removed a publication of the SG from the mosques' walls.[124] SG activity was limited to mosques during the 1960s and 1970s and it did not have a permanent headquarters or a magazine.

Prior to the establishment of Jam'iyat Ihia al-Torath al-Islamiya (Islamic Heritage Revival Society (IHRS)), members of the SG were working within the framework of the SRS on the grounds that this society comprised all Kuwaitis of all Islamic orientations. In the early 1980s, members of the SG succeeded in persuading the Kuwaiti regime in allowing them to have a permanent headquarters. They announced the establishment of the IHRS on 19 December 1981, and Khalid al-Sultan was elected as the first Chairman of the Board of Directors of the IHRS. It should be noted that the SG denies any relationship between them and the IHRS, which represents the official social forefront for the SG. Apparently, the reason behind this denial is to keep the independence of the IHRS in case any of the SG leaders were arrested.[125] The organizational structure of the SG is in complete secrecy, where the names and identities of the group leaders are anonymous. There is a Shura Council, which serves as the supreme command headquarters. It is responsible for creating the policy of the group. It is prohibited to talk about the organizational structure of the SG in public for the safety of its leaders' lives, recalling what has happened to the MBG leaders in Egypt and Jabhat al-Inqhath al-Islamiya (Islamic Salvation Front) in Algeria.[126] There is no particular regulation to join the SG, but the membership is restricted to those who had been chosen by the leaders through a continuous supervision of their attendance at lectures and camps held by the IHRS and then offering the membership to the adequate ones. There is another method to be a member of the SG: the individual shows his desire to join its ranks to one of the public figures of the SG, upon which the leadership will accept his request or reject it.

The SG program focuses on the call for the creation of an Islamic state in accordance with the policy of the legitimate channels through the use of peaceful, constitutional methods and the rejection of the pattern of violence, and gradually to establish an Islamic society through reform of the individual and society. But there is no specific phased program to achieve this.[127]

The SG exploited the facilities provided by the official authorities to extend its influence on the youth centers in Kuwait, which are under the supervision of al-Hay'aa al-'Amma li al-shabab wa al-Riyada (the Public Authority for Youth and Sports). This is a governmental authority that has leaders, such as Saleh al-Nafeesi, one of the active Salafiah student leaders who completed his studies at Kuwait University and became the Deputy Chairman for al-Hay'aa al-'Amma li al-Swhabab wa al-Riyada. Knowing that the purpose of this establishment was to promote sports activities, al-Nafeesi added religious activities through hosting representatives of religious movements such as Nazim al-Mesbah, Sheikh 'Abdul-Rahman 'Abdul-Khaliq, Salman Mandani, Suleimman Ma'rafi and other prominent members of the SG in religious events, such as the month of Ramadan, to give religious lectures under the cover of being cultural forums.[128] During these activities, they announced competitions and valuable prizes after the end of the lectures to attract the largest possible number of young men and women to participate and listen to their lectures.[129]

In addition to its activity in social and religious issues, the SG began its political activity in October 1976 when a number of SG leaders published articles in *al-Watan* newspaper, which gave the group two pages every Friday under the name of al-Shu'n al-Diniya (the religious affairs). In January 1989, the SG managed to publish its own journal: *Majallat al-Forqan* (*Watershed Journal*), which is regarded as the mouthpiece of the SG in Kuwait; Jassim al-'Oun became its chief editor. The journal has embraced all views and opinions of the Salafiah Group supporting the Saudi regime in Saudi Arabia, such as Sheikh 'Abdul-'Aziz bin Baz, al-Sheikh Mohammad bin Othaimeen and al-Sheikh Saleh al-Fozan.

Although the SG has allegedly refused in the past to be dragged into political action and has criticized the MBG, describing them as Asharite whose concern is political activity,[130] those who are in favor of participation in the elections of the National Assembly managed to persuade the majority of the base members in the SG to participate in the elections. On these grounds, the SG participated for the first time in the elections for the National Assembly held in February 1981 by two of its leading members: namely, Jassim al-'Oun and Khalid al-Sultan, and both won memberships in the parliament. Al-Sultan justifies the participation of the SG in the elections by saying that:

> Political work in the parliament was aimed to change Article II of the Constitution and the call for the establishment of the rule of God and change the country with the rule of religion.[131]

After the liberation of Kuwait, the SG participated with other political forces in the political arena in Kuwait to seek the renewal of their political demands, which focused on the call to work within the framework of the 1962 constitution and to hold elections for the National Assembly, which was dissolved in 1986. The representatives of the SG signed a statement issued by all the political groups under the name al-Rai al-Mustaqbali li Benaa' al-Kuwait al-Gadidah (the vision of the future to build new Kuwait).[132] In the meantime, the political arena in Kuwait witnessed an important development on the national level when seven political groups announced themselves in public gatherings with specific names and announced some of their political, economic and social programs. The SG was one of them and took the new name of al-Tajammau' al-Islamyi al-Sha'abi (the Islamic Popular Gathering).[133]

Notification Group (NG)
Jama'at al-Tableeg

This organization was founded in the 1960s in Sabhan District by Sheikh Fouad al-Rifa'i and Sheikh 'Abdul-'Aiziz al-Hagan. The Notification Group (NG) used the Sabhan mosque as a center for its activities in Kuwait. Traditionally, the NG is regarded as an extension of Tableeq Society in India, which was founded by Sheikh Mohammad Ilyas bin Mohammed Isma'il al-Kandaholi,[134] who advocated for his call in the Arabian Peninsula when he came to Saudi Arabia in 1938. His followers continued to be active in all Muslim countries even after his death. The NG approach is to concentrate on religious education, the conservation of the Quran, the establishment of religious schools, and to promote volunteering in Islamic action among the poor. The NG was opposed to the traditional ways of Islam, such as Sufism, as well as to the visits being made to graves; they regarded these actions as a sort of worship to idols.[135] The NG was also against participation in the government and political activities, and for this reason it opposed the politicization of Islam led by Seyyed Qutb, Abu al-A'la al-Mawdudi and Imam Khomeini in the region.[136] The NG's objective was not in establishing Islamic rule; on the contrary, it demanded that its members and supporters stay away from discussing political matters on the basis that politics divide 'brothers' and spread hatred among Muslims. Furthermore, they believed that engagement in political matters might cause a halt to the activities of advocacy. In this sense, the NG does not seek to establish Islamic rule, does not contest elections, does not support or oppose the political regime in any country and avoids discussing these regimes in all lectures or seminars that it sponsors. The NG believes that the problems and difficulties experienced by Muslims are a result of the desertion of Muslims to the provisions of Islam and that the only solution is the commitment of Muslims to their religion. The NG does not believe in political and military solutions for the Palestinian cause, the jihad in Afghanistan, Palestine and Iraq, contrary to other Islamic movements and groups that are engaged in armed action.[137] The NG is distinguished from the rest of the Islamic movements and groups by having its own style and character in a peaceful change through a spiritual approach, and the call to reform the individual. The Greater Jihad for the group is through self-reform rather than calling for a political coup. The NG has no social or political concerns in a battle with the state on the issues of legitimacy and justice and, in this sense, the theoreticians of the MBG criticized the NG, especially al-Mawdudi, who said:

> It is useless to advocate for Islam in the manner of a Christian missionary.[138]

Fathi Yakan expressed that the style of the group is unable to establish an organized gathering capable of opposing al-jahiliya (pre-Islam ages) and the establishment of an Islamic society and an Islamic state and that this method will be limited to mosque attendees and will not be able to face the challenges of ideas and material philosophies.[139] 'Abdullah al-'Atiqi, one of the MBG leaders in Kuwait, addressed several criticisms to the NG: that its staying away from political and economic activity means taking part of Islam and leaving the others, that it lacks the political organization which will lead to the discontinuation of this group, and finally the absence of Shari'a education among the members of the group.[140]

In the beginning, the NG used 'Omar Bin 'Abdul-'Aziz mosque in the Ahmadi district as a center for its activities, then moved to Sabhan mosque, where the group held weekly meetings every Thursday evening and then the members were distributed in the various governorates of Kuwait for advocacy. The group has to do weekly rounds where members work on notifying people through a visit to mosques, homes, shops and institutions distributing religious tapes and pamphlets. As defined by Sheikh al-Kandaholi, the founder of the NG, its advocacy is based on six principles: no God but Allah, Mohammad is his prophet, praying, religious science, respect every Muslim, and loyalty. Through these principles the NG invited people for a maximum of four months to join its ranks.[141] The NG suffered from the arrests and harassment by the authorities and Sheikh Fouad al-Rifa'i, the emir of the group, was arrested several times.[142] The group is currently headed by Sheikh Rashid al-Haqan and still has limited activity in Kuwaiti society.

The Adherence Movement (AM)
Harakat al-Murabitun

This movement was founded by the MBG in Kuwait during the Iraqi occupation of Kuwait. The leading members of the youth sector within the organization who stayed in Kuwait and participated in founding the AM were Sheikh Jassim Muhalhal al-Yassin, 'Isa Majed al-Shaheen and Sami al-Khatrash. The organizational structure of the AM consisted of the security wing, which is divided into two sections – the popular resistance section, which commanded the military work such as gathering information, communication, intelligence documentation and armed operations; and the institutional section, which carried out functions related to health, energy, electricity, water, fire, and transportation – and the civil wing, which carried out a mission of solidarity and is divided into several sections. The most important of these was the residential areas section, where committees of social solidarity in various neighborhoods were formed to do some of its most important activities, which included the care of prisoners and carrying out tasks of the Red Crescent Affairs, such as digging graves and carrying out financing and distribution tasks.[143] The AM participated in the civil resistance movement and played a role in supervising the co-operative societies, urging citizens to resist. After the liberation, the AM was active in the formation of Lijan al-Takaful (care committees), which supervised the operation of basic services for citizens. The bulletin *al-Murabitun* was the official magazine of the AM, issued in London during the Iraqi occupation of Kuwait. It was a weekly magazine headed by Nasser al-Sani', one of the MBG leaders.[144] After the sixth issue of *al-Murabitun*, a decision was taken by the occupied Iraqi authorities to execute any person dealing with any publication. After the liberation, and as a result of the return of the constitutional institutions to work, the MBG abandoned this movement and began operating under a new name: the ICM.

The Islamic Constitutional Movement (ICM)
Al-Haraka al-Dstoria al-Islamiya

On 30 March 1991, the MBG in Kuwait decided to abandon the old organization, the AM, and to establish a new organization: the Islamic Constitutional Movement (ICM). It seems that the reason for taking this designation was the position of the international organization of the MBG towards the Iraqi occupation on the one hand, absorbing the popular wrath towards the international organization, which took Iraq's side in a meeting held by the Islamic Association in Pakistan attended by delegations representing the MBG from all over the world. This meeting did not refer to the Iraqi occupation of Kuwait, but stressed the support of the delegates to the regime of Saddam Hussein.[145] The same action was also repeated during the Islamic Conference, which was held in the Sudanese capital of Khartoum, where resolutions were supportive of those taken in the meeting in Pakistan.[146] Other branches of the MBG in the Arab region took a strong position in favor of the Iraqi regime, such as the MBG branch in Jordan, which issued a statement that called for the support of Iraq, and speeches were given by their leaders for this purpose.[147] In Syria, the MBG described the campaign against Iraq as being targeted against the Arab and Islamic worlds, and not only against Iraq.[148] In Egypt, a number of the MBG leaders supported the Iraqi occupation. Mamoun al-Hudaybi, the spokesman of the MBG in Egypt, said, for example, in an interview with Jordanian radio, that the basic demand of the Muslim Brotherhood is the expulsion of foreign forces from the Gulf,[149] forgetting intentionally that the basic reason for the presence of the foreign forces in the region was the Iraqi occupation in the first place.

Despite its alleged desertion of the international organization of the MBG, the ICM is still committed to the ideology developed by the founder of the MBG, Hassan al Banna. In this context, Mubarak al-Dowaila, one leading figure in the ICM, confirms that the ICM is still committed to the al-Banna line.[150]

There are still strong relations between the MBG in Kuwait and the international organization of the MBG through the participation of a representative of the MBG in Kuwait at the Guidance Office. The MBG in Kuwait did not object to the pro-Iraq positions taken by the international organization of the MBG.[151] The evidence on the lack of credibility of the desertion of the

MBG internationally to support Kuwait fully with the international organization lies in the literature of the MBG in Kuwait, whether through *Majallat al-Mujtama'* or *al-Murabitun* bulletin or within the electoral program of the ICM or *Majallat al-Haraka* (*Movement Journal*), the official journal of the ICM, where they all fail to mention the supportive position for the occupation of Kuwait of the international organization of the MBG. According to *Majallat al-Mossawar*, the Egyptian magazine, the investigations conducted by the Egyptian authorities with the leaders of the MBG in Egypt confirm that the leaders of the MBG held a training course on the SRS premises in Kuwait. In addition, they used sources to provide funding for the organization to revive the MBG international organization in the Islamic world. In 2007, Hamoud al-Rumi, the chairman of the SRS, became the representative of the MBG-Kuwait branch in the Shura Council of the international organization of the Muslim Brotherhood instead of 'Abdullah 'Ali al-Mutawa', the former leader of the MBG in Kuwait, who died in 2007. This council consists of 36 members representing all the MBG branches in the Arab and Islamic countries.[151] 'Abdullah 'Ali al-Mutawa' confirmed in his memoirs the continuation of the close relationship between the MBG and the international organization and mentioned his meetings with Hassan al-Hudaybi, 'Omar al-Talmasani and Mohammad Mahdi 'Akif.[152]

The ICM Conference elected the Central Committee of the ICM, where Sheikh Jassim Muhalhal al-Yasin became its secretary general and 'Isa Majed al-Shaheen the official spokesman for the ICM. In 2003, Badr al-Nashi was elected as the Secretary General for the ICM. In 2009, Nasser al-Sani' was elected as its Secretary General. Al-Yasin confirmed that the new name adopted by the MBG in Kuwait was to create a new framework for a popular political organization for all who adopt the ICM's program, which is expressed in the document issued by the ICM under the name *Nahwa Esteratigiyah Dostouriyah Islamiya li E'adat Benaa' al-Kuwait* (*Towards a Constitutional Islamic Strategy for Rebuilding Kuwait*). The ICM is composed of members of the AM and, after the liberation, a number of citizens who lived abroad during the occupation joined it.[153]

The ICM emphasizes that it is not a non-profit society, or a charity society, or a group for preaching and guidance, but it is a political organization that uses the political action mechanism to serve its objectives represented in the deep faith of Islam and that the movement has chosen Islam as its ideology.[154] At the same time, the ICM abides by the constitution of 1962 as a framework for its political activity and it believes in a multi-party political system.[155]

The ICM has a number of objectives, the most important of which are:[156]

1   Develop a political system for greater popular participation.
2   Amend the constitution in a way that satisfies the optimum application of Islam's rules and principles.
3   Preserve justice in the country, achieve equality among citizens and preserve the Shura (the Islamic Council) principle.

4   Distribute the state's income in accordance with the principles of Islam.
5   Try to establish social, educational and information systems that are based on Islamic foundations.

It is noticeable from the above mentioned objectives of the ICM program that they seek to amend the constitution and the application of the principles of Islam, which means that the ICM does not believe in democracy on which the constitution of Kuwait is built.[157]

In addition to its declared name and its program, the ICM was keen to develop a secret plan to control all aspects of life.[158] This emphasizes the fact that the MBG-Kuwait branch is still active secretly and indefinitely, and that the ICM name is just a disguise and no more than that, as the movement takes from it a forefront for its political activity. It seems that the secret scheme adopted by the leadership of the MBG for domination and control has paved the road for its success in the student movement, the trade union, economic sector, some of the civil society institutions and, finally, among the legislative and executive institutions.

On this basis, the ICM participated in the first general elections that took place in Kuwait after the liberation in October 1992 with five candidates representing the ICM officially. Some of the founders of the ICM participated as independents. It seems that the aim of the ICM behind this action is to prepare some of its figures in case they are successfully chosen to be part of the cabinet as independents and not as party members. The ICM has been able to achieve good results both at the level of official candidates and through the independent candidates supported by the movement formally.

The ICM followed a soft line towards the Kuwaiti regime and succeeded in passing its Islamic projects where the ICM has a plan for its political agenda regarding its activity within the National Assembly. It has distributed the roles between its representatives in the National Assembly to achieve its goal in the Islamization of laws. This plan included a draft law to amend the penal law related to drugs and alcohol, moral crimes and information policy. Moreover, there is a draft law on the establishment of the Social Development Authority. It also includes the draft law on disallowing the use of women in the media, a draft law that imposes segregation in education and other areas. Those MPs who were responsible for submitting these drafts were Jam'an al-'Azmi, Jamal al-Kandari, Nasser al-Sani', Isma'il al-Shatti and Mubarak al-Dowaila. The ICM has succeeded through this relation with the political regime in the implementation of its political agenda in the National Assembly.

The ICM participated in the eighth elections of the National Assembly in 1996, where the political atmosphere differed from the 1992 elections. In this connection, a secret document describing these circumstances states:

> The Islamic movement in Kuwait is witnessing a new phase in its orientation and impact that differs from the period witnessed during the 1992 elections . . . at that period the movement was living a stage of pride due

to its performance and its contribution to the resistance which was appreciated by everyone, including the regime itself. The situation started to change in this period ... On the political side the regime adopted general policies that narrow the impact of the Islamic movement in all levels. In the social aspect the observer can notice a decline in the Islamic awakening in favor of the trend of westernization and secularization that contributed to the increase in moral corruption.[159]

Accordingly, the ICM developed its strategy and objectives as follows:[160]

1   Work on the formation of a parliamentary majority in the Assembly sympathizing with the demands of the Islamic trend.
2   Nominate 10 members who would represent the movement in the next Assembly.
3   Increase the number of representatives of the Islamic bloc in the Assembly.
4   Decrease the percentage of the government and Liberal bloc who oppose the Islamization.

In order to implement this strategy and objectives, the movement had adopted several policies toward Sunni and Shi'ite Islamic forces, merchants and tribes, represented in the following:[161]

- political co-ordination with the IHRS in order to form a majority in the National Assembly
- political co-ordination with the Shi'ites and the adoption of common issues and concerns and do not show any hostility towards them
- political co-ordination with the merchants by trying to persuade those who sympathize with the Islamic trend to participate in the elections
- benefit from the tribes, who are regarded by the movement as a conservative class, and push them to participate in the elections in order to adopt a political program that coincides with the movement's aspirations.

The ICM participated in the elections for the National Assembly in 1999 with 15 candidates. The movement suffered a major defeat as only Nasser al-Sani' and Mohammad al-Busairi managed to win, where the second won according to tribal considerations and not for ideological ones. The representatives of the movement in the National Assembly have succeeded in the formation of al-kutlah al-Islamiya (Islamic Bloc), which included in its ranks representatives of the Islamist Sunni political groups, and its goal was to co-ordinate among each other in order to have common positions against orientations of the liberal representatives in the parliament and to submit drafts for Islamic projects. The representatives of the ICM in the Islamic Bloc in collaboration with some Sunni pro-Islamic fundamentalist movement MPs took a strict attitude towards the law to give women political rights made by the government, and it held symposiums, lectures and issued statements showing its opposition for the adoption of such law.[162] The MPs Dayfullah Abu Ramiah, a member of the Islamic Bloc, held a symposium under the slogan Wefqan li al-Shari'a al-Islamiya . . . Laisa li al-Marah Huquq Seyasiah (in accordance with Islamic Law . . . women do not have political rights).[163] He regarded that law as: 'a disgrace to the nation if approved.'[164] In spite of this campaign, the government managed to pass the law, especially with American pressure exerted on the Kuwaiti regime.[165]

The ICM took a firm stand against the Danish Government when one of the Danish newspapers attacked Islam and the Prophet Mohammad, peace be upon him, demanding the Kuwaiti Government take proper diplomatic and economic measures and to use the weapons of strict economic boycott against those who have adopted this deviant line.[166] The MP Nasser al-Sana', a member of the Political Bureau of the ICM, demanded an immediate investigation by the Danish Government, emphasizing that Western democracy has proved full hostility to Islam and Muslims.[167]

The ICM took a firm stand against the statement made by Pope Benedict XVI against Islam during his visit to Germany, and it considered this statement as an offense to the Prophet of Islam. Mohammad al-'Olaim, the official spokesperson for the movement, emphasized that such statements reflect the hostility and unjustified attacks on Islam and Muslims, the ignorance of others of Islamic principles and foundations, and urged the Pope to apologize for what he said.[168] Mohammad al-Busairi, Deputy Speaker of the Kuwaiti National Assembly and one of the leaders of the movement, also warned that there would be a massive wave of anger in response to the insult of Islam, considered the Pope's apology not enough and urged him to admit his sin.[169] The SRS, the religious front of the ICM, also called for expelling the Vatican ambassador from Kuwait to stop 'Christianization' from taking place in Kuwait and not to allow the building of any new churches in Kuwait. Furthermore, he urged that an official apology be made by the Pope personally on TV channels and force the teaching of Islam as a creed and a law in Kuwaiti private universities.[170] Saa'd al-Shari'a, one of the ICM supporters and representatives of al-Kutlah al-Islamiya al-Mostakillah (the Independent Islamic Bloc) in the National Assembly, demanded that all churches be removed from Kuwait.[171]

The Russian Government banned the activity of SRS on Russian territory along with 17 organizations supporting terrorism in Russia, such as al-Qaeda, Jamma'at Ansar al-Islam (Islamic Supporters Group) in Lebanon and Jamma'at al-Jihad (Jihadiast Group) in Egypt.[172] Akdaeier al-Enezi, one of the representatives of the ICM in the Kuwaiti National Assembly, said that Zionist groups are behind these accusations seeking to distort the image of Islamic charity and activity in the world and that the accusations made by the Russian Government are mere fabrications.[173] Because of its support to the Islamist political groups, the Kuwaiti regime defended the SRS and the IHRS, where the Foreign Ministry sent an official note to the Russian Government in protest against the inclusion by the Russian Government of the SRS and the IHRS on the terrorist list, summoning the Russian Chargé of Affaires in Kuwait.[174] The Director of the Department of Co-ordination and Follow-up at the Kuwaiti Foreign Ministry, Khalid al-Maqamis, said:

> It is unjust to confuse between . . . pure charity work and a terrorist act. . . . The SRS and the IHRS are known for their humanitarian and charity work.[175]

After there was a dispute between the government and Kutlat al-Tis'ah wal'shron Nab (Bloc of 29 MPs), which included representatives of the ICM MPs in the National Assembly,[176] due to the division of constituencies where the Bloc of 29 MPs rejected the current division of constituencies represented by the 25 constituencies, endorsing the slogan Nabiha Khamsa (we want it five) raised by Harakat Nabiha Khamsa (We Want it Five Movement).[177] The meaning of this slogan is the division of constituencies to five instead of 25 constituencies. The Bloc of 29 MPs believed that the old division of constituencies was behind the massive corruption in the political system. The government and its loyal MPs rejected the division of the five constituencies and referred the proposal to the Constitutional Court. Following these developments, three MPs from the Bloc of 29 MPs requested the questioning of the Prime Minister, Sheikh Nasser al-Mohammad al-Sabah, resulting in the dissolution of the National Assembly. Then the Emir issued an Emiri resolution calling for new parliamentary elections to take place on 29 June 2006. The elections resulted in most of the candidates of the ICM and its supporters winning. The movement abandoned its allies in the Bloc of 29 deputies and was absent from the mass meeting held on 7 July 2006 in Sahat al-Irada (Determination Square), opposite the Kuwaiti National Assembly. This was attended by members of the National Assembly belonging to the NDA, the National Islamic Alliance (NIA), the KDF, the SM and some independent Islamist members; they announced their support for Ahmad al-So'doun, the head of the Kutlat al-'Amal al-Sh'abi for the presidency of the National Assembly against the former Speaker of the Assembly, Jassim al-Kharafi, who was supported by the government and its loyal MPs. During the election for the Speaker of the National Assembly and his Vice-Speaker, the alliance between the ICM and the government was clear, as Ahmad al-So'doun failed in winning the post of Speaker of the Assembly, while the ICM movement's candidate, Mohammad al-Busairi, won the post of Vice-Speaker with the support of the government votes. Ismai'l al-Shatti was appointed Deputy Prime Minister and Minister of State for Cabinet Affairs. He was then replaced by Mohammad al-'Olaim, the Spokesperson of the ICM, as the Minister of Electricity and al-Shatti was appointed as a consultant in the Prime Minister's office. In addition, when the Kutlat al-'Amal al-Sh'abi and Kutlat al-'Amal al-Watani (the National Action Bloc) – representing the liberal trend in the Assembly – submitted a question for the Minister of Oil, Sheikh 'Ali al-Jarrah al-Sabah, on the ground of his relationship with Sheikh 'Ali al-Khalifa al-Sabah (who was accused in the oil tanks embezzlement case, which the former mentioned in an interview with *al-Qabas* newspaper)[178] the ICM representatives in the National Assembly took a supportive stand with the Minister of Oil.

Following this dispute, the Emir dissolved the National Assembly and called for the election of a new parliament on 17 May 2008 according to the new electoral law. The outcome of the election resulted in the victory of three MPs for the ICM out of eight candidates. Thus, the ICM registered a significant decline compared with the 2006 parliamentary elections, where its number of representatives was six. There are a number of factors that contributed to this significant decline:

1   The failure of some of the ICM leaders in the primary (tribal) elections in the tribal areas, bearing in mind that there was a law issued in 1998 that prohibits conducting such elections.
2   The refusal of the tribes to support political movements.
3   The absence of the spiritual leader of the MBG, the late 'Abdullah 'Ali al Mutawa', which caused the loss of great social impact.
4   The failure of the movement to arrange family and tribal alliances that would increase the number of votes, especially in the third and second constituencies.
5   The poor performance of some candidates from the movement and their lack of outstanding leadership could be included among the causes of the decline and the failure of the ICM in these elections.
6   When there is no coalition and co-ordination between the candidates of the Salafi Islamic Gathering (SIG) and the ICM, a considerable decline of representatives of the ICM will occur, as happened in the 2003 elections where there were 15 ICM candidates but only two won.
7   Strict positions of the ICM on a number of issues reflected negatively on its supporters, such as their opposition to co-education and their issuing of a statement that hurt the feelings of parents of the students, which contributed to the decline of their base and their popularity.

Since the founding of the ICM, it has not raised issues of major importance. It has only dealt with issues such as wearing veils on university premises; the Committee for the Propagation of Virtue and the Prevention of Vice; standing with the proposal submitted by the MP Dhaifallah Abu Ramiah to abolish teaching music in public schools;[179] the prevention of concerts held in the month of Ramadan; preventing the opening of dance training centers; preventing fashion shows and Internet cafes; and other trivial issues so as to distract citizens from the key issues, especially those related to the disaster of plundering public money. The National Democratic Alliance, which represents the liberal stream in Kuwait, attacked the Islamist political groups sharply by describing them as forces of religious bigotry that are leading an organized campaign to intervene and prevent all forms of innocent entertainment, including television series and movies that do not agree with the views of the forces of religious bigotry.[180] The Alliance also criticized the Information Minister, Mohammad al-Sen'ausi, for 'looking for legitimate justifications (fatwas) and forgetting that Kuwait is a State of Law and Constitution, rather than a State of religious forces which make fatwas for everything without controls or mechanisms.'[181] The Alliance also stressed in its statement that it would counter any attempt to drag in the smaller matters at the expense of important national issues.[182]

Islamic Popular Gathering (IPG)
Al-Tajammau' al-Islami al-Sha'abi

After the liberation of Kuwait, the SG adapted the new name of al-Tajammau' al-Islami (Islamic Gathering), which has been used officially in the signing of the subsequent statements issued at the beginning of the liberation. The name was changed later to the Islamic Popular Gathering (IPG), as a definition and description of the SG that formed al-Lijan al-Sha'baih (popular committees) during the occupation.[183] The official announcement of the IPG, the official political front of the SG in Kuwait, is regarded as an important development in the ideology of the SG, whereas the idea of the declaration of the organization was by itself controversial among the SG ranks.[184]

In its first statement – which carried the title Hawl Tahkeem al-Shari'a al-Islamiya (on the Islamic Shari'a arbitration) – the IPG criticized the officials who exploited their positions for personal purposes and did not observe God in their work, and stated that the biggest fault of the regime was moving away from God. The statement also criticized depriving the Kuwaiti people of their right to participate in decision-making and keeping them away from supervising the executive authority. The statement demanded to review all the legislation that violated the Islamic Shari'a and to replace it with Islamic legislation.[185] The IPG also called on the Kuwaiti regime to establish Islamic Shari'a, the arbitration law of God in Kuwait, to reform the existing system and to create a climate of freedom and democracy through the Shari'a and the constitution. The IPG criticized the first Kuwaiti Cabinet formed after the liberation and stated that the selection of members of the government should be based on certain criteria, describing the reshuffle as random and incompatible with the aspirations of the Kuwaiti people. The IPG also demanded that the post-liberation government should be a government of national unity in which all political trends should be represented. The IPG endorsed the call for the separation of the Crown Prince from the presidency of the ministers, since the Constitution separates the two positions in accordance with Article no. 56, which states that 'The Amir shall, after the traditional Consultation, appoint the Prime Minister and relieve him of office. . . .'[186]

The IPG participated in the parliamentary elections that took place after the liberation of Kuwait on 5 October 1992 to elect members of the National

Assembly with seven candidates, and announced its support for another 11 candidates. For the first time the SG declared its own electoral program, which was considered a step forward in the field of political participation; this included a set of points that affect the social, political and economic aspects, mainly:[187]

1 Amend Article II of the Constitution such that the Islamic Shari'a is the main source of legislation.
2 Amend all existing legislation that violates the Islamic Shari'a.
3 The executive authority has to take into account the provisions of Islamic Shari'a in all its policies.
4 The implementation of Islamic Shari'a should not be a slogan merely raised for local consumption or for a political purpose.
5 Recognition of the principle of popular participation in running the country's affairs and reject autocratic rule.
6 Support the security agreements signed by the government with Western countries that have been described by the IPG as friendly countries that have contributed to the liberation of Kuwait.
7 The submission of the Cabinet reshuffle to the parliamentary majority and to allow all the people to hold ministerial posts, including the ministries of sovereignty.
8 Amendment of the law of gatherings to achieve freedom of meeting without restrictions.
9 Kuwaiti economic systems must be based on Islamic doctrine.
10 Emphasize the Arab identity of the Kuwaiti people.
11 Emphasize that the Islamic doctrine is the base for the foreign policy of Kuwait, that Kuwait should interact with the issues of Muslims in the world and preach Islam to the world.

Majallat al-Forqan urged the Kuwaiti people in its opening article to vote for the candidate who has the strength and the faith and not to vote for candidates who belonged to suspicious parties and groups that enforced sectarianism and are loyal to foreign hostile regimes, or those parties that believe in the secular approach. It was considered that the winning of the secular and sectarian approach in the parliamentary elections is the greatest betrayal of the nation.[188]

This election resulted in the victory of three IPG candidates and four of the SM candidates that were not officially listed with the IPG candidates but were backed up by them.[189]

After announcing the results of the elections, which showed a clear dominance of the representatives of the religious trend in the National Assembly, the representatives of the IPG proposed a draft law calling for the establishment of the Public Authority for al-Amr bi al-Ma 'ruf wa al-Nahi 'an al-Munkar (the promotion of virtue and the prohibition of vice).[190] The aim of this proposal was to provide legal cover; this body had already been initiated when the SG, after the liberation, founded the legitimate body for the promotion of virtue and the prohibition of vice, where 80 people from religious groups requested the Kuwaiti regime to form this committee and their request was declined. However, the committee continued illegally and imposed itself on Kuwaiti society. The Secretariat General of the committee is Walid al-Tabtabae, a teacher at the Faculty of Shari'a and a current member of the National Assembly.[191] Consequently, the IPG representatives in the National Assembly proposed a draft law to form the Public Authority for the Propagation of Virtue and Prevention of Vice,[192] which states:

> The need to revive the Propagation of Virtue ... through planning, supervision and oversight and to compel the Ministry of Interior to send monthly reports to the Authority, which in turn has offices and branches in all the governorates of Kuwait.[193]

The draft faced an anti-campaign by liberal writers in the newspapers, who regarded the project as a contradiction to the public freedoms guaranteed by the Constitution. They considered the draft of the Salafiah Group as incompatible with the principles of the separation of powers as stated in the Constitution of Kuwait and felt that it limited the powers of the Prime Minister and regarded al-Amr bi al-Ma 'Ruf wa al-Nahi 'an al-Munkar (the promotion of virtue and the prohibition of vice) as a state within a state.[194] This project is very serious because it was submitted by a group with one religious orientation, which means the imposition of its concepts on others regardless of their religious affiliation. This is why the Shi'ite sect has declared its rejection of the establishment of this Authority and expressed fears towards the adoption of this law by the National Assembly; it distributed leaflets inside Kuwait University attacking this project, describing it as a draft that confiscates freedoms and that sectarian terrorism is practiced without taking into consideration the national unity.[195] In return, the organizations dominated by the Sunni fundamentalist groups issued a statement supporting the proposal of the representatives of the Islamic political groups in the National Assembly.[196]

After this campaign, the IPG withdrew the draft law,[197] but they succeeded in adopting a number of religious laws, such as preventing co-education in all levels of education in government schools except foreign schools. Furthermore, IPG MPs, with other Islamic MPs, succeeded in establishing Lajnat Derasat al-Dhawaher al-Salbiya fi al-Mujtma' (Committee for Studying Negative Phenomena in the Society), and the Parliament voted completely with it except for four liberal MPs. This committee's main focus was to implement Islamic laws in all detail of the society. The phenomena the committee is considering include private parties, TV shows, bisexuals and many other matters. This would mean that members of the parliament are intervening in every person's life even if they are not invited to do so, as the Public Authority for al-Amr bi al-Ma 'ruf wa al-Nahi 'an al-Munkar (the promotion of virtue and the prohibition of vice) is doing in Saudi Arabia. Also, many lawyers and constitutional experts agree on the point that this committee is not constitutional.

The IPG, either through its representatives in the National Assembly or through articles that have appeared in *Majallat al-Forqan*, has shown strict positions against giving women their political rights, including the right to vote and to stand for elections. It's worth mentioning that the issue of women's participation in political life was raised directly after the liberation and the women's movement has headed the campaign to give them their political rights represented in holding women's gatherings, which called for the exercise of women's political rights and submit petitions to the National Assembly.[198]

When the government announced the elections of the municipal council on 6 June 1995, the IPG participated in this election with four candidates for the 2nd, 3rd, 8th and 9th constituencies. All political groups competed in these elections on the grounds that they give a voice in the elections for the National Assembly in 1996. The IPG candidates suffered a severe defeat – none of its candidates won.[199]

On 7 October 1996, elections for the eighth National Assembly were held – the second parliamentary elections in Kuwait after the liberation – and the SG participated in these elections without the formal announcement of any representatives of the IPG, since the IPG suffered from the conflicts with the SG members.[200] They succeeded in winning three seats.

The representatives of the IPG in alliance with representatives of other Islamist political groups and pro-government MPs worked on depriving the liberal and leftist representatives from holding positions in the main commit-tees of the National Assembly. The representatives of the IPG with other religious forces held a campaign to collect signatures of members of the National Assembly on a petition demanding the Emir approve the amend-ment of Article II of the Constitution to make Islamic Shari'a the sole source of legislation. Mubarak al-Dowaila, a representative of the ICM, urged the representatives of the religious forces to compose a delegation to meet the Emir to support their demands, but before the composition of that delega-tion, an indirect refusal came from the Emir through his annual speech in Ramadan, saying that there is al-Lajna al-Istishariya al-'Olia Lial'amal Li al'amal 'Ala Istikmal Tatbig Ahkam al-Shari'a al-Islamiya (Supreme Advisory Committee to work on completing the implementation of the provisions of Islamic Shari'a), which was formed on 2 December 1991, in an indication that the Kuwaiti regime is working in that direction.[201] Representatives of the IPG also submitted a draft for a law that imposed *zakat* on all companies and economic institutions working in Kuwait, and almost succeeded in the adoption of a law that banned concerts, songs and fashion shows, namely:[202]

- non-establishment or advertising for a concert without taking official permission

- commitment to good conduct and decent clothing by women from both the performers and the audience
- prevention of dancing in all its forms, whether from the performers or from the audience
- prevention of concerts in the month of Ramadan
- preventing foreign institutions that have programs in violation of the traditions of the country to participate in concerts such as the Star Academy and Miss Lebanon
- an official permission to hold a concert has to be obtained from the Ministry of Information
- if a serious matter is conducted in a concert, the concert will be halted and those responsible will be arrested and brought to the Public Prosecutor
- officials should attend concerts and monitor them
- granting the right of judicial police inspectors during the concerts, rather than simply writing reports, as is the case now
- prevention of girls below the age of 21 years to enter concerts except those accompanied by parents.

The fatwa committee in the Ministry of Awqaf and Islamic Affairs dominated by groups of political Islamists issued a fatwa regarding the singing performances, which included strict regulations, such as forbidding mixing between sexes among the audience and that a male singer should sing for male audiences only and the same thing be adopted for females.[203]

In 1999, the IPG participated in the general elections for the National Assembly with seven candidates; only two of them won: Ahmad Baqir, representing the fifth constituency, and Ahmad Mohammad al-Di'aij, representing the seventh constituency, Kaifan. The group leader was among those candidates who lost the elections.

In addition to its activities and the organizational work in the Kuwaiti arena, the IPG had clear political activity in most countries, where it supported many of the Salafiah organizations in various countries around the world.[204]

In 2000, differences among the IPG ranks occurred and some of its leaders abandoned the organization to form an independent organization called al-Haraka al-Salafiah al-'Ilmiyya (the Scientific Salafiah Movement (SSM)); then the IPG changed its name to al-Tajammu' al-Islami al-Salafi (the Salafi Islamic Gathering (SIG)). Salem al-Nashi was chosen as its Secretary General, followed by Khalid al-Sultan, who confirmed that the SIG is part of the political action of the Salafiah advocacy and serves its activities on the political level; that the political activity of this gathering is not a goal in itself but a means to achieve the objectives of collective action to the Salafiah cause; and its objectives are adopted from the Salafiah advocacy program.[205] He added that the gathering is not limited to certain people and does not have narrow partisan interests. Furthermore, he stated that SIG is not a gathering of interests, but is a gathering that works for the benefit of Islam and Muslims carrying the Salafi advocacy.[206] According to al-Sultan, the objectives of the SIG are:[207]

1 Islamize laws and apply Islamic Shari'a.
2 Expand political influence in order to open the prospects for the Islamic faith.
3 Preserve the nation from Westernization.
4 Protect the charity activity and the activity of the Islamic faith from internal and external pressures, which aims to narrow the charity and Islamic advocacy.
5 Combat bad phenomena and promote virtue and prevention of vice.
6 Defend the Islamic creed and consolidate it in society.
7 Highlight the role of the Salafi advocacy in addressing the nation's issues and its challenges.
8 Adopt a plan to support the return of Muslims' dignity.
9 Narrow the effectiveness and the role of the hostile groups to Islam and undermine their schemes to Westernize the society.
10 Demand the participation of the members of the National Assembly in the process of choosing the Prime Minister and the ministers.
11 Restructure the distribution of constituencies and fight against the intervention of the regime in election results and the buying of votes in order to ensure a good selection of members in the National Assembly.

The SIG is close to the political regime, where its representative in the National Assembly, Ahmad Mohammad al-Di'aij, abstained from the vote of confidence on the Minister of Finance, Yousef al-Ibrahim, away from the overwhelming majority of the representatives of the Islamist political groups in the National Assembly. In addition, Ahmad Baqir, a prominent MP representing the SIG, was appointed as the Minister of Awqaf, then the Minister of Justice and Minister of Municipality. The SIG took a strict stand against the announcement of the political parties in accordance with the government position regarding this issue.

In 2003, the SIG participated in the general elections for the tenth National Assembly with eight candidates and only two of them won: Ahmad Baqir, representing the fifth constituency, and Fahad al-Khanah, representing the sixth constituency, al-Faiha. The gathering played a role in the failure of the liberal candidates such as 'Abdullah al-Nibari, Ahamad al-Rub'i and others. In this regard, Salem al-Nashi, the Secretary General of the SIG, says:

> We sought for the failure of the liberal candidates and we succeeded in doing so. We even do not have candidates in their constituencies, so that we have enough time to fail them, and they are great symbols of the liberals.[208]

The former president of the IHRS and the current Secretary General for the SIG, Khalid al-Sultan, criticized the liberals and accused them of turning the external forces against the Islamic trend, in which he said:

It is clear that the secularists and liberals are not seeking rights . . . But their activity is a tool of the enemies of Islam and the enemies of the nation. They stand today with the massacres committed by the Jews in Palestine and turned their backs on their nation . . . So they are sick and this ideology is an intruder to the nation and a tumor that has to be removed from the nation . . . The Kuwaiti secularism and liberalism used a dangerous method by referring to external forces and its stark incitement to the Kuwaiti political forces on the Kuwaiti regime . . . And asked them to put pressure on the government to secularize the Kuwaiti regime under the pretext of human rights and women's political and social rights and limitation of the charitable and religious work and that these are a threat to the future of this country.[209]

The representative of the SIG in the National Assembly, Fahad al-Khanah, regarded the demands of the Human Rights Association to stop the death penalty as contrary to common sense and a contradiction to God's law. He accused the Association of carrying Western ideas and called for the dissolution and disintegration in violation of instinct in Shari'a and that it does not represent the Kuwaiti society, but represents the views of the corrupt and is inconsistent with the principles of Islam. He demanded the Association apologize to the people of Kuwait for their repetition of ideas contrary to religion.[210]

The SIG took a tough position against the United States, where it addressed a severe criticism to the American practices in the city of Fallujah, stating that its troops do not differentiate between a baby, the elderly or a weak woman, and this was inconsistent with defending human rights that it alleges to do. SIG demanded the Arab and Islamic countries carry out their duty to condemn such outrageous crimes and denounce what is happening in the city of Fallujah. It also called for the rejection of foreign domination exercised by the United States of America against Iraq.[211] The SIG criticized Osama bin Laden severely and blamed him for the damage to Islam and Muslims. In this regard, the Secretary-General of the SIG emphasized that Osama bin Laden harmed Islam and Muslims by following a devastating terrorist ideology contrary to the reality of Islam and that is a great mistake; he also urged Muslims to focus on the correct methodology in Islamic advocacy.[212]

The SIG demanded that the Pope of the Vatican, Benedict XVI, apologize to Muslims and recognize Islam as a divine religion. The SIG stated that he had made a dangerous precedent and this was an indication of the lack of understanding of the Islamic religion and disregard for the principles of respect and appreciation for human values and international regulations.[213] Khalid al-Sultan said that the United States encouraged the enemies of Islam to harm it, and the Pope of the Vatican, Benedict XVI, followed the American scheme.[214]

In 2006, the SIG participated in the general elections for the eleventh National Assembly with seven candidates; only two of them won: Ahmad Baqir, representing the fifth constituency, al-Qadisiya, and 'Ali al-'Omair representing the eleventh constituency, al-Khaldiya. Most of SIG's dominant candidates – such as Fahad al-Khanah, a candidate for the sixth constituency, and Mufarej Nahhar al-Mutairi, the candidate for the nineteenth constituency, New Jahra – failed.

In the 2008 parliamentary elections, the SIG in particular and the Salafiah movement in general achieved an overwhelming victory over their traditional rival, the ICM, where four of their five candidates won, in addition to three of their supporters. It can be said that the IPG MPs won through primary (tribal) elections in the tribal areas,[223] as well as some candidates winning by sectarian and ethnic votes. Khalid al-Sultan, the Secretary General of the IPG, won through his family connections, influence and alliance with other families in the second constituency.

There are a number of factors behind the success of the SIG:

1   The SIG, for example, has an effective presence in co-operative societies and charity social committees and mosques, as well as a presence in social activities such as zakat committees, pilgrimage trips, social action committees, advocacy committees and youth centers.
2   The weakness of the liberal stream, which only strengthens during the elections and disappears in other times.
3   It benefited from the primary (tribal) elections.
4   The victory of the SIG in the second and third constituencies is due to the fact that they are strongholds of this stream and have already produced a number of MPs of their stream, such as Ahmad Baqir, Walid al-Tabtabae . . . etc.

Regardless of the outcome of these elections, the reality is that ethnicity, tribal, family, political manipulation and money have affected the results and not the party affiliation. On this basis, it cannot be said that the IPG has achieved victory as a political organization, but for reasons already mentioned, and, in particular to religious ideology, that the conduct of the Kuwaiti voter does not care for political affiliation.

The SIG is considered as one of the hard-line religious groups on religious issues, such as shortening the formal clothes, growing beards, and not congratulating the Christians on Christmas or on sending them greeting cards and not to import, sell or distribute these cards, according to one of the SIG statements.[215] The SIG supervised, printed and distributed the book entitled *Fatawa fi Mu'amalat Alkuffar* (*Religious Ruling in the Treatment of the Infidels*), which included the provisions of Islam concerning the treatment of the infidels and prohibition of the employment of non-Muslims.[216] The Committee of

Advocacy and Guidance of the IHRS, al-Faiha branch, which is one of the strongholds of the SIG, warned through its chairman, 'Ali al-Huseinan, about congratulating the Christians on their feasts.[217] The SIG used to issue warning statements each year on the occasion of Christmas and New Year celebrations, and held symposiums warning the citizens from participating in these events.

The SIG also took a strict position towards the Shi'ites, where Jassim al-'Oun emphasized that the difference between the SIG and the Shi'ites is in the basic issues.[218] The active students belonging to the SIG in the Faculty of Shari'a at the University of Kuwait organized a fair for the sale of books, cassettes and tapes, which insulted the followers of Ahl al-Bayt (the Prophet's family), describing them as Jews and Christians, resulting in a strong reaction from the Shi'ite students, who urged the university administration to stand against such sectarianism practices, which represent a threat to the national unity.[219] During the Shi'ite commemoration of 'Ashura, the Committee of Advocacy and Guidance of the IHRS, al-Andalus branch, issued a statement distributed extensively in most mosques of Kuwait calling for boycotting the Shi'ites ceremony in their grief.[220]

When the Bohras sect (Ismaili Shi'ism), which constitutes about 200,000 people, applied to the Kuwaiti Government requesting the building of a mosque made especially for them in Kuwait, the Kuwaiti Government agreed to this request. However, the Sunni Islamist political groups launched an attack through their representatives in the National Assembly objecting to this request. As a result of this campaign and the pressure applied by the Sunni fundamentalist groups, the government withdrew the license for this mosque. The Secretary-General of the SIG, Khalid al-Sultan, described the establishment of this mosque *shirk akbar* (the major blasphemy).[221] Knowing that Bohras is a Muslim sect that has lived in Kuwait for more than 50 years, they have the right as Muslims to practice their own creeds. They are Muslims who believe in the Quran, the Prophet Mohammad and in making the required pilgrimage to Mecca. There are a lot of mosques for this sect in many Arab countries, such as the United Arab Emirates, Bahrain, Iraq, Egypt and Syria.[222] The Sunni fundamentalists not only made statements and wrote articles in the local newspapers regarding this matter, but they also provoked the Kuwaitis through spreading leaflets against the Bohras, such as the leaflet issued by Ahmad Bin 'Abdul-'Aziz al-Haseen in which he described Bohrahs as *shirk akbar*.[223]

The SIG is still exercising a political role in the events of Kuwait and has had many representatives in subsequent cabinets.

The Salafiah Youth Call (SYC)
Shabab al-Da'wa al-Salafiah

This organization was founded in the mid-1990s by 'Abdullah al-'Asaker, 'Abdul-Rahman-al-Shayji, Mish'al al-Saee'id, and Walid al-Tabtabae, after the differences that ravaged the unity of the SG when Jassim al-'Oun, one of the leaders of the SG, became Minister of Communications. Al-'oun was criticized by the Salafiah Youth Call (SYC) in public. On 5 April 1994, a letter was sent to al-'Oun by the SYC under the title *Naseehat al-Ikhwaen* (the Advice of the Brothers), criticizing his abandonment of the Salafiah line when honoring the female artists by shaking hands with them.[224] These differences had a significant impact on the cohesion of the SG and, accordingly, on its electoral base in the Kaifan district, which was regarded as the grassroots district for the SYC. Eight of its candidates were nominated for the elections of the National Assembly and almost all of them lost, except al-Tabtabae, who came in second with great difficulties – the difference between him and the liberal nominee, Kalid al-Sani', was only 14 votes.

Clearing the Islamic Ranks Movement (CIRM)
Harakat Tanqiat al-Sofoof al-Islamiya

This movement emerged in 1995. A group of young Muslim extremists in this movement attempted to carry out an attack on the premises of the Dar al-Seyassah (al-Seyassah House) in an attempt to assassinate one of the workers in the *Arab Times*, the English newspaper issued by Dar al-Seyassah. They accused him of publishing a caricature cartoon mocking God. They were arrested by the Kuwaiti authorities, which described them as extremists and terrorists. The Clearing the Islamic Ranks Movement (CIRM) demanded the release of its detainees and not to be referred to the State Security Court.[225] After a period of activity through the distribution of its publication, this organization disappeared from the political arena.

Consultative Supporters Group (CSG)
Gama'at Ansaar al-Shura

This organization was founded in 1997 with Ahmad al-Muzaini becoming its Secretary General. The Consultative Supporters Group (CSG) emphasized in its charter that it is an independent group that rejects democracy and urges the application of the *shura* concept in Kuwait using peaceful methods. It regards democracy as a danger to national unity, describing it as a godless rule because it is based on separating religion from the state. The CSG rejects the democratic civil society and calls for resisting its institutions. It also calls for the abrogation of the Constitution, which, according to the CSG, is behind the evils of democracy.[226] The CSG stresses that democracy is imposed by the minority on the majority in 1962, and that it is the reason behind the crisis of Kuwait because it is based on the lack of trust between the ruler and the people. The CSG has called for replacing democracy with *shura*.[227]

The CSG believes that *shura* is the natural alternative for the 'imported' democracy and believes in the need to abolish the Constitution of 1962 and in the use of the constitutional Islamic model issued by al-Azhar. This model calls for the establishment of two Shura Councils. The first is called the Fatwa Council, whose membership includes religious people. Its function is doctrinal, scientific and legislative. The second council is composed of the shura people who are responsible for choosing the government and supervising its tasks, controlling and questioning those responsible for implementation. Those people are elected from its members in the non-profit organizations, trade unions and other organizations.[228] The CSG expressed strong criticism of the Islamist political groups who participated in the parliamentary assemblies, such as the ICM and the SG, by saying that they have fallen into the fame of democracy, which the CSG considers as the biggest danger to national unity. The CSG accused these groups of distorting the image and the reputation of Islam because Islam is more important than democracy.[229]

The CSG sees that the only way to defend the GCC from external aggression is by using the mass destruction weapons, such as chemical weapons, and in this regard, Ahmad al-Muzaini says:

> We have proven that chemical weapons have a deterrent effect and serve as a good way to preserve the security of the Gulf. Therefore, the GCC states have to provide Dir' al-Jazeera (the Peninsula Shield) with this weapon.[230]

The CSG adopted a hard-line position towards the radical Islamic groups, which permitted the killing of American troops and non-Muslims. It describes the fatwas issued by some Muslim scholars, such as Yousef al-Qaradawi, which calls for the killing of Americans, that they lead to confusion and raise the enthusiasm of the youth to harm the Islamic nation. Furthermore, that they distort the image of Islam and give the impression that Islam is a religion of terrorism and violence, and that such fatwas are neither based on Quranic verses nor on the Hadiths of the Prophet.[231]

The CSG calls the leaders of the GCC to convene a peace agreement with the Zionist State, according to the fatwa of Sheikh 'Abdul-'Aziz Bin Baz, former mufti of Saudi Arabia, which allowed both the absolute and the provisional reconciliation with enemies if it was in the best interest of the Muslim nation seen by the 'Ulama. Al-Muzaini emphasized that it was wise for the Arab states to reconcile with the Zionists because they cannot resist its military, and this peace would have great benefits where the funds spent on the purchase of weapons used for war would be better used in other areas.[232]

The CSG does not enjoy any popularity and its founders are not known except for the Secretary General of the CSG, al-Muzaini, who used to make political statements carrying his signature, distributing brochures and holding press conferences regarding local and Arab affairs and he is still doing so. The latest statement issued by the CSG declared that it has taken a new name for itself, Gam'at Ansaar al-Shuar wa al-Salam (Supporters of Shuar and

Peace Group), to match its belief in reconciliation with the Zionist state, as expressed in its statements.[233] It demanded the acceptance of the Zionist State in the Arab League.[234]

Al-Salafiah Movement (SM)
Al-Harakh al-Salafiah

This movement was formed on 15 November 1997 after the disputes between the members of the IPG. These disputes were ignited when Walid al-Tabtabae refused the nomination of Mish'aal al-Sa'ad, an IPG member, in the Kaifan constituency for the Parliamentary elections in 1996, knowing that Kaifan is a stronghold for al-Tabtabae. In addition, there was a dispute between Sheikh 'Abdul-Rahman 'Abdul-Khaliq and Sheikh 'Abdullah al-Sabt, one of the leaders of the SG in Kuwait; there was also a dispute regarding the definition of al-Hakimiyyah (sovereignty), which was adopted by 'Abd al-khaliq. Al-Sabt thought of this definition as a way to *takfir* the rulership. Al-Sabt accused 'Abdul-Khaliq and his supporters of being Khawarij al-'asr (contemporary Kharijites).[235] 'Abdul-Razzaq al-Shayji, a professor in the Faculty of Shari'a and one of 'Abdul-Khaliq's supporters, criticized some of the leaders of the IPG, who were supporters of al-Sabt, saying that they deviated from the Salafiah ideology after the liberation of Kuwait from the Iraqi invasion. He also accused them of supporting some of the Arab political systems,[236] and that the IPG changed its ideologies according to the pressure made on it, while the Salafiah trend refuses this and follows the Quran and Sunna.

As a result of these differences, a splinter group, led by Sheikh Hamid 'Abdullah al-'Ali, 'Abdul-Razzaq al-Shayji, and Walid al-Tabtabae, established al-Haraka al-Salafiah al-'Ilmiyya (the Scientific Salafiah Movement), which was changed later on to the SM. Al-Shayji emphasized that the change was due to: first its easiness and second there is no Islamic group under this name, Salafiah Movement, which is sufficient to express their creed based on the Salafiah ideology.[237] Sheikh Hamid 'Abdullah al-'Ali was elected as the Secretary-General of the SM and in 2000 Hakim al-Mutairi became its Secretary General. The SM announced in its foundation press conference that it would be preaching the intellectual literary association. This statement identified the goals of the movement, which centered around the following main points:[238]

1   Call to God.
2   Deployment of forensic science.
3   Exposing the seriousness of the intellectual deviations by the unbeliever currents, which aims to wipe out the nation's identity and demolish its important characteristics.
4   Contribute to finding solutions to social, educational and cultural problems.

The SM in its constituent statement defined the means to achieve its principles and objectives through legitimate channels, such as the press, scientific symposia, studies, research and through issuing statements against all illegal means.[239] Sajid al-'Abdaly, Secretary General for Public Information of the SM, denies the accusation that the movement is a split of any other movement, but that its founders are the elite of scholars and students of science and that some of them were independent, while others have links to other Islamic movements, and that the movement is not a traditional group that imposes al-Bay'ah (pledge Covenant) on its members, but is a voluntary association. Each member of the movement has the right to withdraw from it at any time and, therefore, it is a means and not an end; the goal is Islam and Shari'a.[240] The SM believes in the necessity of a radical change in the existing political practices, which are hampering any reform process, and believes that the National Assembly is only a political club where people say what they like to do and the government does what it wants. The SM confirms that the movement cannot succeed in its Islamic project in the light of the political dictatorship and the marginalization of the will of the nation, whether in the name of religion, or the guardian of obedience, or on behalf of the Constitution and the law. According to the SM, this is why the Islamic political discourse has to be renewed in a similar way to the State of the Righteous Caliphs and the revival of the principles of the nation's right to choose the regime, the right to the Shura Council, and the right to change the regime when it deviates from God's path.[241]

The organizational structure of the SM is:[242]

The Constituent Shura Council is the regulatory organ, which supervises the affairs of the movement. Its meetings are held once a month on a regular basis headed by the Secretary General. The Shura Council achieves its resolutions by an absolute majority and its most important task is the election of the Secretary General and the acceptance or rejection of the nomination of any new member of the Secretariat. To be a member in the Shura Council, the following terms and conditions have to be fulfilled:

- The nominee's age should not be less than 30 years old.
- The nominee has to spend three years as a member in the movement.
- The nominee's name has to be approved by the Constituent Shura Council.

Followed in hierarchy is the Office of the Secretariat, which is working to achieve the goals of the movement. It is composed of the Secretary General, who represents the movement and is the only authorized person issuing statements on its behalf and is elected by the Shura Council for a period of three years, renewable only once. This is followed by the official spokesperson for the movement. Then the chairman of the Political Bureau, who is responsible for monitoring the developments and changes in the political arena and contacting the members of the National Assembly and the political forces.

The spokesperson is followed by the head of the Press Bureau, who is responsible for monitoring the media, followed by the head of the Scientific and Cultural Bureau, who is responsible for supervising the scientific, cultural, educational and advocacy activities. The General Conference of the SM is the highest authority in the organization and includes members of the Constituent Shura Council, members of the Office of the Secretariat, and the elected members from all the provinces who are to be nominated and approved by the members of the Shura Council.

In June 2003, the SM submitted its political discourse, which represents a reformist vision of the movement on a range of domestic and foreign issues, focused on:[243]

1   Amending Article II of the Constitution to make the Islamic Shari'a the sole source of legislation by amending everything contrary to the provisions of Shari'a in economic, social, political and media areas such that the Shari'a is its reference point.
2   Adopting political multi-party systems and opening the door for the Kuwaiti people to participate in the selection of a government mandated by the majority party to form the government.
3   Working on a bill regulating the work of the parties similar to the constitutional monarchy regimes.
4   Making Kuwait a single electoral constituency for the elimination of sectarianism, tribalism and regionalism.
5   Adopting the Islamic penal code.
6   Demolishing laws that limit public freedom, such as the Press and Publication law.
7   Ending the foreign military presence, which now threatens the independence of the countries of the region.

The SM participated in the elections of the National Assembly in 1999 and Walid al-Tabtabae won a seat representing the seventh constituency, Kaifan. In the 2003 elections, al-Tabtabae again won representing the same constituency, and 'Awad Barad won representing the nineteenth constituency, al-Jahra al-Jadida, the latter won on a tribal basis and not due to his political orientation. Hussein al-Sa'di, the head of the Political Bureau of the movement, failed in these elections. In the 2006 elections, only al-Tabtabae won, representing Kaifan.

The SM publishes its principles and views through the *al-Mishkah* magazine and al-Mishkah Media Center, as well as *al-Watan* newspaper, which has dedicated a page to disseminate views and orientations of the SM; this is in addition to the religious pages in *al-Rai al-'Am* and *al-Qabas* newspapers. Islamic supplements are issued by the *al-Watan* and *al-Anba* newspapers. One of the most prominent activities of the SM is attacking the liberals through the media and through its representative in the Parliament, 'Abdul-Rassaq al-Shayji, accusing it of trying to Westernize Kuwaiti society and transform it into an American colony.[244] The SM participated in the interrogation of the Minister of Information, Sheikh Sa'ud Nasser al-Sabah, and has succeeded in pushing him to resign. It also succeeded in submitting several Islamic bills, such as the Islamic Penal Code draft law, consisting of 280 articles, which aims to establish the laws based on Shari'a, such as flogging, amputation and others.[245] It also stood against the political rights of women. 'Abdul-Razzaq al-Shayji, one of the SM ideologists, says that women do not have any political rights because Shari'a did not give them that right.[246] Sheikh Hamid 'Abdullah al-'Ali, the former Secretary General of the SM, claimed that the decree giving women political rights has been imposed on Kuwait by the Americans[247] and considered such decree as a fatal blow to Islamic Shari'a. He refused the joining of women to the army on the grounds that Shari'a does not permit them for its high risks.[248] During the general election of 2009, the member of the Political Bureau of the SM, Mish'aal al-Muallath, urged the voters not to vote for women, adding that voting for them can be sinful because it is regarded as a wilaya 'Ama (high leadership) under the Islamic law (Shari'a). However, for the first time in the history of Kuwait's National Assembly, women won four seats in Parliament in the 2009 elections: Aseel al-'Awadhi, Rola Dashti, Salwa al-Jassar and Ma'souma al-Mubarak; all of them have doctorate degrees from American universities.

Islamist political groups suffered a great loss in this election, and MP 'Ali al-'Omair, who is considered one of the leaders of the Salafi trend, stated that these elections are a disaster for the religious stream.[249] There are a few reasons behind this defeat, mainly:

1 They stood against the nomination of women for the elections.
2 They supported the Hamas movement and raised funds for it. They also sent a delegation to Damascus from the party's religious leaders to congratulate Hamas leaders in Damascus for their resistance against the Zionist army siege and attack on the Gaza Strip. This caused public hatred towards the Kuwaiti Islamist political groups, especially the fact that Hamas stood with Saddam Hussein during the occupation of Kuwait.
3 The strict stands taken by the representatives of the Islamist political groups in the National Assembly against public freedom.
4 The propaganda led by some local private TV channels against the Islamist political groups had a great effect on public opinion. An example of such channels was Scope TV.

All these factors led to a reaction among the majority of people.

The SM urged the Kuwaiti Government and the Kuwaiti National Assembly to lift the injustice and discrimination of the *bedoon jinsiyya* (people without citizenship) by demanding the abolition of Decree Law No. 98 of 1996, which demands not to pass any official papers of the bedoon without the authorization of the Central Committee. It also urged the government to commit to the United Nations Treaty of 1954 regarding the people without citizenship, which grants the bedoon full human rights enjoyed by citizens, such as work, movement, study and marriage, until the acquisition of citizenship, which is in agreement with the Islamic Shari'a and its provisions.[250]

The SM has taken strict positions against normalization with the Zionist State, and for this reason it was one of the founders of Lajnat Moqawamat al-Tatbi' Ma'a al-Kayan al-Sahuoni (the Resistance Committee to Normalization with the Zionist State). The SM supports martyrdom operations carried out by the Islamic movements in occupied Palestine against the Zionists and considers such operations a legitimate act of jihad for the sake of God and the SM considers that all the Zionists are enemies.[251]

The SM severely criticized the Kuwait Central Bank's decision to freeze the accounts of the Harakat al-Muqawama al-Islamiya (Islamic Resistance Movement (Hamas)) and al-Jihad al-Islami (the Islamic Jihad), considering it a provocation to the feelings of the Kuwaiti people who believe in legitimate jihad in the Palestinian territories. The SM considers this decision as a Zionist breakthrough in the Arabian Gulf region and as foreign interference in its affairs. It linked this interference with the American presence in Iraq and urged the Kuwaiti Government to change that decision and to commit to the Arab and Islamic principles regarding the Palestinian issue. It also appealed to the Kuwaiti people in all their political streams to stand together to reject such a step, which, in their minds, represents a threat to the Gulf Arab front, a front that represents a strategic depth of support for the Palestinian people.[252]

After the winning of Hamas movement, a parliamentary majority enabled it to form a government in Palestine. Then the SM in Kuwait issued an initiative to support the Hamas movement by urging the Kuwaiti Government to commit to its apportioned share of the Arab League in support of the Palestinian Authority, to increase financial aid, to open the door for popular donations, to deduct a percentage from the salaries of government employees and transfer it to the government of Hamas, to open a Palestinian embassy in Kuwait, to allow the establishment of an Information Office, and to hold festivals in solidarity with the Hamas movement. The SM resisted the normalization with the Zionist enemy and refused to make any concessions before the restoration of all Palestinian rights. It stressed the rights of the Hamas movement to retain arms until the establishment of a Palestinian state on all Palestinian territories. It appealed to the Kuwaiti Government and the Kuwaiti people to turn the page on past tensions and remove any turbulence in the relations between Kuwait and Palestine.[253]

The SM condemned the air strikes committed by the United States and the international coalition forces against the Taliban regime in Afghanistan and regarded such action as an ambiguous confrontation and that the campaign against terrorism must be conducted in accordance with the resolutions of international legitimacy.[254] Hakem al-Mutairi, the Secretary General of the SM, emphasizes the attitude of the movement towards al-Qaeda and says:

Regardless of our disagreement with the al-Qaeda organization in juris-prudence and Shari'a Law in dealing with the issues of the Islamic nation, it remains a jihadist Islamic movement.[255]

Fhaid al-Hailim, the chairman of the Political Bureau of the SM, regards Osama Bin Laden as a unique example that needs to be praised. He believes that Bin Laden is one of the heroes and he prays to God to help him to achieve victory.[256]

After the United States of America released five Kuwaiti terrorists from Guantanamo Bay prison, the SM held a rally in March 2006 in al-'Ardiya district celebrating those terrorists' release. Among those who participated in the celebrations were representatives of the Islamist political groups in Kuwait such as the ICM and other Sunni Islamist political groups. In the speech delivered by the head of the Information Office of the SM, Fhaid al-Hailim, he shaped those terrorists as heroes.[257]

Four of the leading members of the SM – Hakem al-Mutairi, Sajid al-'Abdaly, Sheikh Hamid 'Abdullah al-'Ali and 'Abdul-Razzaq al-Shayji – par-ticipated in the establishment of Hayat al-Hamlah al-'Alamiya li-Muqawamat al-'Odwan al-Amriky (the Global Campaign to Resist the American Aggres-sion Commission) and launched it from Saudi Arabia. In addition to the previously mentioned names, many leaders of Islamist political groups, movements and parties from various Arab and Islamic countries joined this Commission.[258] The Commission, as stated in its founding statement, aims to confront the American aggression represented in the forces of Zionism and the American administration led by the extreme right wing, which is working to establish domination over nations and people, loot their resources, eradi-cate their will and change their educational and social systems. It also con-sidered the American presence in Iraq and Afghanistan as the worst form of armed invasion, and that this aggression reintroduces the era of colonialism where law of the jungle is dominant. It stressed that this Commission is a framework that combines the efforts of the nation and it is the duty of everyone to defend themselves against the aggressor through every possible legal means.[259] Its most important objectives are:[260]

1   Make the Islamic nation aware of its enemies' schemes and urge it to preserve its identity.
2   Resist the aggressors by all legitimate means.
3   Awaken the Islamic spirit among the people to defend their religion and their rights.
4   Clarify the true image of Islam and expose the fake campaigns against it.
5   Effectively communicate with the people and institutions and various religious bodies rejecting the injustice and oppression of the Islamic people's destiny.

The Association elected its executive committee composed of nine members, and it also elected Dr. Safar al-Hawali to become Secretary General of the Commission, and Dr. Khalid al-'Ajimi to become Deputy Secretary General and Muhsin al-'Awajy to become the official spokesman on behalf of the committee.[261]

The SM took a strict position towards the war waged by the United States of America and the forces of the international coalition against the Saddam Hussein regime. It considered it a war of aggression and urged the governments and people of Islamic ranks to face the military campaigns and the colonial crusade. Furthermore, it denied participating in this aggression and appealed to Muslims not to pay attention to the suspicious fatwas designated by the colonial powers in the service of its objectives, which will have the greatest danger to the present and future of the Islamic world.[262] The movement launched a fatwa considering that the support of America, even verbally in its military operations against Iraq, is prohibited.[263] This coincided with another fatwa issued by an unknown Islamist political group via an Internet site to provoke the assassinations of Deputy Prime Minister and former Interior Minister Sheikh Mohammad al-Khalid al-Sabah, the Attorney General Hamid al-'Othman, a number of senior officers and officials of the Ministry of Interior, a number of advisers and some judges; it called for their assassination due to their abstaining from the arbitration initiated by God and due to their pro-crusaders position. It saluted those whom it called (Islamic Jihad youth) champions in Afghanistan, Bosnia and Chechnya.[264]

The SM organized an Islamic rally of solidarity with the people of Fallujah in the main ceremonies hall in the building of the National Assembly. The MPs Walid al-Tabtabae and 'Abdullah 'Okash, in addition to Sheikh Ahmad al-Qattan, one of the MBG leaders, participated in this rally, where they made speeches demanding that the National Assembly and the Kuwaiti Government take positions and make resolutions that support the just demands of the Iraqi people, including the withdrawal of the occupation forces as described by the speakers.[265] Al-Tabtabae requested that the American Government review its policies in Iraq and abide by the principles of human rights and described the American forces in Iraq as a brutal force that kills children and innocent people. It demanded material and moral solidarity with the people in Iraq from the Kuwaitis.[266] 'Abdullah 'Okash described what is happening in Iraq as a violation of human rights by the United States of America, which claims to be just, but in reality it crushes children, the elderly and women; then he demanded that the Kuwaiti people must seriously get rid of the invasion complex.[267] A statement issued by al-Lajnah al-Sha'biyah al-Barlamaniyah li Munasarat wa Inqath al-Sha'ab al-Iraqi (People's Parliamentary Committee for the Support and Relief of the Iraqi People) was distributed in a rally and called for the support of the just causes of the Iraqi people through the media and direct charitable committees, and the assistance of competent committees and governmental institutions to make voluntary contributions to the Iraqi people. The statement also called on imams and mosque preachers to guide citizens and introduce them to their Islamic duty towards the Iraqi people.[268]

The SM held an Islamic rally under the slogan of Kulluna Fadak ya Rasool Allah (We are All Martyrs of the Messenger of God) in response to statements made by the Vatican Pope. It demanded the closure of churches in Kuwait and the expulsion of the Vatican ambassador in protest against the Pope's statements. They demanded that there should be clear legislation in the National Assembly regarding establishing churches in Kuwait.[269]

The SM was exposed to several failures as a result of the arrest of its former Secretary, Sheikh Hamid 'Abdullah al-'Ali, on charges of belonging to al-Qaeda, and the positions of the SM regarding the American coalition forces and its support for the armed resistance in Iraq. One of the most prominent founders of the SM, 'Abdul-Razzaq al-Shayji, took a soft line with the political regime and retired from political work. The former Secretary of the SM, Hakem al-Mutairi, together with most of the leadership of the SM, withdrew from the movement to form a new one called Hizb al-Umma (Nation Party).[270] The movement's representative in the National Assembly, 'Awwad Barad, voted with giving women their political rights contrary to the official position of the movement, and he was criticized severely for it. Most of the movement's candidates in the parliamentary elections that took place on 29 June 2006, failed. All these failures led to a decline in SM activity and its impact in the Kuwaiti political arena.

Defending the Nation's Principles Gathering (DNPG)
Tajammu' al-Defa' 'An Thawabit al-Ummah

This organization was founded in late 2003 in al-Jahra district, one of the strongholds of the extremist religious line, by a number of Islamic activists, including a number of professors in the Faculty of Shari'a, medical doctors, lawyers and MPs of the National Assembly belonging to the Islamic trend. The DNPG held a first meeting in Bader al-Hajraf Diwan where they chose Mohammad Hayif al-Mutairi as a secretary general for the DNPG and Hamad 'Omar al-'Omar as its spokesperson. The aim of this organization is to form a nucleus of public pressure towards a number of issues associated with the Islamic community, and it issued several statements and distributed them to the press.

The DNPG objectives as mentioned in its electoral program are:[271]

1 Make Islam the only source of legislation and the DNPG finds that the application of Islamic law applied in full is the comprehensive solution to all the problems of the Islamic nation.
2 Preach Islam through the media.
3 Emphasize public freedoms that are not inconsistent with the principles of Islam.

4   Abolish any restrictions on the freedom of the press that are not inconsistent with Islamic Shari'a.
5   Issue laws that ensure the protection of the fundamentals of the nation and the doctrine of assault by secularists and anti-Islamists.
6   Clear the Kuwaiti banking system from all forms of usury and expand the licensing of Islamic financial institutions in accordance with the principles of Islamic Shari'a.
7   Activate the prevention of mixed education in all educational institutions.
8   Form committees to guide the media in line with Islamic Shari'a and work on establishing a television channel that introduces Islam to non-Muslims; work on purifying all radio and television programs from all corrupt programs, songs and dancing; and strictly prohibit the showing of foreign films that promote obscenity and immorality.
9   Prevent the importation of books that distort Islamic history.
10   Protect Kuwaiti women from Westernization and secularism.
11   Spread the spirit of jihad in the ranks of the army.

The DNPG took hard positions towards women's right to political participation and emphasized that all the scholars of Islam issued fatwas that prohibit women from voting or electing because the parliament is a Wilaya 'Ama (high leadership). The DNPG accuses the government and the liberal stream of seeking to destroy all these views and fatwas.[272] Its Secretary General also criticized the position of the Nation Party towards granting women their political rights, which are not based on any evidence drawn from the Shari'a, and argued that giving Muslim women these alleged rights is immoral and a great evil on the nation. He demanded the non-mixing of women in all positions, whether in the university or at work.[273]

The DNPG took a firm stance against the Shi'ite community when the former Minister of Information, Mohammad Abu al-Hassan, who belongs to the Shi'ite sect, allowed the broadcast of a program on the occasion of 'Ashura (Shi'ite mourning ritual) on Kuwaiti television. This act was described by al-Mutairi as being a sectarian act and he warned that the Sunnis believe that the broadcast of such programs is bid'ah (innovation), which must be prohibited, and criticized the establishment of Shi'ite funerals.[274] He added that:

> What he is doing is an absurd sectarianism where he tried to ignore the Sunnis in favor of a particular sect and make it above everything else.[275]

Saleh 'Ashour, an MP in the National Assembly and one of the representatives of the Shi'ite stream, criticized the statement issued by the DNPG, saying that it has an irrational sectarian breath that might destroy the national unity, and he urged for a mutual respect between all communities in the Kuwaiti society.[276] 'Ashour stressed that:

As some people think that the Shi'ite have unaccepted practices, the Shi'ites in turn see that the practices of Salafiah and the Muslim Brotherhood are unacceptable and that it is better not to discuss such matters in order to preserve the cohesion of society.[277]

The DNPG participated in the demonstration called by the extremist religious groups against the 'Star Academy' concert held at the Mishref district fair grounds. The Deputy Secretary for the DNPG, Hamad al-'Omar, stated that 'those who stand behind this concert are the ones who are advocating for the Greater Middle East and want to kill any Muslim nation.'[278] The DNPG addressed severe criticism of the Kuwaiti Association for Human Rights, which in its letter to the Kuwaiti Government demanded the suspension of the death sentence on the grounds that it contradicts human rights; the DNPG considered this orientation as a violation of the principles of Islam and considered the Human Rights Association as a tail for the West and its anti-Islam policy.[279] The DNPG requested the Minister of Awqaf and Islamic Affairs return the 35 imams who were dismissed from their jobs (they were dismissed because of extremist advocations that they made) in mosques and warned that the political arena will witness an escalation against the Minister of Awqaf and Islamic Affairs, 'Abdullh al-M'atooq, and regarded the confrontation for the dismissal decision as a Shari'a duty.[280]

The DNPG stood with the terrorist groups and the Ba'athists in Fallujah, where its Secretary General described it (the war of Fallujah) as an ideological war against Arabs and Muslims, and that what is being done by America in Fallujah resembles what the Jews do to the Palestinians.[281] The DNPG held a rally in the diwan of its leader, al-Mutairi, under the slogan 'supporting the Iraqi people in confronting the occupation', in which the MP Walid al-Tabtabae accused the government of trying to isolate the Kuwaiti people from what is happening in Iraq. The MP, Faisal al-Mislim, also criticized the government's silence towards the massacres in Iraq, considering the siege of Fallujah as a collective punishment rejected by all laws and creeds.[282]

The DNPG held a rally attended by the Islamist political groups under the slogan Ayat al-Rahman Tukathib Baba al-Fatikan (Rahman mandates disavowing the Vatican Pope), in which the participants launched a sharp attack on the Islamic governments, including the Kuwaiti Government, on the grounds that these governments have failed to reach the required level of respect. The Secretary General of the DNPG emphasized that the attacks on Islam and Muslims started when President George Bush announced that the war on terrorism is a crusade, and then it was subsequently followed with publications of pictures of the Prophet in comic drawings in Denmark.[283]

The DNPG denounced the approval of the Council of Ministers on converting one of the public schools to a temporary church and considered that such approval would create a new situation in the country and lead to a change in the composition of society in terms of religion and ethics.[284]

The DNPG regarded the inclusion of the SRS and the SRIH on the terrorist list by the Russian Government as an accusation of the Kuwaiti people of being terrorists. He urged the members of the Kuwaiti National Assembly to hold an emergency meeting to discuss this matter and to send a message to the Russian Government that shows that the common interests between the two countries are incompatible with this unfair decision. The DNPG described the situation in the Russian Islamic Republic as being continually governed with an iron fist by the Russian autocracy and that the Russian troops exercise the worst violations of human rights.[285]

In December 2009, the Egyptian scholar Nasr Hamid Abu zaid, who holds the Ibn Rushd Chair of Humanism and Islam at the Utrecht University for Humanistic in Holland, was invited by a group of liberals who belong to Markaz al-Hiwar lil Thaqafah (The Cultural Dialogue Centre), to attend a number of cultural seminars in Kuwait, but he was banned from entering the country upon his arrival despite having a valid visa and was sent back to Cairo the same day, without any explanation and this was due to the pressure made by the MPs of the DNPG and other Islamists Political Groups on the interior minister, Sheikh Jaber al-Khalid al-Sabah, who had publicly urged him, to deny Abu Zaid's entry, during a time when al-Khalid needed parliamentary support to fight a motion that could remove him from office and called Abu Zaid a zindiq (atheist). In January 2010, Kuwaiti authorities also banned Mohammad al-'Uraifi, a prominent Sunni Saudi cleric, from entering the country, under the pressure of the MPs of the Shi'ites Islamists Political Groups. In February 2010 the Kuwaiti authorities also canceled the visa of Madawi al-Rrsheed, of Saudi origin and professor of social anthropology at King's College London.

Consequently and in a new step towards a Taliban state road, 22 MPs representing the DNPG and other Islamist Political Groups submitted a proposal that puts restrictions on the entry to the state of Kuwait and to ban anyone who insults God, Prophet Mohammad, his wives, al-Sahabah and ahl al-Bayt from entering Kuwait.

The Human Rights Watch demanded from the Kuwaiti regime to encourage civil society organizations in Kuwait to play an active role in regional debates instead of trying to silence them.[286]

Mohammed Hayif Al-Mutairi participated in the parliamentary elections that took place on 29 June 2006 under the slogan of 'The Holy Quran is our Constitution,' but he did not succeed, coming in third place. It is worth mentioning that he also participated in the elections of the National Assembly in 1999 and 2003 but was unable to win, coming in third place in both elections, But he won in the election of the National Assembly in 2008. The DNPG still exists and plays a role in the political events in Kuwait.

The Nation Party (NP)
Hizb al-Umma

This party was initiated on 29 January 2005 by Hakem al-Mutairi, former Secretary General of the SM, Hussein al-Saa'idi, former Secretary of the SM, Sajid al-'Abdaly, former Deputy Secretary General of the SM, and others.[287] The Nation Party (NP) is an extension of the SM and its constituent meeting was open to the local, Arab and international media. Furthermore, representatives from the American Embassy in Kuwait were there,[288] which asserted that the presence of its representatives should not be understood as necessarily an endorsement of the principles of this party or its establishment.[289] The NP's statement emphasized the need for participation of the nation in achieving political, economic, cultural, social and legislative reforms that guarantee the rights of peoples to freedom and popular participation in the selection of their governments in accordance with the principle of the multi-party system and the rotation of political power.[290] In its first bulletin, the NP emphasized that it represents a broad front of the conservative trend. The party believes that the nation is the source of authority and power selected through free elections. It also believes in the political multi-party system, the peaceful transfer of power and the principles of separation of powers and the preservation of liberties. The NP rejects all forms of political autocracy and believes in the right of every individual to justice, liberty and equality, without any racial discrimination due to race, color or sex, and it stressed its respect for human rights, in addition to political, religious, intellectual, professional and economic freedom. The NP also stressed its rejection of all forms of colonialism, namely: military, political, economic and cultural, and of the need for the continuation of the dialogue between civilizations for the benefit and good of humanity.[291] The NP confirms that the party literature does not deviate from the Constitution of Kuwait.[292] Al-'Abdaly expressed a strong criticism of the Salafiah groups that took care of the Salafiah ideology before the foundation of the NP.[293]

The party is based on the following principles:[294]

1 Islamic faith is the religion of the State and Shari'a is the source of legislation.
2 Islamic Shari'a is the reference for the maintenance of public freedoms.
3 Shura is the way to reach the rulership.
4 Faith in a multi-party system and peaceful rotation of power.
5 Combat all forms of racial, sectarian and class discrimination.
6 Reject all forms of foreign colonialism.
7 Build a society of Islamic beliefs.
8 Announce political parties.

The party's major objectives include:[295]

1 Establishment of an Islamic society.

2   Achieving freedom and political multi-party systems through the peaceful rotation of power.
3   The right of the nation in choosing its ruler.
4   Adoption of announcing the political parties.
5   Complete implementation of the provisions of Islamic Shari'a in all aspects of life: political, economic, legislative and social.
6   Ending foreign military presence in the peninsula and the Gulf, which threatens its sovereignty and independence, and freeing the region from all manifestations of colonialism.
7   Supporting the Islamic people.
8   Give women their legitimate rights.

The party's program confirmed that the achievement of these goals will be through peaceful means, such as participation in the general elections and the establishment of lectures, symposia, rallies, protests and strikes.[296]

By reading the party's political program, it can be noted that the party ignored the clear term of democracy and replaced it with the word Shura, and this means a complete disagreement between the principles and ideas of the party with those of the provisions of the Constitution of Kuwait, in which Article (6) clearly states that: 'The System of Government in Kuwait shall be democratic.'[297] It is also noticeable in the party's program that the ultimate objective of the party is to establish the religious state and this is in contradiction with the constitutional texts of the State of Kuwait.

The organizational structure of the NP is headed by the General Conference, the highest authority in the party, which sets out the strategy for the party; followed by the Shura Council, which consists of 15 members elected or recommended by the General Conference and is responsible for the party's general conference. The third in the hierarchy is the General Secretariat, the highest executive authority in the party, who is responsible for supervising the implementation of the policy and the decisions of the party. The party's branches have divisions, which in turn elect the members of the General Conference. There is a special section for women members and the party has different bureaus, such as the Political Bureau, the Cultural Bureau, the Information Bureau, the Public Relations Bureau and the Bureau of Research and Studies.[298]

The leadership of the party in co-ordination with the representatives of the Islamist political groups in the National Assembly actively submitted a draft of a new law for the establishment of political parties. The party addressed the President of the National Assembly and the Prime Minister and urged them to speed up the issuance of a law that regulates political parties in Kuwait.[299]

After a short period of the establishment of the NP, its leadership has been referred to the Public Prosecution for the charge that the party aimed at changing the system of government and accused them of violating the Press, Publication and Gatherings Acts. The party denied all of these accusations, affirming its commitment to peaceful political work in the framework of the general system of the State and according to constitutional channels, as stated in its constituent statements and official pronouncements made by the party leaders. Accordingly, the party urged all political forces to reject such arbitrary practices and work hand in hand to push towards the desired political reforms by working towards an elected Parliamentary government, multiparty systems and the peaceful rotation of power in the general mainframe of the State and its Constitution, which guarantees these freedoms and rights. The party also urged the government to go along with the political reform in the region and take the initiative to achieve the aspiration of the Kuwaiti people towards a better future with full freedom to choose their government, in which the law and the principle of equality without discrimination is applied.[300] For general information, the constitutional legislator in drafting the Constitution was convinced that organized political action cannot move on the right track without the announcement of political parties and that it was imperative to tackle this subject someday, which left the door open to the possibility of legislation regulating the establishment of legal political parties. Article 43 of the Kuwaiti Constitution states that:

> Freedom to form associations and unions on a national basis and by peaceful means shall be guaranteed in accordance with the conditions and manner specified by law. No one may be compelled to join any association or union.[301]

This article did not mention the political parties in order to avoid the constitutional obligation to legalize the creation of these parties. In addition, the omitting of this commitment in the text of the article does not mean a constitutional ban for an indefinite period and does not prevent the legislature from allowing the formation of parties if they see that it is the proper time. In conclusion, the above-mentioned article neither commits to the formation of political parties nor bans them, but according to the explanatory memorandum to the Constitution of the State of Kuwait, it authorized the ordinary legislator without directing him in this regard positively or negatively.[302]

There are many political groups and movements that have announced their political programs in official conferences since the liberation of Kuwait from Iraq in 1991, such as the CIM, the SM, the Kuwaiti Democratic Forum, the National Democratic Alliance, and others. Ministers in the government followed these groups since the liberation of Kuwait and until now are leading members in these groups and their movements.[303] The programs of some of these groups do not differ from that of the NP, but the Council of Ministers did not take any action towards its members or refer its leaderships to prosecution for violating the law. The step taken by the NP had exceeded all the political groups and movements in the history of Kuwait since its independence, such as the ANM, which was represented in the first National Assembly in 1963 but none of its MPs proposed a draft law regarding the establishment of political parties in Kuwait, as well as the MBG when they were represented in the 1981 National Assembly.

Despite the actions taken by the government towards the founders of the NP and regarding it as illegal, the party has continued its activities through issuing statements regarding the local, Arab and Islamic issues, such as its participation in the meetings held by the political forces. Among the most prominent positions taken by the party is the participation of its Assistant Secretary General, Mansour al-khazam, in a seminar on women's political rights; he addressed the critics of the party from the political Islamic groups and stressed that the party supported the granting of political rights to women and that the issue of women's rights is not rejected by the Constitution, but there are views in favor of and in opposition to those rights, and that the participation of women is not incompatible with the customs and traditions and it will contribute to the political reform.[304] In a debate organized by the NP regarding women's political rights, the majority of the members were supportive of giving women the right to nominate and to vote, except Hakem al-Mutairi, the Secretary General, who voted against this right on the basis that the issue of women is otherwise for the principle of a general authority.[305] The party rejects the primary (tribal) elections and sees it as a damaging factor to the political process, because it leads to injustice for the qualified people of the tribes. In addition, it leads to denying the rights of minorities in the constituency.[306]

The NP rejects the current electoral law and is in favor of the one constituency system.[307]

The NP underestimated the importance of the bloody events in some areas of Kuwait among a number of terrorists belonging to al-Qaeda and police in the first months of 2005, where a number of terrorists and some policemen were killed. The party believes that these events have been magnified as if Kuwait was Afghanistan, full of fighters and hidden weapons.[308] The party believes that the reason behind the emergence of young radicals in Kuwait is due to the presence of Osama Bin Laden, the situation in Iraq and the foreign presence in the region.[309] The party urged the members of the National Assembly and the Committee on Human Rights to intervene and exercise their power to stop the constitutional violations and accelerate the formation of a Committee of Inquiry into the death of the leader of the al-Qaeda cell, 'Amer Khalif al-Enezi, and the NP demanded the adoption of the separation of the Investigations Department and forensic medicine from the Ministry of Interior and attach them to the Ministry of Justice.[310] It is noticeable that statements of the party issued by its leadership avoided calling those convicted youth 'terrorists' and simply called them 'young people.'[311]

Al-Mutairi strongly criticized those who are advocating for the necessity to co-ordinate with the ruling establishment to draw the political future of Kuwait. He described this advocacy as a serious deviation from the Kuwaiti Constitution, which states that the nation is the source of all authorities and not what is called Moassat al-Hukm (the ruling institution) and the Majlas

al-Usrah al-Hakamh (ruling family council), and that the Constitution provided only three powers: legislative, executive and judiciary, which is chaired
by His Highness the Emir of the country only. Al-Mutairi expressed the
seriousness of such a call because it calls for the legalization of a political
institution that does not exist constitutionally or legally. He urged the political forces to work seriously in co-ordination with the deputies of the
National Assembly for the submission of draft laws, such as the amendment
of electoral constituencies, the political parties and groupings to achieve political multi-systems, and a parliamentary government elected by the people
and other laws that promote public freedoms and address the political crisis
that has prevailed in Kuwait for decades and has led to failure in all aspects.
Al-Mutairi said that any talk about political reform outside this framework is
only an obstacle for the process of political reform and a confiscation of the
Kuwaiti people's right to exercise their political rights guaranteed by the
Constitution.[312] In the background of the constitutional crisis, which faced
Sheikh Salem al-'Ali al-Sabah, in his interview with *al-Qabas* newspaper, the
NP demanded the resignation of the government and the formation of a
transitional government to resolve the crisis. The NP took it upon themselves
to make drastic reforms on both the political and social systems, severely
criticizing the government by accusing it of failure in the management of
state affairs and with the failure to achieve political, economic and management reforms. Moreover, it declared the lack of the government's ability to
maintain the rights and freedoms guaranteed by the Kuwaiti Constitution and
the inability to safeguard the interests of the Kuwaiti people and resources.
It also stated that there is a lack of seriousness in eliminating the political,
economic and administrative corruption that has spread throughout the
state's institutions.[313] According to the party, this is all due to the autocratic
practices of the government and the marginalization of the legislative and
regulatory role of the National Assembly and overstepping the will of the
nation, which is the source of all authorities confirmed by some prominent
symbols of the regime. The party also confirms that the people of Kuwait are
the source of all powers who are looking for fundamental solutions to the
political and constitutional crisis that exceeds the traditional and sectarian
practices exercised by the government.[313] The party urged in its statement
the establishment of a popular government elected in accordance with the
provisions and principles of the Constitution.[314]

Al-Mutairi violently criticized the political systems in the GCC states,
considering the relationship between the people of the region and the ruling
regimes – which he described as tribal regimes – are neither based on a
legitimate basis nor on Shari'a.[315]

> It is not a brotherhood relationship as stated by Islam, and not a relation
> based on the loyalty to the state as determined by the contemporary
> constitutions!!! It is a fellowship relation in which the ignorant class is so
> clear . . . i.e. on a class and feudal basis, where the land – namely, the

Gulf and the Arabian Peninsula – is owned by the six ruling families or clans, which employ the people![316]

Al-Mutairi emphasized that building a contemporary modern state in the Arab Gulf had not been achieved yet, and the ruling regimes are still tribal regimes where governments are formed on a tribal basis according to which the sons of the six ruling clans are always at the head of the governments and all the ministries of sovereignty.[317] He pointed out that those six ruling families deduct what is the equivalent of one-third of the income of the oil wealth for the benefit of the clan, with an income of around $6,000 billion, which is equivalent to the budgets of the countries of the region for nearly 100 years.[318] Al-Mutairi wondered:

> What are the legal or constitutional rights that allow thousands of members of ruling families and clans to enjoy these privileges while denying this right to the rest of the people, while stating that all individuals have equal rights and duties as stated in the Islamic Shari'a and the Constitutions?[319]

Al-Mutairi believes that the legitimacy of these regimes has been shaken in popularity due to the protest movements that reject the relationship of dependency and efforts should be made to reform this situation, whereby six families control the faith of 30 million inhabitants. He added that this is not happening anywhere else in the contemporary world, and urges the people of the region to take their rights to choose their governments in a peaceful way, if possible, or in a revolutionary manner, if they are suppressed.[320] On the occasion of the summit of the GCC, the NP demanded the leaders of these countries work to achieve political benefits for all its citizens, which is the achievement of political freedoms and especially the right of the people of the Arabian Gulf in the selection and participation in the management of their affairs. In addition, it called for the right of announcing political parties and the establishment of elected councils with the separation of powers and independence of the judiciary system. It also demanded to push towards the unity of the people of the region under a unified parliament, the opening of borders between the GCC countries, the unification of the Gulf market, opening the door to investments without any restrictions, and the establishment a common currency. In addition, it called for unification of the educational process between the members of the GCC and equality in the posts between the citizens of the GCC. Moreover, it suggested the establishment of a unified army and the abolishment of the foreign presence in the Arabian Gulf region. It also requested allowing the Yemen Arab Republic to join the GCC due to its social and cultural homogeneity and the strategic location of Yemen to the Arabian Gulf region.[321] The party warned of the danger of the draft proposed by the United States under the slogan supporting moderation in the Middle East and in co-ordination with the GCC, Egypt and Jordan, describing it as a suspicious project that aims to recruit the GCC states, Egypt and Jordan in the colonial wars led by the American administration in the Arab and Islamic world as in Palestine, Iraq, Lebanon and Afghanistan. The party emphasized that participation in this project will lead to widening the gap between Arab governments and their people. The statement warned that the decision of these governments in accordance with the imperialist powers could cause them to lose their sovereignty and independence.[322]

The NP rejected the bill regarding exploitation of the northern oilfields by foreign companies and stated that foreign control over Kuwait's oil is a warning of danger of falling under foreign pressure to pass this bill. This concern was raised by the party in public. It stressed that the party position on this project came under the principles of the party, which reject all forms of foreign colonialism whether political or economic, which is clearly reflected in this project. The party warned the government that it will be responsible to the Kuwaiti people if this project is passed and it will be accused of abandoning Kuwait's interests and the fortunes of the Kuwaiti people, which is the duty of any government to maintain.[323]

The NP urged the National Assembly and the government to take the initiative to stand against the governments of Denmark and Norway and to announce their opposition to the reports of the misuse of the Prophet, peace be upon him, in the media, and demanded that the two governments apologize to Muslims all over the world for this abuse, which fuels hostility between the people of the world. The party also urged the Kuwaiti people and the people of the Arab region and the Islamic world to boycott all Danish and Norwegian companies as a protest for this act. The NP also expressed its surprise at the prohibition of any act against the Jews in all European countries under the pretext of anti-Semitism, while allowing anyone to mock the Prophet Mohammad under the freedom of press. They continued with stating that this double standard is responsible for the loss of the European Christian-Western countries' credibility on the subject of freedom and respect for human rights, most especially over the fact that Arabs are also considered to be semitic.[324]

The party condemned the political and economic blockade of the government of Hamas, which aims to starve the Palestinian people by putting them under the Zionist occupation. It regards the imposition of the political and economic boycott as being similar to the fascist campaigns on Libya during the Italian occupation, which affirms that the Western colonial campaigns on the Arab region still exist today under the leadership of an American extremist administration. The party urged the Kuwaiti National Assembly and the Kuwaiti Government to provide assistance to the Palestinian people.[325]

The NP regarded the issue of the Iranian nuclear dossier raised by the colonial powers as an excuse to gain complete control over the region in order to consolidate their influence at the expense of the independence and sovereignty of the people of the region. It stressed the right of the Islamic Republic of Iran to possess peaceful nuclear energy and the right of the countries and people of the region to independence and sovereignty over their own land, wealth, right to enhance their own capabilities, and to reject all forms of foreign intervention. At the same time, the party emphasized criticism towards the Iranian political regime and demanded them to overcome the sectarian spirit in dealing with the Iraqi issue and in respect to the Arab identity of Iraq, to preserve the unity of its land, and the people of Iraq as being an Arab country. It regarded the Iranian interference in Iraq's affairs as a disruption in the emotions of the Arab nation, which could lead to the hostility of the people of the Arab region on one hand, and the Sunni Islamic world, on the other hand, towards Iran.[326]

The party took a stand in favor of supporting the resistance in southern Lebanon while avoiding mentioning the name of Hizbollah (Party of God), which is the leading the armed resistance against the Zionist state, whether through statements or through the press statements of the Party leadership.[327] Al-Mutairi criticized the views, which provoked confusion in the society about the resistance and its legitimacy. He regards every Muslim, regardless of his religious sect, whether Sunni or Shi'ite, fighting the Zionist enemy in the land of Palestine and Lebanon, as a defender of his religion, and if he is killed in the war, then he is a martyr.[328] Al-Mutairi emphasizes:

> . . . it is not right not to support the people of Lebanon in their fight with the Zionist enemy while the people of Iraq are killing each other, it is not right also to convict the Shi'ites of Lebanon, who are resisting the Zionist occupation and the Americans on the ground of the crimes of the Shi'ites of Iraq who stood with the occupation there, this is an injustice and an aggression, which is totally prohibited by Shari'a, and nobody bears others' mistakes and crimes, even though it is his community or family.[329]

After the end of the first Conference of the NP, a split between the party's leadership happened following the controversy that occurred between supporters to boycott the general elections to elect members of the National Assembly scheduled for 29 June 2006 on one hand and their opponents on the other hand. The party emphasized that the participation in these elections contradicts the principles and objectives of the party and that the decision to boycott the elections was due to the corruption of the electoral system, and the need to amend it; for instance, the use of political money, and enforcing factional, sectarian and tribal feelings that undermine the unity of society and the popular will.[330] Following this statement, three leaders of the party, – Hussein al-Sai'di, Jaber al-Marri and Jiliwi al-Jumai'a – issued a statement opposing the party's decision to boycott the elections issued by the Shura Council of the Party. They regarded this decision as an escape from confronting corruption and that it was far from reality. They announced their resignations from the party and that they were joining the SM, which they described as 'the Mother Movement', in order to complete the process of reform and to attain the achievement of the goals and objectives of the SM.[331] At the same time, the official spokesman for the NP, Faisal al-Hamad, announced the establishment of a popular front consisting of former members, politicians, writers and honest citizens to uncover the corrupt practices in the electoral process,[332] and emphasized that 'the government wants a weak Assembly to pass many of its projects'.[333]

After the change of electoral constituencies from 25 constituencies to five, the NP participated in the elections of the National Assembly held on 17 May 2008, with 11 candidates but none of them succeeded, causing the resignation of the party's leader and a number of its leading members. These results confirmed the lack of popularity of the party. It is worth mentioning that the NP ran for Parliamentary elections for the first time. The party still exists and plays a role in the political events in Kuwait.

Kuwaiti Youth Gathering
Tajammu' al-Shabab al-Kuwaiti

This organization was founded in September 2005 and it emphasizes that 'Islam is our religion and we only work within its mainframe.' It calls for denouncing extremism and promoting moderation. The gathering has a number of objectives and principles, mainly:[334]

- sophistication of the youth culture
- work to strengthen the compatibility between the youth and society
- use of methods that strengthen the process of participation for the development of society
- work hard for the aim of benefiting the country
- activate the role of the youth in building their own future
- dedication and devotion to the homeland
- credibility in dealing with young people
- seeking reform.

This is one of the newly emerged gatherings where most of its members belong to the youth. To be a member in this gathering, one should be 15 years old or above and should not have been a participant in any other gathering, or group, or political movement before. Because of the fact that this is a new group, no one has heard much about its activity except its constituent statement as well as the statement issued for the support of Mohammad Haif al-Mutairi, the DNPG candidate for the election of the National Assembly.[335]

The Virtue Gathering (VG)
Tajammu' al-Fadalh

This organization was founded on 15 November 2006 by a number of activists belonging to the Islamist political groups, such as Dr. Tariq al-Tawari and Dr. Sa'ad al-Enezi, both of them teachers in the Faculty of Shari'a at Kuwait

University, among others. There are about 100 VG members, as stated by the founders of the VG.[336]

The constituent statement of the VG urged the deployment of virtue in Kuwaiti society and the fight against depravity under the slogan Min Aijal Kuwait Afdal (For the Best of Kuwait).[337] The founders of the VG emphasized that their gathering's objective is far away from the narrow political goals, targets and personal ambitions.[338] Al-Tawari, the Secretary General of the VG, confirms that:

> It will intensify the reformist trend in the face of corruption . . . seeking the resistance of the deviation and the propagation of virtue whose work is to watch for evil and the manifestations of corruption.[339]

al-Enezi says:

> The Gathering is a new awakening, where most of the Islamic dynamic activity tended to be political in nature, while leaving a small fraction to Da'wa.[340]

Some of the most important objectives of the VG are:[341]

1   Call to God through wisdom and good counsel.
2   Make an Islamic society.
3   Protect the Islamic values and address the ethical and social disintegration.
4   Monitor the negative behavior in Kuwaiti society and provide solutions through studies and research, and correspond with the guardians.
5   Establish values and habits based on religion and warn of what causes its demolition.
6   Protect Shari'a from futility and humiliation.

The VG believes in adopting peaceful methods and rejects armed action; it also believes in non-interference in political affairs and claims that its work is purely peaceful with no political trend. It also rejects any action that raises hatred and strife in Kuwaiti society. The VG calls for communication with the rulership through the executive, legislative and judicial authorities.[342]

The structure of the VG consists of consulting bureaus to support its work, as follows:[343]

1   Electronic Consulting Bureau. Its task is to supervise the website of the VG, receive messages and answer them.
2   The Legal Consultant Bureau is to pursue legal proceedings in the case of the fight against vice and virtue.
3   The Consultant Bureau gathers information, assesses and examines it.

Also, it identifies the titles and the arrangement of the transmissions and the reception of the community.

4 The Consultant Bureau for Information develops the spread of information about the gathering in the media.

5 The Consultant Educational and Social Bureau is to follow up on educational and social services.

6 The Consultant Bureau for Shari'a corresponds with the Shari'a authority.

7 The Follow-up Bureau is to oversee the functioning of the VG.

The VG seeks to amend some legal and penal articles of the Constitution through members of the National Assembly.[344] The VG confirms its readiness to co-operate with all Islamist political groups in Kuwait.[345] By reading the VG constituent statement and organizational structure, we find that it resembles the Committee for the Propagation of Virtue and Prevention of Vice in Saudi Arabia. It seems that the results of the elections of the National Assembly that took place in June 2006 resulted in the winning of 18 candidates representing the Sunni Islamist political groups. This has encouraged some Sunni fundamentalist figures to establish such a gathering. It is worth mentioning that there have been several attempts since 1991 by the Islamic fundamentalist movements to impose the Committee for the Propagation of Virtue and Prevention of Vice in legal terms under various names by representatives of the Islamist political groups in the National Assembly. However, all these attempts have failed due to the opposition of the liberal and Shi'ite groups.

3   Shi'ite Islamist political groups

According to unofficial estimates, Shi'ites represent 15.4% of the world's Muslim population and Sunnis represent 84.6%. The total of Sunnis and Shi'ites in the world is 1,385 billion. In Middle Eastern countries, Shi'ites represent 37.5% of the total population, while Sunnis represent 62.5%, and their total is 253 million. According to unofficial statistics, the Shi'ites represent the majority in each of Bahrain, Lebanon and Iraq. Regarding Kuwait, there is no official statistic of the number of Shi'ites currently, but it was estimated by James Bill to be in the range between 15% and 25% of the population. However, Anthony Cordesman estimated it to be 30%, relying on the American Central Intelligence Agency's (CIA) resources.[1] We emphasize that these statistics are not official; they are mere speculations by those who are interested in the political situation in the Middle East. Although the Shi'ite sect in Kuwait is an essential part of Kuwaiti society, their real number is not known. The British political agent in Kuwait during the 1930s estimated the numbers of Shi'ites to be 18,000 citizens from a total Kuwaiti population of 65,000.[2] Based on this representation, it could be estimated that Shi'ites are approximately 28% of the overall population of Kuwait.

Kuwait Shi'ites settled a long time ago in Kuwait, and well-known families such as Behbehani and Qabazard migrated to Kuwait in the late nineteenth century.[3] Shi'ites in Kuwait are divided on an ethnic basis between Shi'ites of Arab origin and Shi'ites of Iranian origin. Shi'ite Arabs are people who migrated from the Arabian Peninsula and specifically from the eastern region of Saudi Arabia. The Hasawiyah, named after the area of al-Hasa, as well as the Shi'ites who migrated to Kuwait from Bahrain, are called Baharna. In addition, there are some Shi'ite Arabs who had come from southern Iraq.[4] As for the Shi'ites who came from Iran, they are called 'Ajam and they make up a large portion of Kuwaiti Shi'ites. They migrated to Kuwait in the nineteenth century. British colonialism encouraged this kind of migration for political and economic objectives.[5] In spite of their Arabization, they kept some of their cultural elements, especially the Persian language and folklore. There is a small percentage of these minority who no longer remember the mother tongue of Farsi and call on its members in the name (al-Tararih) for their work in the vegetable market, which in Kuwait is called al-Tararih.[6]

Shi'ites in Kuwait are divided into four denominational schools:

First: Sheikhiya, named after Sheikh Ahmad bin Zainuddin al-Ahsai, who carries respectful thoughts towards Ahal al-Bayt (the family of the Prophet). They believe that God had authorized Ahal Albait to distribute faith. However, this is no longer their belief, and they are currently called in Kuwait as Jamma't al-Mirza (Mirza Group). Mirza Hassan al-Ahaqaqi, a Kuwaiti national, is the Imam of al-Sadiq mosque, located in the heart of the capital, as their center. Most of his followers are the Shi'ite Arabs who emigrated from al-Hasa to Kuwait. The most prominent families of this group are al-Arbash, Khraibet, Harban and al-Wazzan. Jamma't al-Mirza was criticized by other Shi'ite groups due to its neutral positions towards political events, both locally and regionally.

Second: al-Akbariya: They are the Baharna, followers of Mirza Ibrahim Jamal al-Din, who is regarded as their Imam. Some of the families that belong to this group are al-Qallaf, al-Khayyat, Makki Juma' and Haji Hamid.

Third: Alosuliya (fundamentalism): This school focuses on the modern Hadith, in other words the Hadith has to be studied instead of accepting it as it is. It is spread between the Shi'ites of Iraq, Iran and Lebanon.

Fourth: al-Khoeih: the rest of Kuwaiti Shi'ites are of Iranian origin. They are the followers of Sayyed Baqir la-Khoei, who lived in Najaf and died recently. Zine al-'Aabideen mosque, Muqames Mosque and al-Naqi mosque in Kuwait are the centers for this group. The most important families are Musawi, Qabazard, Dashti, Ashkanani, Bahman, Behbehani and Ma'rafi.[7]

The demographic distribution of the population of Kuwait shows that the Shi'ites in general are keen on living in areas where they form a majority, such as al-Sharq and Bneid Al-Gar before the discovery of oil. They later moved on to new areas such as al-Qadisiya, al-Mansouria, al-Di'ya, al-Dasma, al-Rumaithya, al-Salmiya, Hawalli and al-Jabriya. These areas are characterized by the presence of Shi'ite mosques and Husseiniyas (the Shi'ite equivalent of the mosque), with the number of Shi'ite mosques and Husseiniyas more than 28 and 60 respectively.[8] Husseiniyas are very important for the Shi'ites. They are more like a social club, school and library through which they celebrate religious occasions, such as the anniversary of 'Ashura in the Muharram month. The Shi'ites play an important role in political events, such as in Kuwait in 1938 when Shi'ites held meetings within the Husseiniya as a protest with the National Legislative Council, as well as the important role in recruiting Shi'ites in political organizations, such as what happened in Bahrain since the beginning of the 1950s.[9]

The economic situation in Kuwait played an important role in reducing the gap between Shi'ites and Sunnis socially and culturally, where Shi'ites benefited from the distribution of oil wealth as the Sunnis did. The early 1950s witnessed a huge land acquisition policy that helped in improving the economic level of Kuwaiti nationals and provided a way for Shi'ites to work in the economic sector, enabling some Shi'ite families to become wealthy merchants. In addition, the economic and social changes in that period enabled the Shi'ites to hold important leading positions in the State. The development of education in Kuwait also contributed to the progress of Kuwaiti people, both Shi'ites and Sunnis, where the State guaranteed free education at all academic levels. Regarding the religious sector, freedom of establishing Husseiniyas was guaranteed even in the Sunni areas.[10] There is no restriction in bringing Shi'ite clerics from Najaf except during the Iraqi–Iranian war, contrary to the conditions of Shi'ites in the Gulf states who suffer from some restrictions in the exercise of religious rights.[11]

The political situation of the Shi'ites in the pre-independence era

The starting point for political participation in Kuwait was in 1921, which witnessed the establishment of the first Consultative Council, founded by a group of merchants and enlightened men. Membership was limited to the Sunni sect of Arab origin, although its Charter states that there will be two members of Kuwaitis of Iranian origin to be elected by Kuwaitis with Iranian origin. According to the following text:

> The Council is formed from: the ruler and his deputy, and in his absence, then two from al-Sabah family and ten from the citizens; two of them are from national 'Ajam. The Deputy of the ruler, from the al-Sabah is elected by the ruler, the other two al-Sabah representatives are elected from the al-Sabah family. The rest of the members are elected by the nation according to the majority of voices. The two 'Ajam members are elected by the national 'Ajam.[12]

It is clear from this text that there is a reference to the Kuwaiti people with Iranian origins, both Shi'ites and Sunnis. It is also noted that the Council did not include any representative of the Shi'ites of Arab origin, such as Baharna and Hasawiyah.[13] This means that the ethnic classifications in the Kuwaiti society have historical roots. Since the Consultative Council did not last for more than two months, it has become difficult to track the reaction of the Shi'ites toward this deliberate exclusion, and the short length of the Council prevented the Shi'ites from showing any dissatisfaction about it. It is especially noteworthy when this situation is compared with what happened in 1938 during the Legislative National Council, as will be explained later. It seems that the reason behind the exclusion of the Shi'ites was due to the disapproval of the Sunnis for the position taken by the Kuwaitis of Iranian origin, who refused to participate in the al-Jahra battle in 1921 between Kuwait and Ibn Saud. A group of them went to the British political resident expressing their refusal to participate in this war on the basis that they are not Kuwaiti citizens, but Iranians.

The first elected Administrative Councils appeared in 1934, represented in Municipal and Education Councils. Its membership was limited to the Kuwaiti Sunnis from Arab origins, excluding the Kuwaitis from Iranian origins (both Sunnis and Shi'ites) from the right of electing and voting. This situation continued until 1938.[14]

Shi'ites and the reform movement in 1938

Kuwaiti society witnessed the first attempt for political reform by members of the National Bloc with the Arab nationalist trend. It adopted a hard line towards Iranian immigration to Kuwait, as it was expressed in its program, published in the Iraqi newspaper *al-Zaman*, which included several demands related to political reform. The domestic situation of Kuwait addressed demands such as the foreign immigrants to Kuwait, who were described by the National Bloc as refugees who do not have any relation with the homeland of Kuwait.[15] It appears that the Kuwaitis with Iranian origin were part of this and that is why the National Bloc excluded the Shi'ites from the nomination for the Legislative National Council, founded in 1938, which limited their right to vote without nomination. The Shi'ites of Iranian origin considered this attitude biased and announced their dissatisfaction with this trend and held a meeting in protest in the Husseiniya led by the Shi'ites' leader at that time, Sayyed Mahdi al-Qaswini. The idea was raised in the meeting to hold demonstrations and announce strikes. However, in the end, they decided to send a protest letter on behalf of Sayyed Mahdi al-Qaswini to the National Legislative Council demanding the following:

- their rights in the Council to be upheld
- the opening of a Persian school
- the assignment of a judge of the Shi'ite sect to examine their cases in court
- to have representatives in the municipal council
- justice in the employment policy in government posts.

The National Legislative Council rejected all these demands and, accordingly, a large number of Shi'ites of Iranian origin met the British political resident in Kuwait requesting British citizenship. This act agitated the National Legislative Council, causing it to issue a resolution to expel all Kuwaitis who assume a foreign nationality, and that they must leave Kuwait in two months' time with the denial of all Kuwaiti rights. This resolution was distributed in all areas of Kuwait. Members of the National Legislative Council met with a representative of the British Government; they showed their concerns regarding granting British citizenship for the Shi'ites and demanded that they have to leave Kuwait if this is true. The British political resident sympathized with those Shi'ites. The National Legislative Council emphasized that it does not recognize the Shi'ites who migrated to Kuwait from Iran after World War I, and the refusal was based on the following:[16]

1   The apprehension of the members of the National Legislative Council from the increasing migration by the Iranians to Kuwait.
2   This idea is not intended to Shi'ites and Kuwaitis of Iranian origin who settled in Kuwait prior to World War I, but immigrants from Iran who emigrated to Kuwait after World War I.

The ignorance of the National Legislative Council towards the Shi'ite minority and their exclusion from the participation in political decision-making led to the support of the Shi'ite sect by al-Sabah in opposition to the National Legislative Council. Sheikh Ahmad al-Jaber al-Sabah and the British took advantage of the attitude of the National Legislative Council towards the Shi'ites in provoking them against the Council, so that they led a strong opposition to the National Legislative Council on the grounds that it does not represent all sects of the society and went out on demonstrations, calling for its fall.

These demonstrations by Shi'ites in Kuwait in 1938 were recorded as the first demonstrations in the history of Kuwait.[17] It is worth mentioning that some Shi'ites of Arab origin did not participate in these demonstrations; on the contrary, some of them, such as Abdul-Razzaq Al-Basir, became members of the National Youth Bloc. The Shi'ite minority, together with the al-Sabah family, the British and some conservative Sunni families, led a strong opposition against the National Legislative Council, causing its fall.[18] After the elimination of the National Legislative Council, an Iranian school was opened with a curriculum brought in from Iran. The opening ceremony was attended by senior members of the ruling family and conservatives who stood against the Council. In addition, financial aid was collected to support the school.[19]

The political situation of the Shi'ites in the post-independence era

On 30 December 1961, the first Constituent Assembly was founded after Kuwait gained independence from Britain in June 1961. The election law ensured the right to vote and nominate for all Kuwaitis, regardless of ethnicity. The Shi'ites succeeded in having two members in this Assembly. The main task of the Assembly was to make a draft for the Constitution of the country, which was later called the Constitution of 1962. This Constitution equalized Kuwaitis in rights and duties.[20]

The Shi'ite Parliamentary Bloc was not distinctive and was not part of the political opposition in Parliament, but an integral part of the group loyal to the Kuwaiti regime represented by al-Sabah. Their group consisted of the majority of the members of the Parliament, who represented Shi'ites and Bedouins, on which the government totally depended to pass laws and resolutions that faced strong opposition from the ANM bloc members and Nasserites. The Shi'ite Parliamentary bloc did not take a clear position on the rigging of elections in 1967,[21] where the Shi'ite Parliamentary bloc participated in this forged Assembly.[22]

On 23 January 1963, the first Parliamentary elections to elect the members of the National Assembly took place, in which the Shi'ites had the right to vote and nominate. It was a memorable day for the Shi'ites, where five of their candidates won seats in the National Assembly from the First Constituency, al-Sharq, and the Seventh Constituency, al-Dasma, which were regarded as the most important Shi'ite strongholds because of their population density. The role of the Shi'ite representatives in this Council was merely represented in passing laws made by the government and putting restrictions on public freedoms, such as civil rights and freedom in the Public Meetings Law, the Civil Service Law, the Press and Publication Law, and the Clubs and Associations Law. The amendment on Article (35) of the Press and Publication Law, for example, gave the Council of Ministers the right to suspend, for a period of one year, any newspaper and to ban any newspaper or magazine without referring to the courts, thus making the Council of Ministers litigant and judge at the same time. The amendment regarding Article (6) of the Clubs and Associations Law was to prohibit any club or association from dealing with politics or even mentioning it. The amendment on Article (149) of the Civil Service Law gave the Council of Ministers the right to dismiss any employee and to deprive him from holding another post in the civil service, or in any of the public institutions or organizations, and also deprive him of his political rights and the right to nominate himself to the membership of the National Assembly, or any other local Council. The dismissed person could only complain to the Council of Ministers, which was again both litigant and judge. Finally, the amendments to the law placed more restriction on public meetings and prohibited any foreigner from participating in demonstrations and public meetings on one hand, and from addressing the political opposition within the Board of mass Arab nationalists and some representatives of the Chamber of Commerce who support them, on the other hand. Shi'ite MPs and the bedouin MPs formed the majority in the pro-government Parliament, thus causing the ANM bloc to resign from the Parliament in 1965 and to accuse the government of converting the 'legislative power from a tool in the hands of the people to achieve more freedoms ... into an instrument in the hands of the government to strangle public freedoms'.[23]

Shi'ite candidates participated in the second National Assembly elections in 1967 and they won nine seats. The government and the Shi'ite Parliamentary Bloc supported the government in its act, as pointed out earlier.

In 1971, the Shi'ites participated with a number of candidates and six of them managed to win seats in the National Assembly. They continued to be a part of the pro-government majority, together with the representatives of the bedouins.

In the 1975 elections, 10 Shi'ite candidates won; this was the highest percentage achieved by the Shi'ites. For the first time, a Shi'ite joined the cabinet where the MP 'Abdul-Muttalib al-Kadhmy became the Minister of Oil. This

Assembly did not last long and the regime dissolved it in 1976.[24] As a result of popular pressure, the Kuwaiti regime issued a new election law in 1981. The Shi'ites believe that the goal of this amendment, which was approved in the absence of the Parliamentary life, was to reduce the Shi'ite representation in the Parliament, especially since the Shi'ites had won 10 seats in the National Assembly of 1975 representing al-Sharq and al-Dasma. Under the new law, the number of representatives of these two constituencies were four MPs. The fact is that changes in the electoral law gave the Shi'ites the opportunity to compete in the constituencies that were closed to them before. For instance, the Fifth Constituency of al-Qadisiya, the Tenth Constituency, which included Qortobah, al-'Adailiya, al-Surrah, al-Jabriya, and the Second Constituency of al-Da'iya, where Shi'ite votes outweighed the winners of the Sunni candidates. The government provided some justification for this amendment, such as the population structure.[25]

On 25 February 1981, elections were held to elect the fifth National Assembly and the election results led to the defeat of all the Shi'ites traditionally loyal to the Kuwaiti regime;[26] they were replaced by new faces represented with Sayyed 'Adnan 'Abdul-Samad and Dr. Nasser Sarkho, which were in Khat al-Imam Khomeini (Khomeini line). It also achieved a good result in the 1985 elections.[27]

Generally speaking, since the 1930s and until the emergence of the Islamic revolution in Iran, the Shi'ites in Kuwait were not a part of the political opposition, contrary to the Shi'ites in Bahrain and Saudi Arabia, who were an integral part of the political opposition to the ruling regime. This was in contrast to the Kuwaiti Shi'ites, who limited their activities from the 1930s until the Islamic revolution in Iran, opposing the Iranian opposition movement that was loyal to the Shah's regime in Iran.[28]

In Bahrain, large numbers of people of the Shi'ite sect were engaged in the political opposition against the rule of al-Khalifa through the celebration of 'Ashura on 13 October 1954; Shi'ite and Sunni sects succeeded in holding a rally in a Husseiniya of the Sanabis village, where they announced the formation of a General Assembly composed of 120 members to represent the two sects. The Assembly appointed eight prominent Bahraini members to the Higher Executive Committee, four from each sect. The most eminent demand was the establishment of a legislative council through free election. The Higher Executive Committee is considered as the first public group in the Arabian Gulf region. It is also considered as the first political group based on a non-sectarian foundation throughout the present history of Bahrain. The most eminent activities of the Higher Executive Committee were to issue statements and to hold rallies by followers of the two sects. It also succeeded in forming a trade union called the Bahraini Labor Union, which included both Shi'ites and Sunni workers among its ranks. Afterwards, other political groups representing Marxist and nationalist trends appeared in the mid-1950s. These included: the Arab Ba'ath Socialist Party, the Arab Nationalists Movement, Jabhat al-Tahrir al-Watani al-Bahrani (the Bahraini National

Liberation Front), al-Haraka al-'Arabia al-Wahida (the Arab Union Movement), and al-Shabab al-Qawmi al-Bahraini (the Bahraini National Youth). In the 1970s, Shi'ites and Sunnis in Bahrain participated in founding underground organizations such as the Marxist Jabhat Tahrir al-Khalij (the Front for the Liberation of the Gulf), Munadamat al-Quwa al-Taqadumiy (the Organization of Progressive Force), Jabhat Tahrir Sharq al-Jazira al-'Arabiya (the Front for the Liberation of the Eastern Arab Peninsula), al-Jabha al-Dimuqratiya fi al-Bahrain (the Democratic Front in Bahrain), Munadamat al-Nidal min ajil Tahrir al-Tabaqa al-'Amila (Organization of the Struggle for the Liberation of the Working Class), Munadamat al-Rif al-Dimuqratiya (the Hinterland Democratic Organization), al-Jabha al-Sha'biya li Tahrir al-Khalij al-'Arabi al-Muhtal (the Popular Front for the Liberation of the Occupied Arabian Gulf), al-Jabha al-Wataniya al-Dimuqratiya li Tahrir 'Oman wa al-Khalij al-'Arabi (the National Democratic Front for the Liberation of Oman and the Arabian Gulf), al-Jabha al-Sha'biya li Tahrir 'Oman wa al-Khalij al-'Arabi (the Popular Front for the Liberation of Oman and the Arabian Gulf), al-Haraka al-Thawriya al-Sha'biya fi 'Oman wa al-Khalij al-'Arabi (the Popular Revolutionary Movement in Oman and the Arabian Gulf) and al-Jabha al-Sha'bia fil Bahrain (the Popular Front in Bahrain). Many Sunni and Shi'ite workers, both educated and non-educated, participated in the formation of these underground groups, which played a great role in narrowing the gap between people from both sects.

In Saudi Arabia, some Shi'ites participated in the establishment and leadership of the revolutionary movements with a tendency of Arab unity, such as the Arab Ba'ath Socialist Party, Itihad Sha'b al-Jazira al-'Arabiya (the Union of the people of the Arabian Peninsula), Ahrar al-Jazira al-'Arabiya (the Liberals of the Arabian Peninsula), Itihad Quwa al-Sha'b al-'Amil (the Union of the Force of the Working People), al-Tali'a al-Tullabiya al-Thawriya (the Revolutionary Student Vanguard). They also contributed to the founding of Marxist organizations, such as al-Lajana al'Ummalliy (the Workers Committee), Jabhat al-Islah al-Watani (the National Reform Front), Jabhat al-Tahrir al-Watani fi al-Sa'udiya (the National Liberation Front in Saudi). In 1975, its name was changed to al-Hizb al-Shiui fi al-Sa'udiya (the Communist Party in Saudia), Itihad al-Quwa al-Dimuqratiya fi al-Jazira al-'arabiya (the Union of the Democratic Front in the Arabian Peninsula), Hizb al-'Amal al-Ishtiraki al-'Arabi fi al-Jazira al-'Arabiya (the Arab Socialist Labour Party in the Arabian Peninsula), Munazamat al-Thawra al-Watanit (the National Revolution Organization), al-Jabha al-Sha'biya al-Dimugratiya fi al-Jazira al-'Arabiya (the Popular Democratic Front in the Arabian Peninsula) and al-Hizb al-Dimuqrati al-Sha'bi fi al-Jazira al-'Arabiya (the Popular Democratic Party in the Arabian Peninsula).[28]

The attitudes taken by the Arab nationalist against the non-Arab 'Agam' played a prominent role in the reluctance of the Shi'ites from engaging in political action and opposition, as well as in taking a hostile position towards the nationalist movement, which was one of the most important movements at that time. These hostile attitudes of the ANM towards the Shi'ites helped to promote sectarian and ethnic divisions in the society. The anti-position taken by the ANM Kuwait Branch towards the Iranian immigration to Kuwait and the Arabian Gulf region did not distinguish between Kuwaitis of Iranian origin who had contributed to the progress, modernization and building of Kuwait, and the new Iranian immigrants. It mobilized the Kuwaiti people on the basis that there was a joint plot between British colonialism, the ruling family, and Iran to erase the Arab identity from the Gulf. The movement's struggle against the British presence was associated with a similar struggle against the Iranian presence by all means and at all levels. The movement felt that the growing Iranian community was a threat to Arabism; they thought:[29]

- making a foreign majority in Kuwait and the rest of the Arabian Gulf region to be a pressing force against its Arab population
- the use of some of its figures to oppose the Arab progressive forces that threatened the colonial privileges in the region
- getting rid of hungry mouths that make a threat to the Shah regime
- achieving the dream of the Iranian empire to expand in the Arabian Gulf region.

The parliamentary representatives of the ANM Bloc in the National Assembly launched a severe campaign against the Kuwaitis of Iranian origin and demanded the formation of a commission to investigate into their files. They also suggested granting Kuwaiti nationality to Arabs only, and the withdrawal of the Kuwaiti nationality from people who were of Iranian origin. They also demanded that the Arabic language as a criterion in granting Kuwaiti nationality.[30] The attitudes of the ANM in Kuwait, which were announced in the Parliament or through its literature, created a violent reaction among the Kuwaiti Shi'ites of Iranian or Arab origin alike, especially when extremist figures of the Shi'ites of Iranian origin, members in Jam'iyat al-Thakafah al-Ijtima'yah (the Social Culture Society (SCS)) succeeded in escalating this division between the Sunnis and Shi'ites of Arab origin. They announced that the action is not intended against immigration organized by the Government of the Shah, but it also meant the Kuwaiti Shi'ites of Iranian origin. At the same time, they encouraged Kuwaiti Shi'ites of Arab origin to live in areas dominated by a sectarian nature. The Society played a role in promoting that the Shah was the protector of the Shi'ites in Kuwait.

The Kuwaiti National Movement was affected negatively due to the positions taken by the ANM towards the Kuwaitis from Iranian origin on the grounds that they are a group of invaders and that there is a historical conflict between Arabs and Persians. These attitudes served the Kuwaiti regime, which succeeded in exploiting the Shi'ites to take positions against the Kuwaiti National Movement.[31]

Islamic revolution in Iran and its impact on the Shi'ites of Kuwait

With the emergence of the Islamic revolution in Iran, led by Ayatollah Khomeini, a hostile spirit began to prevail among Shi'ites in the Arab world towards conservative regimes. This was reflected in Shi'ite gatherings on the Arabian peninsula and the Arabian Gulf. The Kuwaiti arena was not far from this revolutionary wave where Shi'ites were split into two currents: the conservative current and the pro-Khomeini Shi'ite current. The former represented the aristocracy class of merchants who had mutual interests with the ruling family. This current aimed to achieve some religious and social reforms. The second current began taking shape in Kuwait among young Shi'ites, most especially belonging to lower or middle classes. This current aspired to overthrow the conservative regime and replace it with an Islamic republic regime using the Iranian model as an example. The Islamic revolution in Iran became a source of inspiration and awareness of this trend, which represented the vast majority of Kuwaiti Shi'ites. The Revolutionary pro-Khomeini line achieved its first victory by overthrowing the conservative trend that dominated the SCS. In fact, the signs of conflict between the two currents had started before the emergence of the Islamic revolution in Iran. In 1968, a group of young Shi'ites who were members in the society demanded to make a change in the leadership of the society. This struggle between the young Shi'ites and the establishments in the society supported by the Shi'ites aristocratic families continued until 1969, when the former succeeded in removing the latter and succeeded in leading the society. Despite this change, the society continued to work in isolation from the political opposition in Kuwait. After the Iranian revolution in 1979, another current with a different ideology got control over the society and it seems that this current was affected by the Khomeini line.

The Islamic revolution in Iran tried to spread the revolutionary spirit among the Kuwaiti Shi'ites, particularly in the youth sector through provoking them to participate in demonstrations that started from the house of Sayyed 'Abbas al-Mahri, an Iranian firebrand who had lived in Kuwait for many years.[32] He was the spiritual representative of Ayatollah Khomeini in Kuwait and led the group towards the Iranian Embassy where the Iranian flag was replaced with another flag that had Allah Akbar (God is great) written on the top of it. This demonstration was regarded as the first main movement called by the Shi'ite religious leadership in Kuwait since 1938.[33] This was an unprecedented move from the Shi'ites, especially since this demonstration resulted in a clash between them and the special forces, which tried to suppress them and arrested a number of the participants. Al-Mahri headed a delegation to visit Iran after the overthrow of the Shah's regime in which a number of the SCS leadership and some Sunni journalists, such as Isma'il al-Shatti, were among them. This delegation presented congratulations and support for the Islamic Revolution in Iran and they met with the leader of the revolution, Ayatollah Khomeini, in Tehran.[34]

Despite the strict measures taken by the authority against the pro-Khomeini line Shi'ites, the latter continued to challenge the government. On Friday, 30 November 1979, which marked the tenth of Muharram in the memory of the martyrdom of al-Hussein, Shi'ite revolutionaries marched starting from Husseiniyas and went to the American Embassy where the mass rose in slogans condemning the American policy towards Iran and showing solidarity with the Iranian people in the battle to surrender the Shah to Iran for his trial. A clash between the demonstrators and security personnel and the army took place, where demonstrators were dispersed by special forces using tear gas; 20 people who took part in the demonstration were arrested.[35]

The policy pursued by the political forces of the nationalists towards the Shi'ites, both Shi'ites of Iranian origin and Shi'ites of Arab origin, led to the creation of a significant rift between Shi'ites and Sunnis, with the exclusion of Shi'ites from political representation not only in the 1920s and the 1950s, but also in the 1970s. This brought about a feeling of dissatisfaction among the Shi'ites in Kuwait. The subsequent racism campaigns undertaken by the ANM Kuwait Branch throughout the 1950s and 1960s against the Kuwaitis of Iranian origin, who formed the majority of Kuwaiti Shi'ites, did not differentiate between citizens of Iranian origin who belonged to the Shi'ite sect and the illegal migration fueled by the Shah's regime, and even the Shah's ouster in Iran. This action affected the national action in Kuwait, thus leading to the isolation of Shi'ites from participating in political work with the Sunnis. Moreover, this led to the success of the Kuwaitis of Iranian origin in persuading Kuwaiti Shi'ites of Arab origin that the ultimate goal of the racist policy by Arab nationalists in Kuwait was to fight Shi'ites and is not just to resist the illegal immigration flowing from Iran to Kuwait. At the end of the 1960s, the ANM Kuwait Branch started to reconsider its hard-line position towards Iranian immigration to Kuwait.

The ruling family in Kuwait used this situation for its political benefit and took advantage of the Shi'ites to serve its plan to attack the political opposition both through the Shi'ite opposition in the Legislative National Council in 1938, and through the elected and administrative Councils that had emerged in the 1930s and 1950s. In addition, it used the Shi'ite Bloc in the Parliament from 1961 until the Iranian revolution for its favor.

The revolutionary change in Iran was reflected in the change of balance of power within the Shi'ite community in Kuwait from the traditional Shi'ite leadership loyal to the ruling family to the pro-Khomeini line Shi'ites trend affected by the fundamentalist revolution in Iran. The latter rejected the traditional leadership of the Shi'ites in Kuwait in defending the rights of the Shi'ites. In addition, the Iraqi–Iranian war deepened the links with the Shi'ite fundamentalist revolution in Iran. This situation reflected seriously in the cohesion of the internal front and national unity. The Shi'ites in Kuwait were upset with the support of the Government of Kuwait to the Iraqi regime and from the placing of its resources at the disposal of this regime. This situation gave the fundamentalist regime in Iran the chance to recruit Kuwaiti Shi'ites into terrorist organizations, where such organizations sought to destabilize the domestic front. This created a reaction from the Sunnis represented by some extremist figures of the Sunni religious groups by attacking the construction of a new mosque for Shi'ites in the Bayan District with burning the mosque.[35] This tension between Shi'ites and Sunnis continued even after the end of the Iraq–Iran war until the Iraqi occupation of Kuwait on 2 August 1990, when Shi'ites and Sunnis united to resist the occupation.

Despite the confiscation of the political rights of the Shi'ites in Kuwait from the beginning of the twentieth century, and despite the racist attitudes taken by the nationalist forces towards the Kuwaiti Shi'ites of Iranian origin, the Kuwaiti Shi'ites did not suffer social discrimination. They have their own courts and places of worship, such as mosques and Husseiniyas that were built in various parts of Kuwait. They have the freedom of transferring the Khums (the specific Shi'ite Islamic tax consisting of one-fifth of the yearly surplus income of a family) to religious authorities in Qom and Najaf. At the political level, the Shi'ites have occupied some of the highest positions in the State, such as ministers, ambassadors, the army and police, where the former Chief of Staff of the Kuwaiti Army is from the Shi'ite sect and now he is the Kuwaiti ambassador in Iraq, and there are representatives of the Shi'ites in both the Parliament and Municipal Council. On the economic level, there are a large number of Shi'ites who are rich merchants. Furthermore, there is a long history of political and effective participation in all spheres of political, economic and social life in Kuwait. The strong political and economic participation of Shi'ites in Kuwait gave them the power to establish political groups under the category of 'political and cultural associations.'

The appearance of Shi'ite groups

Islamic Movement Party
Hizb al-Haraka al-Islamiya

A group of Shi'ite individuals, who were inspired by the Imam Khomeini's thought, formed an underground cultural–political forum which, in 1962 following Kuwait's independence, became the Islamic Movement Party, representing the first Shi'ite religious group in Kuwait. After a short period, the name was changed to al-Hizb al-Islami or the (Islamic Party) and its main objective was spreading political awareness in the region and observing the political and theoretical changes on regional and global levels. Sayyed Ahmad al-Mahri was its distinguished founder.[36] This party did not last for long and disappeared shortly afterwards from the political arena.

The Social Culture Society (SCS)
Jam'iyat al-Thakafah al-Ijtima'yah

This society was founded in 1963. It is the first public appearance for the Shi'ite religious organizations in Kuwait, representing various Shi'ite groups. The SCS is the social and religious front for the Shi'ites in Kuwait. Although it was officially registered as a charity organization similar to other organizations such as the SRS, Nationalist Cultural Club and the IHRS, which were originally founded as charitable cultural organizations, in fact, they have a political nature and they represent religious and social fronts for various groups.

The declared objectives of SCS are to spread the cultural, social, educational and religious awareness among society. By 1985, the SCS had 900 active members working in its various committees, such as the sports committee, the summer club, and the Religious Guidance Committee.[37] They recruit and educate the Shi'ite youth in a way similar to the Sunni religious societies. Although the SCS is among the organizations that are supervised by the Ministry of Social Affairs and Labor, it does not enjoy the same privileges given to the other Sunni religious societies, such as the SRS and IHRS. Both have branches all over Kuwait, and have the journalistic media which reflect their ideology, such as *Majallat al-Mujtama'* and *Majallat al-Furqan*, in addition to *Majallat al-khairiyah* (the *Charity Journal*), issued by the International Islamic Charitable Organizations, and headed also by one of the leaders of the MBG. At the same time, the request of the SCS in 1963 to issue its own magazine was rejected by the government; even publishing an internal leaflet was banned. The Ministry of Education also refused the request made by the SCS to use one of its secondary schools as a center for teaching the Quran,[38] even though the Sunni Muslim groups have a large number of these centers, such as the SRS, which has 47 centers.[39]

Since the establishment of the SCS in the early 1960s, its activities concentrated on demanding building more Shi'ite mosques and Husseiniyas (Shi'ite religious procession). Its members did not take part in any local political activity and did not participate in signing any political statement regarding local or regional situations. Following the Islamic revolution in Iran, Jamma'h Kat al-Imam al-Khomeini (the Imam Khomeini line Group) managed to control the Board of Directors of the al-Naqi mosque. The first political appearance for the SCS was during the political gatherings called by Ahmad 'Abbas al-Mahri, son of Hujjat al-Islam 'Abbas al-Mahri, in Masjid Shaa'ban (Shaa'ban mosque) in the al-Sharq district near Kuwait City, which took place after the victory of the Islamic revolution in Iran. The SCS played a major role in mobilizing the Shi'ites to these groupings. In the beginning, the gatherings at the Shaa'ban mosque took a sectarian nature, both from attendance, which was limited to some Shi'ite groups in Kuwait, or the issues raised at these meetings, such as demanding the opening of more mosques and Husseiniyas with giving more freedom and equality to Kuwaiti Shi'ites as

Sunnis in terms of rights, where the former felt that they were a minority that was not allowed to occupy high positions in the State. The Shi'ite Revolutionary pro-Jamma'h Kat al-Imam al-Khomeini believed that the issue was not the subject of the rights of the Shi'ites or building Husseiniyas and mosques, but it was regarding the non-democratic situation, and that all the political and social groups in Kuwait had to raise national slogans in the interest of Kuwait. This was a new approach for the Shi'ites in Kuwait.

After the failure of the Kuwaiti regime to stop the Sha'aban Mosque movement peacefully,[40] it proceeded on 9 September 1979 to arrest Ahmad 'Abbas al-Mahri. The regime immediately dropped Sayyed 'Abbas al-Mahri's Kuwaiti nationality together with all his 18 family members and deported them to Iran. Kuwait also withdrew the Kuwaiti passports from three organizers of the Sha'aban mosque movement, charging them with organizing political gatherings and riots in Kuwait. Among them were leaders from the SCS and the Imam Khomeini line Group.[41]

As a result of the violence that occurred in Kuwait in the 1980s from placing explosives in different places of the country, where some members of the SCS were accused of being involved, to organizing political meetings inside the headquarters of the SCS, the authorities arrested a number of Kuwaiti Shi'ites, charging them with being behind the acts of violence that took place in Kuwait. The government also accused them of belonging to Hizbollah-Kuwait and the Islamic Call Party co-operating with the Supreme Council of the Islamic Revolution in Iraq, which took Iran as its center for its activity. Some of them were sentenced to prison, some managed to escape during the Iraqi occupation of Kuwait, some participated in the resistance of the occupation of Kuwait by Iraq, and others fled to Iran.[42] The fact is that this campaign of arrests was carried out at the same time when the Saudi authorities were arresting Shi'ite Kuwaiti pilgrims, accusing them of being involved in the explosions that took place in Saudi Arabia and belonging to the Hizbollah-Kuwait. Among those who were accused were leaders and members of the SCS. Sayyed 'Adnan 'Abdel-Samad, a former member of the Kuwaiti National Assembly, was one of those accused. Sixteen Kuwaiti citizens were executed. Accordingly, the Kuwaiti authorities arrested a number of Kuwaiti Shi'ites and dissolved the elected Board of Directors of the SCS and appointed a new one through the Ministry of Social Affairs and Labor to manage SCS affairs.[43] The SCS closed in 1989 and was reopened in 2009.

Sayyed Shirazi Group (SSG)
Jamm'at al-Sayyed al-Shirazi

This organization was founded in 1970 when its founder, Ayatollah al-Sayyed Mohammad al-Shirazi (1928–2002), sought asylum in Kuwait from Iraq,[44] when he was sentenced to death by the Iraqi regime under Saddam Hussein's regime. Al-Shirazi was the spiritual father for the Monadhamat al-'Amal al-Islami (Islamic Action Organization) in Iraq. Most of the members of the SSG were founding members of the SCS who joined it after the Islamic revolution in Iran. Al-Shirazi became active and succeeded in mobilizing some Shi'ite active figures in the Masjid al-Shirazi (al-Shirazi mosque) in the Bneid al-Gar District and Husseinya, al-Rasool al-Atham (the Great Prophet) in the al-Di'ya District, which were regarded as centers for gathering and polarization.

The SSG succeeded in attracting young Shi'ites to join its ranks by adapting cultural and religious activities. Due to the differences between the SSG and the SCS, the Shi'ite students at Kuwait University were divided into two groups, supporters or opponents of both groups, and thus two groups representing them emerged: al-Qamh al-Islamiya al-Hurra (Free Islamic List), which represented the pro-Khomeini line of Shi'ites, and al-Qamh al-Hurra (Free List), which was supporting the SSG.

In the early 1980s, al-Shirazi was deported from Kuwait to Iran following the assassination of his brother Hassan al-Shirazi in Lebanon.[45] The SSG started to work underground and abandoned its public social–political activities. In the aftermath of the Iran–Iraq war, the SSG started to activate again outside Kuwait, taking London as its base for its activity under the name al-Tajammu' al-Watani al-Kuwaiti (Kuwaiti Nationalist Gathering).[46] After the liberation of Kuwait, the SSG returned to Kuwait to exercise political activity under various names.

The Youth Forum Group (YFG)
Jajma'at Diwaniyat al-Shabab

This forum was formed in the early 1970s by some intellectuals of the Shi'ite community. Among its most distinguished members were Sayyed 'Adnan 'Abdul-Samad, Baqir Asad, Hamed Khajeh, and 'Ali al-Musa, the former Minister of Planning. The most important objectives of this group were:[47]

- focusing on increasing sectarian representation in the National Assembly
- improving political awareness among the Shi'ite community regarding their interests through legal channels provided by the Constitution of 1962
- participating in the SCS elections in order to control the Board of Directors.

Due to its social activities in making regular visits to the notable Shi'ite diwaniyas and holding seminars and public forums, the YFG succeeded in attracting large numbers of educated young Shi'ites to join its ranks.

The role of media was significant in the winning of the bloc of five Shi'ite candidates representing various affiliations of their community in the fifth constituency of the al-Di'ya district seat against the Sunni candidates. For the first time in the history of this constituency, all the Sunni candidates failed to win seats in the elections of the National Assembly in 1975. The YFG also played a role in the municipal council elections in 1975, where it participated in the preparation and adoption of the first primary elections conducted by the Shi'ite community. Hussein al-Qattan, a Shi'ite of Arab descent called Hasawiyah, and Khalil Isma'il, a Shi'ite of Persian descent, competed over a seat for the Municipal Council in the third constituency, which added to the popularity of the YFG to confront the decree issued by the government to limit the personnel status Law during the dissolution period of the National Assembly in 1976. The YFG led a signature campaign obtaining 18,000 signatures on a petition that showed the Shi'ites' concern of negligence towards the Ja'afari doctrine in the new law which was incompatible with the Constitution, which guaranteed the free exercise of religion for all Kuwaiti society.[48] It also rejected the non-constitutional dissolution of the National Assembly in 1976, when 10 members who represented the Shi'ite community were in the dissolved National Assembly; together the Shi'ite and the Sunni members signed a petition demanding the government return the Parliamentary life. This position was a dramatic turning point that showed the new approach of the YFG towards the National Assembly, in particular, and political work, in general, where the YFG went out of its sectarian attitude to the wider national level when it started communications with the Sunni national forces demanding political reforms and the return of the Parliament.[49] The YFG's activity did not last long when its founders abandoned it to join more organized political groups, such as the pro-Khomeini line and Harakat Ansar al-Huriyya (Freedom Supporters Movement).

The Saturday Council Forum
Multaqa Majlis al-Sabt

This forum was formed after several visits made by al-Said Musa al-Sadr, former president of the Majlis al-Shi'i al-A'la (Shi'ite Supreme Council) in Lebanon, to Kuwait from the beginning of the 1970s until 1975. He requested Shi'ite clerics in Kuwait, such as Mohammed Bahr al-'Uloom and Ja'afar al-Qasweeny, to form a Shi'ite Supreme Council similar to the Shi'ite Supreme Council in Lebanon, which looks after the interests and welfare of the Shi'ite community in Kuwait. However, the Kuwaiti Government rejected it, considering it an unfair division of the Kuwaiti society. After that, Shi'ite clerics took the initiative to form an informal forum called The Saturday Council Forum, which gathered the clerics, mosque imams, and Shi'ite preachers; they gathered at the Hussein al-Qattan Diwaniya in al-Sh'aab district and used it as a center for its activity.[50] The main objective for this forum was to unify the views of the Shi'ite clerics and thus address the problems of the Shi'ite sect. Some of the activities carried out by this forum were:[51]

- holding seminars to educate the Shi'ites, with the goal to create closer ties with other religious movements

- supporting the Shi'ite candidates running for the general elections in public, with the goal of having a greater number of Shi'ite members in the Parliament
- participating and contributing in the awareness campaign held in the Shi'ite councils and diwaniyas to expose the danger of the government's attitude in canceling the Ja'fari court
- participating in the protest campaign that accompanied the disappearance of al-Said Musa al-Sadr. The Council sent several letters to the kings and presidents of some Arab countries such as Syria, Jordan, Lebanon and the Palestine Liberation Organization demanding them to intervene with the Libyan authorities to end the crisis.[52]

The Constitutional National Youth (CNY)
Al-Shabab al-Watany al-Dustory

This organization was founded in 1974 by Khalid Khalaf, who had strong ties with the ANM and the owner of *al-Sh'ab* newspaper issued in the 1950s, and Mustafa al-Sarraf, who was a member of the ranks of the ANM. However, the membership in the CNY was limited to the Shi'ite community in Kuwait. Despite the secular trend of its founders, the CNY got the support of the SCS. The CNY is regarded as the first organized Shi'ite political group; its founders confirmed that it had a Shi'ite belonging with a national nature.[53] The program of the CNY consisted of 14 basic points as its target. The most important of these were: constitutional development, the preservation of democratic life, strengthening the separation of powers, and the promotion of national unity.[54] Five CNY candidates ran for the fourth National Assembly elections in 1975 against a number of Shi'ite candidates loyal to the Kuwaiti regime; one of the CNY candidates, Khalid Khalaf, managed to achieve victory. After this election, the CNY soon disappeared from the political arena.

Kuwaiti Nationalist Gathering (KNG)
Al-Tajammu' al-Watani al-Kuwaiti

This organization was founded after the Iraqi occupation of Kuwait in 1990, by Sultan 'Abdul-Hussein, who became the Secretary General for the KNG. The KNG's pamphlets and statements were published in *Majallat al-Thawrah al-Islamiya* (*Islamic Revolution Journal*), issued by the Monadhamat al-Thawra al-Islamiya fi al-Jazira al-'Arabiya (Islamic Revolution Organization in the Arabian Peninsula). On 17 August 1990, the KNG appealed to the leaders of the Islamic Iranian Republic not to reconcile with the Saddam Hussein regime and to support the just cause of Kuwait. The KNG also appealed to the Kuwaiti people, urging them to proclaim civil disobedience against the government of occupation and not to recognize it and to boycott it. It urged them to join the jihadist cells working against the occupation. The KNG was also active abroad during the occupation, where it held seminars and lectures exposing the cause of the Kuwaiti people. It also published a pamphlet called *Risalat al-kuwait* (Kuwait Message), which later became an official journal published in Kuwait.[55] After a period of activity, this organization disappeared from the political arena and some of its founding members participated in establishing Tajammu' al-'Adala Wasalam (Justice and Peace Gathering). See Justice and Peace Gathering.

The Free Kuwaiti Center (FKC)
Al-Markaz al-Kuwaiti al-Hur

This organization was founded in London in 1989 by some Shi'ite activists against the Kuwaiti regime. The FKC identified itself as a free forum through which it expressed its views, allowing the voice of the voiceless to be heard and the opinion of others, which were not permitted in Kuwait, to be written. The FKC called for building a free citizen forum that would be able to express opinions without the fear of the state's security cells, and building a life based on the principle of equal opportunities.[56] It also called for equality in all life's aspects between the rulers and the citizens; socially, economically and politically.[57] Meanwhile, the monthly magazine *al-Kuwaiti* (*The Kuwaiti*), which was regarded as the mouthpiece of the FKC, expressed strong criticism of the Kuwaiti regime's policies and demanded it work within the framework of the Constitution in regard to individuals' freedom, and establish free and fair elections. The FKC also criticized the Kuwaiti regime strongly following the arrest of 29 Kuwaiti Shi'ite pilgrims, where 16 of them were executed by the Saudi authorities on 21 September 1989, charging them with attempting to sabotage the pilgrimage season.[58]

The National Notables Committee
Al-Lajnah al-Watania Lilwujahaa

This committee was founded in 1985 by a group of former Shi'ite MPs, such as Husein Makki, Habib Joher Hayat, and 'Isa Bahman, who represented the conservative trend that had strong ties with the al-Sabah ruling family. The main objective of forming this committee was to take part in the primary election between the Shi'ites to compete with the revolutionary Shi'ites who managed to overcome all the representatives of the conservative trend in the elections of 1981.[59] This attempt failed and the revolutionary candidates were victorious in these elections, causing the disappearance of the Notables Committee from the political arena afterwards.

Kuwaiti Islamic League (KIL)
Al-Rabhtah al-Islamiya al-Kwaitiyah

This organization was established in London during the Iraqi occupation of Kuwait, by Dr. 'Abbas Hajii, a Professor of Islamic Economy at Kuwait

University. It issued a magazine called *Minber al-huriyya* (*Freedom Forum*), where a number of Shi'ite intellectuals published articles about the return of the democratic life, freedom, equality between citizens and rejecting sectarianism.[60] It seemed that the purpose for establishing the KIL was exhausted after the liberation of Kuwait and no one has heard about its activities since then.

Kuwaiti Islamic Gathering
Al-Tajammu' al-Islami al-Kuwaiti

This organization was established on 22 November 1990 following the Iraqi occupation of Kuwait on 2 August 1990, by Hojjat al-Islam Mohammad Baqir al-Mahri,[61] taking support from Tehran as its headquarters, where there were a large number of Kuwaiti Shi'ites who fled to Iran after the Iraqi occupation. Its announced objectives through its constituent statement were:[62]

- commitment to Islamic rules and the principle of the rule of jurisprudence
- commitment to the principle of non-Eastern and non-Western trend towards the regional and international conflicts
- condemning the Iraqi occupation and emphasizing unity of the Kuwaiti territories
- co-operating with all loyal political blocs in Kuwait
- securing social justice for all communities in Kuwaiti society regarding political, religious and civil rights, without discrimination
- holding free parliamentary elections
- denouncing the Western intervention represented in the United States of America and its allies.

After the liberation of Kuwait from Iraqi occupation, no activity for this gathering was heard, and its leader Al-Mahri formed a new gathering called Tajammu' 'Olama al-Moslamin al-Shi'a in Kuwait (Islamic Shi'ite Clerics Gathering in Kuwait).

Free Kuwaiti People Voice (FKPV)
Sout al-Sha'ab al-Kuwaiti al-Hur

This organization emerged during the Iraq–Iran war. The FKPV took a hostile attitude towards the Iraqi Ba'ath regime. Its statements were all about the activity of the Iraqi intelligence in Kuwait and it accused the Iraqi regime of being behind the assassination of Hardan al-Takrity, the former Iraqi Defense Minster, on 30 March 1971 during his visit to Kuwait. The FKPV demanded the Kuwaiti regime take strong measures against such acts, which was considered as an aggression against the sovereignty of Kuwait. The FKPV disappeared from the political scene after a period of activity during which a number of statements were issued.[63]

Islamic Group for Preaching and Combat (IGPC)
Al-Jamm'ah al-Islamiya Lld'awa wa al-Jihad

This group was organized in the mid-1980s. *Risalat al-Kuwait* (*The Kuwait Message*) was its official publication, through which the IGPC identified itself as the national voice of all sincere Kuwaiti people. The IGPC was based in Nicosia, the capital of Cyprus. This was the center for its activity, where it launched its campaign against the Kuwaiti regime.[64]

The Islamic National Coalition (INC)
Al-Itlaaf al-Islami al-Watani

The phenomenon of political gatherings with their publicly announced identities and activities, such as signing public political statements, emerged in the aftermath of the liberation of Kuwait. In this atmosphere, the INC appeared as a political framework that gathered all political, social and religious Shi'ite groups. Among them were members of the SCS, independent Shi't'tes and representatives of Shi'ite mosques in Kuwait. One of the most important requirements to join the ranks of the INC was that the member should represent his own thoughts and not the beliefs of the group to which he belonged. For example, a member who joined the INC ranks from the Hizbollah-Kuwait or SCS should not necessarily reflect their beliefs, but express his own ideas, and this was to ensure the non-destruction of efforts and to keep it within the national framework without any external interference.[65] The INC denies, unofficially, that it has any links with any international organization or association, but it emphasized the intellectual engagement with religious Shi'ites internationally, which is obviously due to the religious vision that dominates the nature of any religious community.[66] The most important principles adopted by the INC are:[67]

- the INC believes in Islam as an ideology and encourages all members of community to work within its framework
- the INC believes in the 1962 Constitution as a platform for its political activity and to enhance it in order to ensure more freedom and equality
- concentrating on the principle of democracy and expanding its base
- confirming the legitimate and constitutional rights for female political participation
- development of political and social awareness among the members of society, and the defense of rights and freedoms within the context of national unity
- equal chances for all national competencies must be given regardless of any sectarian and tribal considerations.

Although the INC meets with other political forces in issues relating to the constitution and public freedom, it still has conflicts with some Sunni religious political forces such as the ICM and the SG in regards to amending the second article of the Constitution. There are other religious concepts with respect to and based on doctrinal and some economic issues (inheritance), women's rights to vote and to run for election and, lastly, the draft proposed by the Sunni political forces in regard to the establishment of the Committee of Propagation of Virtue and Prevention of Vice.[68] The INC is closer to the KDF, which has a secular trend, especially among the KDF members are irreligious-Shi'ites, with some of them occupying leading positions in the executive committee of the KDF.[69] The INC also supports the candidates of the KDF in the constituencies where it has no official candidates of its own.

The INC participated in the Parliamentary elections in 1992 with four candidates. In the meantime, it supported liberal and leftist Shi'ite candidates. Two of the INC candidates were victorious and two candidates supported by the INC also won seats in this election.

The INC's approach was not to confront the government, like other political groups, in important issues such as misappropriation of public funds.

Due to the differences between the members of the INC, most of its founders deserted it, leaving it to a hard-line attitude in the Shi'ite sect, with a new name, al-Tahaluf al-Islami al-Watani (The National Islamic Alliance), which enhanced its relationship with the Sunni Islamic trend.

Al-Rumaithiya Youth of Religious and Social Awareness Committee
Haiat Shabab al-Rumaithiya Lltaw'ia al-Diniai Walajtama'ia

This organization was founded in the mid-1990s by some Shi'ite youth in the Al-Rumeitheya district. It had several sectarian demands, such as:[70]

1   Ashura Day has to be an official holiday.
2   Establish special courts for Shi'ites and establish independent Shi'ite endowments.
3   Name some streets, schools and public institutions after Shi'ite clerics.
4   Establish official public religious schools that teach the Islamic Ja'afari jurisprudence and allow Shi'ite beliefs and ideologies to be discussed in the public media, such as radio and television.
5   Lift restrictions on licensing new mosques and Husseiniyas.

This group stressed that it will support any candidate running for the parliamentary elections who will defend and support these demands.[71]

The National Islamic Alliance (NIA)
Al-Tahaluf al-Islami al-Watani

This organization was formed in 1998 by Sayyed 'Adnan 'Abdul-Samad, 'Abdul Mohsen Jamal and Nasser Sarkhouh, who were representing the hard-liners in the National Islamic Coalition (NIC), as an alternative to the NIA, which was weakened due to the different orientations of the various groups within it. The NIA took the same slogan of the NIC: Kalimat al-Tawhid wa Tawhad al-Kalimah (word of unity and unity of the word). The NIA believes in the theory of the wilayat al-Faqih (jurists' guardianship), which is entitled to address the conspiracies of the enemies of Islam.[72]

The NIA participated in the parliamentary elections in 2003 and it suffered a major defeat for all its candidates. The NIA disputed the Shi'ite groups that represented the moderate line, such as Shi'ite clerics regarding the draft of Ja'afari Waqf and for which Lajnat al-Thalath-'Ashar (the Committee of 13) was formed, claiming that that the Committee does not regard God's legislations as the main source for religious affairs.[73] 'Abdul-Mohsen Jamal, one of the most distinguished prominent leaders of the NIA, emphasized that despite the failure of the NIA's candidates, it played a significant role in the political arena through holding conferences, issuing statements, and controlling a number of co-operative societies, and that the Parliament is not the only arena to judge the popularity of any political bloc.[74] He claimed that 50% of the Shi'ites in Kuwait belonged to the NIA.[75] The truth is that the NIA failed in the elections held after the death of one of the members of the Parliament, Sami al-Menis, in December 2000, when the NIA candidate, Nasser Sarkhouh gained the fourth position, and the winner was Jamal al-'Omar. In the latest elections of the National Assembly, Sayyed 'Adnan 'Abdul-Samad, 'Abdul-Mohsen Jamal, and Nasser Sarkhouh failed in favor of other Shi'ite candidates or other groups.[76] The NIA participated in the elections for the National Assembly, which took place on 29 June 2006, when two of its candidates, Sayyed 'Adnan 'Abdul-Samad and Ahmad Lari, won two seats.

The NIA took a firm stand against the process of normalizing relations with the Zionist state. It participated in the foundation of Lajnat Muqawamat al-Tatbi' Ma'a al-Kayan al-Sahuoni (the Committee of Anti-Normalization with the Zionist State) and stressed its support for Intifidhat al-Aqsa (al-Aqsa Uprising) and urged all Kuwaitis to stand firmly against these attempts and to revive the principal of boycotting the Zionist state.[77] The NIA called on confronting what it called al-Irhab al-Sahuini al-Amriki (American–Zionist terrorism) by unifying the nation's rows against its enemies and that the nation had no choice but to resist, and considered America's support for the Zionist state as full partnership with the Zionists.[78] Sheikh Husein al-Ma'took, one of the NIA leaders, emphasized that Hizbollah, the Islamic Resistance Hamas, and Islamic Jihad are the fronts of the Islamic nation, and there is a spiritual connection with all sincere fighters of these fronts who dedicate themselves to the defense of Islam; any Muslim who likes his religion must stand with them.[79]

The NIA faced fierce criticism by the local press, when the *al-Watan* newspaper (homeland) revealed in its front page a meeting held at the Iranian Embassy premises between the leadership of the NIA and the representatives of 'Ali Khamnai in the presence of the Iranian Ambassador. This meeting was to discuss some of the domestic issues after the negative results in the elections of the National Assembly and to discuss alternative methods to support the NIA in the upcoming elections. The NIA denied that this meeting ever took place.[80]

One of the top commanders of Hizbollah-Lebanon, 'Imad Mughniyeh, was assassinated in Damascus on 12 February 2008. Mughniyeh was one of America's most wanted men, accused of being behind a string of bombings, hijackings and kidnappings during the 1980s and 1990s. Mugnhiyeh was believed to have been behind the attacks in 1983 on the US Embassy and the Marine barracks in Beirut, the terrorist hijacking of the TWA jetliner in 1985, and a series of kidnappings in the 1980s. There have also been accusations against Mugnhiyah that he might have been involved in the bombing of the al-Khobar Towers military residence in Saudi Arabia in 1996, in which 17 Americans were killed.[81] Robert Baer, who hunted Mugnhiyeh for years as a CIA officer, describes Mugnhiyeh as:

> the most dangerous terrorist we've ever faced. He is probably the most intelligent, most capable operative we've ever run across, including the KGB or anybody else. He enters by one door, exits by another, changes his cars daily, only uses people that are related to him that he can trust. He doesn't just recruit people. He is a master terrorist, the grail that we have been after since 1983.[82]

Mugnhiyeh was accused by the Kuwaiti Government as the commander of the hijacking of the Kuwaiti plane, al-Jabriya, in the 1980s, which resulted in the killing of two Kuwaiti citizens, Abdullah al-Khaldi and Khalid al-Ayuab, whose bodies were thrown on the runway of the Cyprus airport by the terrorists who hijacked the plane.[83] Despite this terrorist act against Kuwait, the NIA sent a letter of condolence to Hezbollah Lebanon, describing Mugnhiyeh as a hero and a martyr.[84] The NIA held a memorial service in al-Hussein Husseinya in the al-Salmiya district and called for the death of America and Israel. Sayyed 'Adnan 'Abdul-Samad made a speech in which he attacked America and Israel, and defended Mugnhiyeh, considering him a hero and martyr.[85] The Kuwaiti citizens and regime reacted angrily towards this memorial. Consequently, the security forces arrested the Secretary General of the NIA together with some of its leaders who attended this memorial.[86] The security forces demanded the lifting of the Parliamentary immunity of the two MPs, namely Sayyed 'Adnan 'Abdul-Samad and Ahmad Lari, in order to prosecute them with the charges of belonging to a banned party and conspiring to overthrow the regime.

The attitude taken by the NIA shocked the Kuwaiti community and almost led to a sectarian strife between the Sunni and Shi'ite citizens, but the courts dismissed all charges against them. For the public interest, the prosecution decided not to appeal. This decision was the first of its kind in Kuwaiti history.[87]

These accusations against the NIA made the Shi'ite citizens sympathize with them and want to help achieve a victory in the Parliamentary elections, which took place on 17 May 2008.

Following this victory, the Kuwaiti regime began to open up to the NIA by appointing one of its leaders, Fadhil Safar, as a Minister in successive cabinets. This was followed by the restoring of the SCS, which was closed for about 19 years. It seems that the aim of this openness was the popularity of the NIA among the Shi'ite citizens. In addition to the differences that emerged between the Kuwaiti regime and the ICM, where the latter decided to question Sheikh Nasser al-Mohammad al-Sabah, the Prime Minister, when the agreement with the Dow Chemical Company was in question. The Minster of Oil, Mohammad al-'Olaim, one of the ICM leaders, refused this decision and, accordingly, the Cabinet submitted its resignation to the Emir. The ICM did not participate in the next Cabinet and turned to be on the opposition side, while the NIA became an ally for the government and a defender for the Prime Minister. Accordingly, the Emir of Kuwait, Sheikh Sabah Ahmad al-Jaber al-Sabah, issued an Emiri decree to dissolve the Parliament and called for new elections. It is worth mentioning that the dissolved Parliament did not last for more than eight months.

The NIA is still active and is still issuing statements by its leaders, such as the head of the political bureau, Saleh al-Moussa, Sayyed 'Adnan 'Abdul-Samad, and 'Abdul-Mohsen Jamal.

Justice Supporters Gathering
Tajammu' Ansar al-'Adalah

This group was founded by Mustafa al-Qallaf in 1998 and was regarded as one of the Shi'ite splinter groups from the banned NIC. Al-Qallaf, the official speaker for the Gathering, criticized the leaders of the NIC and described them as being dictators in decision-making. Its main objective was establishing justice between all members of the society.[88]

The Democracy and Justice Movement (DJM)
Harakat al-'Adala wa al-dimuqratiya

This movement was founded in December 1999. It emerged as one of the Shi'ite splinter groups from the banned NIC. Its most prominent founders were 'Abdul-Karim al-Usafai, Mohammed al-Saig, Sulaiman al-Khadari, and others. In its founding statement, the DJM stated that it seeks to fulfill the aspirations of the majority of Kuwaiti citizens through a moderate political approach, to establish justice, and to advocate democracy in various aspects of political and social life in compliance with the Constitution. The DJM stressed that it is a national movement that reflects the goals and aspirations of Kuwaiti society.[89] Al-Usafai, one of the DJM's prominent leaders, confirmed that the movement believes in Kuwaiti democracy and it is based on the principle of justice; it believes in collaboration with other popular gatherings of different backgrounds and beliefs to achieve common goals.[90] The most important goals of the movement are:[91]

- belief in the principles of the democratic system, chosen by the ruler and the people
- finding appropriate solutions to the citizens' problems
- fulfill all kinds of justice
- advocate for equality, liberty and prosperity in respect to human rights.

The DJM criticized the weak performance of both the government and the Parliament and demanded the latter to act within the essence of the Constitution in order to enhance the democratic life, stressing that pluralism and diversity in opinions are integral parts of a healthy political and social life.[92] The DJM did not participate in the 1999 Parliamentary elections; nevertheless, it expressed its view in confirming that the political activity of most of the candidates is capable of playing a major role in supervising public life and that democratic life is not only restricted to the Parliament, but that it also exceeded it to energize other constitutional institutions.[93]

Freedom Supporters Movement (FSM)
Harakat Ansar al-Huria

This movement was founded on 6 December 1999 as one of the Shi'ite movements and groups that emerged in the political arena. Its most prominent founders were: 'Abdul-'Aziz al-Taher, the Secretary General of FSM, Mohammad al-Fili, 'Abd al-Hussein Sultan, and others. The FSM presented itself as a Kuwaiti movement with national thoughts, objectives and leadership, which defends justice and opposes oppression. Its General Secretary confirmed that the movement will seek to achieve social justice, freedom and to defend oppressed people according to the Constitution.[94] He also stressed that the movement believes in the concepts of political pluralism and peaceful actions.[95]

The FSM concepts are centralized in the following:[96]

- achieving the public interest of the Kuwaiti people
- combating injustice and spreading awareness among the citizens in how to deal with the issues that are embodied with injustice
- achieving social justice through democratic methods
- commitment to the values of the Islamic Shari'a and to the rules of the Constitution
- expression of the political, social, economic, intellectual and doctrinal suffering of the oppressed Kuwaiti citizens.

The FSM developed an internal system that contains 44 articles covering all the movement's activities through different organizational units, such as the General Conference and the Women's Bureau.[97]

Despite the denial of al-Taher that the FSM is not confined to a particular religious doctrine, it is a Kuwaiti national liberal movement opened to all people of Kuwait.[98] 'It is a national political thought that has no particular creed or orientation,' he said;[99] the truth, however, is simply revealed when anyone reviews the names of the founders of the FSM where it appears that all of them are Shi'ites.[100] The FSM criticized religious groups who lead the Kuwaiti masses and had a huge influence on the decision-making process, and the FSM called for confronting them.[101]

Committee for Serving al-Mahdi (CSM)
Hayat Khidam al-Mahdi

This group was organized in Kuwait in 2000 by Yasser al-Habib as a voluntary Islamic cultural committee aiming to develop the society according to *resalat ahl al-bayt* (the message of the Prophet's family). The CSM advocated the policy of rejecting violence and adopting the Prophet's family rules, so that the nation can make progress. Al-Habib criticized the leaders of the Islamic movement who followed the al-Shirazi's line, accusing them of not absorbing his ideas and approach.[102]

The CSM opened several branches in various countries around the world, such as the Beirut office, which was headed by Yousef 'Abdul-Hadi Baa'lbaki, and the London office, headed by 'Ali al-Mussawi. It published *Majallat al-Menber* (*The Forum Journal*) in order to express its views and attitudes.

The CSM had adopted a number of principles and objectives, such as:[103]

- reinforcing God to the greatest degree possible
- absolute loyalty to ahl al-bayt
- faith in the al-Shirazi civilized project
- adherence to the spirit of courage
- re-establishing the Shi'ite community and raising the level of consciousness
- ending the state of defeatism, retreat and inactivity in the Shi'ite community
- religious guidance to various communities to the doctrine of the Prophet's family.

Following the attack made by Sunni Islamic fundamentalist movement against Yasser al-Habib, who wrote articles in *Majallat al-Manber* and distributed recordings of some of his speeches criticizing some of the wives of the Prophet Mohammad, he was sentenced to 10 years' imprisonment. Al-Habib was out of jail according to an Ameri Decree, but the government asked him to surrender because there was a mistake in the list of names affected by the Ameri decree. In 1997, al-Habib was also charged with trying to overthrow the regime through his writings in the *al-Qabas* newspaper. However, the judiciary cleared him of these charges. In 2004, the Minister of Information transferred the unlicensed journal *Majallat al-Menber* to the Public Prosecutor because of what was presented in this journal, which was incompatible with Islamic values and principles and was intended to split the ranks of Kuwaiti society.[104] In 2005, the CSM distributed Taqwim al-Kasa (Shi'ite calendar), causing the Sunni Islamic fundamentalist groups to demand the Kuwaiti regime ban the CSM activity. As a result, Faisal al-Muslim, a member in the National Assembly, made a proposal for a draft law to drop the Kuwaiti nationality from those convicted with insulting the Prophet Mohammad, his wives or any of the al-Sahabah (Companions of the Prophet). It seems that the target of this proposed law was Yasser al-Habib, the founder of the CSM.[105] The Kuwaiti authorities took several measures towards the CSM, such as prosecuting its members and closing its head-quarters. The British Government agreed to grant Yaser al-Habib asylum. The CSM is still active in the political arena through statements made by the CSM leader on its website, in addition to holding organized pickets and demonstrations against some Arab embassies in London, such as Saudi Arabia and Egypt.

Al-Zhara House Gathering (ZHG)
Jama'at Dar al-Zhara

This group was founded in the mid-1990s and it represented prominent Shi'ite merchants of the moderate trend. The ZHG appeared as a result of the divisions in the NIC. Its most distinguished founders were: 'Abdul-Wahab al-Wazzan, the former Minister of Trade and Industry, the former Minister of Social Affairs and Labor, Haji Kathiam, and Dr. Yousef al-Zilzila, teacher at the Faculty of Administrative Sciences at Kuwait University, and the for-mer Minister of Commerce. The ZHG believes in moderation, which means loving Kuwait through creed, rationality in dialogue, the acceptance of others, guaranteeing the freedom of opinion, improving national awareness, and non-cancellation of other parties.[106] The ZHG participated in the Parliamentary elections in 2003 and its candidate, Yousef al-Zilzila, won in this election against the candidate of the NIA, Sayyed 'Adnan 'Abdul-Samad. In October 2005 the ZHG participated in the establishment of Iitilaf al-Tajammu'at al-Watania (the Coalition of the National Groups), which included most of the moderate Shi'ite groups.

The ZHG participated in the National Assembly in the 2006 elections with a number of candidates, and Yousef al-Zilzila was among them, but none of them succeeded in winning a seat. The ZHG is still active in the political arena through statements made by its leaders.

Islamic Shi'ite Clerics Gathering in Kuwait (ISCGK)
Tajammu' 'Olama al-Moslimin al-Shia in Kuwait

This group was founded on 7 July 2001. Its most prominent founders were Sheikh Mohammad Baqir al-Mahri, the Secretary General, and Sheikh Ahmad Yaqob, the official speaker, and others. The ISCGK emphasized that it adopts the doctrines of both the Prophet's family and the Imam Ja'far al-Sadeq, without any concessions.[107]

The most important objectives of ISCGK are:[108]

1　Establish trust and harmony in the relationship between Kuwaiti society and the Islamic system, and improve the religious awareness among the community through organized activity, both socially and politically.
2　Educate the Kuwaiti community and participate in establishing and supporting projects for Shi'ites, in particular, and Muslims, in general.
3　Eliminate sources of political and ideological terrorism practiced by some groups who claim Islam.
4　Develop political activity to achieve political stability in Kuwait.
5　Highlight the role played by the Ja'fari community in the evolution of Islam.
6　Spread Islamic cultural awareness in the community through the use of dialogue, which will help to eliminate the sources of intellectual, ideological, social and political terrorism.

The ISCGK emphasized that it does not represent a particular group as others do, but it described itself as a defender of Islam, which is the legitimate duty of every Muslim, especially those students who are carrying the banner of Islam and specialize in religious studies.[109]

The ISCGK membership is divided into two categories: active members and non-active ones. The first category is responsible for the activity of the group, such as gathering information, preparing plans and follow-up on projects. The non-active members are those who believe in the principles of the ISCGK and help consolidate them among the community.[110] The ISCGK stressed in its internal rules that in order for anyone to be qualified to join its ranks, he must not belong to any political group and have high qualifications in accordance with al-Hawza (scientific foundations of the religious learning centers). The 'Ali Ibn Abi Taleb Mosque was the headquarters for the activity of the ISCGK.

The principles and ideas of the ISCGK are:[111]

• Preserve the Islamic identity of Kuwaiti society.
• Any Islamic activity must be based on the Quran.
• The ISCGK has a sacred duty that acts in accordance with al-Hawza without representing them politically.
• The ISCGK is an independent, non-allied group with no external links with any anti-Islam group.

- It believes in the mutual co-operation between the political and religious groups in Kuwait, as long as its aim is the stability of society.
- It works in the interest of the Shi'ite community in Kuwait, trying to correct the social imbalance in the absence of Kuwaiti Shi'ite identity, and to stop the spread of the dissolution of morality and religious extremism.
- It resists religious extremism and sectarian sedition, urging the preservation of national unity.
- It rejects sectarian practices carried out by some extremist groups.
- It gives full rights and freedoms, whether ideologically, culturally or politically.

The ISCGK made a strong criticism to the al-Amanah al-'Ammah lil Awqaf (General Secretariat of the Awqaf foundation) run by the Sunnis, accusing them of distributing the Ja'afari funds in matters that do not coincide with Islamic Shari'a and Ja'afari fuqh (Ja'afari jurisconsult). On this basis, it demanded the establishment of a general secretariat of al-Waqf al-Ja'fari supervised by the Amiri Diwan, or the Council of Ministers in order to ensure its independence of the Ministry of Waqf and its Minister.[112] The ISCGK also demanded that the general administration of al-Awqaf al-Ja'fari must be headed by three Shi'ite 'Ulama (Islamic scholars) and all its employees must be Shi'ites. It also urged the government to regard 'Ashura as a public holiday, to teach Ja'fari jurisprudence and include it in the curriculum, and to allow Shi'ite clerics to teach Ja'fari jurisprudence at the Faculty of Shari'a and Islamic studies.[113]

When the Ministry of Awqaf asked al-Mahri, the leader of the ISCGK, to show his commitment to the Charter of mosques and to the resolutions of the Ministry of Awqaf regarding the mosques' speeches, he reacted violently towards the rules imposed by the ministry at Friday's ceremony, considering it an interference in the mosques' activities, especially that Shi'ite mosques are built by the Shi'ites themselves and the imams of mosques do not receive salaries from the government. Al-Mahri regarded it as a provocation, saying 'the Ministry of Awqaf has no legal right to interfere in the affairs of the Shi'ite mosques,'[114] taking into consideration that there are a lot of Sunni mosques that were built from funds raised by some Kuwaiti Sunni citizens and follow the Charter of mosques.

The ISCGK opposed the cabinet reshuffle made in 2005, which led to the dismissal of the Minister of Information, Mohammad Abo al-Hassan. He was the only Shi'ite minister in that Cabinet, after the claim made by the Islamic groups in the Parliament for him to submit his resignation as they withdrew confidence from him because he allowed the concert 'star academy'; the Radical Sunnis were also secretly angry about Abo al-Hassan allowing the distribution and broadcasting of Shi'ite teachings in public.

The ISCGK also opposed the appointments of the six members for the Municipal Council made by the government in June 2005, where all of them were Sunnis. It warned that this intentional act of the government might lead to a split between the citizens and requested the government to change its decision in order to maintain stability and national unity without differentiation between citizens.[115] The government reacted quickly, when it responded to this demand and decided to appoint Ma'souma al-Mubarak, who became the first woman in the Kuwaiti Cabinet, as the Minister of Planning and Administrative Development. In the new Cabinet, which followed the death of the Emir of Kuwait, Sheikh Jaber al-Ahmad al-Sabah, Yousef Zilzila, who is a Shi'ite, became the Minister of Commerce.

The ISCGK endorsed granting women political rights in the nomination and election for the National Assembly, and it regarded it as a blessed step towards freedom, democracy and application of the Constitution of the State of Kuwait.[116] In this context, Mohammad Baqir al-Mahri says:

> The issue of women's political rights, especially their rights to be members of the Parliament, was a dispute between Muslim 'Ulama and Fuqaha, but we follow the opinion of Sayyed al-Sistani, the highest Shi'ite authority in the world, who permitted the participation of the Kuwaiti women in the elections for the National Assembly, provided that they are religiously committed.[117]

The ISCGK rejected the accusations made by the United States of America in regards to Islam being behind the events of September 11, considering Islam the financier of terrorism, materially and morally. It accused the United States of America of being behind the establishment of some extremist groups using Islam as a cover for its activities. It also confirmed that al-Qaeda cannot do this job without the support of the American Central Intelligence Agency (CIA). The ISCGK supported the American military offensive launched against the regime of Saddam Hussein in 2003.[118]

The ISCGK adopted a clear position towards the terrorist operations carried out by al-Qaeda in Saudi Arabia and Iraq, and considered that these acts of terrorism were aimed at serving the Masonic secularism to implement their plans in the Islamic world. It called on working hard to expose these plans and that the call for jihad is only a propaganda used by al-Qaeda to serve the interests of their master Masons. It requested Muslims to unite in the face of al-Qaeda, and the platform for the jihadist operations is the land of occupied Palestine, and not Saudi Arabia and Iraq. The ISCGK describes the Zionist state as a group of Zionist criminals and the forces of evil were behind the creation of this terrorist state in the Palestinian territories with no regard for human rights and international conventions. It also emphasizes that one must differentiate between some Palestinian people and jihad movements who supported Saddam Hussein and the Ba'athist regime, and the Palestinian issue.[119]

The ISCGK rejected the statement made by the Egyptian President, Hosni Mubarak, about the loyalty of Iraqi Shi'ites to Iran being more than their loyalty to their homeland. It stated that the Shi'ite citizens in the Gulf, in general, and Kuwait, in particular, love their homeland and their State, and are loyal to its political leaders. The Kuwaiti Shi'ite citizens demonstrated loyalty and love for their homeland through history, and they have a strong relationship with the al-Sabah family, the ruling family of Kuwait, and they are ready at any moment to defend their country against any attack.[120]

Mohammad Baqir al-Mahri criticized the statement made by Pope Benedict XVI during his visit to Germany on the fifth anniversary of the September 11 attacks by saying: 'It is contrary to truth and reality,'[121] calling on the Pope to apologize. He said that 'the Pope's unjustified attack on Islam and the Prophet Mohammad is a clear contradiction to the dialogue of civilizations, but instead opened hostility between the divine religions.'[122] The ISCGK is still active through the statements made by its leader Mohamed Baqir al-Mahri.

The Imam al-Sadiq Mosque Group (ISMG)
Jam'at Masjad al-Imam al-Sadiq

This group appeared in the aftermath of the Iraqi occupation in the historical district of al-Sawabir, where the mosque is located. Mirza 'Abdul-Rasul al-Ahaqqaqi is regarded as the spiritual guide for this group. Among the most prominent representatives of the group on the political level are Saleh al-Saffar and Hussein al-Qattan. All members of the ISMG are descended from the eastern region of the Kingdom of Saudi Arabia, in particular the area called al-Hassa, and this is why they are named al-Hasawiya. They migrated a long time ago and settled in the Arabian Gulf region, including Kuwait.[123] This mosque was founded by al-Merza Moussa al-Ahaqqaqi, al-Merza Hassan al-Ahaqqaqi, and al-Merza 'Ali al-ahaqqaqi. The Imam al-Sadeq Mosque is regarded as the headquarters for the religious and political activity of the ISMG. Due to the loyalty of the group to the ruling family, it refused to participate in the events carried out by the Shaa'ban mosque movement, a pro-Iranian movement, which took place in 1979, due to the differences in their ethnic origins, where al-Hasawiya are from Arab descent. Severe criticism has been addressed to the ISMG from other Shi'ite religious groups because of their neutral stand towards the local and regional political events. The ISMG describes itself as a Kuwaiti national group that cares for the interest of its homeland, Kuwait, advocating the slogan of maintaining unity and the defense of Kuwait, and that they are proud of their Arab origin, but their loyalty is to Kuwait, despite their family ties which still exist with their relatives in the al-Hissa.[124]

Most of the activities undertaken by the ISMG are building mosques and Husseiniyas, and participating in the Parliamentary elections. It has permanent polling stations in some districts, where it supervises the process of nomination for the general elections in order to ensure the quality of nominees.[125] This group is still active and continues to support the candidates who have the same orientation as the ISMG.

The National Independent Gathering for Love and Life (NIGLL)
Tajammu' al-Hab Wa al-Haiat al-Watani al-Moestacal

This group was established in 2003 by 'Abas Naqi as an extension of the Qaemt al-Hab wa al-Haiat (List of Love and Life), one of the Shi'ite active student organizations at Kuwait University since 2000. The leader of the NIGLL, 'Abas Naqi, emphasized the independence of the group, rejecting any kind of external leadership directed by a particular political group over its activities, and denying the charge of having sectarian orientation.[126]

The NIGLL is based on the following concepts:[127]

- perception of love in a holistic manner because it depends on the Islamic approach to the definition of love, not the Western definition, which encapsulates love in a sexual relationship, and in this sense, the concept of love according to the NIGLL is: the love of God, love of the Prophet and his family, and the love for himself and other people
- calls for peace and rejects all violent methods
- condemns the ethnic, nationalist and sectarian divisions
- calls for the establishment of a society based on justice and equality.

The most important objectives of the NIGLL are:[128]

- the unity of Muslims in one country with no geographical boundaries, in which Shura principal, justice and non-violence are applied
- facing cultural defeatism and globalization
- launching public freedoms
- application of Islamic laws.

The most prominent activities of the NIGLL were holding lectures and seminars to discuss the local political situations.

Islamic National Consensus Movement (INCM)
Harakat al-Tawafuq al-Watani al-Islamiya

This movement was founded on 7 January 2003. Its most prominent founders were Dr. Nazar Mula Jum'a, the Secretary General, and his deputy Zuhair al-Mahmid. The movement's slogan was the Quranic verse: 'O you men! Surely we have created you of male and a female, and made you tribes and families that you may know each other; surely the most honorable of you with Allah is the one among you most careful (of his duty); surely Allah is knowing, Aware.' The INCM emphasized that it is an Islamic movement, which aims to co-operate with all political groups for the interest of Kuwait. It believes that the differences in views is a richness by itself and not a threat. It takes the principles of Imam 'Ali bin Abi Taleb as a guidance for its activities.[129] The movement believes in the principle of the rule of the jurisprudence and, accordingly, it makes decisions that comply with Islamic Shari'a, through contacting with the Marji'yya (Shi'ite Supreme Religious Authority). The INCM confirms that freedom of worship is not incompatible with the concept of the State and citizenship, and it is a right guaranteed by the Constitution.[130]

The goals of the INCM are:[131]

1   Defend issues of national interest.
2   Enhance mutual national work through the deployment of the culture of tolerance.
3   Demand more freedom for the citizens.
4   Support women's political rights.
5   Support the adoption of multi-party systems.
6   Regard the Palestinian issue as the most important issue of the Islamic and Arab countries.
7   Support human rights issues within the framework of Islam according to al-faqih mandate.

The INCM has put several terms and conditions to join it, namely the faith in the principles and values adopted by the movement and the belief that the Islamic and national laws are a common approach to the rule of the juris-prudent assembly with the guarantee of freedom of reference attributed to each member. The membership is open to both men and women, and non-Kuwaitis are entitled to join the movement and to enjoy all the benefits except the nomination and election to the Shura Council of the movement.[132]

The organizational structure of the movement is: first, the Shura Council, which sets the movement's policy and consists of 11 members, six men and five women. Second, the General Secretariat, elected from the Shura Council, where the General Secretary of the movement supervises all the activities of the movement. The INCM has several offices, such as the Office of Ideological Affairs, the Office of Social Affairs, the Office of the Media, the Political Bureau, the Economic Bureau and the Bureau of Strategic Studies.[133]

One of the most prominent activities of the movement was issuing political statements regarding the political situations in the Arab and Islamic worlds. It held conferences and symposiums on the Palestinian cause, such as Moeatamer Alquds (the Jerusalem Conference), declaring its support for the struggle of the Palestinian people. The movement raised slogans that include parts of the political speeches made by the leaders of the Palestinian jihad movements, such as 'Abdul-'Aziz al-Rantisi, a Hamas leader who was assassinated by the Mossad (Israeli Secret Service), and Ahmad Yassin. It also included the religious leaders of the Shi'ites, such as al-Sayyed Hassan Nasrallah, Secretary General of Hizbollah in Lebanon, Imam Khomeini, the leader of the Islamic Revolution in Iran, and 'Ali Khamenei.[134] The INCM organized a conference on national unity in which some political groups working in Kuwait participated. The movement improved its relationship with the political groups operating in the Kuwaiti arena, such as: the ICM, Kuwait Democratic Forum, the SG, the SM, the National Democratic Alliance, and the National Democratic Gathering, on the basis that they all have one ultimate goal and that is to reach having a charter of joint work between them.[135] The INCM denies any relations with foreign countries and confirms that the relationship with these countries is the responsibility of the Kuwaiti Government, but this does not prevent the movement from watching the developments in the Islamic and Arab worlds in order to benefit from what is going on there.[136]

The INCM participated in the 11th general elections and it suffered a major defeat, where Nizar Mullah Jum'a failed in favor of Hasan Jawhar supported by the NIA, in the eighth constituency; the rest of the movement's candidates in the various constituencies also failed. This movement is still active in the political arena, both through statements and interviews broadcast via Arab satellite channels with its leaders.

Justice and Peace Gathering (JPG)
Tajammu' al-'Adalah wa al-Salam

This organization was founded in December 2004 by 'Abdul-Hussein Sultan, the Secretary General, and Saleh 'Ashour. The roots of the JPG date back to the 1980s under the name of the Maktabat al-Rasool al-A'tham (The Great Prophet Library). The JPG members supported a number of the Shi'ite candidates for Parliamentary elections, such as Ya'qob Hayaty, 'Ali al-Baghli, and Saleh 'Ashour. One of the reasons for the establishment of the JPG was to face the influence of Hizbollah politically and socially, represented by the NIA. There are 30 women among the 110 members of the JPG, among them Fahima al-'Eid and Suhailah al-Jadey.[138] The JPG confirms that it is an Islamic group which believes in multi-party systems with acceptance of others, and in peaceful coexistence. It also rejects all methods of violence. The JPG denies the charges that it was established as an opposition for the NIA, and confirms that it was founded to confront Islamic extremism, stressing that the JPG is Kuwaiti in its origin, objectives and commitments, with no external coalition; it follows Sayyed Mohammad al-Shirazi.[139] The JPG is still active in the political arena, both through its statements, or the interviews through broadcasts via the Arab satellite channels with its leadership.

The National Charter Gathering (NCG)
Tajammu' al-Mithaq al-Watani

This organization was established on 6 July 2005 by a group of Shi'ite activists who participated in founding the SCS, the Shi'ite Islamic student movement at the University of Kuwait. The most prominent members are 'Abdul-Hadi al-Saleh, former Minister of State for the National Assembly Affairs, 'Abbas Majed, and others.[140] Islam and the Constitution of the State of Kuwait are the base from which the NCG confronts corruption and confirms the process of reform in the State's institutions.[141]

The most important objectives of the NCG are:[142]

- faith in Islam
- to preserve national sovereignty and defend it against foreign intervention
- uphold the Constitution of the State of Kuwait and enhance it for more freedom and equality
- faith in the mandate of Ahl al-bait
- rejects fanaticism and sectarian practices carried out by extremist groups
- rejects distinction based on race, sex, origin, or religion
- adopts moderation as a path for coexistence
- believes in the role played by women and rejects their insult
- fights all forms of corruption
- emphasizes the Arab and Islamic identity of the State of Kuwait.

ʿAbdul-Hadi al-Saleh, the Secretary General of the NCG, emphasized that there is no separation between religion and politics, and that the Islamic Shari'a has an opinion in each aspect of life, because Islam is not static. He believes that Shari'a does not just care for performing Faraid (religious duty), such as praying and fasting only. On the contrary, it is dynamic, which means it is in all aspects of life, politically, socially, economically, and even in the humanitarian issues at the global level.[143]

The NCG is characterized in terms of membership with the most important fact that women were elected for its constituent congress of the political office. The NCG is still active in the political arena, both through statements and through interviews broadcast through the Arab satellite channels with its leadership.

The National Humanitarian Message Gathering (NHMG)
Tajammuʿ al-Risala al-Insaniya al-Watani

This organization was established in 2005 as a transformation from Sadeq Mosque Committee in the Sawaber district, inhabited by the Shi'ite majority. It was given this name after the title of the book issued by Mirza Hasan al-Ahqqaqi. Saleh al-Saffar is the most prominent leader of this gathering and is its Secretary General. The NHMG stressed that the transformation is formed from a gathering that cares for religious and social affairs, to an organization that cares for political affairs too, coinciding with a historical stage in the political life in Kuwait, full of active political groups. Its aim is to narrow the differences between Shi'ite groups.

The first public appearance for the NHMG was the participation in the conference held by the coalition of national gatherings for refusing to change the electoral districts from 25 constituencies to five constituencies. This Shi'ite sect believes that the approval of the draft of five constituencies would reduce the chances of the Shi'ite representatives, stressing that this change will enforce sectarianism and inequality. However, the draft of the five constituencies will lead hopefully to the activation of social integration, elimination of sectarianism, tribal regional representation, and election bribes.[144]

The NHMG is still active in the political arena, both through statements or interviews with its leadership by the local press.

The National Groups Coalition (NGC)
Iitilaf al-Tajammuàt al-Wataniya

The NGC was founded in September 2005 by a group of Shi'ites from various gatherings and movements, such as the JPG, the INCM, and the ISCGK.

In its first year, Sha'ban Hussein, one of the JPG members, was chosen to be the Secretary General of the NGC, and 'Abdul-Wahid Khalfan was his deputy, on the basis that the presidency of the NGC will go to one group of the coalition yearly.[145]

The most important objective of the NGC was to demonstrate the Shi'ites' presence in the political, economic and media arenas. It also aimed not to interfere in the religious fatwa and believes solving problems through dialogue and commitment to peace. It also addressed the media campaigns against the Shi'ite sect. The NGC's Charter contains the following points:[146]

- highlighting and strengthening the common issues between the founders of the coalition
- resolving all sorts of political differences among various parties of the coalition through dialogue
- respecting the privacy of the Shi'ite individual in choosing his Shi'ite Marja' (authority) and respecting the views of the Marja'
- keeping the confidentiality of the political approach of each party during the establishment of the coalition within the mainframe of Islamic Shari'a and the Kuwaiti constitution
- respecting opinions of others and committing to dialogue manners
- confronting allegations and campaigns made through the media
- adopting means of resolution in case of any differences that may occur between any of the parties committed to the Charter of the coalition.

The NCG puts itself in the face of the NIA on the grounds that it represents a moderate line within the Shi'ite groupings.

The most distinguished statements made by the NGC were criticizing the Egyptian President, Hosni Mubarak, who accused the Arab Shi'ites of being loyal to Iran rather than to their homelands. The NGC urged him to apologize formally to the Arab Shi'ites through the al-Arabia channel, considering such statements to be aimed at escalating sectarian sedition between Muslims and emphasizing that the loyalty of Shi'ites is always to their homeland.[147]

The NGC announced its rejection of the Zakat law made by the MPs of Sunni fundamentalist groups in the National Assembly, describing it as a law that did not take into consideration the doctrinal differences between Islamic sects. They warned it would cause sectarian discrimination between the Kuwaiti people and stressed that this law is inconsistent with the articles of the Kuwaiti Constitution, which guarantee the freedom of belief for every citizen. The NGC warned that the adoption of this law would disturb Kuwaiti national unity. The NGC emphasized that the aim of this law was to politicize religious values.[148]

The NGC participated in the general elections held on 29 June 2006, but its candidates failed to win any seat in the Parliament. In spite of the defeat of all the NGC candidates, the government appointed its Secretary General, 'Abdul-Hadi al-Saleh, as Minister of the State of the Affairs of the National Assembly in the new Cabinet. This confirms the strong relationship within the NGC, which is one of the moderate Shi'ite groups with the Kuwaiti authority. The NGC is still active in the political arena, both through statements and interviews broadcast through the Arab satellite channels with its leadership.

The Shi'ites Principles Gathering (SPG)
Tajammu' Thawabit al-Shi'ites

The SPG was founded in 2008, its most prominent founder being Faraj al-Khderi, the Secretary General for the SPG. The establishment of the SPG was a reaction to the establishment of the DNPG, the Sunni gathering which has an extreme attitude towards the Shi'ites and regards them as more dangerous than Jews and Christians. The DNPG demanded the government put the Shi'ite Husseiniyas under survelliance.[149] The most important objectives of the SPG are:[150]

- defending Kuwaiti Shi'ites against Sunni extremists
- defending the fundamentals of the Shi'ites against those who want to harm them
- defending the Shi'ite faith.

The major activity of the SPG is issuing statements defending the Shi'ites in Kuwait, such as the statement on the occasion of the visit made by the Shi'ite cleric, Mohammad Baqir al-Fali. He gave a religious lecture at one of the Husseiniyas. The DNPG accused al-Fali of abusing al-Sahaba and called him a zindiq; it demanded the government deport him from Kuwait.[151] Accordingly, the DNPG's MP, Mohammad Hayif al-Mutairi, and the Sunni Islamist Political Groups' MPs, threatened to question the Prime Minister Sheikh Nassr al-Mohammad al-Sabah regarding this matter, causing a political crisis in Kuwait and leading to the resignation of the Cabinet.[152]

Al-Khderi emphasized that the weakness of the government and its silence towards what the Shi'ites are subjected to, encouraged the Sunni extremists to take a provocative attitude towards them; he also added that the SPG does not believe in violence and that mass media is its only means to express its views.[153] In addition, the SPG demanded the government make the 10th of Muharram a national holiday. It also supported the government in establishing rehabilitation centers for those Sunni extremists and blamed some Sunni extremist clerics for being behind the exploitation of the State's Sunni mosques to spread extremist ideas against Shi'ites.[154] The SPG called the Kuwaiti authority to take severe measures towards the elimination of al-Qaeda in Kuwait and the leaders of al-Slafiah al-Jihadi clerics, who were advocating the youth to commit suicide bombings against innocent people.[155]

4   The relationships between the Kuwaiti regime and the Islamist political groups

The post-liberation stage

Although the Kuwaiti Constitution has prevailed on the national side to the Islamic one by stating that Kuwait is an Arab country, the liberal orientations adopted by the intellectual merchants have prevailed since the beginning of the State in 1938. A radical change in the nature of the mutual interests between the Kuwaiti regime and various political gatherings has been taking place. The Islamist political groups are prevailing socially and politically, where they have allied themselves with the Kuwaiti regime, which is represented in the government and some members of the ruling family for a variety of reasons. For instance, they have gained an influence among the Kuwaiti people and have gained in their voting power within the Kuwaiti Parliament. However, their negligence to discuss political and administrative mistakes made by the government, such as wasting the public money on marginal things, has had a negative impact on the overall political activity in Kuwait.

One proof for the existence of such support is the formation of the Cabinet following the death of the Emir of Kuwait, Sheikh Jaber al-Ahmad al-Sabah, where only the Islamist political groups were represented, causing the liberal trend represented by the NDA to disapprove of this Cabinet and protest for being not represented in it. It's as if they have not learned that there is an undeclared alliance between the Islamist political groups and the Kuwaiti regime to change the outcome of the National Assembly elections since January 1967, for more than four decades! Contrary to what some believe, this alliance is strong to the degree that one of the members of the ruling family, Sheikh Sa'ud Nasser al-Sabah, former Minister of Information and Oil, has said that Kuwait is being hijacked by these groups,[1] and announced that:

Some have asked, Do we live in the State of the Taliban?[2]

He warned the Kuwaiti regime of a plan made by these groups which have links with outside organizations. He severely criticized the ICM, the largest of these organizations, which, according to him, is aiming to reach for power and increase its influence and interests.[3]

This chapter focuses on the development of the relationships between the Islamist political groups and the Kuwaiti regime. What is meant here by the Islamist political groups are all groups, movements and parties that take the religious political discourse as an ideology. They call for the Islamization of laws and the application of Islamic Shari'a, and oppose the civil state and try to replace it with a religious one. For example, some of these groups are the ICM, SG, the Shi'ite fundamentals Islamic groups, and others that are growing in Kuwaiti society and dominating the political arena. In contrast, the national, liberal and leftist trend has disappeared from the political scene due to many reasons and factors.[4] Some of these factors are:

- the absence of the organizational commitment of the nationals, leftists, or liberals unlike the Islamist political groups, which is characterized by having bases in every corner of Kuwait and their ability to expand among the citizens
- the liberal trend has seasonal activity using obsolete methods.

Therefore, the liberal trend no longer has a significant representation in Parliament and most civil society institutions have become subject to the Islamist political groups.

The pre-occupation stage

The starting point for the relationship between the Islamist political groups, represented in the MBG, and the Kuwaiti regime, started with the change of the outcome of the elections for the second National Assembly, which took place on 25 January 1967. The ANM in Kuwait prepared itself for the elections by unifying efforts of the opposition in a program called al-Jabha al-Sha' biya (the Popular Front (PF)). The PF determined the issues that it would struggle for: oil revenues, a progressive Arab policy in the commitment of Kuwait towards the progressive countries, the Palestinian issue, backing up the revolutionary movement to liberate Palestine, social justice, and the issue of water supplies in Kuwait.[5] The PF formed a wide alliance in order to guarantee a majority in the new National Assembly. This alliance included – in addition to the committed members of the ANM who were the mainstay of the alliance – the friends of the movement from the liberal and national youth who belonged to the merchant families represented in the Kuwaiti Chamber of Commerce, such as the Chairman, 'Abdul-'Aziz al-Saqer, Mohammad 'Abdul-al-Mohsin al-Kharafi, Humud al-Nisf, Yousef Ibrahim al-Ghanim, and Mohammad Ahmad al-Bahar. In addition, it included the representatives of the trade unions such as Hassan Falah al-'Ajmi, the President of the Oil Workers Union. The candidate of the PF received great backing and response from the masses because of the achievements of the main figures in the national movement in both the Constitution Assembly and the former National Assembly over issues such as expensing royalties, re-opening banned clubs, freeing journalists, the formation of trade unions, and their objections to the laws which would limit the freedom of individuals. It is worth mentioning that during the bi-elections that were called by the government in 1966 to fill the vacant seats of the resigned nationalist MPs from the National Assembly of 1963, the nationalist MPs made an appeal to boycott the elections and the majority of the voters responded to this appeal.[6]

Although all of the above confirmed the ability of the candidates of the PF to have a guaranteed majority in the new Assembly, the authorities foresaw the success of the candidates of the PF and so interfered directly in the process of the election and changed the results on 25 January 1967. Jassim Jerkhi describes the process of the election rigging:

> On election day everything went along normally until the voting finished. According to Article No. 36 of the Election law, after polling finishes, the ballot boxes must be locked and taken to the headquarters of the Principal Committee where they should be opened and the votes counted in the presence of all the chairmen and members of the Principal Committee and sub-committees. However, this did not happen. Armed policemen entered the polling stations and took the ballot boxes before they had been closed. Moreover, the policemen refused to allow any member of the sub-committees to accompany them to the headquarters, a direct violation of the law.[7]

Despite the election's manipulation, seven candidates of the PF succeeded in the elections, but they submitted their resignations as a protest over the rigging.[8] They issued, together with 31 failed candidates, a statement condemning the rigged election:

> The uncovered election rigging, carried out against the people's will and their right to express their views, has created a conviction that the elections are false. It does not represent the people's will and we do not accept its result because it was built on false procedures which violated the law.[9]

The Minister of Education and the winning candidate of district 5, Khalid al-Mas'ud, submitted his resignation from the National Assembly and the government as a protest over the rigging. Statements of condemnation addressing the people of Kuwait were issued by Jam 'iyat al-Muhamin (the Lawyers Association), Jam 'iyat al-Sahafiyin (the Journalists Association), Jam 'iyat al-Khireejin (the Graduates Association), Rabitat al-Udaba, Jam 'iyat al-Muhandisin (the Engineers Society), Itihad al-Muqawilin (the Contractors Union), al-Itihad al-'Am li 'Umal al-Kuwait (Kuwaiti General Workers Union) and the NUKS.[10] Three journals were banned – *Akhbar al-Kuwait* (the *Kuwait News*), *al-Hadaf*, and *al-Risala* (*The Message*) – while the nationalists' weekly journal, *al-Tali'a*, had been banned since 1966. On the contrary,

Yousef Hashim al-Rifa'i, a supporter of the MBG, participated in the Cabinet following this election as the Minister of State for Cabinet Affairs.[11] The SRC did not issue a statement showing its position about the rigging of the elections as other institutions or civil societies did. Nor did the SRC express its solidarity with the statement issued by a number of MPs who won in the elections, and candidates who failed to win who belonged to the leftist, nationalist and liberal forces. The statement also was not signed by any of the candidates belonging or close to the MBG, such as Ahmad Bezee' al-Yasin and Yousef Hashim al-Rifa'i, before the latter became Minster in the Kuwaiti Cabinet. The ANM had accused the MBG of manipulating the people's opinions and views since one of its leading Egyptian members of the MBG, Hassan al-'Ashmawy, participated in the rigging of the election; he was the legal advisor in Idirat al-Fatwa wa al-Tashree'a (the department of fatwa and law).[12]

When the Kuwaiti regime disrupted the Parliamentary life on 29 August 1976, it suspended a number of articles of the Constitution and imposed a series of laws and procedures that restricted civil liberties. Most of the popular associations and organizations stood against these actions, while the position of the MBG was in favor of the Kuwaiti regime in the non-Constitutional resolution of the Parliament. The Chairman of SRS, Yousef al-Haji, participated in the unconstitutional Cabinet that was formed directly after the resolution as a Minister of Awqaf and Islamic Affairs.[13] In addition, the SRS did not condemn the resolution, procedures or suppression of democracy.[14] At the same time, the opposition political groups represented by the leftists, nationalists and liberals were mobilizing people by launching campaigns that demanded the return of democratic freedoms and the preservation of Constitutional guarantees and the return of a democratic life.[15] Also, the SRS and its journal, *al-Mujtama'*, did not take any action against the resolution and did not stand with the other associations and organizations whose boards of directors resolved to stand against the regime's decision, were completely closed, and some of their leaders were put under investigation.[16] On the contrary, the *al-Mujtama'* journal published the Emiri decree immediately after the 29 August action without making any comments.

After these supporting positions of the MBG to the unconstitutional procedures of the regime, the support of the latter for the MBG was clear. It was apparently clear, most especially when the *al-Mujtama'* journal wrote about the meeting between 'Abdullah 'Ali al-Mutawa', the SRS Chairman, and Sheikh Salem Sabah al-Salem al-Sabah, Minister of Social Affairs and Labor, saying:

> The Chairman requested from his Excellency, the Minister, to focus on the need for the government to support the Islamic trend in order to protect Kuwait and its future generations from subversive ideas and principles with external links in nature ... His Excellency, the

Minister replied, that the government supports and encourages the Islamic stream.[17]

As a desire to eliminate the Parliament and reduce the influence of the national and leftist trend, the regime supported Islamist political groups. Therefore, the result was the growing influence of the Islamist political groups, most specifically the MBG, and its effects are still in existence at this time.[18]

When the Kuwaiti regime formed the Lajnat Tankaih al-Dastur (Committee for the Revision of the Constitution) in 1980, the opposition political movement which represented the liberals, nationalists and leftists expressed its rejection of this Committee and considered it an infringement on the Constitution of 1962. It regarded the Committee as a step to marginalize the political participation guaranteed by the Constitution of the State of Kuwait and it refused to prejudice the Constitution or to amend it, and that the process of amending the Constitution is the responsibility of the legislative authority only. On that basis, symposiums were held and political statements were made that led, in the end, to the cancellation of the Committee to consider a revision of the Constitution.[19] Unlike the Islamist political groups, which had expressed support for the regime's intention to revise the Constitution, the MBG led a campaign to collect signatures on petitions calling for an Islamic Constitution and calling for an amendment of Article II of the Constitution. The MBG did this without objection of the intention of the government to revise the Constitution as long as it followed Shari'a law, and they wanted substantial amendments to expand the executive power and reduce the role and powers of the legislative branch.[20] The MBG was active in raising posters in the streets, in mosques, and public places bearing slogans such as Allah Sha'rana Walqran Dastorna (God is our slogan and Quran is our Constitution), demanding that the leadership in Kuwait should be Shura and not a democratic system as stated in Article 6 of the Constitution.[21]

The Islamist political groups welcomed the formation of this committee and launched a campaign of propaganda and put pressure on members of the Committee by submitting petitions and personal letters. They also organized public activities under the slogan of al-Quran Dostorona (The Quran is our Constitution). This campaign succeeded in having an influence on a number of members of the Committee to consider revising the Constitution,[22] whereby 15 members of the Committee made a proposal to amend the second article of the Constitution.[23] They formed a technical committee of nine members to make Islamic Shari'a the main source of legislation and the technical committee's decision was to reject this proposal by five members against four. When this proposal was introduced to the Committee, 18 members were in favor of it while 7 members were against it.[24] After the failure of the Committee to achieve any amendments to the Constitution to reduce the powers of the legislature, in addition to the political changes that may be incurred dealing most especially with some neighboring countries such as the Islamic revolution in Iran with concerns being raised in exporting the revolution affecting the internal political situation of Kuwait.[25] The Kuwaiti regime suddenly declared 23 February 1981 to be the date for electing the fifth National Assembly. Coinciding with this was a new electoral law issued in the absence of the National Assembly that Kuwait be divided into 25 constituencies. Each one was to be represented with two seats in the Parliament, instead of five as in the old electoral law; this was done to ensure the fall of the candidates of the nationalist, leftist and liberal opposition.

The Islamist political groups represented in the MBG, the SG, and the Imam Khomeini line participated in this election. The results were marked with the failure of most of the candidates of the left and nationalists belonging to the Democratic Gathering and the National Gathering, with the success of the candidates of the Islamist political groups winning some of the Parliamentary seats. The Sunni Islamist political groups organized a campaign against the candidates of the left and the nationalists, accusing them of being communists on one hand, and taking advantage of their participation in the Shaa'ban Mosque Movement, when the leader of the Democratic Gathering, Ahmad al-Khatib,[26] participated in the rally organized by the Khomeini line of Shi'ites, on the other hand.[27] Ahmad al-Khatib says:

The Islamist political groups participated for the first time in the 1981 elections after its presence was felt in the political arena. We weren't surprised that its political agenda was basically attacking the nationalists and the pan Arabists calling them with being infidels. They also were supported by the candidates of the government, and we were all surprised when they used developed materials in their promotions, and these promotions almost no other candidate could cover its costs, and it looked like the advertisements in the American elections campaigns.[28]

Yousef al-Haji, one of the MBG leaders and the Minister of Awqaf, described the fall of the left and the nationalist candidates:

They wanted to change the doctrine of this country . . . I find the existence of those was abnormal, and any abnormality should be removed . . . and it has been removed, thank God.[29]

Meanwhile, the *al-Mujtama'* journal attacked the left and the nationalists severely.[30]

The representatives of the Islamist political groups in the National Assembly played a big role in raising issues that had no major significance in regards to the issues of concern to the citizens of Kuwait, such as corruption cases. Instead, they focused on issues that were not of major concern to most Kuwaitis. For instance, a draft law was submitted by two former MPs representing the MBG and the SG, respectively, 'Isa Majed al-Shaheen and Jassim al-'Oun, to ban the exploitation of women in any form of advertisement by any means, such as magazines, radio and television, and that the person violating the law shall be liable to a fine of 100 Kuwaiti dinars, and that this punishment would be doubled if the violation was repeated.[31]

These positions by the Islamist political groups towards the opposition and the conversations that took place in the meetings of the National Assembly, according to the desires of the regime, led the latter to give more material and moral support to these groups and opened all the State's institutions, allowing the Islamists to hold leading positions in it. Moreover, it gave these groups an extensive network in the state's apparatus and a strong existence in the economic and financial institutions.[32]

In 1985, the elections for the sixth National Assembly took place and the results came in favor of the political opposition, which included leftists, nationalists and Shi'ite groups allied with them. The government lost the initiative and, thus, the deputies loyal to the government, traditionally, who formed the majority in all previous Parliamentary councils, became the minority in this Assembly. This Assembly was one of the strongest Parliamentary councils in Parliamentary life in Kuwait since the beginning of the era of independence. Opposition MPs insisted on the accountability of government exercises during the disruption of the Parliamentary life period since 1976.[33] Hence, the Kuwaiti regime decided to dissolve the Sixth National Assembly unconstitutionally. On 22 April 1990, the Kuwaiti regime called the citizens to elect a al-Majlis al-Watani (National Council) as a replacement for the National Assembly for a transitional period of four years, as stated by the government.[34] This was followed by urging voters to elect the National Council and the issuance of its Acts, which was clear from its articles that it was merely a consultative council rather than a legislative one, whereby it was being stripped of all its legislative power. The goal behind the formation of this council was to get rid of democracy and the confiscation of public freedoms. Most of the civil society institutions and popular organizations called a boycott of the elections and about 58% of the voters responded positively to this call.[35]

Despite the rejection of the formation of the unconstitutional National Council in 1990 by the majority of the population, the participation of the Islamist political groups, represented in the MBG and SG, in the call for boycotting the elections was limited. The leaders of the Islamist political groups tried to make a split among the political forces with the call for the boycott and signed a joint statement in which they declared their approval of the formation of the National Council. Among them were 'Abdullah 'Ali al Mutawa', head of the SRS, Ahmad Bezee' al-Yasen, the former Chairman of the Kuwaiti Finance House and Yousef al-Haji.[36] Isma'il al-Shatti – an MBG leader, editor in chief of *Majallat al-Mujtama'* and the current consultant for the Prime Minister – signed the statement issued by 'Abdul-'Aziz al-Saqar, a group of merchants, and political figures calling to boycott the elections; however, at the last moment he quickly retreated and withdrew his signature from the statement.[37] The Islamist political groups, which enjoyed a wide influence among the tribes, also tried to mobilize their supporters not to boycott the National Council elections. It seems that the mutual interests between these groups and the regime had led to the easing of the opposition of these groups of the National Council – most especially when this coincided with the appointment of the youth members of the groups in leading positions in the ministries and state institutions, and membership in state councils, such as the Supreme Planning Council and governorates in which the regime wanted to be an alternative for the dissolved National Assembly.[38]

Some evidence of the support to the Islamist political groups by the Kuwaiti regime are:

1   The absence of the leaders of the Islamist political groups from participating in the gatherings held by the Constitutional Movement every Monday[39] – the participation was symbolically limited to the MPs of the Constitutional Movement.
2   Refusal of the leaders of the National Union of Kuwaiti Students, which is regarded as the student front of the MBG in Kuwait, to participate in the strike organized by the University Faculty Association, in a protest against the arrest of Dr. Ahmad al-Rub'ei, the member of the Constitutional Movement.
3   Acceptance of the Chairman of the IHRS, the religious and social forefront of the SG in Kuwait, a membership in the Supreme Planning Council and the appointment of a leading SG member as Assistant Secretary of the National Council.
4   The IHRS did not sign the petition prepared by the popular and non-profit associations addressing the regime to preserve the Constitution and return the National Assembly.
5   The IHRS did not participate in signing the press statement issued by the popular organizations to stop dialogue with the Kuwaiti regime and to speed the return of the National Assembly.
6   The IHRS boycotted the meeting of the popular organizations, which was organized by the members of the University Faculty Association, calling for a campaign to boycott the elections for the National Council, in addition to its non-participation in the protest called for by the civil society institutions and organizations at Kuwait University.[39] Despite the absence of the Islamist political groups from participating in political protest movements against the regime, the battle for the Constitution – led by the progressive forces – demonstrated the end of the control of the Islamist political groups on the Kuwaiti political arena.

The occupation stage

The relationships between the Islamist political groups and the Kuwaiti regime continued during the occupation. This was clear when the MBG Kuwait branch supported the regime during the Popular Congress in Jeddah, which was held on 13 October 1990 at the invitation of the previous Crown Prince of Kuwait, Sheikh Sa'ad al-'Abdullah al-Salem al-Sabah, aiming to stress the legitimacy of the ruling family. This was done in response to the speech made by the French President, Mitterrand, at the United Nations, to invite the Kuwaiti people for a referendum to choose the appropriate political system for Kuwait.[40] All political forces from the extreme left to the extreme right participated in this congress, including the leadership of the MBG, who mostly were outside Kuwait when the invasion took place. Before the start of the National Congress there was a disagreement between the political forces representing the left, nationalists, liberals, and the political leadership, where the former insisted on the formation of a government in exile that included all political forces to supervise all the matters until the liberation of Kuwait; they wanted a commitment of the Kuwaiti regime to the Constitution of 1962 and its declaration of the illegality of the National Council.[41] After several meetings between the leaders of the political opposition, including the MBG, who threw their weight with the Kuwaiti regime, an agreement was reached between all parties with speeches being made by the Emir, the Crown Prince, and the Prime Minister addressing the commitment to the Constitution of 1962 after the liberation of Kuwait. The liberal, nationalist and leftist groups strongly insisted that 'Abdul-'Aziz al-Saqer, the Speaker of the first National Assembly in the era of independence, make a speech representing the attendees instead of Yusuf al-Haji, who was proposed by the MBG and endorsed by the Kuwaiti regime; these forces succeeded in this.[42] The MBG, as a result of the support they got from the Kuwaiti regime, achieved several gains in the Popular National Congress, where they succeeded in including the document issued at the conference, with a confirmation that the future of Kuwait is based on two main things: Islamic creed and the focus on Islamic education, and then Arab belonging;[43] this contradicted Article 1 of the 1962 Constitution, which states that:

> Kuwait is an independent sovereign Arab State. Neither its sovereignty nor any part of its territory may be relinquished. The people of Kuwait are a part of the Arab Nation.[44]

In addition, the Islamic term Shura was introduced beside the term democracy, while the sixth article of the Constitution affirms that:

> The System of Government in Kuwait shall be democratic.[45]

The post-liberation stage

The Islamist political groups participated in the first general elections that took place in Kuwait after the liberation on 5 October 1992, where it achieved good results. They showed their support for the Kuwaiti regime in order to pass their religious projects and for the Kuwaiti Government not to monitor

their activity. On the other hand, the Kuwaiti regime welcomed and supported these groups to fight against its traditional enemy from the leftist,
nationalist and liberal forces. There are several indications for this viewpoint:

First: the representation of the Islamist political groups in the Cabinet,
which was formed after the liberation of Kuwait from Iraqi occupation.
Among the members of the Cabinet were people responsible for the disaster
of the occupation under the justification of political realism, as was stated by
one of the officials of the ICM, Sami al-Khtrich.[46] Also, its retreat from the
proposal of the separation of the Crown Prince and the Prime Minister post
and that the ministries of sovereignty should not be limited to just members
of the ruling family with the excuse that the general population is not capable
of filling these positions, and that this retreat will not give the enemies of the
nation the opportunity to take advantage of the situation to gain power.[47] As
well, ICM played a key role in having an alliance with the regime to remove
members of the KDF from key committees, such as the Finance Committee
and other important committees in the National Assembly.

Second: the issues raised by these groups were not of high national importance, such as the difference between the Islamist political groups and the
administration of Kuwait University on the subject of wearing the veil in the
university, or the subject of the Committee for the Propagation of Virtue and
the Prevention of Vice to prevent the Star Academy program. The Islamist
political groups also did not want girls to participate in sports; they also
demanded to close theaters, prevent concerts, prevent the establishment of
satellite channels, and other marginal issues, which distracted the citizens
from the main political, economic and social issues, such as the occupation
disaster, corruption, adequate educational systems, security, and other very
important and major concerns. This was not unusual for the Islamist political
groups, whether in Kuwait or in any Arab country. The support of the
regimes for the Islamist political groups usually happens in this way based on
superficial issues, as happened during the rule of the former President of the
Arab Republic of Egypt, Anwar Sadat, against the latter's opponents of
leftist groups, the Alliance of Yemeni President, ʿAli ʿAbdullah Saleh, with
al-Tajammuʿ al-Yamani Lial-Islah (the Yemen Reform Group) (YRG) under
the leadership of Sheikh ʿAbdullah Bin Hussein al-Ahmar, the leader of the
Muslim Brotherhood Group in Yemen against al-Hizb al-Ishtiraky al-Yemeni
(The Yemeni Socialist Party) (YSP), and the co-operation of the former
president of Sudan, Jaʾafar Nimeiri, with the al-Jabhah al-Qawmiya
al-Islamiya (National Islamic Front), led by Hassan al-Turabi.

Third: for the mutual interests between these Islamist political groups and
the regime. The latter agreed to pass some laws proposed by the former in its
political agenda, such as: the prevention of co-education in the university and
private schools, prevention of celebrations in the New Year, and the prevention of concerts. The latter appointed a number of representatives of the
Islamist political groups in the Cabinet and agreed to establish the College
of Shari'a, which is considered by one of the opposition leaders, Ahmad

al-Khatib, as the school for the graduation of the party ranks. The graduates from this college were advocates of extremism and the supporters of economic institutions, such as Baiat al-Tamweel al-Kuwaiti (the Kuwait Finance House), which is not subject to the control of the Central Bank. Those projects come through laws, decrees and proposals put forward in Parliament, which leads, in the end, to establishing a form of religious state and not a democratic one.[48]

Fourth: appointment of many of the leaders of the Islamist political groups and their supporters in leading positions in various state institutions since the liberation until the last Cabinet, when Isma'il al-Shatti, one of the most prominent leaders of the ICM, was appointed as Deputy Prime Minister and Minister of State for Cabinet Affairs; this is the highest post in the Cabinet after the prime minister.

The main objectives of this support from the Kuwaiti regime to the Islamist political groups are:

First: to allow these groups to confront the nationalist and leftist forces, which throughout the history of Kuwait has represented the main political opposition to the Kuwaiti regime, which has dominated the political arena since the 1930s until the late 1970s. For this reason, the Kuwaiti regime strongly rejected the re-opening of Nadi al-Istqlal (the Independence Club), which was dissolved in 1975 and through which the opposition from nationalist to leftist forces expressed their attitudes, while allowing the opening of dozens of religious associations belonging to the Islamist political groups.

Second: the use of the Islamist political groups by the Kuwaiti regime to cover up its mistakes, to justify them to the people and pass laws that limit the freedoms of citizens, such as the law on gatherings through the representatives of the Islamist political groups within the National Assembly.

Third: exploitation of some of the main figures of the Kuwaiti regime for the Islamist political groups to abolish the process of democracy that began with the representation of these groups in the National Assembly in 1981 until now, where the political Islamic discourse is distant from addressing major issues facing Kuwaiti society. Instead, it has a tendency to focus on marginal issues such as co-education and the prevention of concerts, songs, fashion shows, the raising of the veiled female voters and students at the university, the prevention of the use of women in advertising, the prevention of satellite channels that corrupt the morals of society, and other such topics that do not represent the major issues of Kuwaiti society. Such actions create a negative reaction from the Kuwaiti people towards the National Assembly. It was clear that there was a decline in the participation: in the 1981 elections the percentage was 89%; in 1985 it was 85%; in 1992 and 1996 it was 83%; in 1999 and 2003 it was 81%; in 2006 it was 66%; in 2008 it was 60%; and in 2009 it was 58%.[49]

The fact is that the Kuwaiti regime has ignored, in the long run, that it is the first victim of the Islamist political groups. The safety of the state will be hurt by the regime in its unlimited relationship with these groups, which have only one desire: the establishment of an Islamic State or the forcing of the Islamization of the society. It also seems that the regime has not learned any lessons from the way President Anwar al-Sadat's regime in Egypt was used when he tried to use the Islamist political groups against his hostiles from the progressive stream as he became their first victim: he was assassinated at their hands. The Egyptian regime still suffers from a series of terrorist operations carried out on Egyptian soil by these organizations and groups.

It is worth mentioning that there are great similarities between the goals of the Islamist political groups in Kuwait and the Taliban movement as expressed by Mullah Mohammad Omar, the Emir of the Islamic Emirate of Afghanistan, in Kandahar on 4 April 1996.[50]

5   Spread of the Islamist political groups in the social body

The moral and financial support given by the Kuwaiti regime to the Islamist political groups contributed significantly to the spread of the ideology of these groups in the social body; the regime allowed their influence to spread even in state institutions, where schools and educational institutions have become centers for mobilization and recruitment. In addition to the Ministry of Awqaf, health centers, co-operative societies, youth centers and Quran centers have all become dominated and controlled by these groups; they are used as centers for spreading their ideologies through issuing publications and posters. These groups are active among students, laborers, intellectuals and merchants. They are also active in mosques and Haj (major pilgrimage) and ʿUmra (minor pilgrimage) campaigns. They always lead campaigns for collecting Zakat and charity donations from the citizens. They try to convince the girls at schools, and during meetings after schools in one of the houses owned by one of the female leaders, to wear al-Ziyy al-Slami (Islamic clothes). Sheikh Saʾud Nasser al-Sabah criticized the attitude of the Kuwaiti Government towards these groups, and warned of their dangerous practices on both the government and society by saying:

> The only justification for that is to seek and gain the trust of the active Islamic groups in Kuwait . . . I say with bitterness that the country has been abducted by these self-styled Islamic groups, which are in fact exploiting Islam as a cover to conceal their political identity. They seek to climb on the shoulders of the regime and control the political process in the name of Islam, and their activity in Kuwait is the evidence . . . their suspicious behavior is not a barrier in the face of their expansion, but unfortunately, the government has let them be free since the liberation and allowed them to move freely into the foundation of societies, branches, and committees, which has enabled them to play a strong role in Kuwaiti life, thus offending the Kuwaitis. I am confident that I express the opinion of the Kuwaiti street when I say that the silent majority feel this sense . . . They even have the guts to intervene in the Cabinet formation and the choice of ministers. Unfortunately, the regime responds to the conditions ruled by them.

The existing alliance will be harmful for those who have agreed on its setup.[1]

There are several indications that the support of the regime for the Islamist political groups has led to the escalation of the influence of these groups in all aspects of life in Kuwait.

Islamists and the students' movement

The first target of the Islamist political groups in the Kuwaiti political arena during the 1970s and 1980s was to control the trade union organizations and associations, which are considered a stronghold of the leftists and the nationalists. It has been under their control for a long period of time. The MBG identified these institutions as *montadayat Jahiliya* (ignorance forums),[2] which every one has to stay away from. However, in the early 1970s, the leadership of the MBG took a decision to participate in these institutions with a view to overcoming the problem with its growth crisis. For instance, a split inside the student organization of the MBG in Cairo regarding this subject occurred when it began to prepare for the enrollment of the NUKS. Two views emerged. The first was insisting that these institutions are *montadayat Jahiliya* that may not participate in its activity, and as a commitment to the list of duties mentioned in Risalat al-Ta'aleem (the message of guidance) by Hassan al-Banna, the Supreme Guide of the MBG addressed its members with 38 articles. Its 25th article stated that:

All non-Islamic courts, civil courts, clubs, groups, schools and societies that contradict Islamic beliefs, should be completely boycotted.[3]

The second view rejected emotional isolationism and called for joining these institutions to advocate for the organization. The dispute was resolved in favor of the second opinion when Amir al-Jama'a (the leader of the group) invited all members of the organization in Cairo who were studying in the Egyptian universities, and managed to get a large number in the audience.[4] As a result of this meeting, the MBG worked actively within the National Union of Kuwaiti Students, the Cairo branch, and through the cultural committee and the religious committee controlled by the students belonging to the SG in the NUKS. The MBG had an overwhelming success in these elections over the leftists and the nationalists. Following this success, the leadership of the MBG in Kuwait decided to contest the elections for the student branch of the NUKS in Alexandria, and they succeeded.

The SG also tried to mobilize the students of the NUKS in Alexandria and the Cairo branches as its first goal. The most prominent students who played a major role in the formation of the SG student base in Alexandria were Enizi al-Enezi, 'Adel al-Tawhid and Ahmad Baqir. From the Cairo branch, Jassim al-Shareedah, who was the Chairman of the Religious Committee in 1974, emerged.[5] In the branch of Kuwait University, the most prominent SG student leaders was Saleh al-Nafeesi, the President of the Scientific Management Society of the Faculty of Commerce, controlled by the SG student organization. With the beginning of 1976, the SG student organization activated under the name Ansaer al-Wehad al-Tlabi (Supporters of Students Unity), raising the slogan, In Aradt al-Slah Mastata't (I only want reform to my best). It distributed publications and brochures among the students, calling for a revival of the teachings of Islam based on the Quran, Sunna and Salaf, the promotion of the Islamic identity, and the application of the law of God in all aspects of life, and that this had to be done inside and outside the university.

Following the victories of the Islamist political groups over the student organizations at the expense of the leftist and nationalist student groups on the scene in Cairo and Alexandria, they decided to contest the elections of the branch of Kuwait University, which was considered one of the biggest branches of the Union. In 1977, the SG student organization formed an alliance with the MBG student organization to confront the leftist and nationalist forces, and it succeeded in controlling the NUKS and overthrowing the leftists, who had been dominating it since the foundation of the university. It did it again in the elections of 1979.

In 1980, a dispute between the SG student organization and the MBG student organization occurred, which was reflected in the student arena. The SG student organization contested under a new name, Qaimat al-Itihad al-Islamiya (List of the Islamic Union), which was a strong competitor with the al-Qaima al-Itilafiya (List of Coalition). In spite of the differences that emerged, they agreed to support Islamic issues, such as abolishing co-education in the university classes.

The reason behind the success of these groups in the expulsion of the left and nationalists from the leadership of the NUKS at the university was the involvement of the latter in the political aspects without considering the problems that the students suffer at the university. On the other hand, the former was using tactics such as printing memos, giving lectures, distributing those memos at a priceless cost, holding many seminars inside the university with leaders of the Islamist political groups, and conducting flights for pilgrimage and Umrah. All this coincided with the pressure on the university administration to remove the names of students who were put on warning lists, and often the university's administration responded to these demands.

Not only did the Islamist political groups control the student body at the university, but it also exceeded this to the fact that the university's administration appointed them to become administrative leaders at the university through pressure from the representatives of these groups in the National Assembly. However, after a long period of control with the existing coalition between the MBG and SG in Kuwait University in the student body at the university, al-Qaima al-Mustaqila (the Independent List), which does not belong to any political organization, began to compete. The existing coalition feared the good results achieved by the Independent List, which seeked to control the NUKS, and it announced a coalition alliance with the Islamic Union List again to confront it. This alliance won the elections of the NUKS held on 1 October 2007, with a total of 5,735 votes, while al-Qaima al-Mustaqila got 2,774 votes, and al-Qaima al-Islamiya, which represents Shi'ite students at the university, came third with 1,375 votes. Al-Wasat Aldimuqrati, which represents the liberal and left groups, got 1,308 votes.[6] Also, in the elections of the NUKS held on 13 October 2008, a coalition alliance between Qaimat al-Itihad al-Islamiya and al-Qaima al-Itilafiya was established and got 5,677 votes; al-Qaima al-Mustaqila got 2,942 votes, al-Wasat al-Dimuqrati got 1,819 and al-Qaima al-Islamiya got 1,504 votes.[7]

Islamists and the Teachers' Association

After the Islamist political groups gained control of the student movement represented by the NUKS at Kuwait University and its branches in Cairo, Alexandria, the United States of America and Britain, these groups moved to control the Teachers' Association, which is the largest union in Kuwait, with an estimated membership of 14,000 in 2009.[8] The MBG, the SG and Shi'ite groups organizations succeeded in defeating the alliance between the leftist and nationalist groups in the elections for the Board of Directors, where the SG raised the slogan 'towards building an Islamic education' and Qaima al-Mo'lamin (the Teachers' Association) list representative of the MBG, in turn, raised the slogan of Nahwa Bena'a Tarbawi Islami (taking Islamic teaching). In addition, the al-Qaima al-Islamiya (Islamic List) representative of the Shi-'ites advocated the slogan Sorona al-Hakiki al-Wihadah al-Wataniy (Our Real Fence is National Unity). Since then, until the elections of 2009, the Board of Directors for the Teachers' Association is in the hands of the MBG, where in the elections held on 17 March 2009, Qaimat al-Mo'lamin got 2,004 votes and Qaimat al-Mo'lamin al-Mahaniah (the Technical Teachers List) got 619 votes.[9]

Islamists and the educational sector

The educational sector is one of the largest sectors in which the Islamist political groups were keen to extend their influence by trying to control the members of the Supreme Advisory Committee to work on completing the implementation of the provisions of Islamic Shari'a, which follows the Amiri Diwan financially. This Committee tried to impose a curriculum that suits its orientation.[10] Dr. Ahmad al-Khatib mentions in his memoir:

> The government allowed the Islamists to control the Ministry of Education, and their leading ranks started to run the educational process, they changed the curriculum, increased the Islamic studies dose, and established the College of Shari'a to graduate its members and distribute them in the state's institutions.[11]

Despite the attempts made by the liberal Ministers of Education, such as Hassan al-Ibrahim, Ahmad al-Rub'i, Yousef al-Ibrahim, and Nuriya al-Sabih, to limit the dominance of the Islamist political groups in the educational sector, owing to the power and influence of these groups, who have close ties with some members of the ruling family, those efforts have failed based on the efforts made by the representatives of the Islamic fundamentalist groups in the National Assembly. Therefore, those liberal Ministers were forced to submit their resignations after questioning them, except Nuriya al-Sabih, the past Minister of Education who challenged the MPs of Islamist political groups by refusing to wear the veil. In addition, the Islamist political groups objected to appointing a woman to be a minister on the basis that this position is wilaya 'Ama (high leadership), which contradicts their understanding of Islamic Shari'a. Accordingly, those MPs, along with other tribal MPs, demanded the questioning of the Minister of Education and withdrew their confidence from her. However, they failed because the Cabinet stood beside al-Sabih, and the fear of the MPs of the Islamist political groups was in dissolving the Parliament, which caused a split among them.

After the terrorist operations on the streets of Kuwait in February 2005, carried out by al-Qaeda, the Kuwaiti regime realized the seriousness of leaving the educational sector at the mercy of the Islamist political groups. They decided to revise the contents and standards of the educational curriculum that contain extreme ideas as well as to control teachers who were promoting extremist ideas.[12] In this aspect, the liberal newspaper *al-Qabas* criticized the Ministry of Education by saying:

> The Ministry of Education is in front of the moment of truth! It is the best time to make a decision to reshape the educational body and to exclude the extremist thinking from sensitive departments, and some schools. It is no longer a mystery the close relationship between some officials in the ministry and school principals, and religious political groups . . . these officials and principals ignored the fact that they are subject to rules and regulations governing the work at schools, and have imposed laws that suit their own orientations, and they looked at each of the school's regulations as a positive law, which they are not obliged to follow. How many schools in Kuwait do not salute the state's flag? How many schools in Kuwait in which the students march to their classes on religious songs? How many schools in Kuwait in which music teachers have no work to do? . . . How many schools in Kuwait in which leaflets and posters are distributed without the knowledge of the ministry's administration? How many schools celebrate, in particular, religious or political occasions without permission from the ministry . . . The time has come, to get rid of these schools' administrations which encourage the factional, tribal and sectarian role among the students.[13]

Islamists and the mosques

Until 2006, there were officially 1,100 mosques in Kuwait.[14] In addition, there are those mosques that are built by cheap metal; they are called Kerbi mosques.[15] The mosque is a very important place for the Islamist political groups to propagate their ideology. Most of Kuwait's mosques are dominated by them and were turned into their headquarters. In the al-Farwaniya district, for example, these groups, under the name of the district's youth activity, run the mosques' affairs starting with providing paper, tissues, perfumes and carpets, and ending with providing religious books and decorating the walls with posters. Meetings are held in the afternoons, and evening prayers almost weekly. After Friday prayers every week, one of the members of those groups will ask those praying for a donation, without any legitimate cover.[16] A conflict between the Islamist political groups represented by the MBG and the SG appeared in running the mosques' affairs and gaining more supporters through them, which led the MBG to push its members to volunteer to make speeches in the mosques, especially on religious occasions such as Ramadan. Its speakers have to be knowledgeable in all aspects of life and they know how to attract the audience. The MBG succeeded in attracting a lot of ordinary people, especially the youth, and in spreading its ideology through publishing newspapers on the walls of mosques, distributing religious publications,[17] in addition to forming mosque committees that take care of the mosque affairs, such as Shabab Masjad Imam Ahmad Bin Hanabel (Imam Ahmad Bin Hanabel Youth Mosque), Shabab Masjed al-Jahra (al-Jahra Youth Mosque) and Sa'ad Bin Abi Waqqas Youth Mosque in the Kaifan district.

The mosques' committees have played a distinguished role in educating the youth according to their ideology, from holding competitions containing questions about religion to the publication of Salaf literature, as well as publishing the life of Mohammad bin 'Abdul Wahab, the founder of al-Da'wa al-Salafiah in the Arabian Peninsula. These publications accused the Arab nationalism of spreading sectarianism, interest on usury, and monopoly, and for these reasons it is rejected by Islam. They also claim that democracy is an innovation of Christians for the sake of the destruction of the Ottoman Empire.[18] The Islamist political groups used the mosques to attack their nationalists, leftists and liberal opponents through unlicensed seminars, as happened with Sheikh Hamid 'Abdullah al-'Ali, who was convicted of damaging the reputation of an Arab country and describing its leadership as a traitor and loser in one of his speeches during the Friday prayers in al-Sabahiya mosque. He has also criticized Kuwait's ruler for authorizing the international coalition forces to cross the Kuwaiti borders into Iraq, during the liberation of Iraq. The court sentenced Sheikh Hamid 'Abdullah al-'Ali to two years in jail and ordered suspension of the sentence for a period of three years provided that the accused pays bail and adheres to the observance of good conduct.[19] Consequently, the government put restrictions on speeches made in mosques.[20] Preachers have been suspended from working as mosque imams for violating the Charter of the mosque imposed by the Ministry of Awqaf and those who have played an important role in planting ideas of extremism among hundreds of young Kuwaitis have also been suspended.[21] Most of these mosques are considered strongholds of Islamist political groups, such as the MBG, SG, LP and the SM. From these mosques, speeches of hate are taking place almost daily.

In this context, Sheikh Mohammad 'Abdullah al-Rashidi, Talha Mosque imam, expressed strong criticism of democracy:

> Democracy is another religion which differs from the religion of Islam. All wise people admit that democracy is infidelity and void, and that legislative power is the right of God only.[22]

Mosques were also used to hold special religious meetings where video cassettes were spread to provoke fighting against the Americans,[23] and to distribute extreme fatwas, such as the fatwa made by Sheikh Humoud ibn al-'Oqla al-Shuybi, in which he allowed the killing of the famous Kuwaiti singer Abdullah Rewaishid. Among those imams, there were people accused of belonging to terrorist organizations such as Suleimman Abu Ghaith, spokesman of al-Qaida in Afghanistan, imam of al-Rumeitheya mosque, and 'Amer Khalif al-Enezi, leader of al-Qaeda, and others.[24] This put the government in an embarrassing situation towards the liberal political forces, which launched their campaign against what is happening in the mosques under the control of the Ministry of Awqaf. State mosques turned into a theater for distributing pamphlets, leaflets, and booklets belonging to terrorist groups carrying extreme ideas. The best example of this was the confiscation of booklets that carried the title of 'preferred Jihad in the cause of God,' written by Mujahid Sheikh Mohamed bin Abdullah bin Saif, one of the leaders of the Chechen Mujahideen, where 1,000 copies of this text had been distributed and were seized by the Ministry of Awqaf from the mosques in the six Governorates in Kuwait.[25] In this regard, the parent of Fawaz Taliq al-'Otaibi, who was killed in the armed confrontation with the security forces in the Hawalli district, says: 'Malik bin 'Auf mosque . . . was the safe haven of the radical extremist groups'.[26] A relative of Taliq Fawaz al-'Otaibi appealed to the Ministry of Awqaf to seize control of many of the al-Jahra Governorates' mosques, one of the main strongholds of terrorist groups, controlled by suspicious groups.[27] A group of young Islamic fundamentalists calling themselves Shabab Masjad al-Nasim (Youth of al-Nasim mosque), which is located in the Governorate of al-Jahra and is one of the strongholds of the Islamist political groups, distributed a booklet entitled *Hukum al-Dimuqratyh wa al-Dimuqratian* (*Democracy and the Rule of the Democrats*), whose ideas are derived from the published book, *al-Hasaad al-Mur: al-Ikhwan al-Moslmon fi Sitain 'Aam* (*The Bitter Harvest: Muslim Brotherhood in Sixty Years* by Ayman al-Zawahiri),[28] in which they described all who believe in a democratic style of government as kufaar (unbelievers).[29] They also stressed that 'democracy is a religion and whoever believes in it has fallen in the shirk akbar (a major blasphemy).'[30] In this regard, Fahad al-'Ali, one of the liberal columnists, expressed strong criticism of the government policies regarding this issue:

> A political decision to control mosques is required. It is not enough to say that speeches are subject to supervision, and every group and mature people realize that the danger lies behind all those panel discussions taking place inside mosques. If the Ministry of Awqaf monitors imams, then who monitors those who gather small groups encouraging them with praying and ending with brainwashing our youth into takfir to anyone who opposes the Amir of the group?[31]

Consequently, the Minister of Awqaf, 'Abdullah al-Ma'took, denied this accusation, confirming that the extremists do not work under the mosques' roofs, which is controlled by the Ministry. However, they do work in the desert where nobody can watch them.[32] In fact, this denial is far from the truth and the evidence is that a number of leaders of al-Qaeda in Kuwait are imams in mosques, and most young people are recruited through the mosques.

Islamists in the trade unions

Since the late 1940s, the Islamist political groups in Kuwait represented in the MBG have sought to expand among the ranks of the working class and have established a division for the purpose of recruiting workers, but this attempt has not succeeded. One of the leaders of the MBG justified their failure by the absence of a real working class at that time.[33] The beginning of the 1980s witnessed the retreat of leftist and nationalist forces, on one hand, and the rise in the religious tide in Kuwait, on the other, with the support and backing of the Authority in Kuwait for these groups. The Islamist political groups began operating in the ranks of the working class, especially in the trade unions, declaring themselves as the existing Islamic unions, which are, in fact, the front union of the MBG. By 1986, they managed to impose their control over most trade unions in the oil sector and, hence, controlled the oil workers' union, which prompted *Majallat al-Mujtama'* to choose for its editorial opening the title, 'and finally the stronghold of the left fell.'[34] Since the domination of the Islamist political groups over the trade unions in the oil sector, *Majallat al-Mujtama'* started to cover all of the union's activities and the union became a forefront of the MBG. It used the union's headquarters as a place for signing statements issued by the institutions of the civil society dominated by the Islamist political groups, such as the campaign launched by these groups against the Minister of Education and Higher Education, Dr. Hassan al-Ibrahim, who tried to reform the educational sector dominated by these groups. He was forced to submit his resignation when the executive board of the oil trade union issued a statement that complied with the context of statements made by the MBG and expressed opposition to the educational reform, which considered the resignation of the Minister of Education and Higher Education as a national and popular demand.[35]

Islamists and charity activity

Under the cover of charity activities, the MBG formed different committees to collect donations. These included the Committee of Zakat – which has more than 12 branches – the Islamic World Committee, and Committees of the Islamic cause to provide charities to Palestine and Lebanon.[36] The MBG was also dominating the three governmental financial institutions: Islamic Charitable Organization, Bait al-Zakat (Zakat House), and the Kuwaiti Finance House. The SM also played a role in the charitable activities in Kuwait by forming several committees, such as the Committee for the Arab World, the African Committee, the European Committee, and the Central Asia Committee, and other names that included all of the five continents. The IHRS, which supervises these committees, was accused of financing terrorist groups.[37] Dr. Ahmad al-Khatib said in his memoirs:

> They were the only ones who were given the right to collect donations without any censorship. They formed many committees deployed in every corner of Kuwait, with various names for fundraising, and the disposal of these funds was done without government control.[38]

The US Government accused IHRS, which oversees many of these committees, of being the financier of terrorist movements, after announcing that the US Treasury Department had frozen its funds. The IHRS denied the accusations and stressed that such accusations are not based on any physical evidence and affirmed that the IHRS is against al-Qaeda and terrorism.[39] Also, the Macedonian Government accused the IHRS of financing terrorism through Hilmi Bakr, director of Jamm'yat al-Hisan al-Khyriay (Ihsan Charity Society), where the IHRS transferred money through a Kuwaiti bank to German bank accounts for the Jamm'yat al-Hisan al-Khyriay, and the utilization of these funds was for terrorist activities; the IHRS denied this charge too.[40] Furthermore, they affirmed that a number of wealthy Kuwaitis who belonged to the Kuwaiti Islamist political groups offered financial support to many of the Salafiah groups in Lebanon when they visited the Western Bekaa in 2006. They held a variety of states responsible and non-governmental organizations who funded Salafiah Islamic Jihad, stating the money came from Saudi Arabia and Kuwait, in particular. Among the groups that have been funded is al-Harakah al-Islamiya al-Jamahirya (the Islamic Popular Movement), which was receiving military training in the camp of 'Ein el-Hilweh, one of the groups associated with al-Qaeda in Lebanon.[41]

The Egyptian *Rose al-Yousef* magazine accused the IHRS and the SRS of being behind the financing of extremist religious groups in Egypt, claiming that they were declaring jihad.[42] Pressure was exerted by the Egyptian Government, the United States of America, Russia and the European Union, which all accused the Kuwaiti charity societies of being involved in financing terrorist groups in Chechnya, Afghanistan and Europe, as well as the terrorist acts of January 2005 on Kuwaiti soil carried out by al-Qaeda. These accusations pushed the Kuwaiti Government to put some restrictions on the charity activities done by religious associations through raising funds for charity, such as the removal of the mobile caravans that were spread widely in all the streets of Kuwait and were used as centers for collecting donations by the religious groups. The government also restricted the collection of Zakat and donations to the Ministry of Awqaf. Today, any request for charities has to be authorized by the ministry officially. All the accounts of these religious societies and committees were audited by the Central Bank of Kuwait.[43]

In spite of these decisions and measures taken by the Kuwaiti Government towards the charity associations representing the Islamist political groups, the latter continued to disregard these measures, where the first report issued by the Ministry of Social Affairs and Labor revealed 55 violations in the first five days of the month of Ramadan, 27 of them belonging to the SRS and 12 to the IHRS. More than 6,000 violations were found since the imposition of this law. These violations were in the form of monthly deductions, fundraising tables, clothing stalls, unlicensed advertisements and unsealed vouchers. The report issued by the Department of Charitable Associations and Institutions confirms that these associations use suspicious methods, such as kiosks that can be moved from one place to another and hidden from the eyes of the ministry's inspectors, and that many of these associations violate the law of employment in the private sector and the law of residence of foreign employees. The report regarded these violations of laws as a demolition of the regulations issued to organize and control the charitable activities.[44] In addition to all of these violations, the team of control and inspection of the Ministry of Social Affairs and Labor found 125 unlicensed committees that belonged to major mother associations that do not have official files in the ministry to help control their activities. This led to the inability of the officials to know their budgets, the way of disbursement of the money and to whom it was transferred.[45]

The general election of the Kuwaiti National Assembly that took place in 2006 resulted in the candidates of the Islamist political groups winning a large number of seats. The government, represented by the Ministry of Social Affairs and Labor, released some of the restrictions imposed after the events of 11 September 2001 on the charitable associations and committees, under the pressure of these groups. The Ministry decided to allow those associations and committees to carry out cash fundraising during the month of Ramadan, and in this regard Sheikh Nadir al-Nouri, the Secretary-General of the 'Abdullah al-Nouri Charity, expressed his concern from the procedures imposed by the Ministry since the events of 11 September 2001 on the charity associations and stressed that the continuation of collecting the money by any means from the merchants will not stop because he believes this procedure is an act against god's will.[46] This coincided with the disclosure of the largest embezzlement implemented by an accountant in the Accounts Section of the Sanduq li I'nat al-Mardha (Patient Assistance Fund), which is one of the charities controlled by the Islamist political groups. This accountant succeeded in transferring more than 3.5 million Kuwaiti dinars into his bank account; it was discovered by chance when his bank noticed a suspicious movement in his account.[47] A statement issued by the National Democratic Alliance showed its opposition to allowing these religious associations to collect the funds in cash money and was surprised by the sudden decision of the Ministry of Social Affairs to allow the collection of cash during the month of Ramadan, in spite of previous decisions that had worked well in the last couple of years by banning this method of uncontrolled fundraising. The statement expressed its worry that the decision was taken under the pressure of the religious groups.[48] 'Abdul-Rahman al-Ijmai'an, who belongs to the Islamist political groups, criticized the mechanism of the charity action in Kuwait, confirming that:

> Party activity is the base for the charity action and that most of the time the funds collected are disbursed according to the principle al-Wala wal bara (allegiance to fellow Muslims and dissociation from non-Muslims) based on ideology and not religion and creed.[49]

He demanded the change in the leadership of these associations that had been leading the charity activity for almost 30 years.[50]

Islamists and district committees

The lenient policy pursued by the government towards the Islamist political groups led to the spread of li Jan al-'Amal al-Ijtamai' (Committees of Social Work), al-lijan al-Khaiyriya (Charitable Committees), and li Jan al-Da'wa (Commissions Under the Guise of Advocacy). The number of those committees is 15, nine for men and six for women, distributed in all the governorates of Kuwait, and they are all unlicensed. This is in addition to officially licensed committees such as the Zakat Committees, Call and Guidance Committees, management and building mosques, and Islamic projects committees in the districts.[51] They rent houses in the residential areas under the cover of social assistance to the poor citizens, while they serve as parties' offices under the guise of charitable activities in spite of the existence of the state institutions to undertake this task, such as the Ministry of Social Affairs and Labor. However, in fact, they represent the sub-headquarters of the religious groups through which the ideology of these groups is spread among young people in these areas. These committees collect money, gold and clothes from citizens, in addition to the widespread phenomenon of religious lessons that are held weekly in one of the homes of the group's members. In each district, there is a house in which they hold weekly meetings of women through which they explore the prospects of the new women's recruitment of these groups.

Islamists in the co-operative societies

The Islamist political groups have dominated the co-operative sector and most of the sector has fallen into their hands. The participation of the women's sector was significant, bearing in mind that these groups are against women's political rights, but they encourage them to vote in the elections of any co-operative society. These societies have become a forefront for these groups and its walls are full of their slogans. These co-operative societies are dominated by these groups. They have their own regulations, including the prevention of the sale of magazines and books that are not in accordance with their orientations, such as the *Majallt al-Tali'a* of leftist orientation, as well as to prevent the opening of ladies' hairdressers, the selling of song records, and the selling of cigarettes. To some extent, some of these societies place advertisements calling for the co-ops to replace song tapes with religious recordings which handle the Islamic political discourse of these groups. It went to the extent that Jam'iyat al-Mansuriyah al-Ta'awoniya (al-Mansuriyah Co-operative Society) published a statement declaring the change of the laundry official because his religion was 'non-Muslim or Christian,' based on the wishes of the people of the district.[52] Thus, the Director General of the Federation of Co-operative Societies, Farid al-'Awadi, warned that the developments in the co-operative sector are creating sensitivities among the Kuwaitis, making them dislike the co-operative work due to the control of political parties and political currents over these associations.[53] The electoral seasons for these associations became the platforms for the competition between these groups, some subject to the control of the SG, others of the MBG, and some of the Shi'ite Islamic groups. The goal is to take control of the boards of directors of these associations in order to have an impact on the shareholders through the services performed by these associations, and to gain their support for the candidates of these groups in the elections of the National Assembly and the municipal council. Often the religious groups nominate the heads of the boards of directors of the co-operative associations as candidates in these elections.

Islamists and the camps and recreational trips

Islamist political groups used to announce in the local press, in associations, and in clubs dominated by them about entertainment programs for youth from both sexes. For instance, they would be holding spring camps in the desert, in addition to the activities organized by the co-operative societies under their control, such as 'Umra tours. They also organized trips to some

Asian countries, such as Malaysia, European countries such as Switzerland, as well as a trip to Australia called Rahalt Sadiq al-kanqer (Kangaroo Friend Trip). The groups also formed different committees to help families, such as la-Jant al-Sahabh al-Salah (the Company of Good Committee), la-Jant Sanai' al-Kahir (the Good Creatures Committee), la-Jant Masabih al-Huda (Lights of Huda Committee), in addition to training courses for the students during summer holidays. Through these activities and committees, the Islamist political groups try to mobilize the young people and make an impact on them.[54]

Islamists and Islamization of the economy

The Islamist political groups in Kuwait sought to Islamize the economy and they succeeded in establishing a number of Islamic financial institutions, such as the Kuwait Finance House, which is one of the largest Kuwaiti banks.[55] The office of 'Abdullah 'Ali al-Mutawa' in his company and the SRS headquarters, was where the planning and preparation for establishing this bank and achieving this dream took place.[56] The approval for the foundation of Baiat al-Tamwail al-Kuwaiti was issued when 'Abdul-Rahman al-'Atiqi, a member of the MBG, who was the Minister of Finance, and Ahmad Bezee' al-Yasin, a leader of the MBG, who became its first head of the board of directors. In addition, these groups succeeded in founding and converting some existing economic institutions to Islamic ones. Even the traditional financial institutions, such as the National Bank of Kuwait, Commercial Bank, Burgan Bank and others, have Islamic activities now. In this regard, Ahmad Baqir, one of the prominent leaders of the SIG and the current Minster of Commerce, says:

> Thank God that Islamic banks and companies have been founded since 1978.[57]

During the global financial crisis, which caused the fall of many capitalist institutions, the Islamist political groups claimed that the fall of the capitalist system was imminent and that the only solution was in the al-Nathim al-Iqtsadi al-Islami (the Islamic economic system). In this regard, Bagir claimed that usury was behind this crisis and appealed to the Islamic countries to adopt the Islamic economic system instead of the capitalist economic system.[58] The LP–Kuwaiti Branch issued a statement calling on Kuwaiti Muslims to transfer their money from the usury American and European banks to Islamic banks and companies.[59] In another statement, the LP emphasized that Islamic systems are the only cure for the economic crisis.[60] The Islamist columnists also participated in this campaign.[61] It is important to remember that the current global financial crisis did not differentiate between capitalist banks and companies or Islamic ones.

Islamists and the media sector

The Islamist political groups sought to extend their influence to all audio and visual media. They have more than 18 magazines,[62] in addition to the daily newspapers, in which some of the fundamentalists participate in writing articles. At the level of the official visual media, the number of religious programs has increased significantly, run by some leaders of these groups, such as Khalid al-Mathkoor, 'Ajyl al-Nashmi, Mohammad al-'Awadi, Nabil al-'Awadi, and others. As for the audio media, the influence of these groups on the Quranic radio station, which was opened in 1978, was significant, where it is administered by members of these groups.

Islamists with Haj and 'Umra trips

The Islamist political groups were keen to impose their control on most Haj and 'Umra trips through symbolic financial fees in order to spread their ideology between members of the pilgrims. For mobilization purposes, it frees some of its leaders who manage and supervise the operation of these trips. These trips were run by ordinary people who have no political goals, but their aim was to be closer to God Almighty. On these trips, large amounts of religious preaching take place, and the task of education is not the responsibility of the Emir of the group or its leaders, but it is the responsibility of one of the activists, who often lacks the official religious education and sometimes launches provocative judgments. Candidates of the movement for the Parliamentary elections in Bahrain and Kuwait cover the campaigns of 'Umra and Haj financially.[63]

Islamists and the women's movement

The Islamist political groups have paid great attention to the women's movement, either through political organizations or through religious associations such as the SRS, IHRS and other religious associations, committees and branches scattered in all regions of Kuwait. The organized female leadership of these groups tried to attract and recruit the greatest possible number of women through the formation of committees, the holding of lectures and religious lessons, charitable markets, and scientific and cultural competitions throughout the year. Home visits and phone calls are made, and discussion panels in one of the leader's houses are organized. Every district has many women's committees, which play a role in the propaganda of these groups' candidates in general elections, municipal elections, co-operative societies, and other institutions of the civil society. For this reason the ICM established the Office of Women, administered by Wafa al-Ansari, who confirmed that Islamic groups have their own agenda that handles important issues in religious, social, and educational sectors, and she stressed the influential role played by women in the latest Parliamentary elections and the support of women towards the Islamist groups had achieved many seats in the National Assembly.[64] In this regard, al-Ansari says, '. . . that a movement of the group of women activists bears great responsibilities to promote high balanced performance in the ICM and its deputies in the National Assembly . . . so women must have a representation in the decision-making positions in the ICM.'[65] The Office of Women in the ICM consists of a number of committees, whose task is to deploy the movement's programs, such as the Electorate Committee, the Public Relations, the Information Committee, the Developmental Work Committee, and the Training Committee.[66]

This chapter of the study has shed some light on the support of the government for the Islamist political groups within Kuwaiti society – through the exploitation of the Islamic nature of the society on one hand and the facilities provided by the Kuwaiti regime to these groups on the other hand. Through the Islamist political groups' control over the institutions of civil societies founded by the Kuwaiti reformers since the 1920s, it indicates the internal struggle between Islamist political groups and the liberals. The Islamist political groups have tried to destroy all the progressive laws and legislations that have been achieved under the pretext of the Islamization of laws. They have taken advantage of the need of the authorities for support against the liberal, national, and leftist stream, which has dominated the political scene since the 1950s and which called for democracy and participation in the decision-making of the country. However, the government has supported these groups financially and morally by putting the official media sector in their hands, through which religious programs during religious occasions were transmitted, and through which they promote their hidden political Islamic discourse. Through this unlimited support by the authority, the Islamist political groups' activists work in public in all regions of Kuwait under fictitious names such as societies for social solidarity and charity, while, in fact, they are playing politics. In the meantime, the authorities are busy monitoring other political groups, the nationalists and the leftists, which, ironically, may be less harmful than these Islamist political groups.

6 Islamist political groups and religious violence, international terrorism

Religious violence is an old phenomenon represented in the assassination of individuals. Later it became part of the methods used by religious groups against its opponents, as is the case of the MBG in Egypt, or Jama'at al-Takfir wa al-Hijra (Society of Denouncement and Immigration) and al-Jihad al-Islami (the Islamic Jihad) in many Arab and Muslim countries, such as Tunisia, Yemen, Algeria and Pakistan. However, the events of 11 September 2001 and the emergence of al-Qaeda, led by Osama bin Laden,[1] began the emergence of a political–religious phenomenon represented in religious violence, unknown in history. It has not stopped at the borders of the Afghan capital, Kabul, but rather has been extended to become a serious threat to the United States, which had funded the Islamic Jihadist group against the Communist invasion in Afghanistan at an earlier time. This new violence in its new image reached Saudi Arabia and Kuwait, and later on settled in these countries after being utilized in the new Iraq as well.

Although this phenomenon is not entirely new, it has not been subject to research and study within the Kuwaiti society and not globally spread as it is now. Unfortunately, the Kuwaiti regime did not take it seriously, either due to its sympathy with the Islamist political groups or its carelessness in handling some terrorist incidents by some people who belonged to these groups years ago. Therefore, it is important to study this phenomenon as it has become a great worry to every society globally. No one knows when a strike will be launched. It has become clear that the security measures that have been taken to eradicate the roots of this phenomenon were ineffective, and no one and no country is safe from their tactics of violence.

This study is an initial attempt to follow up on the phenomenon of religious violence in Kuwaiti society through its theoretical and practical dimensions. The theoretical dimension is represented in monitoring the groups' literature and writings, while the practical dimension is represented in exposing the terrorist operations carried out by these groups. Nonetheless, we should be aware that this could happen only through making social and psychological studies of the characters of those who have carried out these operations. This can be achieved only by addressing the security investigations and proceedings of the trials that have been conducted. Unfortunately, these proceedings are not available at the present time because of the reluctance of the Kuwaiti Government to publish these facts and records, or to give professional access to these records.

The Islamist political groups and violence

Violence has been around since the start of human history and has always been exercised by various movements and political groups of various ideologies: national, religious and leftist. This phenomenon has been accelerated in many countries and now threatens the stability of political systems and societies around the globe. For this reason, most countries are spending most of their resources to combat it. This religious violence has been transformed into international terrorism, especially after the events of 11 September 2001. There are different definitions for religious violence. For instance, some see it as an organized conduct by some individuals affiliated with religious groups with social and political goals based on specific ideological orientation, and aimed at bringing about radical changes in the social system on the one hand and affecting change to the state's government on the other.[2] Others define religious violence as an extreme behavior that depends on the use of force by social groups who are literal in their interpretation of religious texts and, therefore, they accuse others of being infidels. The extremist groups have undertaken violent confrontation with the community, including the regime and its symbols, in a style and approach in promoting its ideas,[3] using physical as well as verbal violence, which is used in speeches, articles and religious books against the intellectuals who oppose their ideology. One of the most important objectives of religious violence of the extremist religious groups is to get rid of the political and social regime and to replace it with a religious state.

This study is based on Kuwait to discuss the phenomenon of religious violence, which is considered as a new phenomenon to Kuwaiti society. The government has not been exposed to this type of violence before, whether verbally or militarily, as demonstrated by the physical violence that is clear today. Through the study of the practical or impractical behavior that abounds in the literature of the Islamist political groups, we will notice the effect of these practices in Kuwaiti society. The study will try to analyze the phenomenon of religious violence and hence international terrorism.

Violent thought in the Islamist political groups

If we look at the shape of these groups in Kuwait in the form of the MBG, LP, SG and the Shi'ite religious groups,[4] we find that the MBG, which is a major religious group in Kuwait, has been tied to the MBG in Egypt intellectually and structurally.[5] Its founder, Hassan al-Banna, since its inception in the 1920s, promotes fighting those who do not accept the call of the MBG, by saying:

We are in a war with every leader or party leader or association which does not work to uphold Islam, not moving in the restoration of the rule of Islam and the glory of Islam. We will announce it as a hostility that does not make peace . . . until God makes a compromise between us and our people and he is the best conqueror.[6]

In his book, *Muthakirat al-Da'wa wa'l-Da'iyya* (*Memoirs of Mission and the Missionary*), al-Banna divided the Muslim community into two categories: those who belong to the MBG and are considered to be the believers, and the rest, who are not strict Muslims.[7] Since the first years of the formation of the MBG, al-Banna sought to form military formations called Kataeb Ansar Allah (Battalions of Supporters of God), which started in 1940 and adopted the slogan Amer Wata'h (the obedience) and al-Nisam al-Khassah (Special Organization) as a prelude to other stages of the group that would bring it forward to achieve its goal towards rulership.[8] In this regard, al-Banna says:

At the time that they will be ready, Oh ye the Muslim Brotherhood the three hundred battalion, each one equipped spiritually with faith and belief, intellectually with science and learning, and physically with training and athletics, at that time you can demand of me to plunge with you through the turbulent oceans and to rend the skies with you and to conquer with you every obstinate tyrant, God willing, I will do it.[9]

The oath is taken in front of the Supreme Guide for the MBG with the Quran and the gun.[10] Mohammad Hamid Abu-Nasr mentions in his memoirs:

Hassan al-Banna was very happy during my performance of the oath, when I took out my gun, and I said that the gun is the solution.[11]

In fact, the language of violence exists in the literature of the group since its foundation, as Sheikh 'Abdul-Rahman al-Saa'ti, the father of al-Banna, wrote in the first issue of *Majallat al-Natheer* (the *Warner Journal*), issued by the MBG in Egypt in 1938, in an article entitled 'Oh soldiers prepare yourselves,' where he said:

Oh soldiers, prepare yourselves and each of you take an action and prepare his weapon and do not look backward and go to where you are ordered to go . . . Take this nation gently because it needs this care and attention, and describe the medicine for it. How many suffering heart and bodies on the banks of the Nile, prepare it in your pharmacy and to be given by a group of you, if the nation refuses it then put handcuffs in their hands and iron on their backs and give them the medicine by force. If you find a cancerous part, then remove it . . . Oh soldiers, prepare yourselves – many of the people of this nation have deafness in the ears and blindness in the eyes.[12]

After that, the MBG went through a conflict with the palace after the latter discovered their plot, their secret organization and their danger. The palace in Egypt changed its position towards the entire group, but such measures were ineffective as the group had already been allowed to grow and to penetrate into the Egyptian political and social life. Subsequently, the Egyptian Government took strict measures against this violent group, starting with the closure of its Muslim Brotherhood newspaper and concluding with issuing a resolution to dissolve the group on 8 December 1948. In retaliation, the MBG has assassinated the Prime Minister on 28 December 1948, Mahmoud Fahmi al-Nuqrashi Pasha. The regime responded by assassinating the leader of the group, Hassan al-Banna, on 12 February 1949. After three months, the MBG responded to the assassination of al-Banna by attempting to assassinate Ibrahim 'Abdul-Hadi Pasha, who became the Prime Minister after al-Nuqrashi, but this attempt was unsuccessful.[13] Consequently, the ideas published by Sayyed Qutb in his book, *Ma'alim fi al-Tareeq* (*Milestones*), are regarded as the manifesto for the Sunni Islamic radical groups in most Arab and Islamic countries, in which he dealt with the issue of the jahiliyya society (pre-Islamic times). He considered all societies, including contemporary Muslim societies, as the Jahiliyya communities. He defines the jahiliyya society as:

> It is every society that is not faithful in worshiping God alone . . . This worship is represented in the creed and practice . . . In the heavenly creed . . . By this logical definition, all existing communities are regarded to lie in the mainframe of the jahiliyya communities.[14]

He therefore called for the destruction of the human kingdom to establish the kingdom of God on earth by force. Qutb's discourse defines the concept of the divine laws being the slavery of God only and freedom from the governance of human beings, which includes democratic political systems, socialism and secularism. From this standpoint the Qutb discourse emphasizes that:

> Islam is not any doctrine or practice of social status, nor is it any system of a governance situation . . . in all its various names and flags . . . But it is Islam only! Islam is in its distinct, independent, and imaginable image.[15]

Moreover, this doctrine adds that there is no place for coexistence between the God Governorate and the people's. This is why Sayyed Qutb sees that:

> Due to the basic difference between the nature of God and the people's nature, it is impossible for them to meet in the same position. It is impossible to fabricate half from here and half from there. Since God does not forgive the belief in any other than God, then God does not accept any way of life other than the one He prescribes.[16]

From here the extremist ideology has shaped into verbal violence calling for the elimination of the political regimes that had emerged. This was clear in the writings of the Islamist political groups in Kuwait. In an opening article in *Majallat al-Mujtama'*, entitled 'limiting the circle of conflict', it considered that the actual enemy that the Islamic movement has to confront is the political regimes, by saying:

> The actual and day-to-day enemy of the Islamic Movement is the regimes and the actual day-to-day obstacle in the Islamic movement march is the regimes . . . The battle for the Islamic movement is not with the uncommitted girls or westernized women, and not with the low standard programs in the media, not with the banks, which absorb the blood of the poor and inject it in the tummies of the rich and not with concerts . . . This is not the battle of the Islamic movements and not to be restricted in these secondary boundaries . . . The actual battle of the Islamic Movement should be with the regimes, which caused this situation . . . Briefly, we can say that if the Islamic movement wants to make some achievements through its existing approach, which needs to be reviewed, it should first limit the circle of conflict and identify the enemy and its objectives.[17]

Dr. 'Abdullah al-Nafeesi,[18] in his book entitled *'Indama Yahkum al-Iislam* (*When Islam Rules*), confirms the illegality of the rule of the ruling families in the Islamic countries and says:

> The rule of the family whether Mimed, 'Abbasiya, Fatimid, Hamdaniyah, Ottoman, or any ruling family today in the Muslim world, which has no will of its own is a swamp for all illegal ambitions, which history is full of and which has led to all the political, economic, and social collapses of the Islamic nation that we are suffering from in our present time.[19]

He considered all the families that ruled the Islamic countries, from the rule of the Amawi until today, as the most serious deviation that took place in Islamic history.[20] Al-Nafeesi, in his book, later provokes the people of the Islamic countries to make a revolution against the ruling regimes of the Arab countries at the present time by saying:

> By watching the reality of these ruling regimes today in the land of Islam, an important fact is discovered, that is that these regimes did not take over the land of the Muslims accidentally. These regimes are a natural extension of infidel Western colonialism, and if our legitimate duty is to fight the infidel Western colonial powers so that the entire religion is to God, then it is obvious that we fight these regimes that are on the front line of the infidel Western colonial powers. It is regrettable that some Islamic groups are worried about the revolutionary methods in the process of change.[21]

'Ajil al-Nashmi, one of the moderate leaders of the MBG, emphasizes in a study on al-Harka al-Islamia Wadorah fi Yaqdath al-'Alm al-Islami (Islamic Movements and their Role in the Vigilance of the Islamic World) that:

> The call of the Muslim Brotherhood was based on the principle of inclusiveness, i.e. Islam is comprehensive for religious and life affairs, and distinguished their call through the commitment to a number of bases, including the use of force to achieve their goals from the strength of belief and faith, to the strength of unity and link, and then to the strength of arms and disarmament.[22]

Dr. Hamdi Shua'ib, in his article in *Majallat al-Mujtama'* entitled Nahwa Moata Sharifah (Towards Honest Death: the nation that is good in the industry of death is rewarded with life), urged all Muslims to disseminate the culture of death and to engage themselves in the manufacture of death and to follow Sayyed Qutb. He states:

> As stated in the literature of the Islamic movement: that the nation that improves the industry of death and learns how to die an honorable death, God will gift her with a blessed life and eternal bliss in the Hereafter. The illusion which humiliated us is only the love of life and hatred of death. Prepare yourselves for a great work. Be keen for death and life will be gifted to you ... Let the objective which we put on the top of our list be: one of two options: ... either life that makes our friends happy or a death that makes our enemy furious, or as Sayyed Qutb says, choose either to have a victory over the creatures or to have a life with God in heavens.[23]

The LP ideology is based on the ideas and concepts developed by the founder of the party, Taqi al-Deen al-Nabhani; these are radical ideas that refuse the existing regimes and call for their elimination on the basis that they are weak entities and proposes the establishment of an Islamic Caliphate State. The party calls for the demolition of these regimes, the constitutions, and the existing laws that are based on the infidels, and work to alert the people that the mere existence of such governments, governance, and laws is munkar (evil) that must be removed.[24] The party tried to amplify these ideas by putting them into practice in 1974, when the party in Egypt tried to seize power under the leadership of Saleh Sariya.[25] He regarded 'the current regimes in all Muslim countries as disbelievers, there is no doubt about that.'[26] He believes that the only way to change the infidel regimes is through declaring jihad. He said, 'The Jihad to change these governments and the establishment of an Islamic state is an obligation of every Muslim, because jihad continues until the Day of Resurrection.'[27]

As Sheikh Hamid 'Abdullah al-'Ali, the former Secretary of the SM,[28] believes:

The infidel Imam . . . is incorrect, because it is based on corruption and perversion of the Muslim religion, because it is a call for corrupting the provisions of legitimacy, . . . It also decided that the ruler of the Muslims who must be obeyed is the one who guards the religion of Muslims, and the one who governs with the secular Constitution, is the guardian for what he says and not the guardian of the Muslims.[29]

He calls for Takfir (excommunication) of the ruler if he kept the inherited manmade laws.[34] 'Abdul-Razzaq al-Shayji, a prominent member of the Salafiyah Group, supports the assassination of the liberal intellectuals, where on the occasion of the assassination of Faraj Fouda, he says:

They forgot or were trying to forget the fact that clearing the land from these secularists is a duty, if possible . . . jihad against those is similar to jihad against the infidels . . . The interests of religion and Shari'a lies in clearing the land from those secularists.[30]

In another article, the al-Shayji group describe themselves as vanguards who are not afraid of death for the sake of God and are not afraid from the enemies of Islam.[31]

In a continuation of this line of verbal violence provoking the revolution, Hakem al-Mutairi, former Secretary General of the SM and the Secretary General of the NP currently, confirms in his book *al-Hrurriya aw al-Toofan* (*The Freedom or Destruction*) that 'If the Quran and the Sunnah decree are in order, then the Sword must follow God's decree.'[32] After that, he concluded that the Arab and Islamic nations are required to make a revolution on the existing regimes and to work on the establishment of a religious state. He says:

The Islamic nation and the Arab, particularly today, is in need of a theoretical revolution, that blasts the concepts of the forged political discourse and shall have to work to revive the concepts of religious polit- ical discourse, as the right of the nation in the selection of the regime through Shura . . . And its right to remove it when it deviates . . . All the movements and ideologies in the world achieved their reform projects after gaining power, as happened in the French Revolution, the Russian Revolution, and the American Revolution . . . History did not witness any reform movement that succeeded in achieving its reforms in a differ- ent way . . . And the nation has to find a way to achieve renaissance by using every legitimate means peaceful or revolutionary, with the consent of the regime and its participation, or without it. The nations have the right to fight for their religion, freedom, rights and dignity . . . The 'Ulama prohibited the confrontation with the tyranny of the regime and its deviation, for fear of the immoral consequences, and the result was an entire nation under colonialism . . . The Islamic world has suffered a setback that it cannot recover from unless it goes through an intellectual and political revolution, and such revolution has become a social and religious necessity.[33]

If we look at the literature and programs of these groups, including those which claim to be moderate groups such as the ICM, the SM, and the NP, it is evident that they call for the application of Islamic Shari'a and for Islam to become the sole source of legislation, not a major source as stipulated in the Constitution of the State of Kuwait. This means that these groups do not recognize the legitimacy of the existing political system and seek to change the social and political basis of the regime.[34] Furthermore, when they speak of freedom and rights, it appears to be only their freedom and rights, and not others'. On this basis, Sheikh Jassim Mhalhal al-Yasin, the former Secretary of the ICM, urged to change all articles that are contrary to God's law in the Kuwaiti Constitution.[35]

The truth is that all these groups exclude all existing political models and they have the desire to achieve the establishment of an Islamic state. In other words, they seek to establish a state based on the application of Shari'a, which means that the political and religious systems must be joined. All of these groups, from Morocco to Indonesia, emphasize that Islam and the state are integral to each other.[36] This is confirmed by Hassan al-Banna's letters, where he states:

> We believe the provision of Islam and its teachings are all inclusive, encompassing the affairs of the people in this world and the hereafter. And those who think that these teachings are concerned only with the spiritual or ritualistic aspects are mistaken in this belief because Islam is a faith and a ritual, a nation (watan) and a nationality and a state, spirit and deed, holy text and sword . . . The Glorious Qur'an . . . considers [these things] to be the core of Islam and its essence . . .[37]

Furthermore, take note that these groups describe themselves as being moderate political groups and ironically have the following ideology:

1   Their support for the armed violence in Iraq, especially after the intensification of fighting in the city of Fallujah between the American forces and terrorist groups of the remaining Ba'athist members of the former regime and al-Qaeda led by Abu Mus'ab al-Zarqawi.[38] They have been active in issuing political statements and press statements by the representatives of some of these groups in the National Assembly, and promoting an incitement campaign against the American presence in Iraq.[39] In this context, one of the representatives of the Islamic Independent Bloc, MP Saa'd al-Sharia', refused to describe Osama Bin Laden, the leader of al-Qaeda, as a terrorist; he saw in him something different from what President George W. Bush does.[40] He also mentioned on the occasion of the killing of Abu Musab al-Zarqawi by an American raid

that he may agree with al-Zarqawi and may differ with him on many points.[41] This statement led the National Democratic coalition to demand al-Shari'a, and for those who praised Osama bin Laden, to apologize in public on the pages of newspapers to the Kuwaiti people and all the victims of this terrorist.[42] The people of Kuwait regarded the praise for this criminal as a provocation to the feelings of the people and an encouragement to his followers, especially among the young people in the Gulf countries towards the path of violence and extremism, most especially since al-Qaeda is a threat to the Gulf States.[43]

2   Despite the denial of these groups and their denial of adopting the method of violence and despite them saying that they fight terrorism and represent a moderate line, they have a noticeable tendency to make excuses for groups of religious extremism – sometimes under the pretext that such violence is a reaction to the violence against these groups, and at other times that foreign hands are behind this violence, as seen by 'Abdullah 'Ali al-Mutawa', when commenting on the bombings that took place in the underground stations in London in 2005. He hinted at the possibility of the involvement of Mussed, the Secret Irish Army, and foreign intelligence fabricating such events to attack Islam and Muslims.[44] In an interview with *Majallat al-Mujtama'*, al-Mutawa' confirms that 'there is no Islamic call in any Arab or Muslim country that calls for terrorism. Terrorism is a lie invented by the Mussed and the foreign intelligence to attack the Islamic awakening, accusing the religious youth of extremism and fundamentalism, which we did not hear about before. Unfortunately, there are some people who believe this in our Arab countries.'[45] Accordingly, it is evident that there is a refusal of these Islamist political groups from issuing any direct and clear convictions for the terrorist attacks made by the extremist wings such as al-Qaeda in Morocco, Algeria, the United States, Britain, Spain, Egypt, Jordan, Bangladesh, Turkey, Iraq and other countries, while at the same time, some other Islamist political groups that claim to be moderate have tried to make excuses for some of the terrorist actions.

These groups claim moderation so as to give themselves political cover and then try to simplify the terrorist operations carried out by the extremist wing within these groups: for instance, the demand of 13 members of the National Assembly who represented the Islamist political groups not to publish the pictures of those who are convicted in cases of a terrorist nature in local newspapers and magazines,[46] only for it to be discovered later that some of them belong to al-Qaeda.[47] In addition, some of these members attempt to intervene and put pressure on the executive and judiciary authorities to release those involved in terrorist operations. They took advantage of being representatives in the National Assembly, as was the case when one of the religious symbols of one of the Islamist political groups was arrested and then accused of the terrorist attacks in Kuwait in early January 2005.[48]

Religious violence can take several forms. First, verbal violence and the incitement against differing opinions through religious speeches in mosques and in the media are both excellent examples of extremism. Another example involves issuing religious Fatwa and hisba (enforcement of religious laws) and calling people Murtadd (apostate) before the courts in order to create fear in people with liberal views. The second type is physical violence, which is represented with political assassinations, armed clashes with security forces and attacking government institutions and Western interests by a show of force with arms. Kuwaiti society has witnessed waves of religious violence, both verbal and physical, as follows:

First, literature releases, statements and publications issued by the leaders of the Islamist political groups in Kuwait encouraged and called Muslims to fight the Americans and the infidel regimes, as well as fatwas accusing the artists, intellectuals, and men of letters as being infidels. Threats of death were received by writers and thinkers, as happened to Dr. Ahmad al-Baghdadi, the professor of Islamic political thought at Kuwait University, Dr. Shamlan al-'Isa and the singer, 'Abdullah Rwaishid, accusing all of them of apostasy, prejudicing the fundamentals of the nation and assaulting God. In addition to the threats by Ansaer Qaedat al-Jihad fi Bilad al-Rafidayn (supporters of al-Qaeda for Jihad in the land of the Two Rivers), they targeted the cast of the play *A Kuwaiti in Fallujah*, which they claimed spoiled the image of jihad in Iraq, as well as the image of the free and honest Kuwaiti Mujahideen in Fallujah. They said:

> We warn strongly all those who contributed to the production of this play from the director, actor, or photographer, and swear to Almighty God that if you do not stop showing such plays, which make a mockery of mujahideen, then we will attack every one who took part in this play impurely, and we will contact the mujahideen brothers in Iraq to attack the headquarters of the Kuwaiti channel and kill its correspondents in Iraq, as well as the al-Arabiya television channel which was struck.

Under this threat, the administration of the theater was forced to change the name of the play to *Love in Fallujah*.[49]

Moreover, threats were sent by a member of the Islamist political groups to the journalist 'Aisha al-Rashaid, who contested the elections of the National Assembly in 2007, warning her to stay away from this participation, asking her to refer to God and his rules according to Shari'a before it is too late, and to not mix with men.[50] There was also the threat of assassinating MP 'Ali al-Rashed, one of the National Democratic Alliance leaders, because he submitted a bill to cancel the prevention of co-education law at Kuwait University.[51]

Second, some citizens belonging to the Islamist political groups have made criminal complaints against a number of writers and literary groups, charging them with murtadd and hisba. Examples of this include:

- The complaint against the writer Laila al-'Othman and the publisher Yahya al-Rubay'an as an objection to what was written in the story *fi Alail Tatai al'aion* (*In the Night, Eyes Come*) and *Araheil* (*Leave*), which they believed called for adultery and vice.
- The complaint against Dr. 'Alia Shua'ib regarding some texts in her book *'Anakab Tarthey Jaerhan* (*Spiders Both Lamented Wound*).
- The complaint against Mohammad Salman Ghanim and the publisher Ahmad al-dieen on what was in the book *Alah we aljam'a* (*God and the Community*).
- Hesba was roughly against Dr. Suleimman al-Bader following an interview with the *al-Anba* newspaper. This was the first hesba lawsuit against a Kuwaiti citizen.
- The lawsuit that came against Ahmad al-Dieen because of an article published opposing the adoption of Shari'a penalties in the penal code.
- The lawsuits against Dr. Ahmad al-Baghdadi in objection to the articles and Islamic studies published in the local press under the name hisba, which led to his conviction and being imprisoned with an ordered suspension of his sentence for a period of three years provided that the accused pays bail and adheres to the observance of good conduct, and that he adheres to the financial deposit and ethical behavior for a three-year period, and the implementation of a retroactive prison sentence if convicted of any misdemeanor or any other releases. Before that, al-Baghdadi was also sentenced to imprisonment for one month.[52] This caused the liberal groups to call for confronting this theoretical religious terrorism, which calls for the silencing of writers and strips them of their freedom of expression guaranteed by the Constitution and by law, and to fight ideological terrorism, work to abolish the concept of hesba from Kuwaiti legal proceedings, and the transfer of press lawsuits to the Ministry of Information. They regarded what happened to Dr. Al-Baghdadi as only a small part of what is happening to Arab intellectuals in Arab communities from sabotage and misinformation through the dissemination of withholding others' opinion, and trying to imprison the wise intellectuals, or to kill, or expel them outside the borders of their homelands. In Kuwait this is an exclusive model, representing the exclusion and distortion of the meaning of Islam exercised by the extremist Salafists spreading throughout the country and the region. Intellectuals consider what is happening an attack aiming to impose its opinion by creating a totalitarian society and an assault on freedom of opinion and expression guaranteed by the Constitution. Furthermore, they describe the attack as not being between the protestors of morality and unbelievers as described by the religious groups, but that it has a political nature that is between the forces that want to impose its project in establishing a religious state and the forces that are defending the Constitution and public freedoms.[53]
- In a symposium organized by Shabab Masjed al-Jahra (the Jahra Youth

Mosque) entitled *al-Mashru'al-'Almanifial-Kuwatiwaal-Khalejal-'Arabai* (*The Secular Project in Kuwait and the Gulf*), Sheikh Hamid 'Abdullah al-'Ali described those who defend the freedom of opinion, such as the Journalists Association, Lajnat al-Dafa' 'an Hrait al-Rai (Defense of Freedom of Opinion Committee) and the liberal writers, as being secular and traitors who receive instructions from the foreign embassies in Kuwait, who violate the Islamic Shari'a and must be demolished.[54] He urged the Islamic groups to use all available means against the secular campaigns, those who misuse Islam, according to him.[55]

From this standpoint, we find that 'Abdul-Razzaq al-Shayji has announced in public that they are carefully monitoring all that is being written in the press, and they are preparing files with the names of writers, authors and poets to put them under their supervision.[56] 'Abdullah 'Ali al-Mutawa' did the same thing when he called for the trial of the liberal authors and opened the files of these intellectuals, demanding the dismissal of the liberal university professors. He emphasized that the intention of the Islamist MPs in the National Assembly is to expel through the available constitutional channels some university professors, which he described as having a deviant orientation. Furthermore, he felt there was a need to protect the community from those groups that operate according to foreign agendas designed to destroy the society through questioning the basic beliefs.[57] He urged the chief editors of the local newspapers to clear their newspapers of these types of writers.[58] This reminds us of the era of the black fascists and Nazi regimes in Europe, which were active in the pursuit of cultural and intellectual leaders, where the European intellectual was the symbol of resistance to fascism.[59] It also reminds us of the fascist regimes that have prevailed in some Arab countries, such as the totalitarian regimes that have chased, arrested and executed Arab intellectuals who were a symbol of resistance to fascism, Nazism and Communism.

This verbal violence is being transformed to physical violence, similar to what is happening in other Arab countries; this is based on the physical liquidation of those who question those who may be incorrectly interpreting Shari'a – for example, the fatwa issued in the early 1980s by Hassan al-Turabi, the leader of the MBG in Sudan, with the application of Murtadd (apostate) on Mahmood Mohammad Taha, who was later executed. In addition, there was the assassination of Faraj Fouda and the attempted assassination of the novelist Nagib Mahfouz in Egypt, who was stabbed with a knife by one of the terrorists because of a fatwa issued convicting him of apostasy in response to what he wrote in his novel *Awlad Haratna* (*The Boys of our Neighborhood*). Furthermore in Algeria, Islamic terrorist groups have assassinated 60 intellectuals, artists and writers.[60]

The roots of the physical violence that has been carried out by the Islamist political groups within Kuwaiti society has expanded since the organized attack by members belonging to the SRS on 13 November 1971 on male and female students in Kuwait University on the occasion of holding a symposium on segregation at Kuwait University. This informational session was organized by NUKS, but then developed to a battle when 400 members of the SRS intervened and distributed themselves in a similar fashion to military troops. The SRS members had left, right and heart positions; they wanted to prevent the continuation of this symposium because, according to them, the organizers (NUKS) and the participants were infidels.[61] This led to a confrontation between the SRS members and the organizers, which resulted in the injury of several students and the intervention of the security police to control the situation. It was described by *Majallat Ajyal* (*Generations Journal*) in its first page as a dangerous way to terrorize the opponents, where beating replaced the dialogue.[62] *Majallat al-Itihad* (the *Union Journal*), the mouthpiece of NUKS, described the SRS group as monkeys who had invaded the university. The reactionary forces did the planning and the blind forces carried it out.[63] This incident made a tremendous impact in the political atmosphere between the Islamist political groups on one hand and the liberal and leftist groups on the other hand. The Council of Ministers took the decision to close the SRS journal, *al-Mujtama'*, for three months, which described the advocates of no segregated education with not representing the nation's conscience, its sense of religion, its values of honor and virtue.[64] However, they were Kuwaiti citizens expressing their opinion.

The return of democratic life in the early 1980s led to political stability, so much so that the country did not witness any terrorist operations – except for some incidents carried out by some Shi'ite groups during the Iraqi–Iran war. It is noted that Kuwaiti society did not deal with the hard-line fatwas at that time and there was not much of an American presence in Kuwait.

After the liberation of Kuwait, the political arena witnessed a remarkable escalation in the pace of acts of violence by extremist religious groups, which had never been seen by Kuwaiti society before. For example:[65]

1   On 6 May 1991 a car bomb explosion took place in the Yarmouk district in front of the house of the Dean of the Faculty of Medicine, Dr. Hilal al-Sayer, who is one of the liberal advocates in Kuwait.
2   On 15 July 1991 an explosion occurred at Markaz al-Funoon (the Center for the Arts), which is a place for the sale of videotapes in the Salimiya district.
3   An armed attack took place at the National Evangelical Church in Kuwait on Christmas Eve in 1992 by a masked group; all hands pointed to an unknown extremist religious group, although the case was registered against unknown elements.
4   On 1 February 1992 an explosion occurred at Sharikat al-Hizam al-Azraq (the Blue Belt Company) for the sale of videotapes in the Farwaniya district.

5 On 8 May 1992 there was an attempt to assassinate the actor, ʿAbdul-Hussein ʿAbdul-Ridha, where he was subjected to a hail of bullets.

6 On 24 May 1992 there was an armed attack aimed at members of the Italian circus; two people were injured.

7 On 20 June 1992 there was an armed attack on the workers in the Roman circus that led to the wounding of four people (of British and Indian nationality).

8 On 26 June 1992 an explosive device was detonated near the home of Dr. Hilal al-Sayer.

9 On 26 June 1992 there was an attempt to assassinate Bashar ʿAbdul-Ridha, the son of the actor ʿAbdul-Hussein ʿAbdul-Ridha.

10 On 5 September 1992 there was an explosion in an audio recording studio and a video shop in the Abraq Khaitan district.

11 On 1 December 1992 a large quantity of weapons and ammunition belonging to members of the Islamist political groups was discovered in the Sulabiya district.

12 On 10 December 1992 an explosion occurred in a videotape shop in the Abraq Khaitan district.

13 On 11 December 1992 an explosion occurred in a videotape shop in Abraq Khaitan.

14 On 12 December 1992 there was an explosion in the Salmeen shop for the sale of musical instruments.

15 On 16 December 1992 there was a report about the existence of a car bomb with dynamite in the College of Medicine; the security forces were able to diffuse it.

16 On 12 March 1993, the Russian circus exploded.

17 In April 1993 members of a sabotage group, who were accused of attempting to assassinate the former President George Bush during his visit to Kuwait, were arrested.

18 In October 1995, the extremist groups threw a tear-gas bomb at the crowd celebrating the victory made by the Democratic List in the elections in the College of Administrative Sciences Association.

19 In April 1996, a group of young radical members of the CIRM attacked the premises of *al-Seyassah* newspaper in an attempt to assassinate one of the employees of the *Arab Times* newspaper issued by Dar al-Seyassah on the grounds that he published a cartoon mocking God Almighty. The group was detained by the security forces, which called them extremists and terrorists.

20 In 1997, a group of extremists called Jamaʿat al-Jald al-Sahrawi (the Desert Scourge Group) abducted a number of people from the Indian community, the Bohra sect, and scourged them. They also abducted a Bengali, moved him to an uninhabited desert area, and savagely beat him, claiming the implementation of a legitimate rule in which they proved he had a relationship with an Asian girl, which according to them is a Zina (adultery) case.[66] In this context, Sheikh Mashʾaal Jarrah

al-Sabah (Head of State's security), emphasized that this is a new phenomenon in Kuwait and that this group had grown up under the blessing of the influential people in the state.[67]

21 Some extremist people of the Sunni sect groups attacked the construction of a new mosque for the Shi'ites in the Bayan district by burning the building. In addition, a number of armed extremists attacked the Ahmad al-Yasin Husaniya in the Mansuriyah district; the security forces managed to arrest 21 of them, who belonged to one of the extremist religious groups in Kuwait.[68]

22 In April 2000, an Islamic extremist group physically assaulted a female student in the College of Business Studies.[69]

23 In December 2000, a sabotage group was arrested for the possession of 133 kilograms of explosives and bombs.

24 Dr. Falah Mendkar al-Kanderi, the professor of Shari'a in Kuwait University, was assaulted by a group of extremist students from the Faculty of Shari'a who stormed into his office. They took the study prepared by him under the title, 'The infidels . . . The danger in terms of origin and history', claiming that this study would be forwarded to the Taliban Movement for a decision on the type of judgment to be applied against him, which they considered as an implementation of hisba.[70] The University Faculty Association regarded this incident as the nucleus of terrorism in Kuwait, which must be eradicated. The attacked professor expressed that there were deviant groups behind this attack.[71] It is well known that Dr. Falah al-Kandari is a follower of the group al-Jama'ah al-Jamiah (al-Jamiah Group) attributed to Sheikh Mohammed Aman al-Jaime.[72] This group does not share in the ideology of the religious extreme groups in their views towards the rulers, whom they consider that their obedience is a must, based on the sayings of Imam Ahmad Bin Hunbel.[73] Furthermore, Sheikh Mohammad al-Madkhli, the pioneer of the al-Jamiyia school, sees the obedience of the rulers as Faridha (duty), even if they are unjust, so as to keep their prestige in front of the people.[74]

25 In September 2007, the office of the MBC satellite station was attacked by an anonymous group due to its intention to broadcast a series called *Lilkhatiah Thaman* (*The Sin Has a Price*); the writer of the series was sent to the prosecutor by the Ministry of Information. Due to these threats, the station decided not to broadcast the series.

There are several factors that have encouraged the extremist Islamic groups to use various methods of violence, whether verbally or physically, to resolve their differences with others, to show contempt and attack the authority of the State, and attempt to impose the religious state by force:

First, the release of a considerable number of these terrorists after being arrested by the Kuwaiti State Security. Among them were those who had participated later in the attacks executed by al-Qaeda in January 2005, such as Mohsin al-Fadli, Khalid al-Dosari, and 'Amer Khalif al-Enezi. In addition, the terrorist attacks in the Kuwaiti arena since the mid-1990s, starting with the Jama'at al-Jald al-Sahrawi incident and ending with the case of recruiting the youth in Kuwait. Another example is the case of the physical assault of a female student at the Institute of Business Studies. One of those who carried out this assault belonged to an Islamist political group. He was sentenced to imprisonment for one year and then was released, leaving for Afghanistan, where the American forces arrested him; he served four years in the Guantanamo Bay prison. Baddy Cruse al-'Ajmi was charged in 1999 for distributing leaflets against February concerts and the case was kept administratively. In 2000, he was accused of participating in the case of the student of the College of Business Studies, and was sentenced to a year, but was released before the completion of his sentence. In 2001, the Criminal Court endorsed by the Appeals Court abstained from the punishment of the same accused man in the case of sabotaging the network whose objective was the bombing of the Israeli trade office in Qatar. Moreover, in 2003 the Criminal Court sentenced him to three years when an American contractor was killed near the Doha Camp, accusing him of providing the first suspect, Sami al-Mutairi, with the weapon used in the crime.[75]

Second, the regime's tolerance and lack of seriousness towards the danger of the Islamic terrorist groups in which the punishments are subject to tribal interventions and the interventions of the representatives of the Islamist political groups in the National Assembly. The Kuwaiti writer 'Abdul-Latif al-Di'aij criticized the Kuwaiti Government as the number one terrorist for its allowance for the extremist groups to spread among Kuwaiti society. In this regard, he says:

> Let our government start with itself, if it is serious in fighting terrorism, unfortunately, the government is the number one terrorist; as it has facilitated the strength of the religious groups, which until now encourages these forces to impose its religious terror on the rest of God's creatures.[76]

Dr. Ahmad al-Khatib, one of the leaders of the KDF, who reflects the point of view of the liberal trend, holds the political regime responsible for not confronting religious extremism. He considers that the coalition between the government and the religious forces will transform Kuwait to another Fallujah, warning that the presence of the religious groups in the government has no limit and will not be deterred from the cancellation of the political regime.[77] Finally, the Kuwaiti regime realized the seriousness of these groups when Sheikh Nasser al-Mohammad al-Sabah, the former Minister of the Amiri Diwan and the current Prime Minister, in an interview with the Egyptian magazine *al-Mussawar*, spotted the danger of the religious groups, saying that:

> Some of their supporters who support the extremist Jihad ideology exploit the atmosphere of democracy and stability in Kuwait and

some of them hold seminars and lectures with the slogan of fighting terrorism, while in fact, it is a false front in an attempt to avert suspicions about them.[78]

He stressed that 'those extremists have one goal, and that is to seize power using various methods to establish God's law in their own way and in accordance with the methods based on extremism, hatred of others, and fighting foreigners, and calling them infidels.'[79]

Third, the political cover created by the Islamist political groups in Kuwait through statements they make or through the press, attempting to alleviate the religious violence carried out by the extremist religious groups is done by trying to make excuses for them. At times the excuse is that the incidents are carried out by youngsters, and at other times there is a conspiracy against Islamic action in Kuwait by the liberal current.

Fourth, the prevailing laws, such as the Press and Publication Act, and the Penal Code, which has paved the way for raising lawsuits, such as Hisba and Murtadd, as described by Dr. Ahmad al-Baghdadi, in an article published in *al-Seyassah* newspaper, on criminal laws.[80] On the basis of such laws, there have been a number of liberal intellectuals and writers who have been served with lawsuits because they expressed their own opinion in the media, and among them was Dr. al-Baghdadi.

Fifth, the negligence of the official media for allowing propaganda to guide and direct the citizens from the danger of the extremist religious groups. On the contrary, the regime has opened its media widely to the extremist religious advocates through increasing the huge doses of religious programs broadcast by advocates of religious extremism.

Sixth, the trips sponsored by the Islamist political groups, which call for moderation in theory and are made under the cover of charity activities since the beginning of the military clashes between the Afghan Government and the mujahideen. However, in practice, they do not promote peace. These groups push some young people to pay visits to countries such as Afghanistan and Pakistan under the justification of charitable activities. However, these trips have hidden political objectives, where, for example, some of them are allowed to attend meetings held by the Taliban leaders in Afghanistan, most especially before its fall. Some might have met leaders of al-Qaeda, such as Osama bin Laden, and Suleimman Abu Ghaith and others. The unknowing 'tourists' most likely have also participated in further meetings with the leaders of the second and third ranks of the movement. The significance of these meetings lies in its ability to create a state of enthusiasm among the participating members of the associations, which can then be invested later when those boys return home. These journeys, before the fall of the Taliban regime, were taking place with the knowledge of the Kuwaiti regime and they did not move to limit this phenomenon; this, in turn, has created a spirit of extremism among some of our Muslim youth.

Seventh, the regime did not take strict actions towards the extremist religious discourse issued by some parties related to the Islamist political groups by allowing them to issue Fatwas, make speeches in mosques, publish leaflets, publish cassettes or tapes, and use any other means calling for Takfir of the writers, men of letters and literature, and other Islamic sects, such as Shi'ites who are part of the community in Kuwait and other Gulf states. This lenient policy has encouraged religious violence among the extremist groups towards those who differ with them in their opinion. The Islamic extremists have demanded tolerance from the regimes of various countries, but they do not practice what they demand.

Finally, the non-existence of an Anti-Terrorism Act, which should be issued by the Kuwaiti regime.

These terrorist acts and the Takfir of the intellectuals and men of literature carried out by groups of religious violence is an assault on the power of the State. It confirms a set of facts, on top of which is the fact that this type of criminal activity has endangered the lives of the citizens of Kuwait and that the dignity of the State and its power have been subjected to many tests for a long time by those who do not believe that the State is a power over their spiritual power. Moreover, they do not even believe in the State's constitution, yet demand they have freedom of speech – again demanding it but not giving it. It seems that these attacks are only the beginning of more violent conduct to come under the pretext of applying Shari'a or imposing it.

7 The armed Islamist Sunni jihadist groups

The roots for the armed Islamist jihadist Sunni groups in Kuwait are based on the fact that some of its members were influenced by the following:

First: the influence of al-Jama'a al-Salafiah al-Muhtasiba (Group of Ethical Control (GEC)), which originated in Madina in the mid-1960s. This group was affected by Sheikh Nasser al-Deen al-Albani, who was born in 1914 in Albania in a poor religious family. He migrated to Damascus with his father and they settled there. Al-Albani was arrested twice by the Syrian security forces; the first time was in 1967 when he was imprisoned for one month in al-Qal'a Jail and was released during the war of 1967 together with other Syrian political prisoners. The second time was shortly after his release, when he stayed for 18 months in the al-Hasaka Jail. Al-Albani made several visits to different Arab and non-Arab countries, such as Kuwait, Saudi Arabia and Spain, where he gave different religious lectures. Sheikh al-Albani wrote many books and he is regarded as a religious authority for the Salafist groups in the Arab and Islamic countries, such as the SIG in Kuwait. Sheikh al-Albani died on 2 October 1999. Al-Albani rejected all schools of Islamic Fiqh (jurisprudence), including Wahhabism, and instead he adopted the Hadiths (the Prophet Mohammad's sayings) as a means for practicing religious duties.[1] The GEC was keen to host him during his visit to Saudi Arabia to perform the pilgrimage in Mecca. He gave lectures to teach the members of the GEC. Sheikh ʿAbdul-ʾAziz Bin Baz was the spiritual leader for the GEC, which is run by a Shura (Consultative) Council composed of five members. Bayt al-Ikhwan (House of the Brotherhood) was founded by the GEC, located in Madina, where the headquarters of the GEC is located.[2]

The group succeeded in attracting many members from various Saudi cities, most of whom were Bedouins, whose ages varied from 20 to 40 years. It had branches in most Saudi cities, such as Riyadh, Dammam, Jeddah, Mecca and others; each branch had its own local leader. The GEC had strong relations with the Ansar al-Sunna al-Mohammadiya (Supporters of Mohammad's Tradition) in Egypt. The GEC used to host their sheikhs yearly during their visit to the Holy Land to perform Haj and also at a reunion of religious lectures in Bayt al-Ikhwan.[3] The GEC rejected all jurisprudential doctrines, including Wahhabism. The dispute with the Wahhabis was mainly on issues relating to worship,[4] but these differences, in time, turned to a political and social protest movement represented by a radical faction of the GEC led by Juhayman al-'Otaibi,[5] also known as the Juhayman al-'Otaibi Movement, which called for takfir (excommunication) of all the political regimes in the region of the Arabian Peninsula and the Gulf. Some Kuwaitis, such as 'Abdul-Lateef al-Derbas and Jabir al-Jalahma (he is in the latest list of terrorists issued by the UN Security Council), belonged to this group.[6] It is now known as Ahl al-Hadith (People of the Hadith). It took advantage of the atmosphere of freedom and openness in Kuwait, which granted them a sense of confidence and the ability to express their opinions, concentrating mainly on the illegality of the regime. Indirectly, prior to the events of the Holy Mosque in Mecca in 1978, a meeting was held by Sheikh bin Baz in which he expressed his disagreement with the GEC and focused on the extreme positions of the GEC towards the regime as well as some doctrinal issues.[7]

Second: the effect of Jama'at al-Takfir wa al-Hijra on the Kuwaiti students studying in Cairo who belonged to the MBG since the 1970s. The idea of takfir emerged in the 1960s by the MBG in Egypt, in the jails and prisons, which contained many of the members of the MBG in the era of Jamal 'Abdel Nasser. A split between supporters and opponents of this idea occurred among the MBG prisoners. Among the detainees was Hassan al-Hudhaibi, the Supreme Guide for the MBG, who took an opponent stand for this ideology and issued a study labeled *Da'a Lagadah* (*Advocates not Judges*).[8] One of the supporters of the ideology of takfir was Shukri Ahmad Mustafa, who was among the detainees in the Abu Zaa'bal prison; after his release, in the era of President Anwar al-Sadat, he took the initiative to form a political organization called Jama'at al-Muslimeen (Muslim community) in October 1971. He became the emir of this group, which later came to be known as Jama'at al-Takfir wa al-Hijra. It included about 2,000 members, all of whom were young, most of whom belonged to the MBG, and who declared their opposition to the policy of the MBG. Shukri Mustafa declared his condemnation for the MBG clearly and accused its leadership of being behind the arrests and executions against members of the organization, saying that they had committed treason against their own members.[9]

The concepts and ideas of takfir adopted by Shukri Mustafa are part of the takfir ideas made by Sayyed Qutb in his famous book *Ma'alim fi al-Tareeq*. The ideas and concepts of Jama'at al-Takfir are based on the idea of Hakimiya and takfir wa al-Hijra. Shukri Mustafa divided the idea of migration into three stages: the delivery stage, the organization being able to disseminate their ideas and call (mission). The second stage called for the exodus from what God had forbidden to worship, such as going away from forbidden traditions and customs, clothing and costumes, and the role of forums and institutions prevailing in the society – in other words, it was escaping from homeland to another. Thus a lot of them went to the mountains, where a Muslim society was established. Through this society the previous communities were publicly pronounced as infidels, and thus they were ready to fight these infidels. The third stage is the phase of capability, where the community leaves its isolation and goes back to the infidel society to liberate it and create it as an Islamic society.[10]

From this standpoint, some of the leading figures of the student organization of the MBG in Kuwait – who were supervising the organizational activity of the group in Cairo since the 1970s – were affected by the ideology of Jama'at al-Takfir wa al-Hijra. They focused on Sayyed Qutb's book *Ma'alim fi al-Tareeq, al-Mastalahat al-Arba'a fi al-Quran* (*The Four Technical Terms of Quran*) by Abu Al-A'la al-Mawdudi, and *al-Tariq il al-Daw'a* (*The Road to the Call*) by Fayez Matar. It seems that the reason behind the affection of those students for the ideology of Jama'at al-Takfir wa al-Hijra was the decision made by the Egyptian Government to execute Saleh Sariya and his comrades, who were accused of belonging to a terrorist organization and their involvement in the technical military case.[11] This organization regarded all governments in the Muslim lands as infidels and all societies in these countries as being ignorant. Furthermore, they believe the only way to change these governments is with the establishment of an Islamic State, which they believed was deemed an obligation to each and every Muslim man or woman through jihad.[12] Some leading figures of the student leadership attended the trial of these detainees and were affected by the outcries they unleashed from jail.[13] These events paved the way for the growth of the ideology of Jama'at al-Takfir wa al-Hijra between the leaders of the student organization of the MBG in Cairo, which led the MBG in Kuwait, to issue orders to dismiss all of those affected by the ideology of the Jama'at al-Takfir wa al-Hijra organization in Cairo in 1976. This group, which joined the Jama'at al-Takfir wa al-Hijra organization, continued to be active and adopted a special program in which it was committed to bringing some of the organization's Egyptian intellectuals to give educational lectures in order to deepen this ideology among the Kuwaiti students belonging to this movement.[14]

The fundamentalist movement, which raised the slogan of the return to God's book, sought to mobilize 'Abdullah al-Nafeesi, the former teacher in the Department of Political Science at Kuwait University. Al-Nafeesi began writing a series of articles in which he criticized the leadership of the MBG who belonged to the merchant class. In the meantime, al-Nafeesi and others from the MBG formed a political movement within the SRS that differed with the international organization of the MBG on a key issue. Represented in this new movement, which was in favor of political action followed by the religious groups' dissidents from the MBG, was the inevitability of confrontation with the Arab political regimes using armed action. In early September 1979, three months before the storming of the Holy Mosque in Mecca, al-Nafeesi was arrested, together with a group of Kuwaitis such as 'Abdul-Lateef al-Derbas and Jabir al-Jalahma, possessing political religious publications. These publications were four letters from Juhayman al-'Otaibi and others, three of them were written by comrades in the GEC.[15] After his release, al-Nafeesi returned to Kuwait and began to publish some of his articles in *Majallat al-Mujtama'*. The first one was after more than four months of ending the attempted seizure of the Holy Mosque. In 1982, the extremist movement and the movement of the historic leadership succeeded in changing the extremist approach into a political maneuver. At the same time, the historic leadership succeeded in isolating the extremists from the decision-making positions in the MBG.[16] It was 1980 when the liquidation of the extremist trend in the MBG leadership occurred, where the leadership insisted on the need for political practice. The MBG then split into two currents: an extremist view that regarded this as a deviation from the approach, while the other believed that the practical approach was a closer road to achieve the call. Due to this controversy, some extremist figures abandoned the organization and the historic leadership of the MBG managed to absorb other categories of the fundamentalist movements, which represented a broad base of young people through pushing them to work in the charities that were deployed in Kuwait in a way that had never been witnessed before under different names. The activities of these associations in Muslim areas in Asia and Africa considered this as a method of jihad.[17] In fact, the youth groups affected by the ideology of Jama'at al-Takfir wa al-Hijra, who were engaged in the charitable activities in the Asian countries, especially in Afghanistan and Pakistan, had a strong takfir orientation. Most especially as they met people there who had spread this ideology under the name of jihad against the infidel regimes.

Third: the communication of some Muslim youth belonging to the Islamist political groups in Kuwait with jihadist terrorist groups in Afghanistan, such as Jama'at al-Jihad al-Masri (the Egyptian Jihad group), al-Jama'a al-Jazaeria al-Mosalah (Algerian Armed Islamic Group), and al-Jamma'ah al-Islamiya al-Moqatilah al-Libia (Libyan Islamic Fighting Group). These groups designed educational programs for Kuwaiti youth focusing on the literature of Sayyed Qutb, especially his book titled *Ma'alim al-Tareeq*, and Abu Al-A'la al-Mawdudi, most especially his books *al-Mustalahat al-Arba'a fi al-Quran* and *Minhaj al-Inqilab al-Islami* (*The Approach of an Islamic Coup*). In addition to the books there were booklets, such as *al-Faritha al-Ghaiba* (*Missing Duty*) by Mohammad 'Abdul-Salam Faraj, and *Manhaj al-'Amal al-Islami* (*Islamic Approach Action*) by al-Jama'a al-Islamiya (the Islamic Group) in Egypt, and *al-Manhaj al-Haraki li Jama'at al-Jihad* (*The Dynamic Approach for Islamic Jihad*), *al-Hasaad al-Mur: al-Ikhwan al-Moslmon fi Sitain 'Aam* by Ayman al-Zawahiri, and *Hukum qital al-Taafah al-Momtani'a* (*The Rule of Fighting Community Response*). Most of the Arab Afghanis believed in the al-Salafiah al-Jihadia ideology, which believed in the necessity of changing the Arab regimes by means of force on the basis that these regimes were illegitimate and that jihad was the only way to change them. They refused to deal with the constitutional institutions of these countries, claiming that they support the infidels of the states and that they must be fought because they do not apply the laws of Islam. They believe that the fall of innocent victims during this fighting is acceptable because they believe that their death would be martyrism.[18]

Fourth: the affection of the extremist Kuwaitis who belonged to the Islamist political groups in Kuwait towards al-Salafiah al-Jihadia, which was launched in the Saudi city Braida by Sheikh Hamoud Bin ʿAqla al-Shuʾaibi, Sheikh ʿAli al-Khadir, and Sheikh Nasser al-Fahad, after the events of 11 September 2001 and the war of liberating Iraq, who claim infidelity of the political regimes.[19] A number of its clerics, such as Sheikh Salman al-ʾWadh, Sheikh Suleiman ʿAlwan, Sheikh Ali al-Khadir, Sheikh Fahad bin Bashar bin Fahad al-Bashar, Sheikh Nasser al-ʾOmar and Sheikh Hamad ʿAbdullah al-ʾAli issued fatwas that condemned the support of the Americans, and takfir on all who helped those against the Muslims.[20] In addition, there were statements issued by the leaders of the al-Salafiah al-Jihadia in support of the Taliban Movement, such as the letter sent by Sheikh Hamoud bin ʿQlah al Shʾuaibi, Sheikh ʿAli Salman al-Khadir, and Salman al-ʾAwadah to the Emir of the Islamic Emirate of Afghanistan, Mullah Mohammad ʿOmar.[21]

Such letters and statements issued by the Sheikhs of the al-Salafiah al-Jihadia were published through the Islamic sites on the Internet, or through cassettes, or through symposiums and lectures that were held in the camps by the Islamist political groups, where they used to organize the youth in the Kuwaiti desert and brainwash the youth through listening to the lecturers of the al-Salafiah al-Jihadia Group. All of these made a great impact on the Muslim youth in Kuwait and other parts of the Arabian Peninsula, which led to the militarization of their feelings.

Fifth: the impact of the writings of Abu Mohammad al-Maqdisi or Essam al-Berquaoui on the Kuwaiti Afghanis. Al-Maqdisi is a Palestinian born in the village of Barqa in Nablus in 1962 and has Jordanian nationality. He migrated to Kuwait in his early years with his family, where he studied in the schools of Kuwait and joined Ahal al-Hadith al-Thawrien (The Revolutionaries People of Hadith), who emerged from the Juhayman al-ʾOtaibi Movement. In 1988, al-Maqdisi made close links with the IHRS, another extremist organization based in Kuwait.[22]

Al-Maqdisi was spreading his infidel ideology towards the governments of the GCC countries in the camps scattered in the Kuwaiti desert and run by Islamist political groups. During his stay in Kuwait, he issued his book *I'dad al-Qada al-Fawaris bi-hajr Fasad al-Madaris* (*Preparation of Leading Knights for the Abandonment of Corruption Schools*), in which he attacked the government public schools, describing them as schools for the infidels that must be demolished. He called on his supporters to stay away from the government posts and to keep their children away from the government schools. Following the intensification of the differences with his colleagues because of his extremism, he left Kuwait for Afghanistan in 1989, then returned to Kuwait, and then left for Jordan.[23] In 1995, al-Maqdisi with Ahmad al-Khalayla (Abu Musʾab al-Zarqawi),[24] founded Gamaʾat al-Tawhid (The Tawheed Group) in the city of Zarqa in Jordan, which is considered a stronghold of the al-Salafiah al-jihadia, and he was named the emir of the group. The majority of the founders of the group had not completed their studies, except al-Maqdisi, who had gotten a university education in Saudi Arabia specializing in Shari'a. In the same year, the group was discovered by the Jordanian authorities and its leaders were arrested, including al-Maqdisi, who was sentenced to prison for 15 years. Four years later he was released by a royal pardon. In 1999, he left Jordan for Afghanistan.[25]

Millat Ibrahim Wad'wat al-Anbia Walmursalin (*Abraham Creed and the Prophets and Messengers Call*) is a book written by al-Maqdisi and is similar to the book *Ma'alim fi al-Tareeq* by Sayyed Qutb in the degree of its ideological influence. His call in this book is the idea of unification and unity with God, and infidelity to anyone governed by the manmade constitutional laws and not the Islamic Shari'a.[26] In his book *al-Kawashif al-Jaliyya fi kufur al-Dawla al-Sa'udiyya* (*The Obvious of the Saudi State's Impiety*), he calls for overthrowing and fighting all Arab regimes, which are governed without God's regulations.[27] Al-Maqdisi specified three methods to achieve this goal, that is to:[28]

1   Takfir (excommunicate) to the ruler if he shows outrageous disbelief, or overthrow him in order to establish God's law and the achievement of full unification.
2   Any weak Muslim has to emigrate and not obey kafir (unbeliever) and his governments; he may not necessarily have to work in the state's military and civilian institutions.
3   Call for jihad to achieve the unity with God.

It is worth mentioning that the mosque of the Kuwaiti Red Crescent Society in Peshawar was the scene of the distribution of this book in Peshawar.[29] In another book, *al-Dimucratia Waldin* (*Democracy and Religion*), al-Maqdisi says that democracy is a religion that is not the religion of God.[30] Al-Maqdisi also decided that democracy means being an infidel and that it contradicts the religion of Islam.[31] At the same time, al-Maqdisi severely criticized the Muslim scholars who fought the ideas of extremism.[32]

His books have spread to all parts of the Arabian Peninsula and they are regarded as the manifest for al-Salafiah al-Jihadia. Those who committed the terrorist operations of al-Khobar and Riyadh in the mid-1990s admitted that they were affected by the al-Maqdisi writings. Moreover, 'Abdul-'Aziz al-Mo'thm, one of the participants in these terrorist actions, had admitted before his execution by the Saudi security authorities that he met al-Maqdisi in Jordan and took drafts of his work to be distributed in the Gulf and the Arabian Peninsula.[33]

Sixth: the influence of the Salafi Wahabis, which originated in Saudi Arabia through the cassettes, brochures, publications and fatwas; it has the vision of the hard-liner Salafi, which has been quickly spread among the Muslim youth. In addition, there was the prevalence of the phenomenon of spring camps, which were set up and sponsored by political Islamist groups in Kuwait, in which it mobilized young people to listen to the lectures given by a number of al-Salafiah al-Jihadia Sheikhs, such as Sheikh Hamoud Bin Aqlah al Shu'aibi, Nassr al-Fahad, Sheikh Nasser al-'Omar and Sheikh Salman al-'Awdah, which included an extreme Salafiah ideology. The presence of those on Kuwaiti soil was criticized by the liberal trend, but the Kuwaiti authorities did not immediately prevent them from playing a big role in influencing the Kuwaiti youth. Consequently, the Kuwaiti regime issued a decree banning 26 Saudi preachers from speaking and giving lectures in the mosques in Kuwait,[34] but this did not prevent groups of Islamist political groups from hosting them in their private camps and centers spread throughout the Kuwaiti desert, where they are still active in teaching the extremist ideas to the Muslim youth.

Seventh: the role played by some Kuwaiti graduates from the colleges in the Kingdom of Saudi Arabia, who were affected by al-Salafiah al-Jihadia ideology, who are now part of the Faculty of Shari'a at Kuwait University. As described by Dr. Hamad al-'Othman, the teacher in the Faculty of Shari'a, they are the owners of deviant thought, as some of them announce in public 'that our rulers today are not heard nor obedient'.[35] Publications and fatwas, which provoked terrorist acts, were distributed in the college, such as the publication that considers anyone opposing the killing of those who have a treaty with the US is a kafir.[36] Dr. Tariq al-Tawari, a teacher in the Faculty of Shari'a, says that the only reliable nation's scholars are: Sheikh Hamoud Bin 'Aqla al Shu'aibi, the owner of the famous fatwa regarding the spilling of the blood of the singer 'Abdullah al-Ruwaishid, Sheikh Nasser al-Fahad, the author of *al-Tabian fi Kufur Man A'an al-Amrikan* (*In the Elaboration of the Infidel who Helped the Americans*) Sheikh Khalid al-Khadir, who issued a fatwa that permits the murdering of security police, Sheikh Nasser al-'Omar and Sheikh Salman al-'Owda.[37] Dr. Hamad al-Othman confirms that the Faculty of Shari'a embraces the extremists and invites them to conferences conducted by the college, such as Dr. Salah al-Sawi.[38] From these terrorist resources, the armed Sunni Islamic groups emerged in Kuwait, represented by the following groups:

Juhayman al-'Otaibi Movement

This movement was founded in Saudi Arabia. Its most prominent founders are Juhayman al-'Otaibi and Mohammad al-Qahtani.[39] There is no exact date for the start of the activity of this group. However, five years prior to the Mecca incidents in 1979, members of the group started to spread in a small neighborhood in the Skernier district, a mosque in Riyadh, then Mohammad's Mosque, the Islamic University in Madina, Mecca, and other religious centers. This group has been active through the dissemination of Islamic ideas based on Sahabah (Companions of the Prophet) and Salaf al-Salih (pious ancestors).[40] This group is regarded as the first armed Islamic

Movement. Some sources described this organization as primitive and fragile, poor physically and theoretically, while other sources believe that the organizational structure of the group is similar to Hizb al-Nukhba (the Elite Party) and Hizb al-Jamaheer (the Masses Party), as they seek to overthrow the regimes. The movement succeeded in hiding from the security authorities for a period of time without being arrested. They have secret meetings limited to the elite figures of the movement. Meetings are held in the landscapes, caves and houses. On the other hand, it was natural that the movement was also known in the public as they make their call because they used mosques and religious pamphlets for this purpose and, therefore, the public meetings were open where its leaders performed the task of religious guidance.[41] The book entitled *Majmu'at al-Tawheed al-Najdiya* (*The Najdi Monotheism Group*) is one of the most important books on which the Juhayman Movement depends, as well as its subsequent writings, which go in the same direction.[42]

Later on, the Movement issued a series of printed letters known as the Juhayman letters, which were printed in Dar al-Tali'a in Kuwait without the permission and knowledge of Harakat al-Taqadumiyin al-Dimuqratiyin al-Kuwaitiyin (the Kuwaiti Progressive Democratic Movement (KPDM)), which owns this publisher press. Some Arab workers carrying Palestinian, Egyptian and other nationalities took it upon themselves to develop this initiative. Bearing in mind that some writers who dealt with the Juhayman al-'Otaibi Movement mentioned in their books that these letters were printed in Dar al-Tali'a, which according to them, proves that the KPDM sympathizes with the Juhayman al-'Otaibi Movement. It appears that a Kuwaiti GEC member, 'Abdul-Latif al-Derbas, has used his family connections to negotiate a deal with the leftist publisher.[43] The truth, according to Dr. Ahmad al-Khatib and 'Abdullah al-Subai'i, leaders of the KPDM, is that there is no link or support for the Juhayman al-'Otaibi Movement from the KPDM because their leftist ideology completely differs from al-'Otaibi's and any religious ideology.[44]

In these published letters, Juhayman al-'Otaibi advocates the need to change the regimes in the Islamic countries that are not ruled by the Quran and Sunna, by means of armed force. He rejects all political regimes in Islamic countries that are not just, considering them loyal to the infidels, and that his group is the believers' group that faces the infidels.[45]

The most important goals announced by the Movement are:[46]

1 Overthrow the Royal Saudi regime and promote the establishment of an Islamic republic.
2 Stop exporting oil to America for its anti-Islamic attitude.
3 Expel the foreign military experts.

The Movement also demanded to eradicate all features of Western influence from the Kingdom, such as television, radio and women's labor.

On 20 November 1979, the Movement announced its rebellion against the ruling family in Saudi Arabia following the armed attack at the Holy Mosque in Mecca, which lasted about two weeks. The leader of the Juhayman al-'Otaibi Movement announced, from the rostrum of Mecca in front of hundreds of thousands of pilgrims, that Mohammad al-Qahtani is the expected Mahdi. Juhayman and his supporters started to take the mubayh' (oath of allegiance) to the expected Mahdi and pledged all the prayers to do so. On the same day of storming the Holy Mosque in Mecca and before the military action against the protesters inside the Holy Mosque in Mecca took place, King Khalid Bin 'Abdul-Aziz al-Saud summoned to his office 30 of the senior 'Ulama, among them were Sheikh 'Abdul-'Aziz Bin Baz, and Sheikh Mohammad Ibrahim ibn Jubayr, who issued, after the meeting, a fatwa that stated that:

> The rulers have to take any legitimate action even if they have to fight them.[47]

Following this fatwa, the Saudi authorities confronted the Juhayman al-'Otaibi Movement with the use of a large number of National Guards, Army, units from the Jordanian Army and the French anti-terrorism forces led by Captain Paul Barril.[48] The attacking forces were able eventually to control the situation and many of them were killed, among them was Mohammad al-Qahtani (expected Mahdi) and 300 were arrested, including the commander of the Juhayman al-'Otaibi Movement. The royal Diwan issued an order of executing 63 members of the Movement in different main cities of the Kingdom, including: Mecca, Riyadh, Madina, Dammam, Burydah, Tabuk, Hail, and Abha, among them 10 Egyptians, 6 Yemenis, 3 Kuwaitis, one from Sudan and one from Iraq.[49] In the opinion of Nasser al-Huzaymi, a member of Juhayman al-'Otaibi Movement, and one of his students who was detained for six years after the incident of Mecca, he stated:

> The death of the Mahdi was catastrophic for everyone, they were all shocked since they believed that he would never die, they started to collapse and surrendered successively including Juhayman.[50]

It is worth mentioning that on the same day of the Mecca attacks by the Juhayman al-'Otaibi Movement, a statement issued by the Movement was distributed in the streets and mosques of Kuwait as well as messages from Juhayman al-'Otaibi himself. During the confrontation between the Saudi army and the Movement, a Kuwaiti citizen was arrested carrying a letter from Kuwait congratulating the emergence of the Mahdi and it seemed that he was the representative of the Juhayman al-'Otaibi Movement in Kuwait.[51] It is also worth mentioning that Mohammad al-'Qahtani, prior to his death, visited the Gulf countries, including Kuwait, where he delivered several lectures in some Kuwaiti mosques and Islamist political groups' forums. Juhayman's literature has been printed in Kuwait and was smuggled across the border into various areas of Saudi Arabia.[52] After three days from the Mecca incident, and in one of the Sabhan district mosques during Friday prayers, two Kuwaiti citizens made speeches expressing support for the act taken by Juhayman in Mecca, but the worshippers at the mosque showed their protest and announced that this was outside the framework of Sharia'.[53] The three Kuwaitis who participated in the Mecca rebellion were executed: Musa'ad Sa'ud al-Musalam, Mohammad 'Abdal-Rahman al-'Ubaidli, and al-jdaan Hazza' Mubarak.[54] This confirms that there are foreign extensions for the movement in the Arab Gulf countries and it was not limited to the borders of the Kingdom. In addition, according to the head of the former State Security in Kuwait, Sheikh Mash'aal al-Jarrah al-Sabah, the events of Mecca were planned in the Sabahiya district in Kuwait.[55] It is clear that there is sympathy and support by Islamist political groups in Kuwait for the Movement of Juhayman al-'Otaibi. As a leading Muslim Brotherhood member in Kuwait, Isma'il al-Shatti, during a lecture prepared by the NUKS, rejected the accusations calling Juhayman insane or one of the Khawarij (rebellion against the ruler), and he said that whoever accused Juhayman of such things will be responsible in front of god for Juhayman's blood.[56]

Despite the fact that this Movement represented the greatest religious extremism, most of the political groups in the Arab Peninsula and the Gulf had announced their support for it, in spite of their ideological differences. The Arab Socialist Labour Party, in the Arabian Peninsula, contributed to the distribution of Juhayman's private and confidential letters. The Communist Party in Saudia issued a special book about the armed rebellion in Mecca. The Organization of the Arab Socialist Ba'ath Party in Saudi Arabia published a special issue of the magazine, *Sout al-Tali'a* (*Voice of the Vanguard*), which included statements and publications issued by the Juhayman al-'Otaibi Movement; Itihad Sha'b al-Jazira al-'Arabiya (the Union of the People of the Arabian Peninsula), considered it as a 'national revolution and national progressive Arab Islamic and not as they claimed it was an expected Mahdi', according to the head of the Union, Nasser al-Sa'ed.[57] The Shi'ite Islamic extremist groups, including Munadhamat al-Thawra al-Islamiya fi al-Jazira al-'Arabiya (the Islamic Revolution Organization in the Arabian Peninsula), also declared its solidarity with this Movement in its attempt to make political and social change in the Kingdom.[58] On this basis, it defended Juhayman and published the Movement's views in three books in Arabic on these events: *Zilzal Juhayman fi Mecca* (*Juhayman Earthquake in Mecca*) and *Intafathat al-Haram* (*al-Haram Uprising*), as well as a third book in English, *The al-Haram Revolt*. The Islamic revolution magazine, the mouthpiece of Munadhamat al-Thawra al-Islamiya fi al-Jazira al-'Arabiya, described Juhayman as a martyr and published a special issue of the magazine on the occasion of the sixth anniversary of the Mecca incidents, considering what happened as a revolution in the heart of Mecca.[59]

Despite the failure of the Juhayman al-'Otaibi Movement in achieving its objectives during the Mecca incidents, and the execution of most of its leaders, its ideas mentioned in the literature of Juhayman al-'Otaibi are still alive after his death. The followers of this Movement from the Wahabis in the Arabian Gulf and in the Peninsula, known today as Hizb al-Quran (the Quran Party) who many of its members have hidden in Yemen, such as Abdul-Lateef al-Derbas, refuse to recognize the legitimacy of the countries of the region.[60] In addition, these ideas are also the same ideas of the ideology that al-Qaeda is based on.

Kuwaiti Afghani Fighters

The United States Government encouraged Muslim youth to be engaged in convoys of the mujahideen. They regarded them as freedom fighters and allowed them to build camps on its lands, such as Mu'skar al-Kifah al-Afghani (the Afghan Struggle Camp) in Brooklyn.[61] Some came from Pakistan and used this camp as a base to fight the Red Army on the streets of Kabul, which was regarded by the United States as a threat to its national security. This was an attempt to overthrow the communist regime in Afghanistan, which was backed by the former Soviet Union. This situation was supported by a number of Arab conservative countries friendly to the USA, such as Egypt, Saudi Arabia, Yemen and Kuwait, who feared the communist tide – especially since the pro-Moscow Socialist Party governed South Yemen during this period and assisted the armed revolution, led by al-Jabha al-Sha'biya li Tahrir al-Khalij al-'Arabi al-Muhtal (the Popular Front for the Liberation of the Occupied Arabian Gulf), al-Jabha al-Wataniya al-Dimuqratiya li Tahrir 'Oman wa al-Khalij al-'Arabi (the National Democratic Front for the Liberation of Oman and the Arabian Gulf), al-Jabha al-Sha'biya li Tahrir 'Oman wa al-Khalij al-'Arabi (the Popular Front for the Liberation of Oman and the Arabian Gulf), and al-Haraka al-Thawriya al-Sha'biya fi 'Oman wa al-Khalij al-'Arabi (the Popular Revolutionary Movement in Oman and the Arabian Gulf), with a Marxist orientation leading to an armed struggle to topple the conservative regimes in the Arabian Peninsula and the Gulf. Osama bin Laden emphasized that the reason behind the support of the Gulf states for jihad in Afghanistan was not for the sake of God Almighty, but the fear of their thrones being relinquished to the Russians.[62] For this reason, those countries allowed, helped and armed their citizens to volunteer in the ranks of the jihadist organizations engaged in guerrilla warfare against the Afghani communist regime and the Red Army in Afghanistan. In this regard, Gilles Kepel says:

> . . . the decisive battlefield proved to be Afghanistan, where a successful jihad was financed by the oil monarchies of the Gulf and Central Intelligence of the United States. As far as the United States was concerned, this holy war in Afghanistan had one explicit goal: to set a Vietnam-like deathtrap for the Soviet forces that had invaded Kabul in December 1979 and, thus, to precipitate the collapse of the Soviet empire.[63]

Among those countries was Kuwait, which had a good close relationship with the former Soviet Union. However, Kuwait had played a major role in relief assistance, such as building hospitals, schools and institutes from which the Arab Afghanis benefited. The political Islamist groups in Kuwait were active in the formation of committees in solidarity with the Afghani Mujahideen and its three leaders, namely: 'Abdullah al-Sabt, Tariq al-'Isa, the chairman of the IHRS, and Jassim al-'Oun, who paid a visit to Afghanistan to support the Afghani Mujahideen against the Communist regime. In this regard, 'Abdullah al-Sabt confirms that the SG was one of the first groups that played a strong role in Afghanistan.[64] In March 1987, the IHRS founded a special committee to support the Afghani Mujahideen called Lajnat Musanadat al-Afgan (the Afghan Support Committee) headed by Mohammad al-Sharhan and the membership of some of the SG members, such as Nazim al-Misbah, Tariq al-'Isa and 'Abdullah al-'Asakir, and others. The most important objectives of the committee were:[65]

- to support and assist the Afghani Mujahideen, materially and morally
- to make propaganda about the Afghani issue
- to disseminate a healthy Islamic culture in Afghani society.

The SRS was also active in supporting and assisting the mujahideen. In January 1984 it established Lajnat al-Da'wa al-Islamiya (Islamic Call Committee) and Majid Badr Sayyed Hashem al-Rifa'i became its chairman. One of its most significant activities was the founding of many Quranic centers and the establishment of the Institute of Higher Shari'a for teachers, preachers, and publishing the advocacy books of Islam.[66]

Fatwas regarding the jihad against the communist forces in Afghanistan were spread and some advocates of political Islamic groups in Kuwait, such as Sheikh Ahmad al-Qattan and Sulaiman Abu Gheith, were active.[67] In addition, others who had the ability to simmer religious feelings were active.[68] They spread books and recordings of 'Abdullah 'Azzam,[69] such as the book entitled *Ayat al-Rahman fi jihad Afghanistan* (*Verses of God in the Afghanistan Jihad*), which played a role in fueling religious feelings among the youth. This led to an influx of volunteers from Muslim youth to the battlefield in Afghanistan, as well as *Majallat al-Jihad*, which was issued each month. In addition, there was a weekly bulletin, *Laheeb al-Ma'raka* (*The Flames of Battle*), which carried news of the battles and victories of the mujahideen weekly, resulting in the increase of radicalism among the youth in the Arab and Islamic countries.[70] 'Azzam issued the first fatwa in regards to jihad in Afghanistan, as he called it fard 'ayn (an obligation incumbent upon every Muslim) and this fatwa was published in the *Majallat al-Mujtama'*.[71] 'Azzam continued in issuing other fatwas, which urged the Muslim youth to transfer jihad to other fronts, saying in this fatwa:

It must be clear to the Mujahideen that when a Muslim arrives in the land of Jihad, he may not leave it until he has risen as a martyr to God or making a victory against enemies, later he will transfer this Jihad to another front until the land of the Muslims is cleansed from the infidels.[72]

In this context, Osama bin Laden says:

> The people of Jihad who came and lived in this war, knew that the Islamic Jihad in Afghanistan had not benefited from anything as much as it benefited from Sheikh ʿAbdullah ʿAzzam, who provoked the nation from East to West to join the jihad especially through his book *Ayat al-Rahman fi jihad Afghanistan.*[73]

A number of Kuwaiti Afghani fighters graduated from training camps in Peshawar and Kandahar, which were supervised by ʿAbdullah ʿAzzam. They participated in the battles led by the Afghan Mujahideen against the Red Army. In the aftermath of the Afghan–Soviet war came the fall of the Afghani capital, Kabul, into the hands of the Mujahideen. Fighting broke out between the Afghan Jihad factions; this led to the splitting of the Arab Afghans, including Kuwaiti Afghani fighters. Some of them joined the forces of Gulbuddin Hekmatyar; others joined the forces of Ahmad Shah Massoud, and the rest participated in the civil war. Some of them refused to participate in this war and decided to return to their home countries to practice terrorism against their governments, as happened in Egypt and Algeria.[74] Some of these people went to other countries to fight with the Muslim people, such as what happened in Bosnia and Herzegovina, the Philippines and Kashmir.

Some Kuwaiti Afghani fighters returned to Kuwait. They were welcomed by the government as the Deputy Prime Minister and the Interior Minister, and then Sheikh Mohammad al-Khalid al-Sabah said welcoming them: 'They are our sons and they will remain so.'[75] Those who returned via Iran and other countries were subjected to investigation by the Department of State Security. There were 13 people that were confirmed during the investigation that had left Kuwait for Afghanistan to support the Mujahideen brothers, and two of them admitted belonging to al-Qaeda, while others denied their affiliation to the organization, emphasizing that they were seeking jihad only.[76] It is worth mentioning that during the devastating attack launched by the forces of the international coalition against the Taliban in Afghanistan, they were able to detain many of the Arab Afghan fighters, of whom a number were Kuwaiti citizens and were suspected of belonging to al-Qaeda. These were transferred to the Guantanamo Bay detention camp in Cuba. Among them was Nasser al-Mutairi, who was released by the United States. However, he was charged by the Kuwaiti prosecutors of seeking to undermine the Kuwait political status and, without the permission of the Kuwaiti Government, engaging in hostile acts against a foreign country that would impair the political relations between Kuwait and that country. Furthermore, he was charged with training in the use of arms and ammunition at the hands of others targeted for illegal purposes. He was sentenced to five years' imprisonment by the Kuwaiti courts, but he was released after a short period.[77]

Kuwaiti al-Qaeda organization

Al-Qaeda in Kuwait is a branch of the mother organization, which emerged from the Arab Afghans fighter group founded in Pakistan in 1989. It is a terrorist organization with links to a global network of militant Islamic organizations, such as the armed groups in Algeria, Egypt, Libya, Syria, Yemen, Pakistan and other such organizations in parts of Asia and Africa. The leaders of these organizations are a group of terrorists from different Arab and Islamic countries, such as Osama bin Laden of Saudi Arabia, Ayman al-Zawahiri of Egypt[78] and Suleimman Abu Ghaith of Kuwait. This organization was responsible for the attack on American soldiers in Somalia in October 1993 that led to the killing of 18 soldiers, and the bombing of the United States embassies in Nairobi and Dar al-Salaam in August 1998. The first incident resulted in the death of 213 people, including 12 Americans and more than 4,500 people wounded; the other terrorist act led to the death of 11 people and 85 wounded. They are also responsible for the attack on the American destroyer USS Cole on 12 October 2000, which killed 17 American Marines.[79] This organization was also behind the formation of al-Jabha al-'Alamia al-Islamia li Jihad al-Yahood wa al-Nansarh (the World Islamic Front for the Jihad against the Jews and the Crusaders), announced by bin Laden in February 1998, in the Khowst Camp, eastern Afghanistan. According to the founding statement of the Front, jihad is a religious obligation for Muslims and killing Americans and their allies, whether civilians or military, is an obligation on every Muslim until their armies leave the Arabian Peninsula.[80] The idea of the globalization of jihad goes back to 1994, when a meeting was held in the holy Mecca Mosque that included leaders of the jihad movements in the Arab and Islamic countries and its branches in the United States and Europe, which set the outline and ideology of the foundation of this Front.[81] The idea of an Islamic nation or the armed Global Islam resembles the leftist national groups that emerged in the 1970s, which included a number of leftist groups, such as the German Baader-Meinhof Group, the Italian Red Brigades, the Japanese Red Army, and other such groups. This idea has been in the minds of the Islamic groups and movements in the Arab region and Islamic world since the 1980s, especially when these groups held a secret conference in London in mid-December 1981. Among those attending the meeting were representatives of the Iranian and Libyan regimes; both encouraged and supported these movements and groups in the Islamic world and the Khomeini leaders calling for exporting the Islamic Revolution with global advocacy. For this reason, training camps in Iran received many belonging to these Islamic groups.[82] The Libyan leader did not hesitate to show support for the movements, which are inspired by Islamic extremists. He was behind the establishment of al-Qiyada al-Sha'biya al-'Alamia al-Islamiya (the World Islamic People's Leadership), a political–religious organization established in 1989, which was designed to improve the image of the Libyan revolution in Islamic countries. Gaddafi pumped great amounts of money into this organization.[83] The Kingdom of Saudi Arabia has also helped many Islamic movements since 1962 in order to fight the Nasserite tide, which was a threat to the Saudi regime. For this reason, King Faisal took the initiative to establish Rabitat al-'Alam al-Islami (the Muslim World League). The idea of Islamic solidarity in the face of the Arab nationalist tide led to the escape of many Egyptians belonging to the MBG from the Egyptian authorities, such as Mohammad Qutb, Dr. Zaki Badawi, Dr. Salah Shaheen and Salem 'Azzam. The aim of the Saudis was to confront Nasserism and launch Wahhabism in all parts of the Muslim world.[84] Such encouragement and support towards these groups encouraged the holding of the first Arab–Islamic Summit under the initiative of the leader of the MBG in Sudan, Hassan al-Turabi, who was aiming to establish a universal Islamic state. The summit was attended by representatives of these groups from Pakistan, the Philippines, Malaysia, Afghanistan and the Islamic movements and groups in Arab countries. It quickly turned into a center that included terrorist Islamic groups and movements.[85]

After the events of 11 September 2001 – the terrorist attack carried out by al-Qaeda on the World Trade Center in New York City and the Pentagon building in Washington that led to the death of thousands – the fall of the Islamic Emirate of Afghanistan was ignited; this accelerated the elimination of al-Qaeda inside Afghan territory. However, the cells of al-Qaeda shifted from Afghanistan to the Arabian Peninsula and the Gulf; these cells included the Arab Afghans from Kuwait, Saudi Arabia, Yemen, Bahrain and other Arab Afghans. It seems that they re-grouped in these areas, most especially Saudi Arabia and Kuwait, according to the first statement issued on 22 September 2001 in the name of Jaisah al-Qaeda al-Islami-Wehdat al-Jazirah al-Arabiah (the al-Qaeda Islamic Army – Arabian Peninsula Unit) – an extension of al-Qaeda – which threatens to attack vital targets in the GCC countries as well as American interests in the world. It warned all Arab governments from assisting or providing any facilities to the United States. It also called for every real Muslim to stand against any Muslim, whatever his position, if that Muslim stood with the infidels and supported the cross against the Quran.[86] This coincided with the influx of American and British forces on GCC soil in preparation for the liberation of Iraq from Saddam Hussein's dictatorship. In addition, a fatwa was issued by 26 sheikhs of the al-Salafiah al-Jihadia, consisting of Shari'a professors in Islamic universities in the Kingdom of Saudi Arabia, which called young Muslims to fight the infidel American forces.[87] This had an impact among some members of the Islamic political groups in Kuwait and Saudi Arabia, where veteran Kuwaiti Afghani fighters were still active in attracting a number of young fighters belonging to Islamist political groups in Kuwait, organizing and training them in camps in the desert.[88]

Organizational structure

The organizational structure of al-Qaeda in Kuwait resembles the organizational construction of Saudi Arabia's al-Qaeda in that it has surrounded the grounds with the organization operating in the area of the Arabian Peninsula and the Gulf. Osama bin Laden and Ayman al-Zawahiri are considered their supreme guides. It is based on small cells, where its members retain their weapons safely in their homes. The organization has specialized committees or sub-groups responsible for education and training, developing strategy, arranging media and advertising, and taking care of religious affairs. The most important unit of the organization is the Media Committee, which supervises the issuance of *Majallat Sout al-Jihad* (*The Voice of Jihad*), which has been part of the organization since July 2003. It also includes the semi-annual publication *Mu'askar al-Battar* (*The Camp of Saber*), which specializes in military affairs.[89] Al-Qaeda depends on the polarization of its membership through mosques, using propaganda, recruitment, and political education policies. The mosques are the most important tool for recruiting members in its ranks, who are usually selected from the youth.

The educational program, prepared by the organization for the young worshipers inside mosques, starts with competitions on how to fight the Americans and ends with watching films containing scenes of cutting the heads of Americans and urging the worshipers that when they meet an American to cut his neck instead of greeting him.[90] Recruitment is also done through holding camps in the remote desert, whether in Kuwait or Saudi Arabia, where there are no strict limitations for movement between the two countries. Thus, the Kuwaiti desert has become a training camp for dozens of young people who are recruited from the mosques in Kuwait; after recruitment in the mosques they have received training on guerrilla warfare and are subject to the training sessions at the hands of Kuwaiti Afghani fighter veterans,[91] and then became members of the al-Qaeda network. The recruitment of a member passes through four stages, beginning with political and religious education, and ending with political recruitment. These stages are:[92]

First stage: a journey of scouting the youth that the organization seeks to join its ranks. This task is the responsibility of what is called Kashafeen (scouts), among them some school teachers who attract from the mosque centers young worshipers, between 12 and 18 years of age. They start at the beginning to invite them to join their physical activities, such as football tournaments and the distribution of prizes that attract children of this age. Later on, they invite these youngsters to participate in the spring camp, which the Islamic political groups used to set up in the desert, where cultural, educational, and sport programs were held, which included hosting the Mashayikh al-Salafiah al-Jihadia (the Jihadist Salafiah Clerics), who came from Saudi Arabia and some Islamic countries. During this phase, members of the organization carry out visits to youngsters' homes inquiring about their living conditions. Moreover, financial and material assistance is provided for these young people, if required. At school, the youth remain under the supervision of some teachers belonging to the organization, and some students older than them in the same organization, so that the boy couldn't be affected by other friends who might change his mind about the group.

Second stage: the process of brainwashing begins, starting with the category of ages ranging from 15 to 18 years. Intensive programs begin with lessons containing religious talk about evil in the society, such as women wearing make-up, women mixing with men, holding concerts, and the presence of Jewish and Christian temples on Muslim land. By this, the leaders of the extremists push those young people to address the above-mentioned issues through the dissemination of extremist ideas in the community and they encourage them not to join the co-educational universities and institutes, but to join the Islamic universities in Saudi Arabia and Pakistan instead.

Third stage: this is represented in planting terrorist ideas and prohibiting the community from dealing with the rulers. They are taught to comply with the orders of the leaders of the organization. In addition, they are tested on their mental and physical willingness to receive orders for the implementation of any action required by the organization's leadership.

Fourth stage: the training for young people is conducted in an unpopulated remote desert and is conducted by using weapons. They are taught the use of weapons, creating local bombs, the use of grenades and bomb vehicles, and the best ways to disguise themselves, if the need arises. This phase also includes programs for members of the organization, such as the documentaries created by the members of the organization's branches spread in most countries of the world, as well as presentation of the wills of the terrorists behind these terrorist operations. Some of the leaders of the organization talk to the youth about Karamat (the miracles) of these mujahideen. Letters and wills of the founders of the al-Qaeda organization, such as Osama bin Laden, are also broadcast in order to create enthusiasm and motivate them to execute any terrorist act they are asked to perform.

The organizational structure of the al-Qaeda organization is a cluster like the Egyptian Islamic Jihad organization and the Saleh Sarriya organization. This means that they are cluster cells that adopt the extreme ideas based on the formation of small cells, such as Khaliyat al-Mutla' (the al-Mutla' Cell). For instance, one of the cells of al-Qaeda in Kuwait is designed so that most of its members do not know each other in order to provide the maximum possible degree of confidentiality, security and integrity of the activities that the organization may want to implement, in case they are either killed or arrested. The leadership of these cells is linked to the leadership of the supreme leadership of the organization, which gives the possibilities of movement to act swiftly and implement whatever is required.[93] Al-Qaeda was dismantled by the hands of the State Security, most especially in Saudi Arabia, Kuwait, Yemen and the United Arab Emirates, and the supervisors of the organization's operations were located in the Arabian Gulf and the Peninsula. Thus they began to develop another strategy to get their cells to perform and creating new leaders. One of these leaders was ʿAbdul-Raheem al-Nashri, known as Abu Bilal al-Mekki, or Mulla Ahmad Bilal, who was arrested by the UAE's security forces in 2002 while he was attempting to attack the Americans in the United Arab Emirates. He was handed over to the Americans. In Yemen, the organization's leader, Abu ʿAli al-Harthi, was killed with other members during an air strike carried out by the CIA in November 2002. In Saudi Arabia, from 7 May 2003 until mid-2007, the security forces succeeded in killing and arresting a number of the al-Qaeda organization leaders, such as Samran al-Saʾidi, Yousef al-ʾUyairi, Khalid ʿAli al-Haj, Rakan al-Saikhan, ʿAbdul-ʾAziz al-Miqrin, Faisal al-Dakheel, Saleh al-ʾUfi, and others. With these arrests, the organization lost much of its leadership who participated in the Afghan, Chechnya, and Bosnia and Herzegovina wars. Many of its members and supporters left to go to Iraq to execute suicidal operations after being unable to move in either Saudi Arabia or Kuwait, such as Mohsin al-Fadli, one of the main leaders of the al-Qaeda branch in Kuwait.

Al-Fadli was born in 1981; he received his education at al-Maʿhad al-Deeni in the Fahaheel district. He was arrested two weeks prior to the confrontation between security forces and Kataib Usood al-Jasiera (the Lions of Peninsula Phalanges), but was released.[94] The American Government classified al-Fadli as a supporter of terrorism who had connections with al-Qaeda and the network of Abu Musʾab al-Zarqawi working in Iraq under the name of Qaedat al-Jihad fi Bilad al-Rafidayn (al-Qaeda for Jihad in the land of the Two Rivers), where he supported the latter financially, according to American sources.[95] He had fought alongside the Taliban and al-Qaeda in Afghanistan and also fought against the Russian forces in Chechnya, where he was trained with the use of weapons. It is believed that al-Fadli had received notice in early September 2001 that a strike on American interests would take place.[96] It is worth mentioning that al-Fadli's first charge was printing a poster that advocated fighting the American forces and also called for boycotting American products. He is on the top of the international terrorist list together with eight other terrorists, as stated by the US Secretary of State Condoleezza Rice during her visit to Kuwait.[97] In 1999, al-Fadli had been detained for a year by the Saudi security authorities and was released after the intervention of one of the religious clerics. In the same year, al-Fadli left Kuwait with a group of friends to fight in Chechnya, and among them was Salem Cruz, who was killed there. Al-Fadli stayed in Chechnya for 10 months, during which he joined the Abu Walid al-Ghamdi group. During his stay, he met the leader of the Arab Afghanis, Thamer al-Suwailem, named Khattab, and then he returned to Kuwait on 5 July 2001. Al-Fadli left for Afghanistan and received training in the Malik Camp in the capital of Kabul, where he met the official spokesman of al-Qaeda, Suleimman Abu Ghaith. After six months, al-Fadli returned to Kuwait.[98] In 2002, he was arrested and interrogated by the State Security, and he confessed before prosecutors that he was in contact with one of the terrorists, Abu ʿAsim al-Makki, the main suspect in the bombing of the American destroyer USS Cole in the Yemeni port of Aden, and that he handed al-Makki large amounts of money through a GCC citizen in Kuwait that amounted to $117,000 to build a training camp for the mujahideen in Yemen. After a while, the authorities discovered his involvement in the jihad in Iraq and his seeking to attack American forces in Kuwait, leading to his arrest. In February 2003, he was sentenced to five years' imprisonment with three of his colleagues on charges of belonging to al-Qaeda, training with weapons in Afghanistan and fighting with the Taliban, funding the attack on the American destroyer USS Cole, and financing the terrorist training camps in Yemen, but they all were released when the Court of Appeal declared that Kuwait's jurisdiction did not have the right to put them on trial.[99] Al-Fadli is still hiding.

Khalid al-Dossari, another fugitive, is 32 years old and lives in the al-Thaher district in the al-Ahmadi Governorate, south of the capital of Kuwait. He got a diploma from one of the governmental institutes[100] and had been arrested in Morocco as a suspect in relationship with the extremist Islamic groups during the Rabat bombings that targeted Jewish synagogues and tourist facilities belonging to a cell called Gibraltar. Two months later, he was released and left Morocco for Kuwait. On arrival, the authorities withdrew his passport and arrested him for more than 15 days. During that period, the political Islamic groups mediated with the authorities and succeeded in releasing him. On 16 July 2003 he formed Jam'iyat Dhahaya al-Ta'theeb wa al-I'tiqul al-Ta'asufi (the Association of Victims of Torture and Arbitrary Detention) and became its official spokesman. The authorities rejected the official recognition of this association due to its violation of the law of establishing an association that has public benefits. The main activity of this association was to defend the detainees who belonged to extremist Islamic groups in Kuwaiti prisons who were arrested after the events of 11 September 2001. Al-Dossari's name emerged on 30 March 2004 when leading a demonstration composed of a group of Islamic extremists in protest at the closure of a bookshop belonging to a Sunni sect in the area of Hawalli by the Ministry of Information. Its staff member was responsible for selling books that provoked sectarianism, the shop and books were confiscated, and he was arrested. Al-Dossari succeeded through pressure from members of the political Islamic groups in Parliament, who gave a warning to the Minister of Information and the Interior Minister, which called for reopening the bookshop and release of the detainee. Al-Dossari also led the demonstration organized by the extremist Islamic groups composing of more than 300 young Islamic extremists to protest against holding the concert of super-star.

Investigations were made by the Public Prosecution in Kuwait of the Kuwaiti youngsters who were handed over to the Kuwaiti authorities by the Syrian government. These youngsters were on their way to carry out suicide attacks in Iraq and they revealed that Khalid al-Dossari was the financier and provoker of the first call for jihad in Iraq. Moreover, he was behind the recruitment of these youngsters who were fighting in the ranks of terrorists from Zarqawi's group against the coalition forces. Hence, al-Dossari shifted from being a political activist to being the first man wanted by the security forces; since then he has disappeared and no one knows his hiding place.

The al-Qaeda leadership started to search for new methods and tactics that would not lead to the exposure of the organization's members by the security services. Therefore, it abandoned the cluster style of cells and adopted a new method where each cell works by itself and is connected directly via its leader, who is abroad. In this way, the organizational links between the newly formed cells are cut off, which facilitates the new cells' movements, reduces the security risk and reduces the material and human costs. It also deliberately recruits new members who have not had any previous activities and whose names are not listed in the investigation rooms. From the latest arrests that took place in Saudi Arabia, which included 97 persons, it was discovered that a large number of them are new to jihad and are under the age of 25.[101] The organization has also given up its old methods and tactics in hiding in the landscapes and the desert; after the exposure of these places, the organization selected sites less suspicious and far from the eyes of the security forces. Instead, now it has chosen sports halls, scattered in cities where dozens of young men are doing exercises without raising any speculation. These halls are used by al-Qaeda as a disguise to prepare its figures physically together with other youth gatherings, and thus staying away from the charge of holding partisan gatherings – which is against Kuwaiti law.[102] Al-Qaeda has also directed some of its members to spread its ideology via the Internet through giving lessons to explain the process of manufacturing explosives, how to use weapons and how to explode cars and buildings.[103]

Al-Qaeda and armed action in Kuwait

The fact is that al-Qaeda started its armed violence in the Arabian Peninsula and the Gulf – which included Saudi Arabia, Kuwait and Yemen – against the American presence in the region since 1995. It was at this time that al-Qaeda launched the Riyadh and al-Khobar attacks in 1996. In November 2000, a group of 11 fundamentalists belonging to various Arab nationalities were arrested in Kuwait and were found to be associated with al-Qaeda; they were planning a big operation, but the security forces managed to abort this attempt.[104] In addition, there was the Yemeni arena, which also witnessed acts of violence carried out by Jam'at al-Jihad al-Islami (Islamic Jihad Group) (IJG) and Jaysh 'Adan Abyan, al-Islami (the Aden Abyan Islamic Army).[105]

The IJG established in the early nineteen, the IJG is regarded as an extremist fundamentalist organization with members trained in Afghanistan during the Afghan Mujahideen war against the former Soviet Union and the communist regime (1987–1990). They were supported and guided by Osama bin Laden, chief of the al-Qaeda organization. The IJG endeavored to change the ruling regime in Yemen and replace it with an Islamic emirate similar to that of the Taliban in Afghanistan. They denounced 'Ali 'Abdullah Saleh's government which they viewed as un-Islamic regime which must be moved and replaced, particularly following his signature of the unification agreement between North and South Yemen in 1990 concluded between al-Mutamar al-Sha'bia al-'Am (the Peoples General Congress Party) (PGCP) and al-Hizb al-Ishtriaky al-Yamani (Yemen Socialist Party (YSP), considering that this unification was established with the communists of South Yemen.

The IJG in Yemen is led by Sheikh Tariq al-Fadli,104 and Jamal al-Hindi. It depends on forming discrete cells where the individual members of the cell do not know each other. They only know their leaders. Following the return from Afghanistan by Sheikh Tariq al-Fadli and some group leaders such as Jamal al-Hindi the al-Tajammu' al-Yamani li al-Islah (Yemen Reform Group) (YRG), then part of the government together with the PGCP was able to persuade the authorities not adopt a hostile attitude towards the IJG. The YRG argued that taking such a position towards them will cause political instability and will push the IJG to resort to unproductive conflict which will create social chaos.

On the other hand, the YRG succeeded in convincing the IJG that the government was not infidel and that it is was unlawful to declare jihad against it. Thus the jihad's priority shifted to eliminating the leadership and members of the YSP, arguing that the ruling party members, being regarded as neither clear infidels nor anti-religious, should be left alone by the IJG.

The authorities exploited Sheikh Tariq al-Fadli's and his group's enthusiasm for the idea of liberating South Yemen from the communists. Thus, the IJG was permitted to operate in a suitable area in Abyan governorate, Sheikh Tariq al-Fadli's birthplace, from where the IJG waged its war against the YSP. He succeeded in forming an Islamic Mujahideen army from the mountains of Muraqasha with the protection and help provided by the authorities to him and his supporters.

During the crisis between the PGCP and the YSP the authorities initiated relations with Sheikh Tariq al-Fadli and his group between 1992–1993. This led to increased activities of the IJG which resorted to assassinating a number of the YSP leaders. even the capital Sanaa witnessed assassination attempts against Saleh Mohammad 'Abbad (Muqbil) the YSP secretary-general and Anas Hussein Yahya, member of its political bureau. Homes of other members were bombed such as the house of Dr. Yaseen Saeed Nu'aman, speaker of the House of Representatives and that of Haider Abu Baker al-'Attas, the Prime Minister.

The IJG also carried out subversive activities in the southern areas like the events of the Gold More and Aden hotels. The YSP accused some government leaders in the North of helping and encouraging the Mujahideen against the YSP. It followed that the armed forces, which were under the YSP's control, attacked the mountain locations controlled by Sheikh Tariq al-Fadli. Eventually, both parties reached a cease-fire following the intervention of some influential personalities from the PGCP and YRG who endeavored to put an end to the crisis. Following this conflict, the leader of IJG, Tariq al-Fadli, surrendered himself to Sheikh 'Abdullah bin Hussein al-Ahamr, leader of the YRG who in turn transferred him to Sanaa. The YSP demanded that he should be put to trial, but the Yemeni government rejected this demand due to al-Fadli's relationship with some government leading figures in Sanaa. Moreover, Sheikh Tariq al-Fadli and some of his colleagues became members of the governing PGCP Central Committee. This led to strenuous relations between the PGCP and the YRG on the one part and the YSP on the other. The YSP deemed this action as a reward by the authorities to the IJG for the role they played in assassinating YSP leaders.

When the war erupted in 1994, the IJG became active and was openly supported by the authorities. The IJG took control of several locations such as police stations, military checkpoints, and certain houses and places belonging to the YSP in areas controlled by the authorities in Aden, Abyan, Lahaj and Mukalla. Furthermore, the IJG members assumed certain duties of the judiciary and the executive authorities. They prohibited alcohol drinking and imposed street curfew in those areas. Despite the fact the IJG members were armed and wore military uniform, yet the authorities refrained from any reaction or condemnation against activities.

Following the end of the civil war between the North and the South, negotiations took place between the new leaders of the IJG and the authorities during which the IJG leaders requested to be assigned official duties within the government as a reward for their support to 'Ali Abdullah Saleh's regime in the civil war. Following the failure of negotiations, the IJG revived its terrorist activities.

Al-Fadli officially announced his joining to al-Haraak al-Janobi (the Southern Mobility) which began in 2006. It started with some popular demands for the people of the Southern governorates, and ended with clashes and demonstrations to put an end for the unity between the North and the South. The authorities have accused al-Fadli of transferring Abyan governorate to a center for al-Qaeda organization activities.

Jaysh 'Adan Abyan al-Islmi (The Aden Abyan Islamic Army) (AAIA) was formed in 1997. Regarded as an offshoot of the Jihad groups in Yemen, this organization was led by Zain al-'Abideen Abubaker al-Mihdar (Abul Hassan) who belongs to a well-known tribe in Shabowa governorate.

It is evident from the literature emanating from this organization that it belongs to an Islamic trend which combines between "Jihad" and "Salafi" thoughts because it proclaims that Arab governments were infidel as they did not implement the Islamic Shari'a Law. The AAIA believes that Jihad is the only means of establishing the Islamic form of government. Thus, the AAIA rejects parliamentary democracy and all legitimate institutions as well as political practices. The AAIA was responsible for the numerous terrorist operations in Yemen such as kidnapping 16 western tourists.

Following those terrorist activities the authorities vehemtly, pursued the members and leadership of the AAIA. In this endevour, the authorities withdrew on the support of their allies in the IJG leadership who were contained by the government. The armed confrontation between government forces and the AAIA resulted in a large number of the AAIA either killed or arrested including some 150 Yemenis, Arabs and foreigners. The government accused the AAIA of engaging in terrorist activities, About 14 members of the AAIA were arraigned before the court, charged with kidnapping 16 western tourists, resisting the authorities in the Modiya in Abyan governorate and killing 4 tourists (three British and one Australian). The AAIA members were also charged with organizing and forming an armed group with the intention of conducting subversive activities in the country.

The court issued death verdict in the case of the AAIA leader Zain al-'Abideen Abubaker al-Mihdar and two of his colleagues, one Tunisian, Hussein Mohammad Saleh (Abu Huraira) and 'Abdullah Saleh al-Junaidi, a Yemeni national and one of the AAIA founders.

The court also sentenced Ahmad Mohammad 'Ali 'Atif to 20 years in prison. The AAIA leader claimed that the court was illegitimate on religious ground; therefore, its ruling was null and void. He also claimed that the Yemeni judiciary was not independent and that its rulings were issued based on pre-conceived political decisions. Moreover, he said that he considered the death sentence passed against him will actually grant him martyrdom in the way of God, that he regarded what he had done as a religious duty imposed by Islam, and that Islam must prevail upon the west by the beginning of the third millennium. He believes, that Muslim will possess nuclear weapons and the military power that will enable them to succeed. Whenever an Islamic state is established, it will prevent the American battleships from crossing through Bab el-Mandeb straight.105

In spite of measures taken by the Yemeni authorities against the AAIA, the group still continues its terrorist activities.

The serious operations of armed violence began to evolve greatly after the return of hundreds of members of al-Qaeda after the fall of the Islamic Emirate of the Taliban in 2001. They were carrying orders from the al-Qaeda leader, Osama bin Laden, to prepare for attacks against American targets in Saudi Arabia, Yemen and Kuwait.[106] Kuwait became a transit station for al-Qaeda fugitives from Afghanistan, where they departed to their homelands from Kuwait to carry out terrorist operations.[107]

After bombing the World Trade Center in New York City on 11 September 2001, the Kuwait political arena witnessed the return of dozens of the Kuwaiti Afghani fighter veterans fleeing from the Afghan territory through Iran. After their arrival in Kuwait, they joined groups of secret Islamic cells and their number exceeded 500 members. Some of them received training in Afghanistan and others were veterans of the Afghani conflict who had returned after the jihad against the Soviet army to practice their usual activities and their regular training courses in the desert, where large quantities of weapons were buried.[108] The first armed action attributed to al-Qaeda in Kuwait was the attack on the American Navy and infantry soldiers on

8 October 2002 while performing military exercises called 'Violent Hammer' on the island of Failaka. It was discovered that the group, known as the Anas al-Kandari group, its leader, Anas al-Kandari, who was born on 23 September 1981 and was killed with his colleague Jassim al-Hajiri during this operation. It was known that al-Kandari and al-Hajiri had close intellectual, military, and organizational relations with the main base of the al-Qaeda organization in Afghanistan. This group was composed of 16 people who had been arrested and confessed that they have ties with al-Qaeda. It is worth mentioning that they were regular worshipers at the Rumaithiya Mosque, where Suleimman Abu Ghaith, the spokesman of the al-Qaeda organization and the leader of the Kuwaiti Afghanis, was its imam. It is believed that al-Kandari and al-Hajiri were close to Suleimman Abu Ghaith, who commissioned the group to organize and prepare dormant cells ready to carry out suicide attacks against American forces if they received orders.[109] Earlier, this group met the leader of the al-Qaeda organization, Osama bin Laden, and the official spokesman for al-Qaeda, Suleimman Abu Ghaith, in the al-Farooq camp in Afghanistan. They agreed to make bin Laden the emir of the camp. The head of the group, Anas al-Kandari, had participated in several operations with the Taliban Movement. Jassim al-Hajiri also participated in the jihad of Bosnia and Herzegovina. Before the attacks of Failaka Island, this group was preparing for a series of attacks aimed at attacking one of the foreign schools in the Salwa district and the bombing of the the the Aliah and Ghaliah Twin Towers in the al-Fantas district, and to attack the Doha Military Camp, which is inhabited by American soldiers. However, the operation of Failaka Island led to the exposure of these terrorist plots and the arrest and prosecution of most members of the cell.[110] Following Failaka's terrorist attacks, a group calling itself al-Haraka al-Kuwaitiya liltaqier (Kuwaiti Movement for Change) distributed more than 5,000 copies of an electronic statement. It was published on seven websites belonging to the extremist Islamic movements, describing those who executed that operation as the heroes of Kuwait, who are the students of Sheikh Suleimman Abu Ghaith, whose vengeance for their brothers in Guantanamo Bay Prison detention camps, Palestine and Chechnya, considered this operation as the starting point for the spirit of change in the region. They also described the American Army in Kuwait as crusaders, warning that the Islamic Jihad will not stop.[111] The statement was signed by the students of Sheikh Suleimman Abu Ghaith. This movement has continued to issue political statements, which have reached more than 15 attacking the political situation in Kuwait, through electronic journals and discussion forums of the extremist Islamic movements in the Arabian Peninsula and the Gulf.[112] By studying these statements, it can be discovered that the movement has a close relationship with al-Qaeda and it absolutely supports its ideology.

In January 2003, the al-Qaeda dormant cells launched its activity when a member of the organization, Sami al-Mutairi, succeeded in killing an American citizen and injuring another near the Doha Camp. The Saudi security forces managed to arrest him after an attempt to escape from Kuwait through the Kuwaiti–Saudi border. He was extradited to the Kuwaiti security authorities and sentenced to death after admitting committing murder and supporting the ideas of al-Qaeda.[113] Subsequently, he was given the death sentence for the murder of the American citizen, Michael Rennie Pellet, a civilian who had worked at a company contracting with the American forces, but Sami Mutairi's death sentence was changed to a life sentence.[114] After a short period, the organization calling itself al-Masadah al-Jihadia (the Jihadi Lion) issued a statement demanding the Kuwaiti authorities release the hero, Sami al-Mutairi. The statement made threats that it will carry out several attacks in Kuwait in response to the arrest and pursuit of the mujahideen.[115] It is worth mentioning that Sami al-Mutairi was a leading figure in the liberal democratic students movement and was arrested by the state security forces because of his leftist ideas, but after the events of 11 September 2001, there was a severe shift in his personality and he became religious, spending most of his time in the mosque in the Sabah al-Nasser district, which is considered a stronghold of the political Islamic groups.[116]

In 2003, a group of terrorists attacked an American military convoy on the highway that linked the port of Shu'aiba with the Kuwaiti–Iraqi borders. The act began by attacking a bus belonging to the National Industries Company, which led to the injury of a lot of people including four American soldiers and seven workers from different Arab and Asian nationalities. The security forces managed to arrest the head of the group and the rest of the members of the group. They also found weapons that were used in the operation in the house of the head of the group.[117]

Following the intensification of fighting between al-Qaeda and the international coalition forces in Iraq, the dormant cells of al-Qaeda in Kuwait activated the recruitment and training of many young Kuwaitis and sent them through the borders to fight with the Iraqis. The number of deaths in these fights from Kuwaitis and Bedouin residents in Kuwait is about 11 people.[118] Among the Kuwaitis was Faisal Zaid al-Mutairi,[119] who wrote a will before his death; this was published in the *al-Seyassah* newspaper:

> I present myself for the sake of God to defend Islam and as a revenge for my brothers who were killed in the name of Allah at the hands of the Crusaders in all corners of the Earth and by the Zionists in Palestine.[120]

Al-Mutairi described the al-Qaeda leaders, such as Osama bin Laden, Ayman al-Zawahiri, and Suleiman Abu Ghaith, as heroes who fight for the Muslim cause.[121] He confirmed that there are hundreds of thousands of Osama bin Laden soldiers waiting to make their lives cheap for the sake of God.[122] Sheikh Hamid 'Abdullah al-'Ali, the former Secretary General of the SM, regarded al-Mutairi as a martyr, describing him as 'a nation in a man'.[123]

Kuwaiti security forces managed to arrest a number of these terrorists, who were behind the cause of jihad in Iraq. At that time, 21 defendants were put on trial, including the fugitive Khalid al-Dossari, who was sentenced by the court to three years in absence of imprisonment. The rest of the defendants were convicted with different sentences and the common charge against them was carrying out hostile action against a foreign country through fighting the foreign forces stationed in the Iraqi territory with armed training. Some of them have participated in the fighting in Fallujah, where they met the leader of al-Qaeda in Iraq, Abu Mus'ab al-Zarqawi. Khalid al-Dossari was responsible for the transfer of the mujahideen to Iraq across the Syrian borders after their submission to brainwashing courses.[124]

After the defeat received by the terrorist groups in the city of Fallujah, most Iraqi areas and the Kingdom of Saudi Arabia began to tighten their security measures. Hence, al-Qaeda began planning for the transfer of its battles to the Kuwaiti territories, most especially since Kuwait is the home to many of the terrorist groups that have a political cover by using Islamic political groups that have good links with the Kuwaiti regime. Kuwait has opened its doors for all groups and members in all aspects, and, eventually, the Kuwaiti regime became unable to control the terrorist groups that had roots in Kuwait as they transformed its territory to an environment filled with their terrorist principles.[125] Examples of what was mentioned above is that Abu Mohammad al-Maqdasi, the mastermind of the al-Salafiah al-Jihadia; and Abu Anas al-Shami, an alias for a Jordanian of Palestinian origin, born in Kuwait in 1969, 'Omar Yousef Jumah, who is considered the Mufti (religious scholar who issues religious edicts) of Qa'idat al-Jihad fi Bilad al-Rafidain; he participated in the battles of Fallujah and was killed while trying to break into the Abu Ghraib prison, together with 30 fighters. Khalid Sheikh Mohammad (Khalid al-Bolushi) was involved in the bombing of the American embassies in Nairobi, Dar al-Salaam, and the mastermind behind the attacks of 11 September. Those three people have one thing in common: they all used Kuwait as a transitional phase in their journey of terror. Mohsen al-Fadli was involved in the attack on the American destroyer USS Cole; Suleimman Abu Ghaith, spokesman of al-Qaeda; Mahmoud Ahmad al-Rashid named ('Omar al-Faruq), were some of the prominent figures in al-Qaeda;[126] Anas al-Kandari; and Khalid al-Dossari, among other terrorists, were all either Kuwaiti citizens or lived in Kuwait for a long time. It seems that Kuwait over many years has produced and exported not only petroleum, but also terrorist groups in every shape, size and color. In addition, whenever any Islamist terrorist is arrested in Canada, the Philippines, Afghanistan and Pakistan, and possibly Sudan or Saudi Arabia, it is often that he was born or studied in Kuwait under special Kuwaiti supervision of some of the most dangerous fundamentalist Islamic extremist clerics. It is certain that a number of extremists and figures of al-Qaeda and others have been prepared, packaged, and grown in Kuwait.[127]

The Lions of Peninsula Phalanges (LPP)
Kataib Usood al-Jasiera

In January 2005 some governorates of Kuwait witnessed armed confrontations between terrorist groups represented by the LPP – which is associated with al-Qaeda – and the Kuwaiti security forces, for a period of 20 days. The scene of confrontations began in the Hawalli governorate opposite a car rental office, where two police officers and one of the terrorists, Fawaz al-'Otaibi, were killed. The second and more violent one took place in the area of Umm al-Himan near the Saudi borders, which is considered the main stronghold of the LPP; this resulted in the death of a member of the LPP, Hammad al-Enezi, a Saudi national; three members of the LPP were also arrested. A list of police officers' names were found with them, together with 329 hand grenades and 349 detonators in this confrontation. The third confrontation occurred on 30 January when the security forces raided some apartment buildings in the al-Salmiya district, which resulted in the death of one security officer, a Bahraini citizen, and Nasser Khalaif al-Enezi, the brother of the leader of the organization, 'Amer Khalif al-Enezi, who was later killed. Nasser Khalaif al-Enezi is regarded as the military leader who got his military training in Iraq. The last confrontation was in the Mubarak al-Kabir governorate, which resulted in the killing of one of the security officers, five members of the LPP, and the arrest of three members of the terrorist group, among them 'Amer Khalif al-Enezi, the leader of the LPP who died in prison two weeks after his arrest.[128]

'Amer Khalif al-Enezi had taken advantage of his work as an imam of Malik bin 'Auf's mosque for spreading the extreme thoughts, which calls for takfir to the ruler and his loyal citizens, and the encouragement to fight foreign forces in Kuwait. It is worth mentioning that during the preparations of the American forces for the war against the regime of Saddam Hussein, 'Amer Khalif al-Enezi was arrested and released. 'Amer Khalif al-Enezi has written a booklet in which he called for the need to kill the Americans, the inadequacy of praying, and for the disruption of jihad. He was a charismatic speaker who publicly incited jihad and was the spiritual guide for the youth who were trying to go to Iraq.[129] He actually participated in fighting the Americans in Iraq. One of 'Amer Khalif al-Enezi's colleagues described him as one of the extremist figures who always criticized the moderate 'Ulama severely.[130] During his arrest in January 2005, he admitted his links with al-Qaeda abroad. He also admitted he had contacts with al-Qaeda in Saudi Arabia and the leader of al-Qaeda in Iraq, Abu Musab al-Zarqawi, who was a friend of Suleimman Abu Ghaith. Al-Zarqawi had met Abu Ghaith at first in Afghanistan; after the fall of Kabul they had met again, but in Iran this time, and both agreed on the establishment of the al-Jihad base in Kuwait.[131]

Al-Zarqawi's creed and ideas, which had become known through his letters and speeches made during his argument before the state security court in

Jordan and during his stay in Iraq, were based on not recognizing any legislator but God, whether this legislator was a governor, or deputy, or chief of a clan. He regarded everyone that worked without God's law and acted according to manmade laws followed by the Arab and Islamic governments as an infidel.[132] Al-Zarqawi put the Arab and Islamic regimes at the top of his enemies' list because they violated the application of God's law and followed the infidel forces.[133] Al-Zarqawi took a firm stand against the Shi'ite sect and called for fighting and killing them and did not believe in the Shi'ites as part of the Nation of Islam. Consequently, he regarded the Shi'ites as infidels and that they were outlaws of Islam; he called them Rafidha (the Wahhabis' pejorative term for the Shi'ites).[134] Al-Zarqawi regarded the United States and the Zionist State as the forces of infidels and tyranny, which fight against justice. He believed that the slaughtering of the people abducted by al-Qaeda was the only commemoration of the principles of Islam. Therefore, he stressed that slaughtering all the abductees was the only method he adopted and that he would never accept money for releasing them as a revenge for the Arab and Islamic honor that had been breached by the infidels and the occupation forces.[135]

What emphasizes the links between the LPP and al-Qaeda in Iraq was the tape found by the Kuwaiti police of a lengthy conversation between one of the members of the LPP and Suleimman Abu Ghaith, who in co-ordination with al-Zarqawi worked on extending the al-Qaeda operations in Kuwait. The plan was, as 'Amer Khalif al-Enezi believed, intended to transfer the confrontation inside Kuwaiti soil against the American forces as ordered by Abu Mus'ab al-Zarqawi.[136] The head of the National Guard, Sheikh Salem al-'Ali al-Sabah, confirmed that this organization had links to al-Qaeda and that they were preparing for the bombing of the headquarters of the state security services and oil installations. The LPP called for terrorist acts such as attacking American forces stationed in Kuwait and the Kuwaiti security forces, if the need arises.[137]

The LPP took a slogan similar to the slogans used by the al-Qaeda branches in the area of the Arabian Peninsula and the Arabian Gulf composed of the picture of two machine guns in an 'x' shape with a picture of the Quran underneath them. In the slogan, the sentences La Ilah ila Allah Mohammad Rasole Allahalh (No God but God and Mohammad is his Prophet) and the phrase 'Shura and Jihad' are also written. 'Amer Khalif al-Enezi was chosen as the emir of the organization and Nasser Ahmad Khalif and Ahmad Mutlaq are his deputies.[138] The committees of the organization are:[139]

Military Planning Committee
Committee of Shari'a
Operation Committee
Monitoring Committee
Follow-up Committee

Leadership Committee
Information Committee
Financial Committee

The responsibilities of these committees were distributed among the leader-ship of the organization.[140]

It is believed that the organization was founded in the mosque of Malik bin 'Awf by a number of fundamentalist clerics in Kuwait, who met members of the LPP in this mosque. Among them are youngsters who are not known for carrying ideas of extremism, as others have in the past track records of fighting in more than one place such as Afghanistan, Chechnya, Bosnia, and Herzegovina.[141]

After the crackdown of the organization cells in Kuwait by the Kuwaiti security forces, al-Qaeda threatened the Kuwaiti regime, through the state-ment issued by a group calling itself Kataib 'Abdul-'Aziz al-Miqrin ('Abdul-'Aziz al-Miqrin Phalanges). They stated that a great war will face Kuwait if it does not withdraw the American forces from Kuwaiti territories, and threatened to take revenge for their members' killings at the hands of the security forces. Furthermore, they called for expelling the infidels and other soldiers from Kuwait. This statement demanded the Kuwaiti people to assist the mujahideen and to stay away from places of the infidels,[142] by saying:

> To the Kuwaiti people, we order you to take caution and to keep silent about the hiding places of the Mujahideen, and to assist them in various ways. Stay away from the places which could be destroyed and these are the places where the infidel soldiers are gathering.[143]

The statement regarded the arrest of the LPP leader, 'Amer Khalif al-Enezi, who died in prison, as not the end of the jihadi operations in Kuwait. The statement also warned the security men who took part in the eradication of the terrorist group.[144]

The members of the LPP, who numbered 37 defendants, including nine fugitives, were convicted with several charges, including the overthrow of the ruling regime and disgracing the Emir. The public prosecutor demanded the death penalty for their crimes of killing and planning to commit a series of terrorist operations in Kuwait and abroad, describing the LPP as a little lost group that has committed terrible criminal acts and has hijacked Kuwaiti society.[145] On 27 December 2005, the Kuwaiti Criminal Court sentenced six of the accused to death and the rest of the sentences ranged between life sentence and innocence.[146] A short time after this conviction, the court changed the death sentences to life sentences for the six LPP members. Among them was one of the prominent detainees of the LPP who had been released, Sheikh Hamid 'Abdullah al-'Ali, the former Secretary General of the SM. His release was on the basis that there is no evidence of his connection to that organization.[147] It is worth mentioning that al-'Ali is among the names on the international terrorism list issued by the UN Security Council, which would prevent him from traveling and has froze his assets; this was done in accordance with evidence from the US Treasury Department showing his relationship with al-Qaeda.[148] Ayman al-Zawahiri describes al-'Ali as being one of the symbols who supports jihad and mujahideen.[149]

Mohsin al-Fadli and Khalid al-Dossari were sentenced to 10 years' imprisonment in their absence.[150] It seems that they escaped to Saudi Arabia. Since then, the Saudi authorities revealed in April 2007 that they had arrested 144 terrorists belonging to seven terrorist cells of al-Qaeda, including five Kuwaitis, who were planning to target military bases and oil installations both inside and outside Saudi Arabia, such as in Kuwait.[151]

The question is: does the issuance of these convictions mean the end of religious violence on our national soil? Are there dormant cells waiting for the opportunity to implement its terrorist plans? Especially since the Minister of Interior, Sheikh Jaber al-Khalid al-Sabah, admits the existence of such dormant cells in Kuwait. Moreover, he confirms that the security forces are ready to deal with them at any moment.[152]

It is most disconcerting that since the early 1990s, as we have already mentioned, some of these terrorists were arrested and then released. Others have been tried in different terrorist cases, but then released, only to return and participate in other terrorist acts inside and outside Kuwait.

Apparently, there were some additional Kuwaiti terrorists in Afghanistan and Iraq who were fighting with al-Qaeda, such as 'Ali al-Sinafi, who was killed while fighting with the Taliban Movement in late 2007.[153] In addition, there was 'Abdullah al-'Ajmi and Nasser al-Dossari, who were killed in Mosul after they carried out a suicide bombing targeting the US troops in Mosul in northern Iraq, which resulted in a large number of people being killed and wounded. A pro-al-Qaeda website described al-'Ajmi as the lion of Guantanamo Bay. Al-'Ajmi, who was only 30 years old, held a diploma in Military Sciences and, before joining al-Qaeda, he was working in the Ministry of Defense. He was introduced to a group of young extremists who took him from a mosque in the Sabhan district to a base to disseminate extremist ideas among the youth.[154] On 28 March 2001 he traveled to Pakistan to teach the Quran and was arrested there. After six months, al-'Ajmi entered Afghanistan and participated in fighting against the American forces with a group of young extremists, who were arrested and transferred by the US Army to the Guantanamo Bay Prison, where al-'Ajmi spent five years. He was then released by the US Government and surrendered to the Kuwaiti Government, where he had been detained in the State's Security facility for a short period and then sent to the central prison. Shortly afterwards – and similar to the other eight Kuwaiti prisoners detained at Guantanamo Bay Prison who have been handed over to the Kuwaiti Government – the Kuwaiti court issued al-'Ajmi's innocence from all charges and he was released. On 21 April 2008, al-Ajmi left Kuwait for Syria with two of his colleagues and then crossed the Iraqi–Syrian border into Iraq. On 28 April 2008, they carried out a suicide operation against the American forces in Mosul. Also, Nasser al-Dossari committed a suicide bombing with al-'Ajmy; he had been arrested by the State Security forces earlier on charges of fighting in Iraq, but was later released. He then shaved his beard as a disguise to express his abandoning the jihadist groups as he had been suspected of having connections with them. His brother, Hussein al-Dossari, was killed in Afghanistan when he was accompanied by 'Abdullah al-'Ajmi. Five days after the operation of Mosul, the American military announced another suicide operation in the city of Mosul carried out by another Kuwaiti citizen named Badr al-Harbi, who was born in 1975; he had been a religious fanatic since he was 14 years old. He worked in the Ministry of Interior between 1992 and 2001 and had visited Afghanistan twice since 2006. Later, he returned to Kuwait and was arrested by the State Security but was released after being interrogated. Then he traveled to Saudi Arabia, United Arab Emirates, Syria, and then to Iraq where he participated in the suicide attack against the American forces.[154] The brother of al-'Ajmi has demanded that the authority tighten control on these dormant cells and begin monitoring their movements more closely.[155] According to Kuwaiti security sources, there are still approximately 38 Kuwaitis in Iraq and Afghanistan fighting American forces there.[156]

Some extremists are still advocating for jihad, publicly calling for fighting the coalition forces in Afghanistan and Iraq, both through Arab satellite channels or via the local press. An example of this is Mubarak al-Bathally, one of the extremists who had previously fought in Bosnia and Herzegovina and Kosovo. In London, he met with Abu Hamza al-Masri and Abu Qatada (before he was arrested); Abu Qatada is now detained in British jails on charges of supporting al-Qaeda.[157] Al-Bathally was arrested at first in Saudi Arabia, after being accused of arranging camps inside its territory in co-operation with Jama'at Ansar al-Sunnh (the Supporters for al-Sunna Group) and was shortly released. Al-Bathally was impressed by the preaching of Sheikh Ahmad al-Qattan, a leader of the MBG and the Imam of the Qurtuba mosque, in respect to the Bosnia and Herzegovina situations.[158] It is worth mentioning that al-Bathally was among the names on the list of international terrorism issued by the UN Security Council that would prevent him from traveling and have frozen his assets, following the availability of evidence and information from the US Treasury Department that demonstrated his links with al-Qaeda.[159] Al-Bathally admitted that he was behind the organization of the entry of the mujahideen to Chechnya and Iraq; among those was Muhsin al-Fadli. In 2001, Al-Bathally sent his son, 'Abdul-Rahman, to Kashmir for training in fighting and he was arrested during his return to Kuwait and was later released. Then 'Abdul-Rahman went to Iraq, where he is still being detained.[160] Al-Bathally called the young Kuwaitis also to join Islamic groups fighting the Thai Government.[161] He also called for support of the Islamic State of Iraq and believes that the kidnapping of a

Muslim who helps the Americans is permissible.[162] Al-Bathally was arrested and accused of hostile action against a foreign state, which would endanger Kuwait's political relations.[163] It is worth mentioning that al-Bathally admitted that he has trained 50 youngsters to fight in Iraq; among them was Nasser Khalaif al-Enezi. And he emphasized that Nasser Khalaif al-Enezi had met Abu Mos'ab al-Zarqawi in Iraq. Despite all of this, al-Bathally was released after less than two months in prison with a 1,000 KD bail and was prevented from traveling.[164]

There are dozens like al-Bathally, and some are leading figures who were introduced to the Kuwaiti political arena through public organizations that raise the slogan of al-Jihad al-Siasi (political jihad) publicly. One of the extremists arrested said that his group had participated in the 2008 elections of the Kuwaiti parliament. Those members considered this participation as a takleef Jihadi (Jihadi obligation).[165]

It seems that due to the growing number of terrorist operations carried out by a number of Kuwaiti terrorists in Iraq and Afghanistan, the American Government, in its report issued in April 2009 about Global Terrorism, criticized the Kuwaiti regime in its measures in combating terrorism. It added that the Kuwaiti regime is having difficulty in prosecuting terrorists and terrorism financiers, and that the risk of terrorist attacks on US military installations and convoys in Kuwait is still high.[166]

Four months after the publication of this report, the Interior Ministry had foiled an al-Qaeda-linked plan to bomb a US Army camp and other important facilities related to US and Kuwaiti interests. An Interior Ministry statement said all six members of the al-Qaeda-linked terrorist cell had confessed after being arrested. Two of the defendants charged with trying to blow up the US military base located at A'rifjan Camp admitted that the group had planned to attack Kuwait's Shua'iba oil refinery during the holy Muslim month of Ramadan. They also said that they, along with four other defendants, object to the US presence in Kuwait. The group also planned to attack State Security Headquarters and confessed that they promulgate the al-Qaeda school of thought.

The leader of this cell was born in 1981. He had given refuge to Mohsin al-Fadli, who is wanted by authorities, for four-and-a-half years in his apartment located in al-Slmiya. Five of the suspects were previously charged with involvement in the Failaka Island case. They were accused of belonging to an outlawed group that promotes fanatic ideologies and of involvement in subversive activities against the State. Verdicts were issued against four of the suspects to pay a bill of 2,000 Kuwaiti Dinars each, while the court abstained from sentencing the fifth and instead ordered him to write an undertaking of good conduct.[167]

8 The armed Islamist Shi'ite jihadist groups

The armed Islamist Shi'ite jihadist groups in Kuwait emerged with the victory of the Islamic revolution in Iran, which was led by Imam Khomeini in 1979. At this time, the Iranian Islamic regime raised the slogan of exporting the revolution to neighboring countries through recruiting a number of Shi'ites in the Arabian Gulf and Arabian Peninsula to their ideology. Among those were Kuwaitis who belonged to terrorist organizations, such as Hizb al-Da'wa al-Islamiya (the Islamic Call Party) and Hizbollah, whose main objective was to promote political instability in Kuwait in response to the aid given by the Kuwaiti regime to Iraq in its war with Iran. At the beginning of the war, Kuwait agreed to assist Iraq to use Shuwaikh and Shu'aiba ports to receive imports of equipment and fuel as transit stations in order to transfer goods through the adjoining land borders.[1] In September 1980, Kuwait provided an interest-free loan worth $4 billion to Iraq. By the end of 1982, Kuwait's share in the sale of oil production in the neutral zone was sold in the interest of Iraq. It is estimated that Iraq's benefit from Kuwait was more than $7 billion during the period 1983–1988.[2] Iran considered these acts – from financial support to logistical facilities to the Iraqi regime – as a hostile attitude and warned the Kuwaiti Government to suffer the consequences. In light of this situation, Kuwait suffered a series of military attacks from November 1980 until 30 March 1988 in the form of attacks on Kuwaiti airspace and its planes, and fires in the border areas and oil fields.[3] On 11 March 1986, the Iranian Government also organized in Tehran a hostile demonstration against Kuwait. On 1 August 1987, the Kuwaiti embassy in Tehran was attacked by Iranian demonstrators.[4] The impact of these attacks on Kuwaiti soil strained political relations between Kuwait and Iran; in response to these attacks and interference in their internal affairs, the Kuwaiti regime expelled six Iranian diplomats.[5] In return for the support of Kuwait to Iraq, Iran pushed its loyal Shi'ite Islamist political groups to tamper with the stability and security of Kuwait. As a result, from 1980–88, Kuwait witnessed waves of political violence in the form of spreading terrorist operations and the distribution of publications that provoked the overthrow of the existing regime in Kuwait to establish an Islamic republic on the Iranian model. Some of these terrorist operations were: first, on 12 December 1983, a truck exploded by the

American Embassy building in the al-Bidi'a district, killing and injuring dozens; a similar explosion occurred at the French Embassy in the al-Jabriya district; a third at the airport, and the fourth in a residential area occupied by Americans. These attacks also took place at vital installations, such as electricity stations, and offices of an American company in the al-Bidi'a district.[6] The trial for these terrorist operations was held on 11 February 1984. Among those on trial were Kuwaiti, Iraqi and Lebanese Shi'ites. The government received threats that if it took tough actions against the detainees, the consequences would be severe.[7] The court convicted 25 of them; six of them were sentenced to death. The Emir of Kuwait had not approved the implementation of the death penalty. It turned out that six of them belonged to Hizb al-Da'wa al-Islamiya, and the rest of the detainees belonged to Munadamat Amal (the Amal Organization) in Lebanon.[8]

On 4 December 1984, the Kuwaiti plane Kazimah – carrying 161 passengers and heading from Kuwait to Pakistan – was hijacked and was directed to Iran, resulting in the death of two American passengers. The hijackers demanded the release of the prisoners in Kuwait. Kuwaiti authorities did not respond to their demands, and on the sixth day of the kidnapping, Iranian security forces stormed the plane and released all the passengers. Two terrorist attacks also took place in Kuwait in the same month, which were defused.[9]

On 23 January 1985, there was an attempted assassination of the political chief editor of the *al-Seyassah* newspaper, Ahmad al-Jarallah.[10] *Majallat al-Thawrah al-Islamiya* commented:

This agent who sold himself to the devil . . . deserves those bullets.[11]

On 25 May 1985, the convoy of the Emir of Kuwait, Sheikh Jaber al-Ahmad al-Sabah, was attacked with a suicide car; the Emir survived the assassination attempt, but three of his guards were killed and 12 others were wounded.[12]

On 12 July 1985, a popular café on the Arabian Gulf Street was bombed, killing eight people and wounding 88 others.[13] On 14 July of that same year, a Kuwaiti diplomat working in the Kuwaiti Embassy in Beirut was kidnapped.[14]

Some Shi'ite Kuwaiti names were associated with the bombings that occurred in 1986 and the bombings in January, May and July 1987. The political violence that took place in the Mishref district on 30 January 1987 was due to the Special Forces trying to arrest 30 people who were suspected of being involved in the bombing incidents, but their families stood with them.[15]

In April 1988 another Kuwaiti airplane, al-Jabriya, was hijacked by terrorists, resulting in the killing of two Kuwaiti passengers and demands that the captain take the plane to Iran and then land in Algeria. The demands of the kidnappers this time were also to liberate the prisoners in Kuwaiti prisons, but the Kuwaiti Government did not show any willingness to make concessions. The whole process ended with an agreement between the Algerian authorities and the kidnappers to release all the passengers, ensure the security of the kidnappers and to leave Algeria safely.[16]

Munadhamt al-Jihad al-Islamiya (the Islamic Jihad Organization) claimed responsibility for these terrorist operations because of Kuwait's support for Iraq in its war against Iran.[17] The Islamic Jihad gave a final ultimatum to the Kuwaiti authorities for the release of all the detainees in the bombing incidents that took place in Kuwait, together with the pictures of six Americans and French citizens kidnapped in Beirut. Among these was William Buckley, the First Secretary of the American Embassy in Beirut. Kuwaiti authorities did not make any concessions to this terrorist group. The detainees managed to escape during the Iraqi occupation of Kuwait in 1990 from the central prison to Iran and then to Lebanon. It is worth mentioning that among those terrorists was Mostafa Badrdin, who is related to 'Imad Mughniyeh and who used the alias of Elias Sa'ab. He was convicted by the Kuwaiti courts with eight charges relating to the terrorist operations that took place on 12 December 1983 and was sentenced to death.[18]

Ayatollah Mohammad Hussein Fadlallah, the spiritual guide for Hizbollah-Lebanon, states that the name of the organization is used by others as a cover for their operations.[19] While some people think that Hizb al-Da'wa al-Islamiya and Hizbollah-Kuwait were behind the terrorist attacks that occurred in the 1980s, the parties' officials denied official involvement in the kidnappings and denied any relations with Munadhamat al-Jihad al-Islamiya. In the meantime, al-Sayyed Hassan Nasrallah, the Secretary General of Hizbollah-Lebanon, confirmed:

> Members of the Islamic Jihad are our brothers, but they have their own style.[20]

In spite of the denial of Hizbollah-Lebanon of any relationship with the kidnapping operations, it did not express absolute condemnation of the kidnappings either.[21] Some resources confirmed that the four kidnappers who hijacked the Kuwaiti plane were members of Hizb al-Da'wa al-Islamiya.[22] The truth is that there are several Islamic organizations that supported the Islamic regime in Iran, which were represented by the following.

Islamic Call Party (ICP)
Hizb al-Da'wa al-Islamiya

This party was founded in Najaf, Iraq, in 1957 by Mohammad Baqir al-Sadr, who wrote educational articles through a series of books, such as *Falsafatina* (*Our Philosophy*) and *Iqitsadana* (*Our Economy*). The ICP planned to work over four phases: the underground activity phase, the public activity phase, the take-power phase, and the phase of practical implementation of Islam.[23] Some of the Kuwaiti Shi'ites were affected by the approach of the ICP's activists who came from Iraq, including a Lebanese, Sheikh 'Ali al-Corani, who started to preach their ideologies through their presence at the al-Naqi mosque. The ICP succeeded in taking control over the SCS via the call for a political Islam that is based on Manhaj Ahl Albait. The ICP started several significant cultural activities, such as issuing *Tareeq al-Noer* (*By the Light*) and *Majallat al-Nba* (*The News*) and holding symposiums and lectures.[24] The ICP concealed the party name when all the activities took place on behalf of the SCS.[25] The ICP also clearly emerged in the student movement at Kuwait University during the issue of segregating education at the university, where the battle was being waged between the leftist and nationalist on one hand and the religious currents on the other hand.[26] The ICP also managed to extend its influence to what is known as FYG through attracting some of its leading figures.[27]

After the Iranian revolution in 1981, the ICP submitted a report to Ayatollah Fad-Lallah Mahalati stating that Kuwait was 'ripe for revolution.'[28] The ICP believed, according to this report, that the Shi'ite Kuwaitis were enthusiastic for the Islamic revolution.[29] On July 1986, the ICP published a statement from Tehran, confirming:

> Islam is at war against the mercenary Kuwaiti regime . . . Kuwait is a zone of combat and will remain so until complete Islamic rule is established there.[30]

Later on the members of the ICP were arrested and prosecuted. They were accused of seeking to establish an Islamic republic in Kuwait similar to the Islamic Republic of Iran, and were also accused of being behind the bombings in Kuwait that occurred during the 1980s. The ICP threatened to target the Kuwaiti interests inside and outside Kuwait, especially Kuwaiti embassies, if their members who had been arrested in Kuwait were tortured in prison.[31]

The Missionaries Vanguard Movement (MVM) Harakat al-Risaliyyen al-Talaiyeen

This movement was founded in 1968 in Karbala by Ayatollah Mohammad al-Shirazi.[32] It is a gathering of the Shi'ite religious forces working in Saudi Arabia, Bahrain, Iraq, Kuwait and Oman. The MVM's main goal is to replace the existing regimes in those countries with Islamic fundamentalist ones similar to the Iranian model. In this regard, Sheikh Hassan al-Saffar,[33] one of the MVM leaders, says:

> The establishment of the Islamic Republic in a limited part of the Islamic world (Iran) does not satisfy the aspirations of Muslim believers, and does not fulfill all their holy objectives . . . the final goal is the establishment of the government of a thousand million Muslims . . . the Islamic Republic can be considered the beginning of the road and the first half of the march.[34]

The MVM specified three phases in order to accomplish this task:[35]

1 deployment phase
2 devotion, governance and organization phase
3 phase of confrontation with other political forces.

The MVM worked underground towards the victory of the Islamic revolution in Iran, which led to the overthrow of the Shah's regime in 1979. This event later led to the announcement of establishing its branches in the GCC countries:

In Bahrain on 2 September 1979, Hujjat al-Islam Hadi al-Mudarrisi held a press conference announcing the formation of al-Jabha al-Islamiya li Tahrir al-Bahrain (the Islamic Front for the Liberation of Bahrain (IFLB)).[36] Faisal Marhoun, one of the IFLB leaders, stated that the IFLB was established before the victory of the Islamic Revolution in Iran, but was not revealed for security reasons.[37] Most of the IFLB members represented Bahraini Shi'ites who descended from Iranian origin, while the Shi'ites from Arab origin were connected to the ICP, which was established in Iraq. They formed Harakat al-Ahrar al-Islamiya al-Bahrainiya (the Bahrain Islamic Freedom Movement (BIFM)) in 1980.

The BIFM was founded by a group of Shi'ite students studying in Britain. It was regarded as an expansion of Jam'iyyat al-Taw'iya al-Islamiya (the Islamic Enlightenment Society). The most distinguished figures in the movement were Dr. Sa'id al-Shihabi, Dr. Majeed al-'Alawi, and Dr. Mansour al-Jamri. The political bulletin, *Sout al-Bahrain* (*Voice of Bahrain*), issued in London, was the mouthpiece of the BIFM. The BIFM was regarded as a reform movement because it did not demand the overthrowing of the ruling family in Bahrain. Its demands were focused on the return of the democratic system and the release of political prisoners, and this made it popular among the Shi'ites in Bahrain. One reason for its popularity was that it published its publications in London and Beirut, contrary to the IFLB, which published in Tehran. The BIFM maintained good relations with the European parliaments and the international human rights committees. Many BIFM members and supporters were arrested by the Bahraini regime and were sentenced to imprisonment.

The Shi'ites in Bahrain are divided into Shi'ites Ikhbariiyeen and Baharana, who are Arabs representing Shi'ites with Arab origin, and Shi'ites al-Asoalin (Fundamentalist Shi'ites), who represent those with Iranian origin. The first signs of a dispute between the Shi'ites descending from Iranian origin and those descending from Arab origin appeared during the referendum supervised by the United Nations regarding the political future of Bahrain. The Bahrainis with Iranian origin accused the Arab Bahrainis of denying the existence of their sect and of being a victim of their nationalist fanaticism, while the Arab Bahrainis accused those of Iranian origin of being Persians, foreigners to Bahrain, reinforcing the historical fact that Bahrain was a country first inhabited by Arabs and that independence is a natural right to them.[38]

The IFLB's demands, published through its statement on 15 October 1979, were to release all political prisoners, to allow religious activities, and to remove American military bases from Bahrain. However, the IFLB also wanted to overthrow the ruling regime in Bahrain and replace it with an Islamic republic.[39]

The Islamic Republic of Iran supported the IFLB and its office in Tehran was very active, producing many publications, such as *al-Sha'b al-Thaer* (*The Revolting People*) and *al-Thawra al-Risaliyya* (*The Missionary Revolution*), which were considered the propaganda machines of the IFLB. Since its establishment, the IFLB has defended itself from the accusations of being sectarian, with assurances that:

> it strives against and under the shadow of the worst sectarian regimes in the world.[40]

'Isa Marhoun pointed out: 'We believe that the popular revolution is the best choice, and it is the best and quickest way to overthrow the reactionary regime in Bahrain.'[41] The IFLB also opposed the parliamentary option. The IFLB regarded the reforms made by the Bahraini Government after the announcement of independence, such as the Constitutional Council and the National Council, as formal reforms whose aims were to deny popular demands in free elections.[42]

The IFLB called for the unification of all Islamic forces in the Gulf, not calling it the Arabian Gulf, and, thus, confirming its connection with Iran. It considered the unity of these forces as the right way to achieve unity of the region. It considered the GCC as an alliance of dominant tribes, practicing repression against people, and being directed by colonial forces.[43]

Among the most distinguished activities of the IFLB was the organization of demonstrations against the Bahraini regime, as in the demonstrations held on 23 August 1979. In addition were the 'Ashura processions in Bahrain that year where IFLB went out to the street to support the uprising led by the Shi'ites in the Eastern Province in Saudi Arabia.[44]

In December 1981, the Bahraini Government revealed a coup attempt to seize power and accused the IFLB of being behind it. Following these events, 73 members and supporters of the IFLB were arrested and sentenced to life imprisonment by the state security court, where they were tortured and some were murdered, according to IFLB sources.[45] The IFLB denied any involvement in the coup attempt and announced that the Bahraini regime aimed to get rid of the religious movement and to break its base, which dominated the Bahraini political arena.[46] The IFLB then transferred its activities outside of Bahrain to Beirut and Tehran.

In 1994, the political arena in Bahrain witnessed a strong activity in which all opposition groups participated. This was the Constitutional Uprising.

Among these were the IFLB, demanding the restoration of the Constitution and the National Council, which was unconstitutionally dissolved in 1975.[47]

On 23 December 2000, when the Emir of Bahrain, Sheikh Hamad Bin 'Isa al-Khalifa, announced a reformative plan called Mithaq al-'Amal al-Watani (the National Action Charter), the IFLB rejected this charter and demanded that Bahraini citizens not participate in voting for this referendum. The IFLB continued its struggle for change and freedom and to establish a democratic system that would demolish the backward tribal system. However, it later on discovered that it was necessary to co-operate with the new events and it formed Jam'iyat al-'Amal al-Islamiya (the Islamic Action Society).

In Saudi Arabia, three underground organizations appeared after the victory of the Islamic Revolution in Iran in 1979. These three organizations were extensions of the MVM. The first one is Munadhamat Fajir al-Thawrya (the Dawn Revolutionary Organization), known as the DRO. This organization appeared during the uprising in the Eastern Province in Saudi Arabia led by the Shi'ite religious clerics who sympathized with the new regime in Iran. The DRO raised many slogans supporting the Islamic Revolution in Iran, such as Thawratna Islamia Khomeini Qaidana (Our Revolution is Islamic and Khomeini is our leader), and saying this while raising pictures of Khomeini. The activities of the DRO started on 27 November 1979 through demonstrations, such as the violent one held in the Sihat district, which was met with force by the security forces. Consequently, demonstrations spread throughout the cities of the Eastern Province, which has an intensive Shi'ite presence. The first strike was held on 1 and 2 December 1979. The DRO distributed pamphlets attacking the Saudi regime and the United States of America and, accordingly, the DRO was repressed by the Saudi authorities.[48] The second organization is Lijan Shuhada al-Hussein (al-Hussein Martyrs Committees), known as the HMC. The HMC participated in the above-mentioned demonstrations, it also distributed pamphlets attacking the Saudi regime and the United States of America. Its faith was similar to the DRO. The Saudi authorities arrested some of the HMC's members, who were later sent to jail.[49] The third organization is Munadhamat al-Thawra al-Islamiya fi al-Jazira al-'Arabiya (the Islamic Revolution Organization in the Arabian Peninsula (IROAP)). The IROAP was founded in 1975 as an extension of the MVM. It adopted the Islamic ideology and it is traditionally regarded as the Shi'ite political party in Saudi Arabia. Among its ranks are a group of Shi'ite intellectuals, teachers, religious men, and educated people, such as Sheikh Hassan al Saffar, who is the spiritual leader of the IROAP; in addition, two of its leaders are Hamza al-Hassan and Tawfiq al-Sheikh.

The IROAP believes in the need to build a strong organization in charge of managing and directing the people's political movements.[50] The IROAP regards itself as part of the global Islamic Revolution led by the Iranian regime. It has participated in several conferences held in Tehran and it stood on the same platform with the Iranian regime in its war with Iraq.[51]

The IROAP has had many relationships with the opposition parties and movements in Saudi Arabia based on their beliefs. Moreover, the IROAP regards the political Islamic groups that support the Islamic Revolution in Iran as allies. Accordingly, it has had good relationships with Shi'ite Islamist political groups in the Arabian Gulf and Iraq. The IROAP supports Juhayman's movement, despite the ideological differences between them.[52] The IROAP rejects the Nationalist and Marxist ideologies and, thus, it criticizes them. The IROAP does not have any relation with the Saudi Communist Party and the Arab Socialist Labour Party in Saudi Arabia.[53] They adopted the slogan la-Sharqya wa la-Garbya (not Eastern and not Western). It describes America and the former Soviet Union as imperialist states and, thus, the IROAP rejects the communist and capitalist ideologies, saying that the American and Russian domination is the main reason behind the problems in the world.[54]

The IROAP announced its social and cultural activities outside Saudi Arabia when it issued its monthly magazine *Majallat al-Thawra al-Islamiya* (*The Islamic Revolution Magazine*) in London in 1980. In 1991, the IROAP issued a new magazine that shares the same ideology of *Majallat al-Thawra al-Islamiya* called *Majallat al-Jazira al-'Arabiya* (*The Arabian Peninsula Magazine*).[55] The IROAP had relationships with nearly all of the nationalist and religious movements in the Arab region, and it participated in the Cyprus conference in November 1980 to support the opposition in the Arabian Peninsula.[56]

The IROAP is active during mourning on the days of 'Ashura in the Eastern Province. This was the first confrontation with the Saudi regime that doesn't agree with the mourning on 'Ashura. At that time, 20,000 soldiers set siege in the Eastern Province, leading to many of the IROAP members and supporters being arrested. The IROAP claimed that 60 of their members died, 800 were wounded and 1,200 arrested.[57]

After the Second Gulf War, the IROAP stopped publishing its journal *Majallat al-Thawra al-Islamiya*. However, *Majallat al-Jazira al-'Arabiya* continued publishing and it showed the change of the IROAP's ideology from being extremist to becoming a reformative movement.[58]

The MVM sought to have a presence in Oman. Therefore, Sayyed Mohammad al-Shirazi sent Sheikh Hassan al-Saffar to Oman in 1974. He stayed approximately five years and succeeded in establishing religious institutions, such as Maktabat al-Rasul al-A'dham (the Library of the Supreme Prophet) in Matrah. In the meantime, the MVM founded al-Jabha al-Islamiya li Tahrir Oman (the Islamic Front for the Liberation of Oman), which did not have any significant activity like its other branches in the Gulf.[59] In Iraq, Munadhamat al-'Amal al-Islamiya (the Islamic Action Organization) was formed.[60]

In Kuwait, the MVM borrowed the name of Madrasat al-Rasul al-A'dham (the Greatest Prophet school), which it then established in 1975 as its headquarters for recruitment and education. Most of the new members were young high school or university students from Kuwait, Bahrain, Saudi

Arabia, Oman and Iraq. The lectures and educational seminars were held for one week in the summer holidays and were given by Ayatollah Mohammad al-Shirazi[61] and Sayyed Mohammad Taqi al-Mudarrisi.[62] It seems that the MVM leadership took Kuwait as its base for organizing and educating new members due to the freedom to move in Kuwait under the cover of freedom of religious activity. In addition, the leaders of the MVM in Saudi Arabia, Bahrain and Iraq were unable to activate; they were arrested and prosecuted by the authorities. However, after the series of bombings in the 1980s, which affected many of the vital locations in Kuwait, and the assassination attempt of the late Emir of Kuwait, Sheikh Jaber al-Ahmad al-Sabah, the Kuwaiti authorities took severe measures, such as the apprehension and prosecution of many members of the MVM. It accused them of being behind these events. The Kuwaiti Government, due to the MVM's violent actions, tightened security measures on the political and cultural activities undertaken by the armed Shi'ite organizations funded by the Islamic regime in Iran. Following this the Islamic Action Organization in Iraq threatened to carry out military operations against the interests of Kuwait in the Arabian Gulf region and abroad if the Kuwaiti authorities did not take this warning seriously.[63]

The MVM then threatened the Kuwaiti authorities that they would respond violently towards the allowance of the presence of the Iraqi Ba'ath activists in Kuwait, including the activity of the Iraqi intelligence, which they regarded as support from the Kuwaiti Government towards the Iraqi regime. On this basis, the MVM considered that both the Kuwaiti and Iraqi governments should have the same interests.[64] Since 1980, Iraqi intelligence took Kuwait as a theater of operations to settle their differences with the Islamic regime in Iran. On 4 June 1980, an RPJ rocket was fired towards the Iranian Embassy building in al-Istiqlal street, which resulted in the injury of one person. On 29 April 1980, there was an attempt to assassinate the Iranian Foreign Minister, Sadeq Ghotb Zadeh, during his visit to Kuwait by firing on his convoy; this resulted in three injuries among the Iranian delegation. On 26 June 1980, the Iranian Airlines office on Fahad al-Salem Street was bombed, causing material damages. On 28 March 1981, the Iranian Shipping Company exploded, resulting in the death of one person.[65] Sayyed Mohammad Taqi al-Mudarrisi, the official organizer in Kuwait, was in charge of all the Shi'ite terrorist organizations in the Arabian Gulf region,[66] which aimed to change the political systems in these countries through armed violence.

Party of God – Kuwait (PGK)
Hizbollah-Kuwait

After the Iranian Revolution, the Iranian regime sought to export the revolution to the GCC countries. In Saudi Arabia, Hizbollah-Hijaz (Party of God-Hijaz (PGH)) was established in 1987 by Shi'ite students who studied in Najaf and Qom. Earlier, in 1983, a group of Saudi students were studying in Qom and they established an assembly called Tajammu' 'Olama al-Hijaz (the Assembly for the Hijazi Clerics), which is regarded as the roots of the PGH. Among these was Sheikh Ja'far Mubarak, who graduated from the city of Qom, was an imam at the Safwa Mosque, and was the most prominent leader of the PGH. In addition, there was Sheikh 'Abdul-Kareem Jubail, who graduated from Qom, and Hashim al Shukhus.[67] The PGH believed in using violence to overthrow the Saudi regime, which the party believed did not represent Islam and was allied to Western regimes.[68] The PGH was similar to Hizbollah in Lebanon; it issued some pamphlets and magazines, such as *Majallat Risalat al-Haramain* (*The Letter of the Two Holy Mosques*), *al-Manber* and *al-Fath*, which expressed its ideologies.

The PGH had a strong relationship with Iran and worked according to the Iranian political agenda in order to establish an Islamic republic in the Arabian Peninsula.[69]

Ayatollah Khomeini and Ayatollah 'Ali Khamenei are the religious marji' (authority) for the PGH, contrary to the IROAP, whose religious marji' is Mohammad al-Shirazi, and its political marji' is Sheikh Hassan al-Saffar. The first armed operation of this group was in retaliation for the Saudi Government's killing of several hundred Iranian citizens during their pilgrimage to Mecca in 1987. In 1996 the American military camp in al-khobar was attacked. The Saudi authorities accused the PGH for these attacks. Following the al-Khobar events, around 150 members of the PGH were arrested, including some of its prominent leaders.[70] After the Iraqi occupation of Kuwait, Iranian–Saudi relations were improved and, accordingly, the PGH replaced armed violence with peaceful methods in its struggle with the Saudi regime. The PGH opposed the agreement made between the Saudi regime and al-Harakah al-Islahia in 1993, which allowed the return of all members of the Shi'ite opposition who lived in exile to Saudi Arabia, including the members of the PGH and the release of its prisoners. However, the PGH members were the first ones who took advantage of this agreement and returned home to Saudi Arabia.[71]

Hizbollah–Bahrain (Party of God – Bahrain (PGB)) was established in 1993 in co-ordination with the Iranian Revolutionary Guard by Bahraini students who were studying in al-Hawza in Qom. Some of the founders were 'Ali al-Mutaqawi, Sheikh 'Adil al-Shi'lah, Sheikh Khalil Sultan, Sheikh Jassem al-Khayyat, and Sheikh Mohammad Habib, a resident in Kuwait who supervised the activity of the Bahraini students in Kuwait.[72]

The PGB formed several committees, such as the Committee of Training, headed by Sheikh 'Adel al-Shi'lah; the Media Committee, headed by Sheikh Khalil Sultan; and the Security Committee, headed by Jassem Hassan Mansour. The target of the military wing of the PGB was to recruit and train about 3,000 young people to be the base to overthrow the Bahraini regime with an armed struggle and to establish an Islamic republic.[73] To achieve this purpose, the PGB sent a group of youngsters to Mu'askar Karj (the Karj Camp) in northern Iran to get military training; it sent another group to the camps of Hizbollah-Lebanon, such as Mu'askar Thaar Allah (the God Revenge Camp) in the Bekaa' Valley and the Ba'albak area. The Iranian Embassy in Damascus was supervising these groups and facilitating their arrival to these camps.[74]

The PGB started to hold anti-regime demonstrations in Bahrain to distribute publications against the regime and to write slogans on the walls of houses. The activity of the party was developed to carry out terrorist operations against tourist installations, such as hotels in the al-'Aker Village, al-'Adlia, the diplomatic district, and the Bani Jamra village.[75]

In June 1996, the Bahraini authorities revealed the existence of Hizbollah-Bahrain, and 56 Bahraini Shi'ites were arrested, including 12 leading figures, and were charged with belonging to the PGB.[76]

Majallat al-Nasr, the mouthpiece of the PGB, criticized the Shi'ite religious groups who refused to participate in violent actions against the Bahraini regime, such as the ICP in Bahrain due to their reformative attitudes. They accused the ICP of abandoning jihad to liberate the country from al-Khalifa rule and the American colonialism by adopting lean reformations that concentrated on democracy and the Bahraini Constitution, which, according to the magazine, is a deviation from the Khomeini line.[77]

In Kuwait, Hizbollah-Kuwait (Party of God – Kuwait (PGK)) was founded after the Islamic Revolution in Iran by a group of young revolutionary Kuwaiti Shi'ites who received their education in the scientific shrine in Qom. Most of the members of the PGK were linked to the Revolutionary Committees of the Revolutionary Guards in Iran.

The PGK was activated in Iran through facilities given to it by the Islamic regime, such as al-Markaz al-Islami al-Kuwaiti lil'alam (the Kuwaiti Islamic Media Center), which published *Majallat al-Nasr* (*The Victory Journal*), reflecting the ideology of the PGK; it called itself the sincere Mahammadan voice in Kuwait.[78]

The PGK calls for establishing a free independent Republic of Kuwait and performing a referendum so that Kuwaiti society can choose the type of leadership it wants. It has criticized the existing electoral system, the denial of the Shi'ites to publish their own newspapers and magazines, the banning of some Shi'ite clerics from entering Kuwait, and, lastly, not naming public schools and streets after Shi'ite imams and clerics. The PGK believes that this sectarian policy adopted by the authorities in Kuwait will, in the end, turn Kuwait into a second Lebanon.[79] Sheikh Mash'al Jarrah al-Sabah, the former head of State Security, confirms that the party was active in mosques and they had members in the Kuwaiti National Assembly.[80]

The Shi'ite revolutionaries in Kuwait took a firm stand against the policy adopted by the Kuwaiti Government in supporting the Iraqi regime in its war with Iran – financially, informatively, militarily, and for not showing sympathy with Iran. The Islamic regime in Iran took advantage of this support and the sympathy shown by a minority of the Shi'ites, not only in Kuwait, but also in all areas of the Arabian Gulf and Peninsula, by creating a base of supporters among some lower–middle-class Kuwaiti Shi'ites. The fundamentalist regime in Iran tried, under the slogan of exporting the revolution, to recruit a number of Kuwaitis into the Shi'ite terrorist organizations whose main objective was political instability in Kuwait in response to Kuwaiti aid to Iraq.

During the Islamic Summit held in Kuwait, the Iranian regime opposed its proceedings because it believed that it was held in favor of Iraq,[81] Harakt al-Rafidain – Tali'at Hizbollah fi al-Iraq (Two Rivers Movement – the Vanguard for the Party of God in Iraq), announced that the interests of Kuwait in all parts of the world would be targeted with military-type operations if the summit took place.[82]

State Security in Kuwait cracked down on the PGK and, in this regard, Sheikh Mash'aal Jarrah al-Sabah said:

> . . . We in Kuwait had contributed in the strike against the Shi'ite groups who carried out terrorist acts in Bahrain . . . We have contributed to the elimination of this organization.[83]

A number of its members were arrested for planting explosives in different areas of the country and seeking to overthrow the regime in Kuwait. In addition, the government took the decision to dissolve the elected board of directors of the SCS and to appoint new members for it.

The PGK stood against the Kuwait liberation war led by the United States and the international coalition forces because it believed that its aim was the elimination of Iraq and regarded it as interference in the region's abilities. It warned that the party's mujahideen would target the American interests anywhere if they touch Muslim holy places in Najaf, Karbala, al-Kazimiyah, and Samarra.[84] In a published statement, the PGK warned the United States, the Western countries, Saddam Hussein, and some of the leaders of the GCC from the consequences of this war and stressed that the PGK 'will react severely.'[85] The PGK confirmed in that statement that it is with the withdrawal of the Iraqi forces from Kuwait, but it rejects that it be done at the hands of the 'Great Satan' and regarded it as a humiliation, according to the statement.[86] The PGK appealed to the Kuwaiti people to join its cells and the Islamic resistance militia forces of al-Tajammu' al-Islami al-Kuwaiti (the Kuwaiti Islamic Gathering).[87]

The PGK condemned the Security Agreement signed by the Kuwaiti Government with the United States after the liberation of Kuwait, describing it in a published statement as a return to colonialism. The PGK publicly and clearly demanded expelling the foreign forces from Kuwaiti territories and appealed to the Kuwaiti people to act quickly against this 'shame'.[88]

After the liberation of Kuwait, the Kuwaiti Government allowed the return of a number of expelled members and supporters of the PGK to Kuwait who had been charged with planting explosives in Kuwait in the past, recognising the role played by the Shi'ite Kuwaitis in resisting the Iraqi occupation. The campaign to return the exiled Shi'ites to Kuwait was launched by the Shi'ite community in Kuwait. The changes in Iran that had occurred after the death of Ayatollah Khomeini with the new leadership led by Hashemi Rafsanjani, who was not in harmony with the conservative hardliners in the Islamic fundamentalist regime in Iran, contributed to the weakening of this trend, whereas Rafsanjani sought to improve relationships with the GCC at the expense of this trend. He expelled members of the PGK from Iran, closed the Kuwaiti Islamic Media in Tehran, and banned the issuance of *Majallat al-Nasr* from Iran.[89] In this regard, *Majallat al-Nasr* confirms that the decision to stop the magazine from publication was painful and was beyond the control of the party. It was not due to financial difficulties,[90] but:

> It was an accurate diagnosis of the priorities we reached in the light of the developments in the Islamic revolution arena. These legitimate priorities led us to a crossroads of two options: either to change the magazine line and start new tactics, or to stop publication and have absolute silence. We chose the second option bitterly retaining the dignity of the holy Revolution.[91]

In 1996, the PGK was split into three different trends. The first was the conservative traditional religious line, whose members gather in the mosque of Imam 'Ali bin Abi Talib, located in the al'Owmaria district. The second trend is the most popular one and they gather in Imam al-Hassan mosque in the Bayan district, the Shaa'ban mosque in the al-Sharq district, and the al-Hussian Mosque in the Maidan Hawalli district. The third trend is the newest and the most radical one; it does not have any headquarters except Husseinyas. As a reflection of the parliamentary elections, which took place in Kuwait in 1996, as well as due to the resolution of the SCS board of directors, which is considered the official umbrella of the PGK, divisions among these three trends appeared. Consequently, the international leadership of Hizbollah in Tehran held a conference in the Iranian city of Mashhad in October 1996, which was attended by the PGK leadership representing the three trends, but the conference did not reach a resolution to reunify the party.[92]

In conclusion, all Hizbollah branches in the Arab region are supported by Iran financially. For example, Hizbollah-Lebanon receives about $100 million yearly in aid from Iran.[93] Tehran is the spiritual inspiration for the branches of Hizbollah in the Arab countries. They all follow the Iranian ideology that believes in the rule of wilayat al-faqih (rule by the Islamic jurist). These branches derive their legitimacy from the spiritual guide of the Islamic Revolution in Iran, Ayatollah 'Ali Khamenei.[94] Hizbollah is on top of the list of terrorism issued by the United States. The Director of the CIA, George Tenet, has regarded Hizbollah as a widespread organization with international influence similar to al-Qaeda, if not stronger.[95]

Vanguard for Regime Change (the Kuwaiti Republic)
Tali'a Taqier al-Nidam (al-Jumhuria al-Kuwaitia)

This organization was founded in 1980 by a group of pro-Iranian Kuwaiti Shi'ites. It was active in issuing hostile statements against the Kuwaiti regime in the period 1980–81. Its objective was to change the political system in Kuwait. According to its statements, this organization was behind the blasts against the Kuwait Oil Company offices in London and the Kuwait Airways office in Paris. This organization later disappeared and nothing has been heard of its activity since.[96]

Prophet Mohammed and the God Gorces Revolutionary Organization in Kuwait
Al-Munadhama al-Thawria Liquwat Mohamad Rasul Allh in Kuwait

This organization was founded during the Iraq–Iran war. It was an armed Kuwaiti Shi'ite group loyal to the Islamic Revolutionary regime in Iran. It started its underground activity in January 1987 during the preparations for the fifth Islamic Summit Conference in Kuwait. The Kuwaiti Government's goal was to hold such a conference to achieve a unified Islamic position towards the Iraq–Iran war in order to stop the war between the two countries. The Iranian regime adopted a hostile position towards this summit, where it accused the government of Kuwait of standing with the Iraqi regime and assisting it in its war with Iran.[97] Therefore, it encouraged its loyal Shi'ite groups to carry out terrorist operations inside Kuwaiti territory. This organization issued a statement announcing its responsibility for the terrorist acts that had taken place at the oil installations, threatening to attack any aircraft approaching the airspace of Kuwait, and to execute the heads of states' delegations attending the Islamic Conference, saying in its statement:

> We have previously expressed our rejection of the Islamic summit held in Kuwait, which meets for the legalization of the Zionist regime in Palestine, Iraq, and to support the traitor Hosni Mubarak, and the killer, Saddam Hussein.[98]

This organization disappeared from the political arena after the Iraq-Iran war.

The Supreme Council for Islamic Revolution in Iraq–Kuwaiti Organization (SCIRIKO)
Al-Majlas al-A'la Llthawarah al-Islamiya fi al-'Iarq-al-Tandhim al-Kuwaiti

The SCIRIKO was founded by a group of Kuwaiti Shi'ites with the support of the Islamic regime in Iran and the SCIRIKO in Iraq.[99] This armed organization used Kuwait as a base to conduct terrorist operations. Its leadership succeeded in attracting a number of Shi'ite students.[100] It used the Shi'ite mosques and camps for mobilization,[101] where religious lectures were held. In terms of membership in this organization, the member had to be committed to Islam and be fully prepared to carry out the tasks entrusted to him and be ready to serve the issues of Islam.[102] All members of the organization belonged to the Ja'fari doctrine and were mere followers of Ayatollah Khomeini.[103] Some of the organization leaders made several visits to Iran prior to the formation of the organization, where they met some leaders of the Iranian Revolution. They also made visits to Mu'askar Bader (Badr Camp), which belonged to the SCIRIKO in Iran.[104] The members also had in the use of weapons in the camps of the Iranian Revolutionary Guards and Bader Camp.[105] Weapons were smuggled from Iran across the sea to Kuwait and then part of them were smuggled to the fighters of the Bader Camp across the Kuwait–Iraq borders; they were waging guerrilla warfare against Saddam Hussein's regime in southern Iraq. The rest of these weapons were used to carry out terrorist operations targeting oil installations in Kuwait, according to orders issued by the SCIRIKO.[106] On 17 June 1986, explosives were put into the Mina 'Abdulla refinery and Maqoua' containing many oil wells, the Port of al-Shu'aiba, and the al-Ahmadi Port, as well as in electricity transformers in al-Salhiya; they were all blown up.[107] On 19 January 1987, some oil facilities in the industrial district in Kuwait City were blown up.[108] The SCIRIKO in Kuwait was behind all of these terrorist attacks; they also planned to attack the Iraqi Embassy in Kuwait and to assassinate the Ba'athist figures in Kuwait.[109]

After a period of terrorist activity conducted by the SCIRIKO in Kuwait, State Security managed to arrest most of the 16 members of the organization, who confessed to the Public Prosecutor that they joined the SCIRIKO in Kuwait as a reaction to the aid given to the Iraqi regime. In addition, they wanted to obstruct the Islamic summit in Kuwait and to end the discrimination against the Shi'ite community in Kuwait through the ongoing prosecutions and arrests.[110] Members of the organization were submitted to the State Security Court and were charged with committing acts leading to prejudice in the country's unity and territorial integrity through secret organizations that aimed to spread principles that would destroy the state's integrity and demolish its existing social and economic systems.[111] The State Security Court issued different sentences for the members, but during Iraq's occupation of Kuwait members of the organization were able to escape from the central prison.

Despite the improved relationship between Kuwait and Iran since the liberation and the disappearance of these armed groups from the Kuwaiti political scene, this still does not guarantee that these armed groups will not activate again when the conflict intensifies between the United States and Iran, where the latter considers the United States as the axis of evil. This is especially likely after the American accusations of Iran possessing weapons of mass destruction, its interference in Iraq's interior affairs, and its support for Hizbollah in the Lebanon and the Syrian area. Moreover, the United States accuses them of supporting terrorist operations in Iraq. In addition, the US Government has accused Iran in the export of arms and aids to Shi'ite groups in Iraq loyal to Iran. The US also condemned the hard statements made by the Iranian President, Mahmoud Ahmadinejad, against the Zionist State. According to all these circumstances, it is possible that Iran will deliberately try once again to awaken the underground groups in the Arabian Gulf and Peninsula to work on the instability in the region if the alleged American policy succeeds in dividing the Iraqis on the establishment of a Shi'ite state loyal to Iran in southern Iraq. As was stated by the Saudi Foreign Minister, S'aud al-Faisal,[112] and supported by Iyad 'Allawi, the former Prime Minister of Iraq, these fears are real and are no secret to anyone.[113] The Iranian reaction to these accusations was to cancel the scheduled visit by its Foreign Minister, Manuchehr Muttaqi, to the Kingdom of Saudi Arabia for an indefinite period. Also, the subsequent reactions of the former Iraqi Interior Minister, Bayan Jabr, who accused Saudi Arabia of intervening in the internal affairs of Iraq and condemned the discrimination made by the Saudi Government towards the Saudi Shi'ites.[114] In addition, there were statements made by Hussein Shariat-Madari, the representative of the guide of the Iranian Revolution, 'Ali Khamenei, in the Keyhan Press Institution and its managing editor in response to the statement issued by the Ministers of Defense and Foreign Affairs of the GCC; Shariat-Madari claimed that Bahrain is part of Iran and that the basic demand of the people of Bahrain is the return of this region, which has been separated from Iran through an illegal settlement between the Shah and the governments of the United States and Britain. He regarded the GCC states as illegal governments established during the colonial era and the direct intervention of the super powers, as the people of these states had no say in the decision-making and the appointment of these governments. He also demanded the people to overthrow these governments controlled by the ruling families and replace them with Islamic systems similar to the Iranian model.[115] Furthermore, the commander of the Iranian Revolutionary Guards, General 'Ali Fdaoi, warned that the Islamic militia (Baseej Mobilization) could launch suicide operations in the Gulf in the event of any military action against his country.[116] At the same time, 'Adel Asadi, the former Iranian counsel in Dubai, said that the Iranian intelligence devices in the Iranian embassies in the Arabian Gulf are always recruiting Shi'ite extremists loyal to the Iranian regime at the expense of their loyalty to their own homelands and that these cells are spread in all the GCC countries.[117] This is a reminder of the political scene in 1979, following the victory of the Islamic revolution in Iran, and the raising of the slogans of exporting the revolution to the GCC countries and making itself a defender of its people with the Shi'ite sects.

Conclusion

What is the future of the Islamic radical terrorist groups in the Gulf States? As noted in the study, the future of politically violent groups will not differ from the faith of other such known movements, such as the Baader-Meinhof, the Red Brigades, the Spanish Aieta, the Irish Republican Army, and other armed movements. Most of these have been demolished, whereby the international circumstances and community have forced them to abandon their weapons and engage in more appropriate political activity. To abandon terrorism, the Islamic radical terrorist groups need to be studied carefully, because the religious ideology varies from the political ideology – not only in its religious context, but also in the unbreakable relation between the Muslim soul and religion. It can be said that the Muslim personality is unique in this respect in the modern era. The religious motive is deep in the Muslim human soul, which makes it in need of a particular scientific treatment beyond the scope of security. In that, the Quran teaches Muslims to defend (not attack) their religion.

The Gulf countries are in need of information centers dedicated to handling the religious groups, such as information gathering, analysis, compilation, and follow-up. Unfortunately, such centers are currently unavailable. The scientific and religious confrontation requires belief in the slogan 'knowledge is power,' and without this knowledge the Gulf states will continue to deal with these groups according to the principle of armed force and military confrontation. No doubt these groups have been successful to a certain extent up until now; however, they are operating outside the scope of legitimate human rights. Furthermore, they are not recognized by these states, which have not paid enough attention when dealing with such groups to address their concerns while at the same time being able to protect the state's existence. There is no doubt that there is not a rapidly effective solution; however, there can be a comprehensive solution, which must be provided by the regimes and the religious groups. Accordingly, the Quran states that it is a guide for governments; the religious groups need to evaluate this concept further.

The war with terrorism will be long and will continue for years to come as long as there is a misunderstanding between regimes and religious groups.

However, as has been proven historically, using armed force ultimately is not successful and, in the long run, even the force that conquers a regime will also not last due to its ideology being antiquated with time, most especially if it occurs with a small group and is not the general consensus of the society at large.

There is no doubt that terrorism is a fierce confrontation, but it is definitely not moving in favor of the armed groups of being approved by the masses, in particular the terrorist ones that hurt, kill, and maim the innocent. For instance, the Hamas movement represents the necessary legitimate violence to resist the occupation, yet now suffers from the problem of harmonization between the requirements of political action, which came out of the ballot boxes, and the pressure of the idea of armed struggle. Apparently, it will not be long until the Hamas movement engages in the peace process on the Palestinian issue – then what will happen to the terrorist groups whose sole aim was to overthrow the political systems and change societies for the so-called Islamic state?

Glossary

adabi   literary
ahadeeth al-rassool   the Prophet sayings
ahl al-Bayt   the Prophet's family   ·
ahliya   public
ahyarr   liberals
`ajam   Shi'ites and Sunni of Iranian origin
akbar   great
alosuliya   fundamentalism
al-Sahabah   companions of Prophet
al-Wala wa-l-bara   allegiance to fellow Muslims and dissociation from non-Muslims
`amila   working
ansar   supporters
baharna Shi'ites   Arabs who had come from southern Iraq
bid`ah   innovation
deeni   religious
dostoory   constitutional
ettihad   union
firgat   troops
haj   major pilgrimage
haraka   movement
hasawiyah   Shi'ites who migrated to Kuwait from eastern region of Saudi Arabia
hawza   scientific foundations of the religious learning centers
hisba   enforcement of religious laws
huritta   freedom
hurra   free
husseiniya   the Shi'ite equivalent of mosque
ihia   revival
ikhbariya   Bahrna followers of Mirza Ibrahim Jamal al-Din
`ilmi   scientific
ingath   saving
intifadah   uprising

irshad   guidance
ishtiraki   socialist
islah   reform
itilafiya   coalition
jabha   front
jahiliya   pre-Islam ages
jald   scourge
jama'ah   group
jamaheer   masses
jam'iyat   society
kafir   unbeliever
karamat   miracles
kashafeen   scouts
kataib   Phalanges
khairiah   charity
khawarij   rebellion against the ruler
khawarij al-'asr   contemporary kharijites
khums   the specific Shi'ite Islamic tax consisting of one-fifth of the yearly
   surplus income of a family
kufaar   unbelievers
kutlah   bloc
lajnat   committee
liwa   brigade
madrasat   school
ma'had   institute
mahaliyya   local
majallat   journal
majlis   council
maktaba   library
manber   forum
marji'yya   Shiite Supreme Religious Authority
markaz   centre
mo'alimin   teachers
montadayat jahiliya   ignorance forums
mubayh'   oath of allegiance
mujahedeen   fighters for a religious cause
mulla   teacher of religion
multaqa   forum
munadhamat   organization
muraqib 'Am   general observer
murtadd   apostate
mustaqileen   independent
nadi   club
nedham   system
nukhba   elite

qaidana our leader
qaima list
qawmiyeen nationalists
qibla western
quwa force
rabitah league
reef hinterland
resalah message
sa`ada happiness
sahrawi desert
shabab youth
sha`biya popular
sharq eastern
shirk akbar a major blasphemy
shu`ba section
shun affair
shura consultative
souq market
tahrir liberation
tajammu` gathering
takatul al-Nuwwab parliamentary bloc
takfir excommunication
talabah students
tarareeh name for their work in vegetable market
tashre`i legislative
tasisi constituent
thabaqa class
thagafah culture
thawra revolution
thawriyya revolutionary
tujjar merchants
turath heritage
umah national
`umra minor pilgrimage
`usba league
`uthma great
watani national
wilaya `ama high leadership
worood roses
yarmouk the rover
zakat compulsory almsgiving
zindiq atheist
ziyy al-Islami Islamic clothes

Notes

1 The roots of the Islamist political groups

1 For more information about the impact of the Arab Reform Movement in Kuwaiti society see al-Zaid, Khalid Sa'ud, Udaba al-Kuwait fi Qarnain (Kuwait Men of Letters in Two Centuries), (Kuwait, al-Matba'a al-'Asriya, 1967). 'Abdullah, Mohammad Hassan, al-Haraka al-Adabiya wa al-Fikriya fi al-Kuwait (the Literary and Theoretical Movement in Kuwait), (Kuwait: Rabitat al-Udaba, 1973). Al-Rashaid, 'Abdul-'Aziz, Tarikh al-Kuwait (Kuwait History), (Beirut, 1971). Al-Shamlan, Saif Marzuq, Men Tarikh al-Kuwait (From the History of Kuwait), (Cairo: Matbaat Nahdat Masr, 1959).

2 Sheikh 'Abdul-'Aziz al-Rashaid was born in 1887; he was sent by his father to the Mulla Zakariya al-Ansari to learn the principles of the Quran and then he learned about reading, writing, and math at the age of 6; when he reached the age of 10 he helped his father in his business. Al-Rashaid was fond of reading and by the age of 14 he became a student of Sheikh 'Abdullah al-Khalaf. In 1902, he decided to go to Zubayr for further education and was a student of Sheikh Mohammed bin 'Abdullah al-'Aujan, the teacher of Hambali fiqh (Hambali Islamic jurisprudence) at al-zuhir school. In 1911, he had completed 24 studies and then went on to Baghdad to continue studies at the hands of the most prominent scholars of Iraq in that period, such as Mahmoud Shukri al-Alose. After leaving Baghdad, al-Rashaid headed to Cairo to study in the 'House of advocacy and counseling.' However, he failed to enroll in the school. Instead he went to Mecca, where he attended seminars around the Ka'ba. In 1917, al-Rashaid became a member of the staff at al-Mubarakia School; after being at the school he was influenced by the extremist religious trend and opened the al'Meriya school with some of his colleagues. He taught later at the al-Ahmadiah school. In 1921, he was appointed as a member of the Shura Council. He went to Bahrain and gave some lectures at the Islamic forum and taught in Madrast al-Hadai (guidance school) in Manama and later moved between several countries until he settled in Indonesia, where he died on 3 February 1938. Al-Rashaid had written many articles, published in the newspapers and journals at that time, such as *Majallat al-Kuwait* (*Kuwait Journal*) in 1928, *Majallat al-Kuwaiti Walaraqi* (*Kuwaiti and Iraqi Journal*) in 1932, and *Majallat al-Tawhid* (*al-Tawhid Journal*) in 1933.

3 Sheikh Yousef Bin 'Isa al-Qina'i was born in Kuwait City in 1876. He learned Quran at the age of 7, then began learning mathematics followed by studying the principles of jurisprudence. In 1902, he went to al-Ihsa for further education and returned to Kuwait to open the first school for the teaching of Arabic, math, jurisprudence, and religion. Sheikh al-Qina'i contributed to the establishment of many institutions of the civil society such as the al-Mubarakia School, where he taught at first but was then expelled because of his enlightened views. He estab-

lished the public library and al-Ahmadia school. In 1921, he was appointed a member of the Shura Council, and in 1936 was elected a member of the Board of Education and the Municipal Councils. In 1938, he was elected as a member of the first and second Legislative Councils; subsequently, he was appointed a member to the Shura Council after the dissolution of the Legislative Council. He also worked in the judiciary and was well known and used to be called the mufti (highest religious authority) of Kuwait. Al-Qinai died on 6 July 1973.

4 Al-ʾAdsani, Khalid, Private Papers, unpublished typewritten, p.3.
5 Al-Rashaid, op. cit., p.114.
6 Al-Nuri, ʾAbdullah, Qissat al-Taʾlim fi al-Kuwait fi Nisf Qarn (The Story of Education in Kuwait in Half a Century), (Cairo: Matbaʾat al-Istiqama, undated), pp.57–58.
7 Ibid., p.57.
8 Al-ʾAdsani, op. cit., p.4.
9 Al-Rashaid, op. cit., p.114.
10 ʾAbdullah, op. cit., p.185.
11 Al-Rashaid, op.cit., vol.1, part 1, p.106.
12 Khalaf, Fadil, Dirasat Kuwaitiya (Kuwaiti Studies), (Kuwait, al-Matbʾa al-ʾAsrya, 1968), p.20.
13 Al-Rashaid, ʾAbdul-ʾAziz, 'The New and the Old. What Should Kuwait Follow?',(in Arabic), Majallat al-Kuwait, 1929, p.358.
14 Al-Zaid, op.cit., pp.95–96.
15 Al-Rashaid, op.cit., p.105.
16 Ismaʾli, Fahad, al-Qissa al-ʾArabiya fi al-Kuwait, Qiraʾa Naqidya (The Arab Story in Kuwait, a Critical Study), (Beirut, Dar al-ʾAwda, 1980), p.14.
17 Husain, op. cit., p.106.
18 Al-Saleh, ʾAbdul-Malik, Tatawur al-Taʾleem fi al-Kuwait (the Development of Education in Kuwait), Kuwait, al-Mosam al-Thaqafy, Rabitat al-Ijtimaʾian, 1968), p.7.
19 Hassan, op. cit., p.109.
20 Al-Haji, Yaʾcoub, al-Sheikh ʾAbdul-ʾAziz al-Rashaid, Sirat Hayatah (Sheikh ʾAbdul-ʾAziz al-Rashaid, Biography of his Life), (Kuwait: Markaz al-Buhuth Wadirasat al-Kuwaitia, 1993), pp.82–84.
21 Qanun Madrasat al-Ahmadiya lil Nasha al-Wataniya (The Law of the al-Ahmadia School for the National Youth), unpublished manuscript, 1921.
22 Al-Nuri, op. cit., p.62.
23 Al-Haji, op. cit,. p.85.
24 Ibid., p.82.
25 Al-ʾAdsani, op. cit., p.16.
26 An interview with Sheikh ʾAbdullh al-Jabir al-Sabah, (in Arabic), Majallat al-Kuwait (the Kuwait Journal), 16 April 1972.
27 Ibid.
28 Hassan, op. cit., p.108.
29 For more details about the reform movement in Kuwaiti society in 1938, see Al-Rumaihi, Mohammad 'The 1938 reform movements in Kuwait, Bahrain and Dubai,' (in Arabic), Dirasat al-Khalij wa al-Jasira al-ʾArabiya, vol. No. 4, October 1975. pp.29–68.
    Al-Jassim, Najat, al-Tatawur al-Siyasi wa al-Iqtisadi li al-Kuwait bain al Harbain, 1914–39 (Political and Economic Development in Kuwait between the Two Wars, 1914–39), (Cairo: al-Matbaʾa al-Fanniya al-Haditha, 1973), pp. 205–52.
30 I.O.R. L/ P & S/ 12/3757: P.Z. 7757, 1963, No.1. 14 OF 1936, Kuwait Intelligence Summary.
31 I.O.R. L/ P & S/ July 12, 3351: P 25749/ 37: Political Agent, Copy Enclosed in Political Kuwait, to Political Resident Office to India, 26 July 1937.

32 I.O.R. 127804/ 37: Political Agent, Kuwait, to Political Resident, 2 Nov. 1937.
I.O.R. L / P & S / July 12, 3351: P 25749 / 37: Political Agent, Kuwait, to Political
Resident Copy Enclosed in Political Resident Office to India, 26 July 1937.

2 Sunni Islamist political groups

1 For more information about 1938 events refer to: al-'Adsani, Khalid, op. cit.,
al-'Adsani, Khalid Nisf 'Am li al-Hukm al-Niyabi fi al-Kuwait (Half a Year of
Representative Rule in Kuwait), (Beirut, Matba'at al-Kashaf, 1947).
2 Hussein, 'Abdul-'Aziz, Muhadarat 'an al-Mujtama' al-'Arabi bi al-Kuwait (Lectures
About the Arab Society in Kuwait), (Cairo, al-Jami'ah al-'Arabia, 1960), p.98.
3 For more information about Kuwaiti political groups, refer to: al-Mdaires Falah,
Malamih Awaliyah Hawl Nashat al-Tagamu'at wa al-Tanzimat al-Siyasiyah fi al-
Kuwait (1938–75) (The Emergence of the Political Groups and Organizations in
Kuwait: Initial Outline (1938–75), (Kuwait: Dar Qurtas, 1999).
4 Al-Shirbasi, Ahmad, Ayyam al-Kuwait (Kuwait Days), (Cairo: Dar al-Kitab
al-'Arabi, 1953), p.324.
5 Baha al-Deen, Ahamd,' a Week in Kuwait' (in Arabic), Majallat Sabah al-Khair,
25 April 1957.
6 Al-Mdaires, Falah, al-Tawajuhat al-Markisiyah fi al-Kuwait (The Marxist Orientations in Kuwait), (Kuwait: Dar Qurtas, 2003). Al-Mdaires Falah, Malamih
Awaliyah Hawl Nashat al-Tagamu'at wa al-Tanzimat al-Siyasiyah fi al-Kuwait:
(1938–75), op. cit.
7 A personal interview with al-Shatti Isma'il, one of the leaders of the Muslim
Brotherhood in Kuwait, and the former representative of the ICM in the National
Assembly, 22 March 1983, Kuwait. Majallat al-Majallah, 26 February 1995.
al-Sawaf, Mohammad, Mahmoud, Min Sejel Thekraiaty (From My Memories),
(Cairo: Dar al-kalafa, 1987), p.136. For more information about the beginning of
the organizational activities of the MBG in Kuwait, refer to: al-Mdaires, Falah,
Jama'at al-Ikhwan al-Muslimin fi al-Kuwait (The Muslim Brotherhood in
Kuwait), (Kuwait: Dar Qurtas, 1990), pp.12–13. al Mutawa' 'Abdullah 'Ali,
Thekraiaty (My Memories), published in Majallat al-Haraka, 19 December 2005.
Majallat al-Majallah 26 February 1995.
8 Al-'Aqail, 'Abdullah, Men 'Alam al-Da'wa wa al-Haraka al-Islamiya al-Mo'asirah
(A Prominent Advocacy and Contemporary Islamic Movement), (Cairo, 2006),
p.380.
9 'Abdullah 'Ali al Mutawa' was born in 1926 and grew up in a religiously conservative family. He studied in Mulla 'Othman School, which is a private school limited
to teaching religion and math. He studied modern sciences at the al-Mubarakia
and al-Ahmadia Schools supervised by the State. Al-Mutawa' engaged in Islamic
activity giving that he was affected by his brother 'Abdul-'Aziz 'Ali al-Mutawa', who
was a member of the MBG in Egypt. In 1946, he met Hassan al Banna in Mecca
and attended his lectures in Medina. In 1952, he contributed to the establishment
of the IGS, which is the religious and social forefront of the MBG branch
in Kuwait. 'Abdullah 'Ali al-Mutawa' participated in the administrative council
elections that took place in 1958, which supervised the activity of government departments, but he failed due to the domination of the national trend.
After the independence of Kuwait, al Mutawa' participated in the elections for
the first National Assembly in 1963, a candidate for the 9th Constituency, but he
did not succeed in these elections. He contributed to the establishment of the
Social Reform Society, which is the religious and social front of the MBG in
Kuwait, and after a period of time, he became the Chairman. Al-Mutawa' died on
4 September 2006.

10 Al-Rai al-'Am, 12 April 1997.
11 'Abdullah al 'Atiqi, al-Manhaj Atarbawi Lil Harakah al-Islamiya al-Mo'asirah wa Atharah Labuniat al-Muajtam' al-Kuwayti (Educational Methodology of the Islamic Contemporary Movement and its Impact on the Kuwaiti Society), (Kuwait: Maktabat al-Manar al-Islmaiya, 2006), pp.340–41.
12 Hewins, Ralph, A Golden Dream: The Miracle of Kuwait (London, W.H. Allen, 1963), pp.182–87. Al-Shaitti, op. cit.
13 Al-Shatti, op. cit.
14 Shalabi, Rauf, al-Saikh Hassan al-Banna: Wemadrest al-IKhwan al-Moslmon (Sheikh Hassan al-Banna: School of the Muslim Brotherhood), Cairo: Dar al-Ansar, 1978, p.99.
15 Hanna, 'Abdullah, 'the General Features of the Movement in Syria from Renaissance to the Beginning of the Sixties,' (in Arabic), Majallat Qthai Fakria, 16 October 1989, Cairo, p.222. Al-Mdaires Falah, al-Harkat Waltajam'at al-Seyassa fi al-Bahrain 1938–2002 (Political Movements and Groups in Bahrain 1938–2002), (Beirut, Dar al-Konooz al-Adabia, 2004), p.123.
16 Al-Shirbasi, op. cit., p.314.
17 Al-Mdaires, Falah, Jama'at al-Ikhwan al-Muslimin fi al-Kuwait, op. cit., pp.20–21.
18 Al-Shirbasi, op. cit., pp.315–18.
19 Ibid., pp.315–18.
20 Al-Khaldi, Sami, al-Ahzab al-Islamiya fi al-Kuwait (Islamic Parties in Kuwait), (Kuwait: Dar al-Nab, 1999), p.164.
21 A personal interview with al-Di'aij, Ahmad, a founder of the Muslim Brotherhood in Kuwait, 17 March 1983, Kuwait.
22 Ibid.
23 Majallat al-Majallah, 26 February 1995. Sharaf al-Din, Raslan, Mdkal li Dirast al-Ahazab al-Siasia al-'Arabia (An Introduction to the Study of Arab Political Parties), (Beirut: Dar al-Farabi, 2006), pp.229–30. For more information about the organizational structure of the Muslim Brotherhood, refer to: Majallat al-Majallah, 26 February 1995. Mitchell, R.P., The Society of the Muslim Brothers (London, 1969). Huseini, Ishak Musa, The Moslem Brethren: The Greatest of Modern Islamic Movement (Beirut, Khayats, 1956). Lia, Brynjar, The Society of Muslim Brothers in Egypt: The Rise of an Islamic Mass Movement 1928–42, (Ithaca Press: UK, 2006).
24 Al-'Atiqi, op. cit., p.202
25 Majallat al-Irshad, February 1957.
26 A personal interview with al-Sani', Faisal, the leader of the 'Arab, Ba'ath Socialist Party, Kuwait branch, 19 March 1983, Kuwait.
27 Ibid.
28 Al-Shatti, op. cit.
29 Al-Di'aij, op. cit.
30 Al-'Ajami, Mohammad, al-Haraka al-'Ummaliya wa al-Nigabiya fi al-Kuwait (the Labor and Trade Movement in Kuwait), (Kuwait, al-Rubai'an for Publication and Distribution, 1982). pp.86–87.
31 Al-Di'aij, op. cit.
32 Supporters of Democracy in Kuwait, al-Tamar 'ala al-Dimuqratiya fi al-Kuwait (A Conspiracy on Democracy in Kuwait), 1978, p.45.
33 Shukri, Hassan, 'The Muslim Brotherhood in Yemen, by Linking with Religious Education 1939–75', (in Arabic), Majallat al-Tali'a al-Yamaniya, vol. 8, September –October. 1984, p.74.
34 Al-Shatti, op. cit.
35 Majallat al-Irshad, April, 1958.
36 Al-'Atiqi, op. cit., pp.130–41.
37 Al-Shatti, op. cit.

38 Petition to Sheikh 'Abdullah al-Salem al-Sabah, from the IGS about the ways of reform in Kuwait, July 1958.
39 Al-Mdaires Falah, Malamih Awaliyah Hawl Nashat al-Tagamu'at wa al-Tanzimat al-Siyasiyah fi al-Kuwait (1938–75), op. cit., p. 23.
40 Adwa 'Ala Alma'raka (Spots on the Battle), Pamphlet No. 2, issued by the IGS, 1956, p.3.
41 Adwa 'Ala Alma'raka (Spots on the Battle), Pamphlet No. 1, issued by the IGS, 1956, p.2.
42 Majallat al-Irshad, Aug. 1957.
43 Majallat al-Irshad, Aug. 1956.
44 Ibid.
45 Al-Di'aij, op. cit.
46 Al-Shatti, op. cit. Al-Di'aij, op. cit.
47 Al-Di'aij, op. cit.
48 Majallat al-Majallah, 26 February 1995.
49 Al-Sawaf, op. cit., pp.135–36. Majallat al-Majallah, 26 February 1995.
50 Abu 'Azah, 'Abdullah, m'a al-Harakah al-Islamiya fi al-Duwal al-'Arabia (with the Islamic Movement in the Arab Countries) (Kuwait: Dar al-Qalam for Publishing and Distribution, 1986), p.112.
51 Taqrir Sader 'an Wazart al-Shon al-Ijtima'iah wa al-'Amal, Qata' al-Tanmia al-Ijtima'iah 2008 (A Report Issued by the Ministry of Social Affairs and Public Labour, Social Development Sector 2008).
52 Al-Nizam al-Asasi li Jam 'iyt al-Aslah al-Lijtimai (The Internal Rules of the Social Reform Society), pp.5–6.
53 al Mutawa' 'Abdullah 'Ali, Thekraiaty (My Memories), published in Majallat al-Haraka, 26 December 2005.
54 Al-'Atiqi, op. cit., pp.393–95.
55 Ibid., p.392.
56 Ibid.,p.384.
57 Al-Mdaires, Falah, Jama'at al-Ikhwan al-Muslimin fi al-Kuwait, op. cit., p.26.
58 Ibid.
59 Al-Khaldi, op. cit., p.176. Sout al-Kuwait, al-Qawanin al-Qair Dastoriya (the Unconstitutional Laws), (Kuwait: Sout al-Kuwait, 2009), p.6.
60 Rashid, Hadi, Haal Majlas al-Amh wa al-Haraka al-Dustoria fi al-kuwait (The Dissolution of the National Assembly and the Constitutional Movement in Kuwait), (1992), p.18.
61 Ibid., p.19.
62 Barnamaj al-Haraka al-Dustoria (The Constitutional Movement Program), unpublished manuscript. For more details about the activity of the Constitutional Movement refer to: al-Mdaires Falah, al-Haraka al-Dustori fi al-kuwait (The Constitutional Movement in Kuwait) (Kuwait: Dar Qurtas, 2002).
63 Rashid, Hadi, op. cit., p.37. Awraq Min Mofakert Mosharak: al-Theakrah al-Rab'ah Ii Ntalaqat Athnaniat al-Damoqratia (From Participant Private Papers: the Fourth Anniversary of the Mondays Democracy), Majallat al-Tali'a, 8 December 1993.
64 Al-Khatib, Ahmad, Muthakarati: al-Kuwait min al-Dawalh li al-Imarah (My Memoirs Kuwait from a State to an Emirate), (Beirut: al-Markaz al-Thaqafi al-'Arabi, 2009), Part II p.108. Rashid, op. cit., pp.24–25.
65 Al-Mawso'a al-Falastainia (the Palestinian Encyclopedia), (Damascus: 1984), p.564. Al-Moso'a al-Moiasarah fi al-Adian wa al-Mthahib al-Mo'asirah (Simplified Encyclopedia in Religions and Contemporary Sects), (Riyadh: Symposium Global Islamic Youth, 1972), p.135.
66 Al-Moso'a al-Falastainia, op. cit., p.564. Al-Moso'a al-Moiasarah fi al-Adian wa al-Mathahib al-Mo'asirah, op. cit, p.135. Abu Fakhr, Saqar, (al-Harakh

al-Watanyya al-Falastinia mn al-Nidhal al-Msalah ila Dawlah Manzu'at al-Salah (the Palestinian National Movement: from Armed Struggle into a Demilitarized State), (Beirut: al-Moassa al-'Arabia lil Dirasat wa al-Nasher, 2003), p.137.
67 Barot, Jamal and Daraj, Faisal, al-'Ahzab wa al-Harakat wa al-Jama't al-Islamiya (Islamic Parties, Movements and Groups), (Damascus: Markaz al-Dirasat al-'Arabia al-Istratigiya, 1999), Part II, p.46.
68 al-Baghdadi, Ahmad, 'Liberation Party in Kuwaiti Society (1952–96),' (in Arabic), Dirasat al-Khalij wa al-Jazira al-'Arabiya, No.93, April, 1999, p.120. Al-Sheikh, Mamdouh 'Hizb al-Tahrir,' (in Arabic) Majallat al-'Sar, 8 May 2002. P.1. Barot, and Daraj, op. cit., pp.29, 76, 77.
69 Al-Qabas, 18 August 2007. Mohammad Suleiman, 'Liberation Party After the death of 'Abdul-Qadim Zaloom: the Most Prominent Political and Organizational Challenges,' (in Arabic), Majallat al-'Sar, 2 June 2003, p.1. Zaloom, 'Abdul-Qadim, Kayfa Hudimat Alkilafah (How the Caliphate was demolished), (Beirut: 1962). A statement issued by the LP, undated.
70 Al-Nabhani, Taqi Eddin, al-Takatul al-Hizbi, (The Party Block), undated, p.29.
71 Hizb al-Tahrir (Liberation Party), (Liberation Party Publications, 1985), pp.78–84.
72 A statement issued by the LP, 31 March 1984.
73 Ibid.
74 Ibid.
75 Ibid.
76 Ibid.
77 Al-Nabhani, Taqi Eddin, al-Takatul al-Hizbi, op. cit., p.29.
78 Nida Har ila Al'alm al-Islami (Strong appeal to the Muslims World), p.78, op. cit., Zaloom, 'Abdul-Qadim, op. cit., p.73.
79 Al-Nabhani, Taqi Eddin, al-Dawlah al-Islamiya (the Islamic State), (Al-Qads: Liberation Party Publications, 1953), p.139. Al-Nabhani, Taqi Eddin, al-Takatul al-Hizbi, op. cit., p.7.
80 Mohadin, Mwafaq, al-Ahzab wa al-Qwah al-Saiasia fi al-Ordun 1927–87 (the Political Parties and Forces in Jordan 1927–87), (Beirut: Dar al-Sadaqah, 1988), p.77.
81 Ibid.
82 Hizb al-Tahrir, op. cit., p.22. al-Sheikh, op. cit., p.2.
83 Sara, Fayez, al-Ahzab wa al-Harakat al-Siasia fi Tunis 1932–84 (Political Parties and Movements in Tunisia 1932–84), (Damascus: 1986), p.231.
84 Abu Fakhr, Saqer, op. cit., p.130. 'Abdul-Wahab al-Kayali, al-Moso'a al-Siasia (Political Encyclopedia), (Beirut: al-Moassah al-'Arabia lil Dirasat wa al-Nasher, 1981), Vol. II, p.603.
85 'Liberation Party a new party in Jordan', Majallat al-Raid (in Arabic) No. 7, November–December, p.92.
86 Al-Fajr, 9 September 1959. Sada al-Iaman, 4 June 1955. Sada al-Iaman, 5 April 1955. Sada al-Iaman, 4 June 1955.
87 Baha al-Deen, op. cit.
88 Hizb al-Tahrir, op. cit., pp.58–61.
89 A statement issued by the Liberation Party in Yemen, 25 April 2003.
90 Ibid.
91 For more information on this subject, refer to: a press statement issued by Information Office of the LP in Yemen, op. cit. A statement issued by the Media Office for the LP, in Yemen, op. cit. A statement issued by the LP, Yemen, 24 October 2002.
92 A statement issued by the LP, 6 August 1990, op. cit. James Piscatori (de.), Islamic Fundamentalisms and Gulf Crisis, (USA: The American Academy of Arts and Sciences, 1991), p.103.
93 A statement issued by the LP, 6 August 1990.

94 Ibid.
95 A statement issued by the LP, Kuwait, 23 April 2001.
96 A statement issued by the LP, 21 December 1998.
97 A statement issued by the LP, Kuwait, September 2003.
98 A statement issued by the LP, Kuwait, 7 November 2003.
99 Ibid.
100 A statement issued by the LP, Kuwait, 11 January 2008.
101 A statement issued by the LP, Kuwait, 24 October 2001.
102 Al-Mdaires, Falah, al-Tajammu'at al-Siyasiyah al-Kuwaytiah: Marhalat ma ba'd al-Tahrir (Kuwaiti Political Groups: Post Liberation Era), (Kuwait: al-Manar, 1996).
103 Al-Baghdadi, op. cit., p.137.
104 Al-Watan, 17 April 2001.
105 Al-Seyassah, 11 October 2004.
106 Ibid.
107 Ibid.
108 Ibid.
109 Al-Qabas, 30 November 2004.
110 Al-Qabas, 26 September 2006. An interview with a member of the Media Office of the LP in Kuwait Hassan al-Dahi, published in al-Watan, 9 February 2007.
111 A statement issued by the LP, Kuwait, 7 November 2003.
112 Al-Baghdadi, op. cit., p.130.
113 Ibid., p.131.
114 Barot, and Daraj, op. cit., p.76.
115 See al-Mdaires, Falah, Jama'at al-Ikhwan al-Muslimin fi al-Kuwait, op. cit., p.19.
116 Al-Baghdadi, op. cit., pp.129–30.
117 A personal interview with al-Najjar, Ghanim, February 1997, Kuwait.
118 Ibid.
119 An interview with Sheikh, al-Sabt, 'Abdullah, published in Majallat al-Forqan, No.39, July 1993, Kuwait.
120 Ibid.
121 Muthakarati ma' Jama'at al-Ikhwan al-Muslimin fi al-Kuwait (My memoirs with the Muslim Brotherhood in Kuwait), handwritten, unpublished, written by an anonymous former member in the MBG, undated, Kuwait, p.42.
122 Ibid.
123 Bashmi,Ibrahim, al-Kuwait al-Waq' wa al-Rua (Kuwait the Present and the Prospect), (Sharjah: Matba'at Dar al-Khalij, 1982), p.56.
124 Muthakarati ma' Jama'at al-Ikhwan al-Muslimin fi al-Kuwait, op. cit., pp.74–77.
125 Al-Mdaires, Falah, al-Tajammu'at al-Siyasiyah al-Kuwaytiah: Marhalat ma ba'd al-Tahrir, op. cit., p.21
126 Ibid.
127 For more information on this subject, refer to: Sheikh 'Abdul-Khaliq, 'Abdul-Rahman, al-Muslmoon wa al-'Amal al-Siyasi (Musloms and Political Action), (Kuwait: al-Dar al-Salafiah, 1986).
128 Manshoer Sader 'an al-Hayaa al-'Amma li al-Shabab wa al-Riyadha (A pamphlet issued by the Public Authority for Youth and Sports), Markaz Shabab al-Faiha), undated.
129 Ibid.
130 Muthakarati ma' Jama'at al-Ikhwan al-Muslimin fi al-Kuwait, op. cit., p.42.
131 An interview with al-Sultan, Khalid, published in Majallat al-Shira', 25 February 1985. For further details about the attitude of the SG towards Parliamentary Elections see 'The Legitimate Justifications for Participating in the Representative Councils' (in Arabic), Majallat al-Forqan, No.27, July 1992. Sheikh 'Abdul-Khaliq, 'Abdul-Rahman, 'The Legitimacy of participating in the Representative

Councils' (in Arabic), Majallat al-Forqan, No.36, April 1993. Sheikh 'Abdul-Khaliq, 'Abdul-Rahman 'The 'Ulama Opinions in Participating in the Representative Councils' (in Arabic), Majallat al-Forqan, No.38, June 1993.

132 Al-Rouya al-Mustaqbalia li Benaa al-Kuwait al-Gadidah (the Future Vision to Build new Kuwait). 12 December 1991.

133 For more information about the political groupings that have emerged on the scene after the liberation of Kuwait from Iraqi occupation refer to: al-Mdaires, Falah, al-Tajammu'at al-Siyasiyah al-Kuwaytiah: Marhalat ma ba'd al-Tahrir, op. cit.

134 Al-Moso'a al-Moiasarah fi al-Adian wa al-Mthahib al-Mo'asirah, op. cit., p.115.

135 Kepel, Gilles, Jihad: The Trail of Political Islam (Cambridge, Massachusetts, 2000). p.45.

136 Ibid.

137 Barot, Daraj, op. cit., p.655. Gilles, Kepel, op. cit., p.61.

138 Barot, Daraj, op. cit., p.663.

139 Yakan,Fathi, Mushkilat al-Da'wa wa-al-Daa'ya (the Problems of Advocacy and Preacher), (Beirut: Moassat al-Rasalah, 1974), pp.217–18.

140 Al-'Atiqi, op. cit., pp.227–29.

141 Ibid., p.227.

142 Bayan Sader 'an Jam'yat Munahadhat al-Tathib Wala'takal al-T'asufy fi al-Kuwait (A statement issued by the Association Against Torture and Arbitrary Arrest in Kuwait), March 2004.

143 Harakat al-Murabitun (the Adherence Movement, Bazaq al-Fajar), (Kuwait: 1992), p.6.

144 An interview with al-Sani', Nasser the chief editor of al-Murabitun Bulletin, published in Majallat al-Majallah, 2 April 1991. For more information about al-Murabitun Movement, attitudes and activities refer to: al-Murabitun Bulletin, which was published during the occupation of Kuwait.

145 Sout al-Kuwait, 9 July 1991. Majallat al-Majallah, 26 February 1995. Al-Seyassah, 18 November 2002.

146 Majallat al-Majallah, 26 February 1995.

147 Ibid.

148 Ibid.

149 Ibid.

150 Al-Rai al-'Am, 3 May 2001.

151 Sout al-Kuwait, 9 July 1991. Al-Seyassah, 18 November 2002. Al-Jarda, 17 May 2009. Majallat al-Mossawar, 17 June 2009.

152 Al-Mutawa' 'Abdullah 'Ali, Thekraiaty (My Memories), published in Majallat al-Haraka, 13 February 2006. For more information on this subject, refer to: al Watan, 11 July 1991. Sout al-Kuwait, 2 July 1991. Al-Seyassah, 18 November 2002.

153 A personal interview with the Secretary General of the ICM al-Sheikh al-Yasin, Mhalhal, Jassim, Kuwait, 5 May 1992.

154 An interview with al-Sheikh al-Yasin, Mhalhal, Jassim, published in Majallat al-Mujtama', 1 April 1994.

155 Al-Haraka al-Dustoria al-Islamiya: Masirt Atna'sher 'Aam 1991–2003 (Islamic Constitutional Movement: The Twelfth Anniversary 1991–2003), (ICM: 2003 Kuwait), p.9.

156 Ibid, pp.12–13.

157 An interview with al-Sheikh al-Yasin, Mhalhal, Jassim, published in Majallat al-Mujtama', 1 April 1994. Al-Haraka al-Dustoria al-Islamiya:Masirt Atna'sher 'Aam 1991–2003, op. cit., pp.10–11.

158 This plan is published by Majallat al-Talia' (Vanguard Journal) as a secret plan. It is noted that there is no physical evidence of the validity of this plan. Since the

ICM did not object to what was published in Majallat al-Talia', this might show that the plan was valid without ignoring the fact that the content might be right or might be wrong. For further details, see Majallat al-Talia', 16 June 1999.

159 Ibid.
160 Ibid.
161 Ibid.
162 For further details about the attitude of the ICM towards the political rights of women refer to: A statement and symposia organized by the movement as well as the National Assembly session, in which the rights for women to vote and to elect was granted and was published in the local press.
163 Al-Watan, 26 February 2005.
164 Ibid.
165 Al-Seyassah, 16 October 1999.
166 A statement issued by the ICM calls on the government and the National Assembly to take diplomatic and economic actions against Denmark, 28 January 2006.
167 A statement issued by MP Nasser al-Sani', published in the website of the ICM, September 2006. See also al-Qabas, 11 September 2006.
168 A statement issued by Mohammad al-'Olaim spokesperson for the ICM, Kuwait, 19 September 2006.
169 Al-Qabas, 25 September 2006.
170 A statement issued by the SRS, Kuwait, 18 September 2006.
171 Al-Rai al'Am, 18 September 2006.
172 Al-Watan, 21 July 2006.
173 Al-Rai al'Am, 3 September 2006.
174 Ibid.
175 Ibid.
176 The 29 MPs block is a block that represents different trends, such as liberal MPs, tribal MPs, Islamist political group MPs, both Sunnis and Shi'ites, and some independent MPs.
177 Harakat Nabiha Khamsa (The Movement of We Wanted it Five) is an initiative made by the youth and students belonging to the NDA, Tajaam' al-Qowah al-Tlabia (the Student Coalition Forces), Jamma'at al-Shabab al-kuwaiti (The Youth of Kuwaiti Society), Shabab Dhid al-fsad (Youth Against Corruption), Tajam' Kuwaitin (Kuwaitis Gathering), and Jam'iat Tanmait al-Damqratia (The Society for the Development of Democracy), those youth took the leadership to put pressure on the government and the National Assembly members to amend the unconstitutional law of distributing the constituencies issued by the government in 1981 in the absence of parliamentary life, which led to the emergence of the tribal and sectarian phenomenon and services MPs loyal to the government and to replace it with a new law that divides Kuwait into five constituencies. They regarded this action as a national issue and they succeeded in this. Harakat Nabiha Khamsa rose orange slogans and all the political forces stood behind this slogan, including the Islamists. They held rallies almost daily in al-Irada square opposite to the National Assembly building. In the end, the government and the Parliament responded to this demand and changed the constituencies to five instead of 25.
178 Al-Qabas, 12 May 2007.
179 Al-Anba, 9 February 2005. See also A statement issued by one of the National Assembly MP and one of the leaders of ICM, Mubarak al-Dowaila, during the press interview conducted by the Kuwait Times on 23 October 1993. He declared the intention of the Islamic trend to vote no confidence in the Parliament against the Minister of Education and Higher Education because of preventing four female students from entering health laboratories wearing the veil. It is worth

mentioning that the issue of the veil had taken considerable time of the National Assembly meetings, while ignoring the major issues of concern to Kuwaiti society.

180 A statement issued by the NDA, Kuwait, 23 September 2006.

181 Ibid.

182 Ibid.

183 A personal interview with Beqir, Ahmad, Kuwait, 5 May 1992.

184 Al-Najjar, Ghanim, 'Parliamentary Elections in Kuwait 1992' (in Arabic), Social Affairs Journal, No.47, Sharjah, Autumn 1995, p.131.

185 Hawl Tahkeem al-Shari'ah al-Islamiya (On the Islamic Shari'a Arbitration), A statement issued by the IPG, Kuwait, undated.

186 Ibid.

187 Al-Barenamj al-Iantkabi li al-Tajammau' al-Islami al-Sha'abi (Electoral Program of the Islamic Popular Gathering), Kuwait, 1992.

188 Majallat al-Forqan, Kuwait, October 1992.

189 Ibid.

190 An interview with MP Walid al-Tabtabae, published in Majallat al-Forqan, No.21, Kuwait, December 1991.

191 Names of the MPs for the proposal submitted to the National Assembly, 24 February 1993, regarding the draft law for establishing al-Haya al-'Amh li al-Amr bi al-Ma'roof wa al-Nahy 'an al-Munkar (The General Authority for the Propagation of Virtue and Prevention of Vice) are: Ahmad Baqir, Khalid al-'Adwah, Mferij Nhaar al-Mutairi, Shar' al 'Ajami, and 'Aidh al-Mutairi, published in the Majallat al-Dira, 27 April 1993.

192 Text of the proposal for establishing al-Haya al-'Amh li al-Amr bi al-Ma'roof wa al-Nahy 'N al-Munkar (The Public Authority for the Propagation of Virtue and Prevention of Vice), and submitted to the National Assembly, 24 February 1993.

193 Ibid.

194 Al-Di'aij, 'Abdul-Latif, Ma'ark Qalam (the Battles of Writing), (Kuwait: Dar Qurtas 1996).

195 The position of the Shi'ites towards the al-Haya al-'Amh li-al-Amr bi al-Ma'roof wa al-Nahy 'N al-Munkar, can be noticed in the following as an example: Risalat al-Hura (Free Message) bulletin issued by the supporters of the al-Qamyh al-Harah (Free List) at Kuwait University, 29 March 1993. Majallat Rasalat al-Kuwait (Kuwait Letter), No. 33, 17 April 1993. Majallat Manber al-Huraia (Freedom Forum), No. 28, April 1993. Majallat al-Nasar, No. 33, May 1993.

196 The IHRS, the SRS, the NUKS-Kuwait University branch, the Executive Committee of the NUKS, Jam'yt al-Shari'a al-Islamiya (the Islamic Shari'a Association), Rabtat Kulliat al-Tatb (Students of Medicine League), Jam'yat al-Mo'alimin al-Kuwaitiah (the Teachers Kuwaiti Society), Ansar al-Shari'a al-Islamiya (the Supporters of the Islamic Shari'a), Rabtat Kulyat Haiat al-Tadris fi Al-Ta'lim al-Tatbiqi) (the League of the faculty of Applied Education).

197 Al-Mdaires,Falah, al-Jam'ah al-Salafiah fi al-Kuwait: al-Nashah wa al-Fikr wa al-Tatawur (The Salafiah Group in Kuwait: Origins, Ideology and Development), (Kuwait: Dar Qurtas, 1999), p.38.

198 For more information about the attitude of the SG towards women's political rights, see for example: al-Shayji, 'Abdul Razaq, Intkhab al-Maraa Nadhra Dusturia (The Election of Woman in Constitutional Vision), (Kuwait: Maktabt al-Imam al-Thahabi, 1992). Baqir, Ahmad and Sheikh al-Msbah, Nazim lecture 'the Political Rights of Women in Islam' (in Arabic), published in Majallat al-Forqan, No.32, December 1992, Kuwait. Al-Maraa Wal'mal al-Seyasi (Women and Political Activity), Majallat al-Forqan, No. 23, 1993.

199 Al-Seyassah, 14 June 1995.

200 Al-Mdaires,Falah, al-Jam'ah al-Salafiah fi al-Kuwait: al-Nashah wa al-Fikr wa al-Tatawur, op. cit., p.58.

201 Al-Watan, 1 July 1997. al-Anba, 2 February 1997.
202 Dhawabt al-Aqhani (the Songs Restrictions) published in al-Qabas, 13 May 2004. The Fatwa Committee in the Ministry of Awqaf and Islamic Affairs dominated by groups of political Islamists issued a fatwa regarding the singing performances, which included strict regulations.
203 Fatwas issued by Ministry of Awqaf and Islamic Affairs regarding singing concerts, Fatwas No. (1675) and (1345).
204 Al-Mdaires,Falah, al-Jam'ah al-Salafiah fi al-Kuwait: al-Nashah wa al-Fikr wa al-Tatawur, op. cit., pp.44–45.
205 Al-Rai al'Am,13 July 2003.
206 Ibid.
207 Ibid.
208 An interview with the Secretary General of the SIG, Salem al-Nashi, published in al-Seyassah, 1 February 2001.
209 Al-Seyassah, 2 June 2002.
210 Al-Rai al'Am, 30 October 2005.
211 A statement issued by the SIG, Kuwait, 14 April 2004.
212 An interview with al-Nashi, op. cit.
213 A statement issued by the SIG, Kuwait, 18 September 2006. See also the statement issued by the SIG, the NIA, the ICM and SM, Kuwait, 21 December 2004.
214 Al-Qabas, 20 September 2006.
215 A pamphlet issued by Shabab Masjed Ahmad bin Hambal, about Tahrim Musharakt al-Nasarah fi Munaasbat al-Kirsmas (Prohibiting Joining the Christians in Celebrating Christmas), Kuwait, undated. A pamphlet issued by SIG, Hukum Tahnat al-Kufaar Bia'yaduhum (The Rule of Congratulating the Infidels on their Religious Occasions), al-Jahra branch, Kuwait, undated.
216 IPG, Fatawa fi Mu'amalat al-Kuffar (Religious Ruling in the Treatment of the Infidels), (Kuwait: IPG Publications, undated).
217 Al-Qabas, 28 December 2007.
218 Al-Mdaires,Falah, al-Jam'ah al-Salafiah fi al-Kuwait: al-Nashah wa al-Fikr wa al-Tatawur, op. cit., p.14.
219 Al-Huda, A pamphlet No. 30, May 1994. A pamphlet issued by al-Qaimah al-Hurah, 29 March 1994.
220 SIG, Lajnat al-Da'wa wa al-Irshad, al-Ndals branch, Kuwait, undated.
221 Al-Qabas,13 October 2007.
222 A statement issued by Noerldain Jassim al-'Atar, Hawl Iqamat Masjad li alBohra, published in al-Qabas, 10 October 2007.
223 Al-Hasin, Ahmad, al-Bohra al-Isma'ilyah Muslmon am Kuffar (the Bohras al-Ismailis are Muslims or Infidels), (undated, 2007), p.54.
224 Risalh li Jassim al-'Oun: Risalat al-Nasah (Letter to Jassim al-'Oan: an Advice from the Muslim Brotherhood).
225 A pamphlet issued by Harakat Tanqiat al-Sofoof al-Islamiya (Clearing the Islamic Ranks Movement), published in Majallat al-Tali'a, 24 July 1996. Al-Seyassah, 15 June 1996.
226 Al-Muzaini, Ahmad, Minhaj Gama'at Ansaar al-shura (the Approach of the Consultative Supporters Group), (Kuwait: 2000), pp.21–32.
227 A pamphlet issued by the CSG, Kuwait, 2 February 2001.
228 Al-Anba, 22 May 1997, Kuwait.
229 Al-Seyassah, 15 June 1998.
230 Al-Seyassah, 13 August 1998.
231 Al-Qabas, 7 September 2004.
232 Al-Seyassah, 19 December 2003.
233 A pamphlet issued by the CSG, Kuwait, 21 February 2006.
234 Ibid.

235 Al-Baghli, Mohammad, al-Harakah al-Salafiah al-'Almia (Salafiah Scientific Movement), unpublished research, undated, p.4. See also al-Rai al'Am, 16 March 1997. Saleh al-S'aidi,al-Harakah al-Salafiah (al-Salafiah Movement), Al-Qabas, 19 April 1998. Al-Anba, 1 July 1996.
236 An interview with al-Shayji, 'Abdul-Razzaq published in Mirat al-Umah, 6 February 1999.
237 Ibid.
238 A statement issued by al-Harakah al-Salafiah al-'Almia (Salafiah Scientific Movement), Kuwait, 15 November 1993.
239 Ibid.
240 An interview with al-'Aabdili, Sajid, published in al-Ryaih (flag), 24 May 2002.
241 Ibid.
242 Al-Nidham al-Asasi li al-Harakah al-Salafiah (The Internal Rules for the Salafiah Movement).
243 Al-Ruyaai al-Islahia li al-Harakah al-Salafiah (Reformative Vision of the Salafiah Movement), 29 June 2003.
244 An interview with al-Shayji, 'Abdul-Razzaq, al-Sharq al-Awsat, 28 May 1999.
245 A proposal of penalties punishment law submitted by the MPs Walid Tabtabae and Mukhalid al-'Azmi to the National Assembly, 24 June 1996.
246 Al-Shayji, op. cit.
247 Al-Seyassah, 16 October 1999.
248 Al-Rai al'am, 9 July 1999.
249 Al-Watan Daily, 4 May 2009. An interview with al-'Omair, 'Ali, published in al-Qabas, 23 August 2009. For more information about the attitude of the Islamist Movements in Palestine towards the Occupation of Kuwait see Yasin, Sayyed, al-Taqrir al-Istratiji al-'Arabi, 1990 (Arab Strategic Report 1990), (Cairo: Markaz al-Darasat al-Saiasiah wa al-Stratijiah bi al-Aharam, 1991). Al-Rumaihi, Mohammad, Asda Harb al-Kuwait: Rudud al-Fa'al al-'Arabiah 'Ala al-Qazu wa Ma Talah, (Beirut: Dar al-Saqi, 1994).
250 A statement issued by the SM, Kuwait, 23 April 2004.
251 For more information about the position of the SM toward the Zionist State refer to: The statements issued by the leaders of the SM and published in the local press. A statement issued by SM, al-Moamarah 'al-al-Jihad al-Islami fi Falastine (The Conspiracy Against the Islamic Jihad in Palestine), Kuwait, 2 November 1998.
252 A statement issued by the SM, Kuwait, 24 September 2003.
253 A statement issued by the SM, Itlaq Mobadarat Da'm wa Msandt mn al-Kuwait li Harakat al-Muqawamah al-Islamiya Hamas (Launching an Initiative of Support from the State of Kuwait to Islamic Resistance Movement Hamas, Kuwait, 2006.
254 See pamphlets and statements issued by SM about al-Jihad in Afghanistan in the local press.
255 Al-Afqan al-'Arab wa Asra al-Qaeda wa al-Mustaqbel(Arab Afqans and Al-Qaeda and Future (http://www.islamonline.net/livedial org/arabic), 23 January 2002.
256 Al-Nahar, 28 October 2007.
257 Al-Watan,13 March 2006.
258 Such as Sheikh Salman al-'Waadh, Safer al-Hawali, Nasser al-'Omaer, and 'Abdul-Rahman al-Mdkaly from Saudi Arabia; Ahmad al-Rsani President of the Justice and Development party and Sheikh Mohammad al-Mrony, head of the Society Movement for the Sake of the Nation from Morocco; Harith al-Dari a leading member of the gathering of Sunni Muslim Scholars, and Ahmad 'Abdul-Razzaq al-Kobaisi from Iraq; Sheikh Fazlul Rahman, the leader of Jamiat 'Ulema Islam, Sheikh Afdal Khan, Amir of the Islamic Group from Pakistan and others. See: Baian Sader 'an Hayat al-Hamlah al-'Alamiya li Muqawamat

al-'Odwan al-Amriky (A statement issued by the Global Campaign to Resist the American Aggression Commission), 28 April 2003.

259 Ibid.

260 Ibid.

261 Ibid.

262 A statement issued by the SM, Kuwait, 11 March 2002.

263 Ibid.

264 Al-Watan, 14 March 2003.

265 Al-Watan, 14 April 2004.

266 Ibid.

267 Ibid.

268 Ibid.

269 Al-Qabas, 20 September 2006.

270 After the establishment of the NP by most of the leaders of the SM, the Shura Council of the latter announced the reformation of al-Maktab al-Siasy al-'Am (the General Political Bureau) as follows: Sheikh Falah al-Dhifiri Secretary General of the SM, Sheikh Bader al-Shibib the official spokesman, Nawaf al-'Adwani, Fhaid al-Hailim head of the press office.

271 Al-Barnamaj al-Intikhay li Tajammu' al-Defa' 'An Thawabit al-Ummah (Electoral Program for Tajammu' al-Defa' 'An Thawabit al-Ummah).

272 Al-Qabas, 7 April 2005.

273 Al-Seyassah, 27 February 2005.

274 Al-Seyassah, 20 February 2004.

275 Ibid.

276 Ibid.

277 Ibid.

278 Al-Qabas, 7 May 2004.

279 A statement issued by the DNPG, Kuwait, 30 October 2006.

280 Al-Islam al-Yoam, 31 January 2005. Al-Qabas, 15 March 2005.

281 Al-Qabas, 19 November 2004.

282 Ibid.

283 Al-Qabas, 20 September 2006.

284 A statement issued by the DNPG, Kuwait, undated.

285 A statement issued by the Secretary General of the DNPG Mohammad al-Mutairi, published in al-Rai al-'Am, 3 September 2006.

286 Al-Qabas, 21 January 2010. Al-Seyassah 21 January 2010. Al-Watan 16 December 2009. Al-Watan, 16 December 2009.

287 For more information about the NP refer to: al-Bayan al-Taasisi Sadir 'an Hizb al-Umma (Constituent Statement issued by the Nation Party), 29 January 2005. al-Qabes, 30 January 2005.

288 Al-Qabas, 30 January 2005.

289 A statement issued by the American Embassy on its participation in the meeting of the NP, one of the Declaration, published in al-Qabas, 31 January 2005.

290 Al-Bayan al-Taasisi Sadir 'an Hizb al-Ummah, op. cit.

291 A pamphlet issued by the NP, Kuwait, undated.

292 An interview with al-'Aabdili, Sajid chairman of the Political Bureau of the NP, published in Majallat al-Tali'a, 14 June 2006.

293 Ibid.

294 Al-Nidham al-Asasi li Hizb al-Ummah (The Internal Rules for the National Party), Kuwait, 7 January 2005.

295 Ibid.

296 Ibid.

297 The Constituent Assembly, the Constitution of the State of Kuwait and the Electoral Law, the Government of Kuwait, 1962, Kuwait, p.18.

298 Al-Nidham al-Asasi li Hizb al-Ummah, op. cit.
299 Letter from the NP to the President of the National Assembly and the Kuwaiti Government on the law on political parties.
300 A statement issued by the NP, Kuwait, undated.
301 The Constituent Assembly, the Constitution of the State of Kuwait and the Election Law, op. cit., pp.71–72.
302 Ibid.
303 Yousef al-Ibrahim, Sa'd bn Taflah 'Abdullah al-Twil, of the National Democratic Alliance. Ahmad Baqir of the IPG. Yousef al-Zilzila of the Dar Azahra. Ismail al-Shat'ti, 'Adel al-Sabih, Mohammad al-Jarallah, of the ICM.
304 Al-Qabas, 9 March 2005.
305 Al-'Abdaili, op. cit.
306 Ibid.
307 Ibid.
308 Ibid.
309 Ibid.
310 A statement issued by the NP on the investigation of the organization of Kataib Usood al-Jasira, Kuwait, 12 March 2005.
311 Al-'Abdaili, op. cit. A statement issued by the NP on the investigation of the organization of Kataib Usood al-Jasira, op. cit.
312 A statement issued by Secretary General of the NP, information office, Kuwait, undated.
313 A pamphlet issued by the NP, Kuwait, 3 February 2006.
314 Ibid.
315 Al-Mutairi, Hakem, 'Freedom and Identity Crisis in the Gulf and the Arabian Peninsula' (in Arabic), an unpublished study submitted to the symposium held in the Graduates Society in Kuwait, 29–30 April 2006, p.6.
316 Ibid., pp.7–9.
317 Ibid., p.10.
318 Ibid., p.10.
319 Ibid., p.11.
320 Ibid., pp.19–20.
321 A pamphlet issued by the NP, 'on the occasion of the summit of the GCC', Kuwait, 2006.
322 A pamphlet issued by the NP, Kuwait, 3 October 2006.
323 A statement issued by Hussein al-Sa'idi, official spokesperson of the NP, Kuwait, 28 December 2005.
324 A statement issued by the NP, Kuwait, 28 January 2006.
325 A pamphlet issued by the NP, Kuwait, 19 April 2006.
326 A pamphlet issued by the NP, Kuwait, 26 December 2006.
327 Al-Mutairi, Hakem, Ahkam al-Muqawmah wa al-Shahada: Bayan Wujub Nasrat al-Muqawamah fi Falastin wa Labnan (the Rules of Resistance and Martyrdom: the Necessity of Supporting the Resistance in Lebanon and Palestine), Kuwait, undated.
328 Ibid.
329 Ibid.
330 A pamphlet issued by the NP, Kuwait, 24 May 2006.
331 Al-Qabas, 25 May 2006.
332 Al-Rai al-'Am, 1 July 2006.
333 Ibid.
334 A pamphlet issued by Tajammu' al-Shabab al-Kuwaiti, Kuwait, undated.
335 Ibid.
336 Al-Rai al-'Am, 16 November 2006.
337 A pamphlet issued by the VG, Kuwait, 15 November 2006.

338 Al-Rai al-'Am, 16 November 2006.
339 Ibid.
340 Ibid.
341 A pamphlet issued by the VG, op. cit.
342 Al-Rai al-'Am, 16 November 2006.
343 A pamphlet issued by the VG, op. cit.
344 Al-Rai al-'Am, 16 November 2006.
345 Ibid.

3 Shi'ite Islamist political groups

 1 Bill, James, 'A Resurgent Islam in the Persian Gulf,' Foreign Affairs (Fall 1984), p.120. Newsweek, 5 December 2006. Cordesman, Anthony, H. Kuwait: Recovery and Security after the Gulf War (US: Westview Press, 1997), p.59.
 2 I.O.R. L / P & S/12/3894A, Confidential No. 5415, the Residency Bushire to Peel, 29 Oct. 1938.
 3 Freeth, Zahra, A New Look at Kuwait (London: George Allen and Unwin, 1972), p.34.
 4 Majallat al-Azmina al-'Arabia, 26 September 1979.
 5 Al-Timimi, 'Abd al-Malik, al-Istatan al-Ajnaby fi al-Watan al-'Arabi (The Foreign Settlement in the Arab World), (Kuwait: 1989), p.189.
 6 A personal interview with Dr. Ghulum Yousif, sociology teacher at Kuwait University and former secretary of the SCS, Winter 1983, London.
 7 Majallat al-Azmina al-'Arabia, op. cit.
 8 Gharib, 'Abdullah, Waja Dor al-Majus: al-Ab'ad al-Taraikhya wl 'Aqaidiya wl Siasia lil Thawrah al-Iraniya (The Role of the Magus: Historical, Ideological, Political Dimensions: for the Iranian Revolution), (Cairo: Dar al-jeel, 1981), pp.320–26.
 9 Al-Hasan, Yousuf, 'Our Attitude Towards the Religious Movements in Bahrain' (in Arabic), Majallat al-Nahj, No. 15, 1987, Cyprus, p.57. Khuri, Fuad, I, Tribe and State in Bahrain: The Transformation of Social and Political Authority in an Arab State (Chicago and London: The University of Chicago Press, 1980), p.173.
10 We find that Husseiniyas and Shi'ite mosques are built in areas where Sunni population density is dominated by the Sunni sect, such as 'Abdullah al-Salem, Sulaibikhat, Kaifan, al-Shamia, and other areas.
11 For more information about the social, economic and political situation for Shi'ites in the GCC, see for example: Al-Hassan, Hamza, al-Shi'a fi al-Mamlaka al-'Arabia al-Sa'dia (Shi'ites in the Kingdom of Saudi Arabia), (London: 1993).
      Rabtat 'Amom al-Shi'a fi al-Sa'dia, al-Shi'a fi al-Sa'dia: al-Waq' al-Sa'b wa Tal'at al-Mashro'h (Shi'ites in Saudi Arabia: Difficult Reality and the Legitimate Aspirations), (London: 1991). Goldberg, Jacob 'The Shi'i Minority in Saudi Arabia' in: Cole, Juan R.I. and Keddie, Nikki R, (ed.), Shi'ism and Social Protest (New Haven and London: Yale University Press, 1986), pp.230–46. Lawson, Fred H., Opposition Movements and U.S. Policy Towards the Arab Gulf States (New York: Council on Foreign Relations Press, 1992), pp.7–32.
12 Mithaq al-Majlis al-Istishari (The Charter for the Consultative Council), unpublished, manuscript, 4 March 1921, pp.2–3.
13 Through a review of the names of members of the Consultative Council, indicated that all members belong to the Sunni Arab sect, such as the al-Saqer, al-Badr, al-Naqib, al-Mutairi, and al-Ghanim.
14 A group of youths who played a big role in establishing the National Bloc and the National Youth Bloc were behind the idea of having different administrative boards with the consent of Sheikh Ahmad al-Jaber al-Sabah. Elections for these

councils, such as al-Majlas al-Baladi (the Municipal Council) and Majalas al-Ma'raf (the Educational Council) were limited. The membership was limited to Sunni Nationalist notables only. The active members of the Municipal Council carried out a campaign against the Iranian immigrants under the justification of protecting the Arab identity of Kuwait from Iranian danger. A personal interview with al-Saqar, Jassim Hamad, a member of the National Youth Bloc, which was founded in 1938, Kuwait, 2 April 1983.

15 Al-Jassim, op. cit., p.216.

16 Al-'Adsani, Khalid, private papers, unpublished, typewritten, op. cit., pp.46, 47, 48. Al-Najjar,Ghanim, 'Decision-Making Process in Kuwait: the Land Acquisition Policy as a Case Study', Ph.D. thesis, University of Exeter, 1984, p.84. Private diary, handwritten, unpublished, written by a member of the National Youth Bloc.

17 One of the shoutings was:

> Nathir al'Ash Laikbar farkha (Destroy the Nest Before the Bird Grows up). See al-Hatim, 'Abdullah, Min Huna Bada't al-Kuwait (Kuwait Started from Here), (Kuwait, Dar al-Qabas, 1980), p.59. Private diary, handwritten, unpublished, written by a Member of the National Youth Bloc.

18 The families who stood against the Legislative Council movement lived in the Sharq area (eastern sector) of Kuwait City, represented in al-Rodan, al-Rumi, al-'Asusi, al-Mudhaf, al-Nusf and al-Ghanim families. Members of the al-Ghanim family were divided into supporters and opponents for the Legislative Council movement. These families are traditional allies of the ruling family and all the political movements in that period originated from the Jibla area (western sector). Some families from the western sector whose interests were affected by the reforms of the Legislative Council also opposed it, such as al-Kharafi, al-Bahar, and al-Shai'.

19 Al-Nahar, 13 May 1939.

20 Masirat al-Dimaqratia fi al-Kuwait (The March of Democracy in Kuwait), Kuwaiti news agency, February 1981, p.81.

21 Most popular associations and societies participated in issuing statements condemning the rigging of elections except CSC, which, on the contrary, backed its candidates who participated in forged National Assembly elections, while members representing the nationalist forces and the Chamber of Commerce withdrew from the Assembly and signed a statement condemning the fraud process. It's worth mentioning that none of the Shi'ite candidates signed this statement.

22 Al-Nafeesi, 'Abdullah, al-Kuwait al-Rai al-Akar (Kuwait: the other opinion), (London: Taha House Publishing, 1978), pp.95–113.

23 Ibid., pp.95–113.

24 Al-Mdaires, Falah, al-Harakh al-Sh'ih fi al-Kuwait (Shi'ite Movement in Kuwait), (Kuwait: Dar Qurtas, 1999), p.35.

25 Assiri, 'Abdul-Reda, and al-Menoufi, Kamal, 'the Sixth Parliamentary Elections (1985) in Kuwait: Political Analysis' (in Arabic), Social Sciences Journal, Vol. 14, No. 1, Spring 1986, p.99.

26 Following the strong existence of the Revolutionary pro-Khomeni line Shi'ites movement, the Sunni religious groups in Di'ya constituency carried out a sectarian primary election to stand against this movement, and there were similar attempts in other constituencies such as al-Qadisiya and al-Adailiya, but the strength of the nationalist, liberal and leftist movements failed at such attempts.

27 Representatives of the Shi'ites in the fifth National Assembly were limited to the Shi'ite Revolutionary movement pro-Khomeni line, such as Sayyed 'Adnan 'Abdul-Samad, Nasser Sarkhouh, 'Abdul-Mohsen Jamal, and the traditional Shi'ites, those who had a close relationship with the al-Sabah ruling family, such as 'Abdul

Latif al-Kazemi, Ibrahim Khraibit, Jassem al-Qattan, Isma'il Dashti disappeared from the political scene then.

28 For more information refer to: al-Mdaires, Falah, 'Shi'ism and Political Protest in Bahrain,' Digest of Middle East Studies, Spring 2002, Vol. No.1, pp.25–26. Al-Mdaires, Falah, al-Harkat Waltajam'at al-Seyassa fi al-Bahrain 1938–2002 (Political Movements and Groups in Bahrain 1938–2002), (Beirut: Dar al-Konooz al-Adabia, 2004). Al-Mdaeirs, Falah, al-Harakh al-Sh'ih fi al-Kuwait, op. cit., pp.55–56.

29 For more information about this sectarian campaign against the Iranians launched by the ANM in Kuwait, both inside the National Assembly and through the mass media owned by the ANM in Kuwait refer to: The executive Committee of the NUKS, Madha Yajri fi Khalijina al-'Arabi? (What is Going on in our Arabian Gulf?), (Kuwait, 1967). The executive Committee of the NUKS, al-Khalij al-'Arabi aw Falastin Thaniya (The Arabian Gulf or a second Palestine) (Beirut: 1969). The executive Committee of the NUKS, Nazra ila Dore Iran fi al-Khalij al-'Arabi (A Look at Iran's Role in the Arabian Gulf), (Kuwait: 1976). Majallat al-Tali'a, since the issuance in 1961 and even in 1970. Majallat al-Itahad, No. 3, November 1965. Majallat al-Itahad, No. 17, March 1967. Majallat al-Itahad, No. 18, April 1967. Al-Fjer, 9 August 1958. Al-Khatib, Ahmad, 'We and Iran', (in Arabic), Majallat al-Iman, No. 5, 5 May 1953, pp.6, 8.

30 Minutes of meetings of the National Assembly's No. 33, 23 November 1963, pp.16–17 and No. 42, 4 June 1964, p.5.

31 Al-Mdaires, Falah, al-Harakh al-Shi'ih fi al-Kuwait, op. cit., pp.21–22.

32 Taheri, Amir, Holy Terror: The Inside story of Islamic Terrorism (London: Sphere Books Limited, 1987), p.54.

33 Majallat al-Nasr, No. 25, March 1991.

34 Al-Nafeesi, Abdullah (ed.), Al-Haraka al-Islamiya: Ruwyi Mustaqbaliyah: Awraq fi al-Naqd al-Dhati (The Islamic Movement: A Future Vision: Papers in Self-Criticism), (Kuwait: 1989), pp.248–49. Majallat al-Nasr, No. 25, March 1991.

35 Majallat al-Nasr, No. 25, March 1991. Majallat al-Tali'a, No. 630, 5 December 1979.

36 Al-Khaldi, op. cit., pp.129–57.

37 An interview with the former secretary of SCS 'Abdalbaqhi, Baqir, al-Watan, 15 February 1986.

38 'Abdalbaqhi, op. cit., Ghulum, op. cit.

39 SRS, Jam'yat al-Islah al-Ijtamaya fi 'Ishrin 'Aam (Social Reform Society in 20 years), (Kuwait: undated), p.12.

40 For further details about the events of the Sha'ban Mosque Movement see al-Mdaires, Falah, al-Harakha al-Sh'ih fi al-Kuwait, op. cit., pp.24–29. Al-Khaldi, op. cit., pp.114–15.

41 Middle East Contemporary Survey 1978–79, pp.450–51, and Assiri, Abdul-Reda Kuwait's Foreign Policy: City-State in World Politics (Boulder, San Francisco & London: Westview Press, 1990), p.58. Al-Qabas, 25 September 1979.

42 Wazarat al-'Adil, Taqrir Itiham Muqadam min Niyabat Amn al-Dawalah to Mahkamat Amn al-Dawalah fi Qadiyat al-jinaya Raqam 410/87–332/87 Salhiya 1/87 Amn al-Dawalah (Ministry of Justice, the report submitted by the state security prosecutor to the state security court in the case of crime 410/87–32/87 Salhia No. 1 / 87 State Security). Wazarat al-'Adil, Mahadher al-Tahqiqat Niyabat Amn al-Dawalah. (Ministry of Justice, records of the investigation on behalf of state security).

43 Majallat al-Kuwaiti, No. 6, November 1989. Majallat al-Nasr, No. 29, August 1991.

44 Al-Ghraib, 'Awataf. 'Al-Taqirat Alty Tarat 'Ala 'laqat al-Sulta al-Siayassiah fi al-Kuwait bi al-Shi'aih Mabain 'Amain 1980–90 (The Developments in the

Relationship between the Political Authority and Shi'ites in Kuwait between 1980–90), unpublished paper, 1992, pp.9–10.

45 Ibid.

46 Al-Khalidi, op. cit., pp.110–11.

47 Ibid., pp.104–5.

48 Ibid., p.106.

49 Ibid., p.105.

50 Ibid., p.101.

51 Ibid., p.101.

52 Ibid., p.102.

53 Al-Barnamaj al-Intikhabi li-Shabab al-Watani al-Dasturi (The Electoral Program for CNY), 1975.

54 A statement issued by the CNY, Dhikra Istishad al-Hussein (Anniversary of al-Hussein martyrdom), 1975, Kuwait.

55 A statement issued by the KNG, 1990.

56 Majallat al-Kuwaiti, No. 1, May 1989.

57 Ibid.

58 Majallat al-Kuwaiti, No. 6, November 1989. For more information about the FKC activities and attitudes refer to: Majallat al-Kuwaiti, from 1989–90.

59 al-Harbi, Dbai, Man Yantakhib Man . . . wa Limatha: Wasail wa 'wamil al-Tatheir 'Ala al-Nakhib al-Kuwaiti (Who Elect Who . . . and Why: Means that Influence factors on the Kuwaiti voter), (Kuwait: Dar al-Qabas li Atiba'ah wa Lnasher wa al-Tawzi', 1996), p.58.

60 For further information about the KIL attitudes and activities refer to: Majallat Minber al-Huriyya from 1991 to 1993.

61 Mohammad Baqir al-Mahri Imam of 'Ali bin Abi Talib mosque in al-'Mariya District. He lived his early years in Najaf, with his father Ayatollah 'Abbas al-Mussawi. He was detained by Kuwaiti security in 1989 on charges of planning to overthrow the regime, but he was released by the court. During the Iraqi occupation of Kuwait, he played an important role in the management of the Kuwaiti community, which flowed into Iran because of the occupation. He had some publications, such as Hayat al-Sadar (Sadr Life).

62 A statement issued by the KIG, 22 November 1990, Kuwait.

63 A statement issued by the FKPV, undated, Kuwait.

64 A leaflet issued by the IGPC, January 1986, Kuwait.

65 A personal interview with al-Wazzan, 'Abdul-Wahab, one of the founders of the NIC, Kuwait, October 1992.

66 Ibid.

67 A statement issued by the Islamic National Coalition, 1991, Kuwait.

68 Majallat al-Nasr, No. 33, May 1993. Risalat al-Hura (Free Message) pamphlet issued by the supporters of the al-Qamyh al-Harah (Free List), op. cit.

69 Al-Mdaires, Falah, al-Harakha al-Shi'ah fi al-Kuwait, op. cit., p.42.

70 A leaflet issued by Hayat Shabab al-Rumeitheya lil Taw'ia al-Diniya wa Liajtam'a), No.3, Kuwait, 1996.

71 Ibid.

72 An interview with Sheikh al-Ma'tooq, Hussein, published in Al-Qabas, 9 June 2003.

73 A statement issued by the NIA, Kuwait, 16 February 2002.

74 An interview with Jamal, 'Abdul-Mohsen, published in al-Seyassah, 21 May 2005.

75 Ibid.

76 Al-Qabas, 3 June 2005.

77 Al-Nidham al-Asasy li Muatamer al-khleej al-Sha'by li Muqawamat al-Mashruw' al-Sahiuny (the Internal Rules for the Gulf popular resistance to the Zionist project), undated. For more information about the NIA attitude towards the Zionist State refer to: Statements issued by the leadership of the NIA in this regard.

78 A statement issued by the NIA, published in al-Qabas, Kuwait, 9 October 2004. See also al-Qabas, 21 May 2005.
79 An interview with Sheikh al-Ma'took, Hussein, op. cit.
80 Al-Qabas, 8 May 2004.
81 The Time Magazine, 13 February 2008.
82 Ibid.
83 Al-Watan, 16 February 2008.
84 Bayan Sader 'an al-Tahaluf al-Islami al-Watani Bimunasabt Istishad 'Imad Mughuniyeh (A statement issued by the National Islamic Alliance on the occasion of 'Imad Mughuniyeh Martyrdom), published in al-Watan, 16 February 2008. Al-Mnar, Satellite Channel, 16 February 2008. Al-Shahid, 17 February 2008.
85 Al-Sahad, 17 February 2008.
86 Al-Jarida, 19 February 2008. Al-Watan, 21 February 2008. Al-Nahar, 21 February 2008. Al-Seyassah, 19 February 2008.
87 Al-Seyassah, 28 February 2008. Al-Qabas, 2 March 2009.
88 Al-Seyassah, 6 June 1998. al-Seyassah, 7 June 1998.
89 A statement issued by the DJM, 11 December 1998. See also al-Qabas, 12 December 1998, Kuwait.
90 Al-Qabas, 13 January 1999.
91 Ibid.
92 A statement issued by the DJM, Kuwait, 23 May 1999.
93 Ibid.
94 Al-Qabas, 17 February 1999. Also refer to: al-Barnamj al-Seaiasy li Harakt Ansar al-Hurai (Political Program for the Supporters Freedom Movement), undated.
95 Ibid.
96 Al-Barnamj al-Seaiasy li Harakt Ansar al-Hurai, op. cit.
97 Ibid.
98 Ibid.
99 Interview with the Secretary General of the FSM, published in al-Anba, 11 September 1999.
100 Ibid.
101 Ibid.
102 Watheqat al-Mabadi Walmuntalaqat li Tawjah Haiat Kiadam al-Mahdi (A document of principles and perspectives to guide the Committee for Serving al-Mahdi).
103 Ibid.
104 Al-Watan, 23 November 2004.
105 Al Watan, 12 July 2005. al-Watan, 19 July 2005.
106 An interview with al-Wazzan, 'Abdul-Wahab, published in al-Qabas, 25 June 2003.
107 Wathiqat al-Mbadi wa al-Nidham al-Asasy li Tajammu' 'Olama al-Moslamin al-Shi'a in Kuwait (Islamic Shi'ite Clerics Gathering in Kuwait), 2005. Interview with one of the ISCGK leaders, published in Al-Qabas, op. cit.
108 Wathiqat al-Mbad wa al-Nidham al-Asasy li Tajammu' 'Olama al-Moslamin al-Shi'a in Kuwait, op. cit.
109 Ibid.
110 Ibid.
111 Ibid.
112 A statement issued by the ISCGK, Kuwait, 21 September 2004.
113 A statement issued by the ISCGK, Kuwait.
114 Al-Seyassah, 16 March 2005.
115 A statement issued by the ISCGK, Kuwait, 25 January 2005.
116 Al-Qabas, 17 May 2004.

117 Ibid.
118 A statement issued by the ISCGK, Kuwait, 10 September 2002.
119 A statement issued by the ISCGK, Kuwait, 21 November 2003. See also al-Rai al'Am, 19 November 2003.
120 A statement issued by the ISCGK, Kuwait, 10 April 2006.
121 Al-Wasat, 15 September 2006.
122 Ibid.
123 An interview with al-Saffar, Saleh, the representative of the ISMG, published in al-Qabas, 13 June 2003.
124 Ibid.
125 Ibid.
126 An interview with Naqai, 'Abas the NIGLL leader, published in al-Seyassah, 20 September 2002.
127 A leaflet issued by the NIGLL, Kuwait, 2001.
128 Ibid.
129 Harakat al-Tawafuq al-Watani al-Islamiya, Ta'araf 'la Harakat al-Tawafuq al-Watani al-Islamiya (Be Introduced to the Islamic National Consensus Movement), undated, Kuwait, p.3.
130 Ibid., p.5.
131 Ibid., pp.33–36.
132 Ibid., p.16.
133 Ibid., pp.21–26.
134 Harakat al-Tawafuq al-Watani al-Islamiya, Moutamer al-Quds al-Thani: Mohoer al-Istratijiat (Second Jerusalem Conference: strategies Axis), (Kuwait: Mataba'al-Mahamid al-'Alamih, 2004), pp.55–67.
135 Harakat al-Tawafuq al-Watani al-Islamiya, Ta'araf 'la Harakat al-Tawafuq al-Watani al-Islamiya, op. cit., p.4.
136 Ibid., p.5.
137 Al-Rai al-'Am, 17 November 2003. al-Watan, 17 November 2003.
138 An interview with Sultan, Abdul-Hussein, Secretary General for the JPG, published in al-Qabas, 9 January 2005.
139 Al-Qabas, 30 December 2004. al-Seyassah, 30 December 2004.
140 An interview with al-Saleh, 'Abdul-Hadi, the Secretary General of the NCG published in al-Qabas, 12 December 2005.
141 A statement issued by NCG, Kuwait, 16 July 2005.
142 Ibid.
143 An interview with al-Saleh, 'Abdul-Hadi, op. cit.
144 Al-Qabas, 13 September 2005.
145 Press conference for the NGC, 22 October 2005, Kuwait.
146 Ibid.
147 A statement issued by the NGC, Kuwait, 11 April 2006.
148 A statement issued by the NGC, Kuwait, 5 November 2006.
149 An interview with al-Khdarai, Faraj the Secretary General of the SPG, published in al-Dar, 2 February 2009.
150 Ibid.
151 A statement issued by Tajammu' al-Defa' 'An Thawabit al-Ummah, Kuwait, 23 September 2008.
152 A statement issued by Tajammu' Thawabit Shi'ites, undated, Kuwait.
153 A statement issued by Tajammu' Thawabit Shi'ites, Kuwait, 20 January 2009.
154 Al-Dar, 1 March 2009.
155 A statement issued by Tajammu' Thawabit Shi'ites, Kuwait, 13 August 2009.

4 The relationships between the Kuwaiti regime and the Islamist political groups

1 An interview with Sheikh al-Sabah, Sa'ud Nasser, former Minister of Information and Oil published in al-Sharq al-Awsat, 13 October 2001.
2 Ibid.
3 An interview with Sheikh al-Sabah, Sa'ud Nasser, published in al-Seyassah, 23 April 2007.
4 Al-Mdaires, Falah, Jama'at al-Ikhwan al-Muslimin fi al-Kuwaut, op. cit., pp.29–30.
5 ANM, Taqrir Hawl al-Iqlim (Report About the Region), Kuwait, unpublished manuscript, 1967, p.5.
6 Rumaihi, Mohammad, al-Jidhur al-Ijtma'iya li al-Dimuqratiya fi Mujtama'at al-Khalij al-'Arabi al-Mu'asira (The Social Roots for Democracy in the Contemporary Societies of the Arabian Gulf), (Kuwait: Kazma Publications, 1977), pp.39, 52.
7 Jerkhi, Jasem Mohammad, 'The Electoral Process in Kuwait: A Geographical Study', Ph.D. thesis, University of Exeter, 1984, op. cit., pp.188–90.
8 Those were: 'Abd al-'Aziz al-Saqer, Rashid al-Farhan, 'Abd al-Razzaq al-Khalid, Mohammad 'Abd al-Muhsin al-Kharafi, 'Ali 'Abd al-Rahman al-'Omar, and Mohammad al'Adsani.
9 A statement issued by the candidates of the general elections held on 25 January 1967.
10 A leaflet issued by Jam'iyat al-Muhamin, Jam'iyat al-Sahafiyin, Jam'iyat al-Khireejin, Rabitat al-Udaba, Jam'iyat al-Muhandisin, Itihad al-Mugawilin, al-Itihad al-'Am li 'Umal al-Kuwait, and the NUKS.
11 Al-Menoufi, Kamal, al-Hakwmat al-Kuwaiti (The Kuwaiti Government), (Kuwait: al-Rubai'an for Publication and Distribution, 1982), p.58.
12 A statement issued by the candidates of the general elections, op. cit. A leaflet issued by Jam'iyat al-Muhamin, Jam Jam'iyat al-Sahafiyin, Jam 'Iyat al-Khireejin, Rabitat al-Udaba, Jam 'Iyat al-Muhandisin, Itihad al-Mugawilin, al-Itihad al-'Am li 'Umal al-Kuwait, and the NUKS. Itihad al-Shabiba al-Dimuqratiya fi al-Kuwait, Lamahat min Trarikh al-Nidal al-Dimuqrati fi al-Kuwait (Pictures of the History of Democratic Struggle in Kuwait), (Itihad al-Shabiba al-Dimuqratiya fi al-Kuwait: 1982), pp.5–6. al-Talia', 13 October 1999.
13 Al-Menoufi, Kamal, op. cit., pp.62–63.
14 Majallat al-Mujtama', 31 August 1976.
15 Alnajjar, Ghanim, Muqdma li Attawr al-Saiasi fi Al-Kuwait (Introduction to the Political Development in Kuwait), (Kuwait: Dar Qurtas, 1994), pp.96–101.
16 Al-Tali'a, al-Tali'a fi Ma'rakat al-Dimuqratiya (The Vanguard in the Battle for Democracy), (Kuwait: al-Tali'a Publications,1984), pp.132–33. Petition submitted by the MPs of the National Assembly dissolved in 29 August 1976, to the Emir of Kuwait, Sheikh Sabah al-Salem al-Sabah. A leaflet issued by the Kuwaiti popular organization as protest on the dissolution of the National Assembly, this statement signed by the General Union of Workers of Kuwait, the Literary Association, the Lawyers Association, the Journalists Association, the Independence Club, the Kuwaiti Teachers Association, the NUKS.
17 Majallat al-Mujtama', 31 August 1976.
18 Mohammad 'Abdul-Qader al-Jassim, Mizan, 18 July 2005. http://www.aljasem.org.
19 Jam 'iyat al-Khireejin, Masierat al-Tasis Wal'ataa 1964–94 (The Graduates Association, the Establishment Pace and the Giving 1964–94), p.27. See also: al-Tali'a, al-Tali'a fi Ma'rakat al-Dimuqratiya, op. cit.
20 Al-Najjar, Ghanim, Muqdma li Attawr al-Saiasi fi al-Kuwait, op. cit., pp.101–2.
21 Ibid.

22 Ibid.
23 Baqir, Ahmad, Dirasa Hawl al-Madah al-Thanya min Dastwer al-Kuwait (A Study about the Second Article of the Constitution of Kuwait) (Kuwait: al-Dar al-Salafya, 1984), p.19.
24 Al-Watan, 23 July 1980.
25 For more information on this subject refer to: al-Mdaires, Falah, al-Harakh al-Shi'iah fi al-Kuwait, op. cit., pp.22–34.
26 Ahmad al-Khatib was born in 1927 and to a middle class family that used to live in a poor district called al-Dahla. He was educated in al-'Anjery School as an elementary student and the Ahmadiyah and al-Mbarkia School. During his studies, the educational mission arrived from Palestine and began to affect al-Khatib. These teachers explained the critical situation in Palestine between the Zionists and British colonial forces. When he was 14 years old he went to Beirut to continue his studies in the international college in Beirut. In 1942 he joined the American University of Beirut (AUB) to study medicine. The AUB was known for its nationalist movements, which affected al-Khatib. Also, the displacement of the Palestinian people and occupation of their lands by the Zionist and the declaration of the Zionist State in 1948 affected al-Khatib. From then al-Khatib began to be politically active; he was one of the leaders of al-'Urwa al-Wuthqa (the Firm Bond Society), which was taken over by nationalist students in the AUB. Al-Khatib during his study was suspended from the AUB for participating in demonstrations in Beirut against the American intervention in the Middle East. Al-Khatib with George Habash, Wadi' Haddad, and Hani al-Hindi participated in the establishment of the ANM. After he graduated he returned to Kuwait, and then al-Khatib set up a branch for the ANM in Kuwait; he established a number of organizations of civil society, such as al-Nadi al-Ahli (The National Club), al-Nadi al-Thaqafi al-Qawmi, and al-Rabita al-Kuwaitiya. In 1952, al-Khatib worked in the hospital, and in 1957 he resigned from his job because of the succession of Sheikh Fahad al-Salim al-Sabah, head of the public health at the time, where the Public Health Service published a circular to expel workers in the constituency if they exercised in a political act. Al-Khatib then opened a private clinic in the Salhia district located in the western part of Kuwait City. In 1958 he was elected a member of the Adminstrative Council, and in 1962 he was elected a member of the Constituent Assembly and was elected Vice President of the Constituent Assembly and later became a member of most of the elected councils in Kuwait, and then he became a co-founder of the Kuwaiti Progressive Democratic Movement. Al-Khatib participated in 1989 in the establishment of the constitutional movement. In 1990 he was arrested by State Security because of his opposition to the non-constitutional dissolution of the National Assembly in 1986, and the establishment of the National Council. After the liberation of Kuwait from Iraq, al-Khatib took part in the establishment of the Kuwait Democratic Forum and the National Democratic Alliance. Al-Khatib is still active in the Kuwaiti political arena, but has not participated in the elections since 1992. See al-Khatib, Ahmad, Muthakarati: al-Kuwait min al-Imarah il al-Dawalh (My Memoirs Kuwait from an Emirate to a State), (Beirut: al-Markaz al-Thaqafi al-'Arabi, 2007), Part I.
27 Majallat al-Nasr, No. 25, March 1991. Al-Jarida, 17 September 2008. For more information about the Islamist political groups campaign against the leftists; see for example Hadad, Amir, Majmu'at al-Tali'a: Mabadi-Mawaqif-Da'awat (al-Tali'a Group: Principles, Attitudes, Calls), (Kuwait: al-Dar al-Slifiah, 1985).
28 Al-Khatib, Ahmad, Muthakarati: al-Kuwait min al-Dawalh li al-Imarah, op. cit., p.31.
29 An interview with al-Hjai, Yousef, published in Majallat al-Mujtama', 25 August 1981.

30 Majallat Al-Mujtama', 17 March 1981.
31 Al-Watan, 19 May 1983.
32 Al-Jarida, 2 October 2007.
33 Al-Mdaires, Falah, al-Harakah al-Dusturiyah fi al-Kuwait: Nashatuha wa Tatawuruha (The Constuitional Movement in Kuwait: Origins and Development), (Kuwait: Dar Qurtas, 2002), pp.14–15.
34 A statement issued by the CM Qatuo' Intakhabat al-Majlis al-Watani (Boycott the National Council Elections), Kuwait, 5 July 1990. Bayan Sadar 'an al-Jaan al-Sh'bia li Al-Harakah al-Dusturiyah fi al-Kuwait, Nida men Ajal al-watan: Qatuo' Intakhabat al-Majlis al-Watani (A statement issued by the Popular Committee for the Constitutional Movement in Kuwait: An Appeal for our Citizens to Boycott the National Council Elections). Kuwait, 4 June 1990.
35 A statement issued by the CM Hawl Haqiqat Intakhabat al-Majlas al-Watani (The Trouth About the National Council Elections), undated.
36 A petition addressed by the leaders of the MBG in Kuwait to the Emir of Kuwait Sheikh Jaber al-Ahmad al-Sabah, 1990.
37 A statement issued by CM Hawl Asbab Mqata't al-Majlis al-Watani (the Reasons for Boycotting the National Council), 16 May 1990.
38 A statement issued by Political Forces, Hawl Haqiqat Jamiyat al-Islah al-Ijtima'i (Fact About the Social Reform Society), undated. A statement issued by the Political Forces Hawl Haqaqat Maqwqif Jam'iyat Ihia al-Turath al-Islamiya (Fact about Islamic Heritage Revival Society), undated.
39 Bayan Sader 'an Jam'iat Haaiat al-Tadries Hawl Da'wa li la'tasam (A statement issued by the University Faculty Association, Calling for Picketing), May 1990.
40 Ibid.
41 Middle East International, September 1990, No. 348, p.9.
42 A Personal interview with al-Menayes, Sami, former Secretary General of the KDF, 1 October 1993.
43 Al-Bayan Al-Khitamai li al-Moatamer al-Kuwaiti al-Sha'bi (The final Statement issued by the Popular Kuwaiti Congress), from 13 to 15 October 1990, Jeddah, pp.7–6.
44 The Constitutional Assembly, the Constitution of the State of Kuwait and the Electoral Law (Kuwait Government, 1962), pp.11–12.
45 Ibid.
46 Al-Haiat, 10 April 1993.
47 Al-Qabes, 4 October 1993. al-Seyassah, 4 October 1993.
48 Al-Jarida, 2 October 2007.
49 Taqrir Hawl Nisbat al-Musharakah fi al-Intikhabat 'ber al-Majalis al-Niabiah (A Report about the Percentage of the Participation in the Parliamentary Elections), Markaz al-Qabes al-Ma'lumat wa al-Darasat, 2008. Al-Talia', 21 May 2008. Al-Qabes, 17 May 2009.
50 Al-Amir, Yahia, Akhraju al-Watan min Jazyret al-'Arab: Ayam al-Irhab fi al-S'udia (They Expelled Homeland from the Arabian Peninsula: Days of Terrorism in Saudi Arabia), (Beirut: al-Markaz al-Thaqafi al-'Arabi, 2007), pp.40–41.

5 Spread of the Islamist political groups in the social body

1 An interview with Sheikh al-Sabah, Sa'ud Nasser, op. cit.
2 Muthakarati ma'a Jama'at al-Ikhwan al-Muslimin fi al-Kuwait, op. cit., pp.28–9.
3 Majmu'at al-Rasaal li al-limam al-Shahid Hassan al-Banna (Collection of Letters of the Martyr Hassan al-Banna), (Beirut: Muasasat al-Risalah: undated), pp.28–29.
4 Muthakarati ma'a Jama'at al-Ikhwan al-Muslimin fi al-Kuwait, op. cit., pp16–17.
5 An interview with al-Najjar, Ghanim, February 1997, Kuwait.

6 Al-Jarida, 10 October 2007.
7 Al-Jarida, 10 October 2008.
8 A statement issued by 'Abdullah al-Kanderi, the former Chairman of the Teachers' Association, 24 August 2009.
9 Majallat al-Mo'alm, 5 May 1993. (http://www.moalem.org/default.aspx.)
10 Al-Qabas, 5 February 2005.
11 Al-Khatib, Ahmad, Muthakarati: al-Kuwait min al-Dawalh li al-Imarah, op. cit., p.30.
12 Al-Qabas, 7 February 2005.
13 Al-Qabas, 29 January 2005.
14 The Ministry of Endowments and Islamic Affairs, the Department of Public Information.
15 When the demolishing illegal structures committee applied the law in removing the offending building, including mosques that had been established on the territory of the State without a permit, the Islamic extremist groups launched a media campaign against the head of the demolishing illegal structures committee, Lieutenant General Mohammad al-Badr. One of these extremist MPs, Mohammad Hayif al Mutairi, demanded the submission of al-Bader to the Public Prosecution or he will question the Prime Minister Sheikh Nasser al Mohammad al Sabah, in this respect. As a result, the government retreated from applying the law on these mosques despite the fact that some of them are centers for extremists.
16 Al-Qabas, 16 January 2005.
17 Muthakarati ma'a Jama'at al-Ikhwan al-Muslimin fi al-Kuwait, op. cit., pp.16–17.
18 Musabaqat kaifan al-Thaqafiah (Kaifan cultural competition), held by the Youth of Sa'ad Bin Abi Waqqas mosque, 1981.
19 Al-Qabas, 6 October 2004.
20 Ibid.
21 Ibid.
22 Al-Qabas, 18 October 2004.
23 Al-Anba, 14 January 2005.
24 Al-Sharq al-Awsat, 9 October 2001. al-Rai al-'Am, 20 July 2001. al-Anba, 14 January 2005.
25 Al-Anba, 7 February 2005.
26 Al-Anba, 14 January 2005.
27 Ibid.
28 For more information refer to: al-Zawahiri, Ayman, al-Hasaad al-Mur: Jama'at al-Ikhwan al-Muslimin fi Sitain 'Aam (The Bitter Harvest: Moslam Brotherhood in Sixty Years), (Dar al-Byraq, undated).
29 Shabab Masjid al-Nasim, Hukm al-Dimaqratya wa-al-Dimuqratyin (The Rule of Democracy and the Democrats), undated. p.3.
30 Ibid., p.8.
31 Al-Qabas, 15 January 2005.
32 Al-Qabas, 26 January 2005.
33 Al-Di'aij, Ahmad, personal interview, op. cit.
34 Majallat al-Mujtama, 11 March 1986.
35 A-Talia', 31 May 1986.
36 Al-Qabas, September 1999.
37 US Treasury: Kuwait Charity Designated for Bankrolling al-Qaida Network, 17 June 2008.
38 Al-Khatib, Ahmad, Muthakarati: al-Kuwait min al-Dawalh li al-Imarah, op. cit., p.31.
39 Arrouiah, 15 June 2008. Al-Qabas, 15 June 2008.
40 Al-Watan, 11 May 2008.

41 'Atanay, Fida, al-Jihadiyoon fi li Bnan: from Quwat al-Fajr ila Fath al-Islam (The Strugglers in Lebanon from The Dawn Forces to Fath al-Islam), (Beirut: Dar al-Saqi, 2008), p.208.
42 Majallat Rose al-Yosif, 9 June 1994. Majallat al-Majallah, 4 October 1994.
43 Al-Qabas, 16 October 2005.
44 Ibid.
45 Al-Qabas, 16 October 2005. al-Qabas, 29 January 2005. al-Qabas, 5 February 2005. al-Qabas, 20 January 2010.
46 An interview with al-Nuri, Nader, published in al-Watan, 25 September 2006.
47 Al-Qabas, 3 October 2006. al-Qabas, 7 October 2006.
48 A statement issued by the National Democratic Alliance, 22 September 2006.
49 Nadwat al-'Amal Al-Khairi al-Kuwaiti: al-Waq' wa Alamal(Charity Activates: Reality And Hope), Published in al-Jarida, 30 November 2007.
50 Ibid.
51 Al-Qabas, 15 September 1999.
52 I'lan Sader 'an Jam'yat al-Mansuriah al-Ta'awiniya Far' al-Masbaqh (An Advertisement issued by the laundry of al-Mansuriah Cooperative Societies).
53 An interview with al-'Awadi, Farid, the director general of the Union of Cooperative Societies, published in al-Qabas, Kuwait, 9 March 1993.
54 Majallat al-Talia', 19 June 2003.
55 Dreyfuss, Robert, Devil's Game: How the United States Helped Unleash Fundamentalist Islam (New York: An Owl Book, 2005), p.186.
56 Al'atiqi, op. cit., p.450.
57 Al-Qabas, 26 October 2008.
58 Ibid.
59 A statement issued by the LP, Kuwait, 7 October 2008.
60 A statement issued by the LP, Kuwait, 7 October 2008.
61 See Arrouiah, 17 October 2008. Al-Rai, 10 October 2008. 'Alam al-Uiom, 28 October 2008.
62 Al-'Atiqi, op. cit., pp.497–519.
63 Al-Najjar, Baqir, al-Harakat al-Dinia fi al-Kaleej al-'Araby (The Religious Movements in the Arabian Gulf), (Beirut: Dar al-saqi, 2007), p.91.
64 Al-Wasat, 16 May 2007.
65 Ibid.
66 Ibid.

6 Islamist political groups and religious violence, international terrorism

1 Osama bin Laden, the founder of the al-Qaeda organization, was born in the city of Riyadh in Saudi Arabia on 30 July 1957. Bin Laden's family roots are from Hadramawt in Yemen. His father is the owner of the largest contracting and construction company in Saudi Arabia, which has a strong relationship with the ruling family in Saudi Arabia. He graduated from King 'Abdul bin 'Abdul-'ziz University in Jeddah and holds a bachelor's degree in civil engineering. With the death of his father, he inherited approximately $300 million, which enabled him to achieve his objectives in supporting the Afghan Mujahideen in their fight against the Communist regime in Kabul and the Soviet army. In 1984, he founded Markas al-kadamat (the service center), which supervises the support and finances to the war effort of the Arab volunteers who arrive in Pakistan. This center has received support from the Arab and Islamic countries, such as Saudi Arabia, Egypt, Pakistan, and even the CIA. In 1988, after the withdrawal of the Soviet army and the fall of the Communist regime of Hafazallh Amain, differences between bin Laden and the Saudi Government arose. He condemned the American presence in Saudi Arabia during the Iraqi occupation of Kuwait; he also attacked the Saudi

regime. Consequently, bin Laden fled to Sudan; he founded a new operation center and succeeded in exporting his ideas to southeast Asia, America, Africa, and Europe. In 1996, he left Sudan, heading to Afghanistan as a result of the strong relationship between him and the Emir of the Emirate of Afghanistan, Mullah Mohammad Omar, and there he founded the al-Qaeda organization with the help of Ayman al-Zawahiri, the assistant Secretary General of the Egyptian Islamic Jihad. The two men launched a fatwa calling for the killing of Americans and their allies. After 11 September 2001, the USA accused bin Laden and al-Qaeda of being behind this act. It led the international coalition forces with the United States of America to launch strikes and air raids against the government of the Taliban and the al-Qaeda organization, which succeeded in overthrowing the Taliban regime in Afghanistan and demolishing al-Qaeda in Afghanistan. Following this, Osama bin Laden disappeared from sight and it is not known if he is still alive, despite the fact that al-Qaeda is still practicing its terrorist activities throughout the world. For more information refer to: Nabil Sharaf al-Din, 'Bin Laden: Taliban. Arab Afghans and Internationalism Fundamentalism, (Cairo: Maktabat Madbouli, 2002). 'Ali, 'Abdul-Rahim, Osama bin Laden: Hilf al-Irhab ... Tandhim al-Qaeda min 'Abdullah 'Azzam li Ayman al-Zawahiri 1979–2003 (Osama bin Laden: Pact of Terrorism ... al-Qaeda's Organization from 'Abdullah 'Azzam to Ayman al-Zawahiri 1979–2003), (Cairo: Maktabat Madbouli, 2004). Suppression, Gunaratna, Inside al-Qaeda: Global Network of Terror (New York: Columbia University Press, 2002). Bergen, Peter L., The Osama bin Laden I Know: An Oral History of al-Qaeda, (New York: Free Press, 2006). Scheuer, Michael, Through Our Enemies' Eyes: Osama bin Laden, Radical Islam, and the Future of America, (Washington, D.C: Potomac Books, 2006). Coll, Steve, The Bin Ladens: Oil, Money, Terrorism and the Secret Saudi World, (Great Britain: Penguin Books, 2009).

2 'Abdul-Majid, Hanan, Tathirat al-Tahawulat al-Ijtama'ya wa Al-Qtasadya 'la-Intshar Dhahart al-U'nf al-Munadam Lada al-Shabab (The Effects of Social and Economic Transformations on the Spread of the Phenomenon of Youth Organized Violence), M.A. thesis, 'Ain Shams University, 1995. In Abu Al'la, Mohammad, al'Nf al-Deeni fi Masar: Dirasa fi 'Im al-Ijtama' al-Siyasi (Religious Violence in Egypt: A Study in Political Sociology, (al-M'ady: Markhaz al-Mahrousa: li al-Buhath wa Atadrib wa al-Nnasher, 1988), p.64.

3 Ibid., p.64.

4 For more information about these groups refer to: al-Mdaires, Falah, Kuwaiti Political Groups (The Post-Liberation), (Kuwait: al-Manar Press, 1996).

5 For more information about the relationship between Hassan al-Banna, and 'Abdul-'Aziz 'Ali al-Mutawa', and his brother, 'Abdullah 'Ali al-Mutawa'. refer to: al Mutawa' 'Abdullah 'Ali, Thekraiaty (My Memories), published in: Majallat al-Harak, 13 February 2006. al-'Qail, 'Abdullah, Men 'Alam al-Da'wa wa al-Harakh al-Islamiya al-Mo'asarah, op. cit., pp.379–84.

6 Al-Banna, Hassan, Muthakirat al-Da'wa wa l-Da'iyya (Memoirs of the Mission and Missionary), undated, p.114.

7 Ibid., p.232.

8 Diab, Mohamed, Sayyed Qutb, al-Khitab wa al-Aidaljyah (Sayyed Qutb, an Ideology Discourse), (Cairo: Dar al-Thaqafah al-Jadidah, 1987), p.78.

9 Majmu'at Rasal al-Imam al-Shahid Hassan al-Banna (A Collection of Letters for Martyr Imam Hassan al-Banna), (Beirut: al-Muasash al-Islamiya li Ataba'h, undated), p.162.

10 Al-S'aid, Raf'at, Qadat al-'Amal al-Saiasy fi Maser Ruwya 'Asryah: Hassan al-Banna Mataa – limatha? (The Political Action Leaders in Egypt Hassan al-Banna: When and Why?), (Adan: al-Hamadany li Ataba'h wa al-Nasher, 1983), p.131.

11 Abu-al-Nasser, Mohammad, Hamid, Haqiqat al-Khilaf bain al-Ikhiwan wa 'AbdeNasser Yarwiha Mohammad Hamid Abu-alNasser, (Mohammad Hamid Abu-alNasser the Truth About the Dispute Between Brethrens and Nasser), (Cairo: Dar al-Tawzi' Wanasher al-Islamiya, 1988), p.10.

12 Majallat al-Natheer, 2 March 1938.

13 Mustafa, Hala, al-Islam al-Siyasi fi Masar: men Harakat al-Islah ila Jama'at al-'Naf (Political Islam in Egypt: From the Reform Movement to the Violent Groups), (Cairo: Markaz al-Drasat al-Saiysiah wa Alistratijia, 1992), pp.113–14. For further details, refer to: al-Sai'd, Raf't, al-Irhab al-Motaslim: li Madh Wamat Wailain? Gama'at al-IKwan al-Mslmon (Islamic Terrorism: Why and When and Where? The Muslim Brotherhood), Part 1 (Cairo: Dar Akhbar al-Youm, 2004). al-Sai'd, Raf't, al-Irhab al-Motaslm: li Madh Wamat Wailain? Hassan al-Banna al-Shkaih al-Mosalh (Islamic Terrorism: Why and When and Where: Hassan al-Banna the Armed Sheikh), (Cairo: Dar al-Akhbar al-Youm, 2004), Part II.

14 Qutub, Sayyed, Ma'alim fi al-Tareeq (Milestones), (Beirut: al-Itihad al-Islami al-'Aalami li Al-Munadhamat al-Tulabi 1978), pp.88–89.

15 Ibid., p.153.

16 Ibid., p.152.

17 Majallat al-Mujtama', 10 November 1981.

18 'Abdulla al-Nafeesi was born in 1945 and received his education at Victoria College in Al-Ma'adi in Egypt, in the period from 1951–1961. He did not continue his study at the Egyptian University because he was expelled from Egypt due to his sympathy with the Muslim Brotherhood in Egypt. In 1963, he joined the American University of Beirut in the Department of Political Science until 1967, where he received a bachelor's degree in Political Science. After that, he continued his postgraduate studies in Britain, where he obtained a doctorate in the field of Political Science from Cambridge University in 1972; the subject of his thesis was 'the role of the Shi'ites in Iraq's political evolution'. He taught in the Department of Political Science at the University of Kuwait from 1972–78 and became the head of the department. He wrote several books and articles, such as 'Indama Yahkum Alislam (When Islam Rules), Tathmain al-Sira' fi Dhofar (Evaluation of the Conflict in Dhofar), al-Kuwait al-Rai al-Akhar (Kuwait: The Other Opinion). Al-Nafeesi then got involved in political and partisan activities when he went to Beirut at the age of 18. One year later he was introduced to Ibrahim al-Masri, holding a Lebanese nationality, by 'Abdulla al-'Aqeel, who was the leader of the MBG in Kuwait and the Arabian Gulf. Al-Masri was a member of the Muslim Brotherhood in Lebanon, which was founded in Tripoli in 1948, under the name of Jaam'hat 'Ibad al-Rahman (God worshipers). In 1964, the group changed its name to al-Jaam'h al-Islamiya (Islamic Group). Al-Masri was the political and intellectual teacher of al-Nafeesi. Since an early age, al-Nafeesi was hostile to the Arab nationalist ideology, Marxism, and the Communist parties. When he was a student at the AUB, he issued a publication called al-Balaq. In Britain, he continued his political activity to reach to the post of the President of the NUKS of the United Kingdom and Ireland branch as a representative of the Islamic trend. During his stay in Beirut and Britain, he published numerous articles in newspapers and magazines of the MBG, such as Majallat al-Mujtama', Majallat al-Shab, Majallat al-Hadharah (Civilization Journal), which was established by Mustafa al-Siba'i, the leader of the MBG in Syria, and Majallat al-Muslimon, which was issued from Geneva by Sa'id Ramadan, one of the founders of the International Organization of the MBG in the late 1970s. In the early 1970s, there was a change in terms of political orientations of al-Nafeesi where he contributed to the establishment of Tajamu' al-Ahrar al-Dimaqratiyin (the Liberal Democrats Gathering) with a group of liberals like Hamada al-Essa and Saif 'Abbas. In 1976, he contributed to the establishment of al-Tajamu' al-Dimuqrati (Democratic

Gathering), which consisted of Ba'athists, Nationalists, and leftists. In 1978, al-Nafeesi published a book on Kuwait, which was faced with a violent reaction by the Kuwaiti regime due to its opponent's views. This led to the application of the law for public office, one of the laws that impedes freedom. Under this notorious Act, he was dismissed from Kuwait University, and was abandoned to work in government institutions, and even his passport was confiscated; he was denied exercising his political rights for a period of five years. In 1979, al-Nafeesi was arrested with a group of Kuwaitis by the Saudi security authorities on Saudi territory possessing political religious publications written by Juhayman al-'Otaibi. After serving some time in prison in the Eastern Province, he was released and started writing a series of articles in Majallat al-Mujtama'. In 1980, he left and went to Britain to teach at the University of Exeter for one year, then he went to the United Arab Emirates to teach from 1982 until 1984. In 1985, al-Nafeesi participated in the general elections as a candidate of the MBG in the Mishref district and managed to win in this election. Following the unconstitutional dissolution of the National Assembly, al-Nafeesi participated in establishing the CM, which called for the return of the Constitution of 1962 and the return of the dissolved National Assembly, causing tension between the CM and the Kuwaiti regime. To make an impact, al-Nafeesi was arrested with a group of leaders of the CM that participated with other national forces in protesting against the establishment of al-Majlis al-Watani (the National Council) in 1990. After the liberation of Kuwait from Iraqi occupation, al-Nafeesi returned to teach at Kuwait University. After a period of time, he began to become active against the normalization with the Zionist state and helped to found the Popular Congress to resist the normalization with the Zionist state in the Arabian Gulf region and was elected as Secretary General. See Majallat al-Majallah, 10–16 October 2004. Al-Seyassah, 4 September 1979. Al-Watan, 2 September 1979.

19 Al-Nafeesi, 'Abdullah, 'Indama Yahkum al-Islam (When Islam Rules), (London: Taha Publications), p.24.

20 Ibid., p.23.

21 Ibid., p.150.

22 Majallat al-Mujtama', 8 September 2007.

23 Al-Watan, 15 April 1997.

24 Al-Mdaires, Falah, Hizb al-Tahrir fi al-Kuwayt 1953–2007 (Liberation Party 1953–2007), (Kuwait: Dar Qurtas, 2008), pp.12–13.

25 Saleh Sariya was born in Jaffa in Palestine. After the Palestinian catastrophe of 1948, he emigrated with his family to Iraq. He studied in Cairo, where he obtained a doctorate degree in Science, and then he joined al-Kuliah al-Harbia (the faculty of war) in Iraq. He became a member of the MBG at the age of 15 before joining the LP later. He rejected the traditional political approach of the MBG, and he was regarded as one of the MBG leaders in Iraq. He was behind the unsuccessful attempt to overthrow the regime in Iraq, then he escaped to Syria. He moved later on to Egypt and contacted the leaders of the MBG while carrying the same ideology, which failed in Iraq, that depended on secret military operations to gain power. Sariya succeeded in forming secret cells in Cairo and Alexandria, known as al-Usar (families) and most of its members were university students who were later known as Jama'at al-Faniya al-'Askaria (the Technical Military Group), which attacked the building of the Technical Military College, causing the death of 11 people. The Egyptian security authorities were able to arrest the members of the organization, including the leader of the group, Saleh Sariya, who was sentenced to death by the court and was executed.

26 Sariya, Saleh, Risalat al-Iman (Message of Faith), (Cairo: 1977), p.28.

27 Ibid., p.37.

28 Sheikh Hamid 'Abdullah al-'Ali is one of the founders of the SM in Kuwait. He is a

professor of Islamic culture in the College of Basic Education, and the imam of the al-Sabahiya District Mosque. He was a student of forensic science at the Islamic University in Medina from 1980 to 1989, and obtained his master's degree in Science and the Quran interpretation. He was the Secretary General of the SM in Kuwait from 1997 to 2000, and then concentrated on writing and teaching forensic science, and lectures. In June 2004, the Kuwaiti Criminal Court sentenced Sheikh Hamid 'Abdullah al-'Ali with a two-year suspended sentence with the commitment of good conduct with a fine of 1,000 Kuwaiti Dinars; he was charged with holding a seminar without a license in one of the mosques, where he attacked Arab rulers and called them traitors and prejudice leaders. See http://www.islamway. com//iwy_s = Scholar&iw_a = info&scholar_id = 500.

29 Al-Qabas, 29 June 2005. Al-Qabas, 8 June 2005.
30 Al-Watan, 14 April 1997.
31 Al-Watan, 17 July 1993.
32 Al-Watan, 25 July 1993.
33 Al-Mutairi, Hakim, al-Huriyya aw al-Tawafan: Dirasah Mawdwhu'ia lilkhtab al-Siasi al-shar' wa Marahilh al-Tarikhia (Freedom or Destruction: Objective Study for the Legal Political Speech Its Historical Stages), (Beirut: al-Muassah al-'Arabiah li al-Dirasat wa al-Nasher, 2004), p.244.
34 Ibid., pp.316–17.
35 See Al-Qabas, 15 February 2005.
36 An interview with Shiekh al-Yassin, Muhalhal, Jassim published in Majallat al-Muajtama', 1 March 1994.
37 Abukra', Lias, al-Jazair al-Ru'b al-Moqadas (Algeria the Worshiped Terror), (Beirut: Dar al-Farabi, 2003), p.180.
38 Al-Banna, op. cit., p.141.
39 For more details about the statements and articles published in support of the jihad in Fallujah by the Islamist political groups in Kuwait, refer to: al-Qabas, 19 November 2004. al-Watan, 14 April 2004. al-Qabas, 15 April 2004. al-Watan, 14 March 2003. al-Watan, 10 November 2004.
40 Al-Qabas, 13 April 2004.
41 An interview with MP al-Sharia', Sa'ad, published in al-Rai al'Am, 21 September 2006.
42 Ibid.
43 A statement issued by the National Democratic Alliance, 22 September 2006, Kuwait.
44 Ibid.
45 Al-Qabas, 14 July 2005.
46 Majallat al-Muajtama', 22 May 1995.
47 Al-Qabas, 12 January 2005.
48 Al-Qabas, 30 January 2005.
49 Al-Qabas, 15 March 2005.
50 Bayan sader 'an Ansar Qa'adt al-Jahad fi Balad Arafidan (A statement issued by the supporters of the Islamic Jihad in the Land of the Two Rivers), 9 November 2004.
51 Risalat Tahdid li al-Sahafiy wa al-Murashaha li Intikhabat Majls al-Umah 2006 'Aisha, al-Rashaid (Threatening Letter to the Journalist and the candidate for the National Assembly elections in 2006, 'Aisha, al-Rashaid), published in al-Rai al'Am, 16 March 2006.
52 Al-Jarida, 11 February 2008
53 Bayan Sader 'an Lajnat al-diufa' 'an Huriat al-Rai Wata'beir, Hawl I'taqal Ahmad al Baghdadi (A statement issued by the defense of freedom and expression Committee about the arrest of Ahmad al Baghdadi). For more information about this arrest refer to: Majallat al-Talia', 6 April 2005. Bayan Sader 'an Jammiat A'dha

Haiat al-Tadris fi Jaami'at al-Kuwait Hawl al-Tahdaid Biqtial idau Haiat al-Tadris (A statement issued by the University Faculty Association-Kuwait University about the threat of the assassination of a member of the faculty), 23 October 1996. An interview with Dr. Suleimman al-Badr published in al-Anba, 10 December 1996.

54 A statement issued by National Democratic Gathering, 2005. Majallat al-Majallha, 31 October 1999.

55 Al-Seyassah, 16 October 1999.

56 An interview with Dr. al-Shayji, 'Abdul-Razzaq published in Marat al-Umah, 6 February 1999.

57 Al-Qabas,13 October 1999. Report about the Situation of Freedom in Kuwait, 1995–2000 (in Arabic).

58 Al-Qabas, 14 February 2005. al-Qabas, 16 February 2005.

59 Ibrahim, Majed, al-Irhab: al-Dhahirah wa Ab'adaha al-Nafsyia (The Terrorism: Phenomenon of the Psychological Dimensions), (Beirut: Dar al-Farabi, 2005), p.91.

60 Ibid., p.90.

61 Ridha, Mohammad, Jawad, Ma'rakat al-Ikhtilat fi al-Kuwait: Dirasah fi al-Thafikir al-Ijtima' al-Kuwaiti (A Battle of the Segregated in Kuwait: A Study in Kuwaiti Social Thought), (Kuwait: al-Rubay'an Advertizing, 1983), p.81.

62 Majallat Ajial (Generations Journal), 15 November 1971.

63 Majallat al-Itihad (Union Journal), 17 November 1971. Ridha, op. cit., p.82.

64 Majallat al-Muajtama', 16 November 1971. Ridha, op. cit., p.86.

65 Al-Qabas, 13 January 2005. Al-Seyassah, 24 December 1992. Al-Seyassah, 15 June 1996. A statement issued by the list of al-Wast al-Damaqrati, 20 October 1995, Kuwait. Bayan Raqam wahd Sader 'an Harakat Tanqiat al-Sofoof al-Islamiya, hawl I'taqal Nakhbah men Shabab al-Kuwait (Statement No. 1 issued by Clearing the Islamic Ranks Movement, about the arrest of Selected group of young people of Kuwait), undated. Bayan Raqam Athnain Sader 'an Harakat Tanqiat al-Sofoof al-Islamiya, Nada men 'Ajal li al-Amier al-alad (Statement No. 2 issued by Clearing the Islamic Ranks Movement, about an urgent appeal to the Amir of the country), Kuwait, 12 April 1996.

66 Al-Sharq al-Awsat, 3 February 2005.

67 An interview with Sheikh al-Sabah Masha'aal, Jarrah, the former head of the State Security, on al-Hurra Television, the Ministry of Information sector news and political programs, the period from 10 to 17 September 2005, p.9.

68 Al-Rai al'Am, 12 April 2000. Al-Tali'a, 12 April 2000. Al-Shabab (the Youth) Nashrah Sadrh 'an Itahad al-Shabab al-Dimuqrati fi al-Kuwait, (Pamphlet issued by Federation of Democratic Youth in Kuwait), No. 51, October 1983, Kuwait.

69 Majallat al-Watan al-'Arabai (The Arab Nation), No. 1207, 21 April 2000. Al-Rai al'Am, 12 August 1997.

70 Al-Seyassah, 5 April 1999.

71 A statement issued by the University Faculty Association, Kuwait University, undated, Kuwait.

72 Mohammad Amam al-Jami was born in 1930 in Ethiopia, where he learned the Quran, then he proceeded to study books of jurisprudence under the doctrine of Imam Shafie'. He studied Arabic in his village, then he left and went to Saudi Arabia to visit Mecca for Hajj in 1949, where he attended workshops on the science of religion. In Mecca, he was introduced to Sheikh 'Abdul-'Aziz Bin Baz and joined him during his visit to Riyadh to open the Scientific Institute. In the early 1970s, he took part in the religious science seminars deployed in Riyadh. He was affected by a Saudi, Sheikh Mohammad bin Ibrahim al-Sheikh, the mufti of Saudi Arabia. He later graduated from the Secondary Scientific Institute in Riyadh, and then joined the Faculty of Shari'a, graduating from it in 1960. He then got a master's degree in Shari'a from the University of Punjab in 1974.

He obtained a doctorate degree from Dar al-'Ulum (the Faculty of Science) in Cairo, then he taught at Samat Scientific Institute in Jizan, and he was commissioned to teach at the Islamic University of Medina, which was established for the dissemination of the Salafiya ideology. He died at the end of December in 1995. See www.sandroses.com.

73 'Thman, Mohammad, Riasat al-Duwal fi al-Fiqh al-Islami (State Presidency in Islamic jurisprudence), (Cairo: Matba'at Dar al-Ma'arif, undated). pp.292–93.

74 An interview with Sheikh Mohammad Hadi al-Madkhaly, published in al-Anba, 19 April 1996.

75 Al-Qabas, 30 January 2005. Al-Sharq al-Awsat, 3 February 2005.

76 Al-Qabas, 15 January 2005.

77 Symposium about Terrorism held by the NDA, published in Majallat al-Tali'a, 19 January 2005. See also: al-Seyassah, 18 January 2005.

78 An interview with Sheikh al-Sabah, Nasser, al-Mohammad, in Majallat al-Mossawar, published in al-Qabas, 24 February 2005.

79 Ibid.

80 Al-Seyassah, 27 June 2005.

7 The armed Islamist Sunni jihadist groups

1 Saudi Arabia Backgrounder: Who Are the Islamists, ICG Middle East Report No. 31, 21 September 2004, p.3.

2 Hegghammer, Thomas and Lacroix, Stephanie, 'Rejectionist Islamism in Saudi Arabia: The Story of Juhayman al-'Otaibi Revisited', International Journal of Middle East Studies, vol. 39, No. 1, 2007, pp.5–6.

3 Ibid.

4 Al-Amir, Yahia, op. cit., p.58.

5 Juhayman al-'Otaibi was born in 1936; he worked in the Saudi National Guard for 18 years. He studied religious philosophy at the University of Islamic Studies in Mecca, and then moved to the Islamic University in Medina, where he met Mohammad al-Qahtani, a student of Sheikh 'Abdul-'Aziz bin Baz. Juhayman believed in the isolation from the society and its civil institutions due to the spread of corruption, profligacy in the community and its deviation from the right path. This is why Juhayman was well known for his rejection of all landmarks of civilization, such as radios and televisions. He believed in the hardliner Wahhabi movement; however, he differed with them on the idea of the expected Mahdi, which he believed in and was not adopted by the Wahhabis. He tried to prove it through his attacks on Mecca.

6 Hegghammer, Thomas and Lacroix, Stephane, op. cit., pp.9–19.

7 Al-Amir, Yahia, op. cit., p.60.

8 For more details refer to: Hudhaibi, Hassan al-Du'at la Qudhat (Advocates not Judges), (Cairo: Dar al-Taba'a wa al-Nashir al-Islamiya, undated).

9 Mubarak, Hisham, al-Irhabiyon Qadimun: Dirasa Muqaranah bain al-Ikhwan al-Mosulmon wa Jama'at al-Jihad min Qadhiat al-'Onf (1938–94) (The Terrorists are Coming: A Comparative Study Between the Muslim Brotherhood and Jihad Groups Towards the Issue of Violence (1938–94), (Cairo: al-Mahroasa lil Nasher wa Khadamat al-Sahafiah, 1995), p.109.

10 Ramadan, 'Abdul'Adhim, Jama'at al-Tkafir fi Masar: al-Osul al-Tarikhyah Walfikrya (Tkafir Groups in Egypt: Historical and Theoretical Origins), (Cairo: al-Haya al-Masriya al-'Amah lil Kitab, 1995), pp.57–61. Ahmad, Rif'at, Sayyed, Quran wa Saif: Min Malafat al-Islam al-Saiyasi: Darasah Muathaqa (The Quran and the Sword: From the Files of Political Islam a Documents Study for the Files of the Political Islam), (Cairo: Maktabat Madbouli, 2002), p.94.

11 Muthakarati ma'a Jama'at al-Ikhwan al-Muslimin, op. cit., pp.18–21, 49–55.

12 Sarya, Saleh, op. cit., p.24. For further details about the ideas of Salih Sarya see Ahmad, Rif'aat, Sayyed, al-Nabiy al-Mosallah (The Armed Prophet), (Beirut: Riyad al-Ryis Books and Publishing, 1991), pp.31–50.

13 Muthakarati ma'a Jama'at al-Ikhwan al-Muslimin, op. cit., pp.18–21, 49–55.

14 Ibid.

15 Muthakarati ma'a Jama'at al-Ikhwan al-Muslimin, op. cit., pp.18–21, 49–55. Majallat al-Majallah, No. 1287, 10–16 October 2004. Al-Seyassah, 4 September 1979. Al-Watan, 2 September 1979.

16 Muthakarati ma'a Jama'at al-Ikhwan al-Muslimin, op. cit., pp.63–69. Majallat al-Majallah, No. 1287, 10–16 October 2004.

17 Muthakarati ma'a Jama'at al-Ikhwan al-Muslimin, op. cit., pp.50–63.

18 'Abdul Majid, Nashat, al'Arab al-Afqhan. Muhawalah li Ata'rif: al-Rwa al-Fakhria wa al-Kharitah al-Tandhimia li al-Afqhan al-'Arab (Afghan Arabs: An Attempt to Define: Ideological Visions and the Organizational Approach of the Afghan Arabs), at Islam Online Net, 7 October 2001.

19 Al-Nogaidan, Mansour, 'The map of the Islamists in Saudi Arabia and the story of Excommunication' (in Arabic), Majallat al-Hejaz, No. 5, 15 March 2003.

20 Al-katib, Ahmad, al-Fikr al-Siyasi al-Wahabai: Qiraa Tahliliyya (Wahabi Political Ideology: Analytical Reading), (Dar al-Shurah lil Dirasat wa al-I'lam, 2004), p.209.

21 A letter sent by Sheikh Humoud ibn 'Oqlah al-Sh'uaybi, Sheikh 'Ali Salman al Khodayr, and Salman al-'Aluda, to the Emir of the Islamic Emirate of Afghanistan, Mullah Mohammad 'Omar, in al-katib, Ahmad, al-Fikr al-Siyasi al-Wahabai: Qiraa Tahliliyya, op. cit., p.209.

22 Brisard, Jean-Charles and Martinez Damien, Zarqawi The New Face of al-Qaeda, (New York: Other Press, 2005), p.18.

23 Majallat Dunia al-Watan, 7 July 2005, www.alwatanvoice.com/print. Php?go = articles&id = 26876.

24 Ahmad al-Khalayla was born on 30 October 1966 in the city of Zarqa and his alias is Abu Mus'ab al-Zarqawi. Al-Zarqawi belonged to the Bani Hassan tribe, one of the biggest clans in Jordan. He studied up to second grade in the secondary school. Later on, 'Abdullah bin 'Abbas Mosque, adjacent to his home, became his second home, where he was introduced to those who belonged to political Islamic groups, which incited young people to be engaged in jihad. In 1989, he left to Afghanistan, where he met 'Abdullah 'Azzam, Osama bin Laden, and Abdul Rasul Sayyaf. He received military training there and fought with Jalal al-Din Haqqani and Gulbuddin Hekmatyar against the Soviet army and the Communist regime in Afghanistan. After the end of the war between the Afghan Mujahideen and the Soviet army with the fall of Kabul and the withdrawal of the Soviet army from Afghanistan, then came the outbreak of war between the mujahideen and the Taliban. However, most Arab Afghans left Afghanistan. Among them was al-Zarqawi, who returned to Jordan and began forming an armed Islamist organization. Al-Zarqawi was imprisoned when the Jordanian security forces discovered this organization. In March 1999, al-Zarqawi was released from prison as a result of a royal pardon by King 'Abdullah II, on the occasion of his accession to the throne. Six months later he left to Pakistan and was detained there for a short period. Then he left to Afghanistan and joined al-Qaeda. After the elimination of the rule of the Taliban and al-Qaeda in Afghanistan following the events of 11 September, he left to Iran and then to Kurdistan in northern Iraq, where he participated in battles waged by Jamma't Ansaer al-Islam (Islam Supporters Group) against the US troops. With the American attack on Iraq in March 2003, he left northern Iraq and joined with a number of Arab Afghans to fight the Americans in Iraq. He formed a base for al-Qaeda in Iraq, which committed and is still committing many massacres against the elderly, youth, women, and children of Iraq. In June 2006 al-Zarqawi was killed by the American forces in Iraq.

For more information see Shahatah, Marwan. 'Al-Qaeda Strategic in Iraq and its leader al-Zarqawi' (in Arabic), Markaz al-Mesbar li al-Darast wa al-Buhoth, No. 26, February 2009, pp.11–47.

25 Majallat Dunia al-Watan, 7 July 2005, www.alwatanvoice.com/print. Php?go = articles&id = 26876., op. cit.

26 Al-Sharq al-Awsat, 14 January 2004.

27 Al-Najdi, Abu al-Bara, al-Kawashif al-Jaliyya fi Kufr al-Dawala al-Sa'udiya (The Obvious of the Saudi State's Impiety), (London: Dar al-Qasaim, 1994), pp.196–98. Abu al-Bara al-Najdi an alias for Abu Mohammad al-Maqdisi. See: al-Rasheed, Madawi, Contesting the Saudi State: Islamic Voices from a New Generation, (Cambridge University Press, 2007), p.121.

28 Ibid.

29 Majallat Dunia al-Watan, 7 July 2005, www.alwatanvoice.com/print. Php?go = articles&id = 26876., op. cit.

30 Al-Maqdisi, Abu Mohammad, al-Dimuqratia wa al-Deen (Democracy and Religion), p.2.

31 Ibid., p.8.

32 Abu al-Bara al-Najdi, op. cit., p.286.

33 Majallat Dunia al-Watan, 7 July 2005, www.alwatanvoice.com/print. Php?go = articles&id = 26876., op. cit.

34 Al-Hayat, 2 February 2005.

35 Al-Qabas, 1 February 2005.

36 Ibid.

37 Ibid.

38 Ibid.

39 Mohammad Bin 'Abdullah al-Qahtani was a laborer in Najd district. He graduated from the Islamic University in Medina and lived in Mecca. He traveled inside and outside Saudi Arabia where he visited Thahran, Kuwait, Bahrain and Qatar. He advocated for Wahabism, while he belonged to the Qahtani tribe, which most of its members are not Wahabis.

40 Al-Jabha al-Sha'biya fil Bahrain, Tatawur al-Haraka al-Wataniya wa Lmuarada fil Jazira al-'Arabiya wal Khalij (The Development of the Nationalists Opposition Movement in the Arabian Peninsula and the Gulf), unpublished type-written, p.7.

41 Majallat al-Majallah, 10–16 October 2004. Sout al-Tali'a, No. 22, May 1980.

42 Al-Amir, Yahia, op. cit., p.62.

43 Hegghammer, Thomas and Lacroix, Stephane, op. cit., p.9.

44 Personal interview with Dr. al-Khatib, Ahmad, leader of the KPDM, Kuwait, 26 April 2009. Personal interview with one of the leading members of the KPDM, and Managing Director of Dar al-Tal'a 'Abdullah al-Suba'ie, Kuwait, 20 April 2009. For more information about Juhayman al-'Otaibi Movement refer to: 'Abdullah, Anwar, al-'Lama wa al-'Arsh: Thunaeit al-Sulta fi al-Saudia (Clerics and the Throne: Bilateral Authority in Saudi Arabia), (Paris: Maktabat al-Sharq, 2004), p.157. Ahmad, Rif'at, Sayyid, Rasail Juhayman al-'Otaibi, Qaid al-Muqtahimin li Masjid al-Haram bi-Makka (The Letters of Juhayman al-'Otaibi: Leader of the Invaders of the Holy Mosque in Mecca), (Cairo: Maktabat Madbouli, 2004). Munadhamat al-Thawra al-Islamiya fi al-Jazira al-Arabiya, Dima fi al-Ka'bah: Haqaiq 'an Ahdath al-Masjid al-Haram 1979 (Bloodshed in Ka'bah: Facts about the Holy Mosque Events 1979), (London: Munadhamat al-Thawra al-Islamiya fi al-Jazira al-'Arabiya, 1986). Trofimov, Yaroslav, The Siege of Mecca: The Forgotten Uprising in Islam's Holiest Shrine and the Birth of al-Qaeda, (New York: Doubleday, 2007).

45 Al-Qahtani, Fahd, Zilzal Juhayman fi Makka (Juhayman's Earthquake in Mecca), (London: Munadhamat al-Thawra al-Islamiya fi al-Jazira al-'Arabiya, 1987),

pp.76–80. Majallat al-Majallah, No. 1287, 10–16 October 2004. 'Abdullah, Anwar, op. cit., p.157.
46 Newsweek, 12 February 1980. The Guardian, 4 February. 1980. al-Nahar, 2 December 1979. Baian Sader 'a Munadhamat al-Thawra al-Islamiya fi al-Jazira al-'Arabiya, Mad Hadath fi Makkah (What is happening in Mecca), A statement issued by Munadhamat al-Thawra al-Islamiya fi al-Jazira al-'Arabiya, 1979.
47 Al-Qahtani, op. cit., pp.176–78.
48 Al-Qahtani, op. cit., pp.218–19. See also Trofimov, Yaroslav, op. cit.
49 Al-Qahtani, op. cit., pp.653–60.
50 Al-Amir, Yahia, op. cit., p.58.
51 Al-Qahtani, op. cit., p.256. Hegghammer, Thomas and Lacroix, Stephane, op. cit., pp.254–56.
52 Al-Qahtani, op. cit., p.256.
53 Al-Qabas, 16 November 1979.
54 Al-Qahtani, op. cit., pp.657–59.
55 An interview with Sheikh al-Sabah, Mash'aal, Jarah, op. cit., p.9.
56 Al-Watan, 2 December 1979.
57 Al-'Akri, 'Abdul-Nabi, al-Tandhimat al-Yasariah fi al-Jazirah wa al-Khalij al-'Arabi (Leftist Organizations in the Peninsula and the Arabian Gulf), (Beirut: Dar al-Konooz al-Adabiya, 2003), p.226. For more information about the Uprising in Mecca refer to: al-Hizb al-Shiu'i fi al-Sa'udiya, Ahdath November 1979 fi al-Sauadia (The Communist Party in Saudia, The Events of November 1979 in Saudi Arabia), Manshurat al-Hizb al-Shiu'i fi al-Sa'udiya, 1980. A statement issued by Itihad Sha'b al-Jazira al-'Arabiya (The Union of the People of the Arabian Peninsula), September 1979. Majallat al-Majallah, op. cit. The Arab Socialist Labour Party in the Arabian Peninsula, Intifadat al-Haram al-Sharif (The Holy Mosque Uprising), Nashrat al-Masira, No. 10, 6 June 1980. Li Takun Thikra Novamber Hafizan li al-Nidhal 'la Tariq al-Taqadum al-Ijtima'i (Let the memory of November to be an incentive for struggle for the Social Progress), A Statement issued by the Communist Party in Saudia, 27 November 1983.
58 Barot, op. cit., p.588.
59 Majallat Shuon S'udiya (Saudi Affairs), No. 25, April 2005. Thawarah fi Qalb Makkh (A Revolution in the Heart of Mecca) (in Arabic), Majallat al-Thawrah al-Islamiya, No. 66, October 1985. Min Fkr al-Shahid Juhiman al-Otaibi (From the Thought of Martyr Juhiman al-'Otaibi) (in Arabic), Majallat al-Thawrah al-Islamiya, No. 39, July 1982.
60 Al-Katib, op. cit., p.214.
61 Dreyfuss, op. cit., p.278.
62 'Ali, 'Abdul-Rahim, Osama bin Laden: Hilf al-Irhab . . . Tandhim al-Qaeda min 'Abdullah 'Azzam li Ayman al-Zawahiri 1979–2003, op. cit., p.230.
63 Kepel, Gilles, Jihad: The Trail of Political Islam (Cambridge, Massachusetts: 2000), p.8.
64 An interview with Sheikh al-Sabat, 'Abdullah, Majallat al-Farqan, No. 40, August 1990.
65 'Abdul-Rahman, Hussein, al-Qadiah al-Fqaniah (Afqani Issue), (Kuwait: 1989), p.149.
66 Ibid., pp.109–12.
67 Suleimman Abu Ghaith was born in 1965 in Kuwait. He worked as a teacher of Islamic studies in 'Abdullah al-'As'usi Secondary School. Abu Ghaith's popularity emerged during the Iraqi occupation of Kuwait in 1990 when he made speeches, against the occupation. Abu Ghaith is one of the active members of the MBG in Kuwait. After the liberation of Kuwait, he cut his relationship with the MBG because of his opposition to their participation in the parliamentary elections. In one of his extreme speeches, he attacked the Kuwaiti Constitution, describing it

as an infidel and any one who follows it is an infidel. In 1994, he left Kuwait, heading to Bosnia to fight the Serbian forces. Shortly, he returned to Kuwait and as a result of his frequent absence from work due to his travel, he was dismissed by the Ministry of Awqaf. Abu Ghaith later settled with his family in Afghanistan and due to the difficult living conditions, the family returned back to Kuwait. After the air raids launched by the international coalition forces led by the United States, the Kuwaitis were surprised to see Abu Ghaith sitting next to Osama bin Laden and Ayman al-Zawahiri as the official spokesman of al-Qaeda on the al-Jazeera channel. He made a statement on behalf of al-Qaeda warning the United States of new attacks on American targets. Consequently, the Kuwaiti Government took a firm decision to withdraw his Kuwaiti nationality in July 2003. Abu Ghaith strongly believes in fanatical ideas. It is believed that he is one of the most radical fundamentalists. After the liberation of Afghanistan from the Taliban forces and al-Qaeda, Abu Ghaith escaped to Iran. See Asharq al-Awsat, 9 October 2001. Al-Qabas, 9 October 2001.

68 Al-'Aqaial, op. cit., pp.706–7.
69 'Abdullah 'Azzam was born in Jenin in Palestine in 1949. He received a diploma from Khadoriya School in Tulkarm. He was appointed as a teacher in the Idr village in the al-Karak area of southern Jordan. He studied Shari'a at Damascus University between 1959 and 1966, where he gained a bachelor's degree. He joined the MBG at the age of 18 and then became its representative at the University of Damascus in 1960. He had links with the Palestinian Liberation Organization and was engaged in the armed struggle against the Zionist State in 1970. He left the PLO ranks because it directed its troops against King Hussein of Jordan instead of the Zionist State. In 1973, he received the doctorate degree from al-Azhar and became a professor of Shari'a at the University of Jordan, in addition to his organizational activities in the MBG. After his dismissal from the university because of his political activity, he left Jordan in 1981 to go to Saudi Arabia. He taught at the King 'Abdul-'Aziz University in Jeddah. One of his students was Osama bin Laden. 'Azzam joined Rabitaht Al'alm al-Islami (the Muslim World League) as a teacher, which then sent him to teach at the International Islamic University in Islamabad, which was co-funded by Arabitah al-Islamiya (the Islamic League) and its staff are members in the MBG. In 1984, he finally settled in Peshawar, where he participated in establishing Majlas al-Tansiq la-Islami (the Islamic Coordination Council) in 1985, which included about 20 Arab charitable organizations to support the Afghani resistance under the supervision of the Kuwaiti and Saudi Red Crescent Societies. In 1984, 'Azzam established the Office of Services to the Mujahideen and became the editor of Majallat al-Jihad. In 1986, 'Azzam established the first training camp for Arab mujahideen inside the Afghan territory called 'Arin al-Assad (The Lion Lair). The relationship in this period strengthened between 'Azzam and bin Laden and they established Masadat al-Ansar. From 1987–1988, 'Azzam declared that al-Qaeda voluntarily fights on behalf of the oppressed Muslims. On 24 November 1989, 'Azzam was assassinated with his two sons, Mohammad and Ibrahim, on their way to perform Friday prayers in Peshawar. Al-Qaeda and Osama bin Laden accused the American and Pakistani intelligence of being behind the assassination. See: 'Ali, 'Abdul-Rahim, Osama bin Laden: Hilf al-Irhab . . . Tandhim al-Qaeda min Abdullah 'Azzam li-Ayman al-Zawahiri 1979–2003, op. cit., pp.19–27. Gilles Kepel, op. cit., pp.144–49.
70 'Ali, 'Abdel-Rahim, Osama bin Laden: Hilf al-Irhab . . . Tandhim al-Qaeda min Abdullah 'Azzam li-Ayman al-Zawahiri 1979–2003, op. cit., p. 23.
71 Sharaf, al-Din, Nabil, Bin Laden: Taliban: al-Afghan al-'Arab wa al-Umaimia al-Isualiah (Bin Laden: Taliban: 'Arab Afghans and Global Fundamentalism), (Cairo: Makatabat Madbouli, 2002), p.96.
72 Ibid., pp.96–97.

73 'Ali, 'Abdul-Rahim, Osama bin Laden: Hilf al-Irhab . . . Tandhim al-Qaeda min 'Abdullah 'Azzam li Ayman al-Zawahiri 1979–2003, op. cit., p.225.
74 'Abdul-Majid, op. cit.
75 Al-Bayan, 18 December 2001.
76 Al Jazeera, 17 December 2001.
77 Al-Seyassah, 2 November 2005.
78 Ayman al-Zawahiri was born in 1951. He received a bachelor's degree in Medicine in 1974, and a master's degree in surgery in 1979. In 1981, he was arrested with charges of belonging to Jamma'ah al-Jihad (Jihadist Group). In 1984, after his release from prison, al-Zawahiri left for Saudi Arabia and then to Afghanistan, where he met Osama bin Laden and became the second man in the al-Qaeda organization and one of the most wanted terrorists, not only by the Egyptian regime, but also with most of the intelligence agencies in the world, particularly the CIA. For more information refer to: al-Zayyat, Montasser, The Road to al-Qaeda: The Story of Bin Laden's Right-Hand Man (Pluto Press: London, 2004).
79 Schanzer, Jonathan, al-Qaeda's Armies: Middle East Affiliate Groups & the Next Generation of Terror, (Washington: The Washington Institute for Near East Policy, 2004), p.79. Gilles Kepel, op. cit., p.320.
80 Bayan Sader 'An al-Jabh al-Islamiya al-'Alamai Li-Jihad al-Yahuad wa al-Nansarh (A Statement issued by the World Islamic Front for the Jihad against Jews and the Crusaders), February 1998. This statement was signed by Osama bin Laden, the leader of al-Qaeda, Ayman al-Zawahiri, the leader of Jama'at al-Jihad al-Masria (the Egyptian Jihad group), Munir Hamza, the secretary of Jama'at 'Ulama Pakistan (Pakistan Clerics Group), Sheikh 'Abdul Salam Mohammad Khan, the Emir of Harkat al-Jihad fi Bangladesh (Jiahad Movement in Bangladesh), Fazlur Rahman Khalil, the Emir of Harkat al-Ansar, fi Pakistan (Supporters Movement in Pakistan) and Abu Yasir Rifa'i Ahmad Taha, one of the leaders of al-Jama'ah al-Islamiya fi Maser (Islamic Group in Egypt).
81 See Mohammad, Suleiman, 'Jordanian Jihadi current . . . harvesting the clashes, Majallat al'aser (in Arabic), 10 January 2004.
82 Al-Watan, 1 December 1982.
83 Abukr', op. cit., p.106.
84 Al-Ameir, op. cit., p.75. Abukr', op. cit., p.105. Saeed Shehabi, The Role of Religious Ideology the Expansionist Policies of Saudi Arabia, p.186, in la-Rasheed, Madawi (ed.), Kingdom without Borders: Saudi Arabia's Political, Religious, and Media Frontiers, (New York: Columbia University Press, 2008).
85 Abukr', op. cit., p.105.
86 Bayan Sader 'An Jaisah al-Qaede al-Islami-Wihdat al-Jazierah al-'Arabia (A statement issued by the al-Qaeda Islamic Army the Arabian Peninsula Unit), 22 September 2001.
87 Bayan Sader 'an al-Tayarr al-Salafi hawl al-Moqawamh fi al-Iraq (A statement issued by Salafi Trend about the Resistance in Iraq, published in Majallat al-Hejaz, No. 25, 15 November 2004.
88 Majallat al-Watan al-'Arabi, 5 November 2004.
89 Saudi Arabia Backgrounder: Who are the Islamists, ICG Middle East Report No. 31, 21 September 2004, pp.14–15.
90 Ibid., p.31.
91 Al-Anba, 14 January 2005.
92 Al-Qabas, 19 January 2005.
93 Al-Anba, 14 January 2005. Al-Anba, 21 January 2005.
94 An interview with Sheikh al-Sabah, Mash'aal, Jarrah, op. cit., p.10.
95 Department of the Treasury, from the Office of Public Affairs, 15 February 2005. Distributed by the Bureau of International Information Programs, U.S. Department of State.

96 Ibid.
97 Al-Qabas, 5 August 2004. Al-Rai al-'Am, 5 February 2005.
98 Ibid.
99 Department of the Treasury, from the Office of Public Affairs, 15 February 2005, op. cit.
100 Salha, Reem, Barnamaj Sina't al-Moat (The Dath Industry Program), http://www.alarabiy.net
101 al-Jarida, 28 April 2007.
102 Ibid.
103 Ibid.
104 Sheikh Tariq al-Fadli, is the son of Nasser Bin Abdullah al-Fadli, one of the sultans of Abyan governorate, in South Yemen. Al-Fadli family escaped from South Yemen in 1967 to Saudi Arabia, following the revolution of 14 October 1963 which erupted from the Radfan mountains under the leadership of the National Front for Liberation of Occupied South Yemen from the British colonial rule, which succeeded in liberating South Yemen and removing the regime of the Sultans who collaborated with the British authorities. Al-Fadli cut off his studies in Saudi Arabia to join Mu'askar Quwat al-Salam (the Camp of peace forces) in North of Tabuk in Saudi Arabia for a period of three years. He left to Afghanistan to join the camp of Arab Mujahideen against the Soviet army and then return to Saudi Arabia and Yemen after the achievements of unity between the North and the South in May 1990. Due to his strong relationship with the PGCP leaders al-Fadli was elected as a member of the General Committee in its Political Bureau and was appointed as a member of Shura Council. See http//www.albaidanews.com.
105 See Al-Saqqaf, Fares, al-Yaman wa al-Irhab: Qabl Ahdath Sibtambar 11 wa ma Ba'daha (Yemen and Terrorism: Before and After the Events of September 11), Sanaa: Markas 'Abbadi li al-Dirast wa al Nashr, Markaz Dirasat al-Mustaqbal, 2003), pp. 35–67. Al-Watan, 17 December 2001. Al-Hayat, 6 May 1999. http//www.albaidanews.com. al-Mdaires, Falah, The Islamic Groups and Movements in Yemen 1929–2004, Vol. 7, May 2005, Center For Strategic Future Studies, Kuwait University, pp.33–34. Schanzer, Jonathan, op. cit., p.67.
106 Al-Qaeda in Saudi Arabia carried out many terrorist attacks. The leader of that organization is 'Abdul-'Aziz al-Miqrin replacing Khalid bin 'Ali Al-Hajj, the former official of the Al-Qaeda Organization in the Arabian Gulf and Peninsula, who was assassinated on 15 March 2003 by the Saudi police in Riyadh. Al-Miqrin left school and traveled to Afghanistan in the period from 1990 to 1994, where he took his training in one of the al-Qaeda camps before being put in charge of the Afghan Arabs. He was transferred later to Algeria to fight with Jama'at al-Jaish al-Islamiya (the Armed Islamic Group) in the mid-1990s. During his stay, he supervised the smuggling of arms from Spain via Morocco to Algeria. Jama'at al-Jaish al-Islamiya had smuggled him from Algeria when the Algerian security forces were about to arrest him. Then he spent some time traveling between Saudi Arabia and Afghanistan. He then moved to Bosnia and Herzegovina, and then returned to Saudi Arabia, where he was arrested by the Saudi security forces and was tried and imprisoned for 10 years. After his release from prison, he moved to Yemen and Afghanistan before returning back to Saudi Arabia where he trained new members of the al-Qaeda network in secret areas in central and western Saudi Arabia. In a statement issued by al-Qaeda, it warned Muslims to stay away from the American civilian communities, emphasizing that Jews and American crusaders are the target of its operation and the government of Saudi Arabia will not be able to protect their interests or to provide security for them. He also added that al-Qaeda will abide by its declared policy of jihad targeting Jews, Americans, and crusaders. A few days later, al-Qaeda attacked oil

fields in Yanbu, resulting in the killing of five American engineers, two British citizens, and an Australian. The attack was a new development in the operations of al-Qaeda. The al-Qaeda Organization claimed its responsibility for this attack. Shortly after this operation, Kataib al-Haramain fi al-Jazerah al-'Arabia (al-Haramain Phalenyes in the Arabian Peninsula) announced its responsibility for the al-Washim operation, which had destroyed a security compound in Riyadh and resulted in the deaths of about 150 civilians and security men. The statement issued by the Kataib al-Haramain fi al-Jazerah al-'Arabia emphasized that the suicide attack was a reaction to those who killed mujahideen and imprisoned 'Ulama. Following the death sentence of an American hostage, Paul Johnson, with his beheading, the Saudi security forces in Riyadh managed to kill the leader of al-Qaeda, 'Abdul-'Aziz al-Muqrin, and Salih al-'Ofi became his successor. Al-'Ofi, who is 38 years old, graduated from the state school, Saif al-Dawalah al-Hamadani. He then graduated from the Intermediate State School in Medina. He served on the police force in al-Khuber prison. Three years later, he was dismissed. Al-'ofi participated in both Afghanistan and Chechnya fighting, where he was wounded and returned to Saudi Arabia in 1995. On 18 August 2005, the Saudi security forces succeeded in assassinating al-'Ofi in Medina. In spite of the assassinations, detentions, and prosecutions launched by the Saudi authority on the al-Qaeda organization, this organization is still continuing its terrorist operations. For more information refer to: Meijer, Roel, 'Yousef al-Uyari and the Transnationalisation of Saudi Jihadism', pp.221–41. In al-Rasheed, Madawi (ed.), Kingdom without Borders: Saudi Arabia's Political, Religious, and Media Frontiers, (Columbia University Press: New York, 2008).

107 An interview with Sheikh al-Sabah, Mash'aal, Jarrah, op. cit., p.7.
108 Majallat al-Watan al-'Arabi, 18 October 2002.
109 Al-Qabas, 28 October 2002. Majallat al-Watan al-'Arabi, 18 October 2002.
110 Al-Anba, 10 October 2002.
111 Bayan Sader 'an al-Haraka al-kuwaitiah li Taqier (Statement issued by the Kuwaiti Movement for Change), 10 October 2002.
112 Ibid.
113 Amnesty International Report, 2004.
114 Ibid.
115 Bayan Sader 'an al-Masadah al-Jihadia (A statement issued by al-Masadah jihadia), 8 October 2004.
116 Al-Sharq al-Awsat, 1 February 2005. Majallat al-Majallah. No. 1199, 2–8 February 2003. Al-Mulaifi, Ibrahim, Halat al-Huriya wa al-Ta'bir fi al-Kuwait 1995–2007 (The Case of Freedom and Expression in Kuwait 1995–2007), (Kuwait: Jam'iat al-Khirijeen, 2009). Personal interview with Ibrahim al-Mulaifi, one of the leaders of the leftist Student Movement, 31 May 2009.
117 Al-Watan, 17 December 2003.
118 Al-Watan, 28 January 2005.
119 Al-Seyassah, 12 June 2004.
120 Ibid.
121 Ibid.
122 Ibid.
123 Ibid.
124 Al-Qabas, 31 May 2005.
125 Al-Watan, 2 June 2003.
126 'Omar al-Faroq, is an alias for Mohammad Ahmad al-Rashed, was born in Kuwait and took part in the resistance against the Iraqi occupation. He left Kuwait for jihad in Bosnia, and then to Indonesia, where he married an Indonesian. He was arrested in 2002 for his direct link in the operations

carried out by the al-Qaeda organization. He has admitted that he was involved in the planning of terrorist attacks on Western embassies in South-East Asia and was sent to prison by the American forces at the Bagram base in Afghanistan. In 2005, he managed to escape and went to Iraq through Iran. He entered through the Iraqi–Kuwaiti borders illegally. In September 2006, he was killed at the hands of British troops in Basra during his visit to his family. 'Omar al-Faruq was one of the leaders of al-Qaeda al-Jihadiya in the land of the Two Rivers in Iraq.

127 Al-Watan, 2 June 2003.
128 Salha, op. cit.
129 Ibid.
130 Ibid.
131 Majallat al-Watan al-'Arabi, No. 1444, 5 November 2004.
132 Hussein, Fuad, al-Zarqawi al-Jeel al-Thani li al-Qaeda (al-Zarqawi the second generation for al-Qaeda), (Beirut: Dar al-Khayal, 2005), p.73.
133 Ibid., p.79.
134 Ibid., p.80.
135 Ibid., pp.78–81.
136 Majallat Dunia, al-watn, 10 July 2005, op. cit.
137 Al-Qabas, 14 January 2005.
138 Murafa'at al-Niabah al-'Amah fi Qadiat Kataib Asowad Al-Jaziera (Defense prosecutors in the case of the Lions of Peninsula Phalanges), published in al-Qabas, 25 September 2005.
139 Ibid.
140 Ibid.
141 Salha, op. cit.
142 Bayan Sader 'a Kataib 'Abdul-'Aziz al-Maqren (A Statement issued by the Phalanges of 'Abdul-A'ziz al-Maqren), 2 February 2005.
143 Ibid.
144 Ibid.
145 Murafa'at al-Niabah al-'Amah fi Qadiat Kataib Asowad Aljasiera (Defense prosecutors in the case of the Lions of Peninsula Phalanges), published in Al-Qabas, 25 September 2005.
146 Ibid.
147 Ibid.
148 Al-Watan, 18 October 2008.
149 Al-Watan, 23 April 2008.
150 Hukum Mahkamat al-Jinayat fi Qadiat al-Khalayah al-Irhabia li-Kataib Asoad al-Jaziera (Verdict of the Criminal Courts in the case of the Peninsula Phalanges Lions terrorist cell), for more information refer to: al-Qabas, 29 December 2005.
151 Al-Qabas, 28 April 2007.
152 Al-Jarida, 27 June 2008.
153 Al-Watan, 3 February 2008.
154 Al-Qabas, 6 May 2008. Al-Jarida, 2 May 2008.
155 Al-Qabas, 6 May 2008.
156 Al-Qabas, 25 June 2008.
157 An interview with al-Bathally Mubarak, published in al-Watan, 7 May 2008. For more information about Abu Hamza al-Masri refer to: O'Neill, Sean, and McGrory, Daniel, The Suicide Factory: Abu Hamza and the Finsbury Park Mosque, (Harper Perennial: London, 2006).
158 An interview with al-Bathally Mubarak, published in al-Watan, 7 May 2008.
159 An interview with al-Bathally Mubarak, published in al-Watan, 7 May 2008. An interview with al-Bathally Mubarak, published in Al-Qabas, 19 January 2008.

160 An interview with al-Bathally Mubarak, published in al-Watan, 7 May 2008.
161 An interview with al-Bathally Mubarak, published in Al-Qabas, 7 May 2008
162 Al-Qabas, 14 May 2008.
163 Al-Jarida, 5 June 2008.
164 Anahar, 8 June 2008.
165 Country Reports on Terrorism 2008, April 2009, p.125.
166 A statement issued by the Ministry of Interior, 11 August 2009.
167 Al-Watan Dally, 12 August 2009. Al-Watan Dally, 13 August 2009. Al-Jarida,
    13 August 2009. Al-Watan Dally, 18 August 2009.

8 The armed Islamist Shi'ite jihadist groups

1 Assiri, op. cit., p.70.
2 Al-Ibraheem, Hassan, Kuwait and the Gulf (Center for Contemporary Arab
    Studies, Georgetown University, 1984), p.100. Assiri, op. cit., pp.70–71.
3 Assiri, op. cit., pp.158–66.
4 Ibid., p.163.
5 Ibid., p.164.
6 Ibid.
7 'Azi, Ghassan, Hizb Allah men al-Hilm al-Idulji ila Waqaih al-Siasia (Hizb
    Allah from Ideological Dream to Political Realism), (Kuwait: Dar Qurtas, 1998),
    p.58.
8 Ibid., pp.58–59.
9 Ibid., p.59.
10 Taheri, op. cit., pp.145–155, 280.
11 Majallat al-Thawrah al-Islamiya, No. 62, 1985, p.33.
12 'Azi, op. cit., p.60.
13 Ibid., p.60.
14 Ibid.
15 Middle East Contemporary Survey 1983–84, pp.405–406, and 1984–85, pp.404–5,
    and 1987, pp.370–71. Assiri, op. cit., pp.72–73. Al-Wagayan, Najib, and Sabah al-
    Shimmari, Ashhar al-Jaraim al-Siasiya fi al-Kuwait (the Famous Political Crimes
    in Kuwait), (Kuwait: 1996), pp.252–55.
16 Assiri, op. cit., p.166.
17 'Azi, op. cit., p.59.
18 Ibid.
19 Ibid., p.57.
20 Majallat al-Majallh, 24 August 1997.
21 Al-Lahi, Maso'ud, al-Islamiyon fi Mojtama' Ta'ddi: Hizbollah fi Libnan Namuthaj
    (the Islamists in a Multi-Society: Part of God in Lebanon as a Model), (Beirut:
    Markas al-Istisharat wa al-Bbuhuth, 2004), p.261.
22 Ranstorp, Magnus, Hizb Allah in Lebanon (New York: St. Martins Press, 1997),
    p.93.
23 Rauf, 'Adel, al-'Amal al-lislami fi al-'Iraq Baina al-Marj'yia wa al-Hezbyia: Qara
    Nakdiya Iimaserat Nisf Qarn (1950–2000) (The Islamic Action in Iraq between
    Authority and Partisan: A Critic Study for a Half Century Activity (1950–2000),
    (Damascus: al-Markaz al-'Irqi li al'lam Wadarasat, 2000), p.187. For more informa-
    tion about the origin and development of Hizb al-Da'wa al-Islamya, refer to:
    Prnamijuna: al-Bian wa al-Barnamaj al-Siasai Li-Hizb al-Da'wa al-Islamiya (Our
    Program: Statement and Political Program of the Islamic Da'wa Party, in 1992.
    Rauf, 'Adel, op. cit.
24 Al-Khalidi, op. cit., p.107.
25 Ibid.
26 Ibid.

27 Ibid.
28 Taheri, Amir, op. cit., p.154.
29 Ibid., p.154.
30 Ibid., p.155.
31 'Azi, op. cit., p.60. A statement issued by Islamic Call Party, 21 December 1983.
32 For more details about the role played by Ayatollah Mohammad al-Shirazi in establishing Harakat al-Risaliyyen al-Talaiyeen refer to: Ibrahim, Fouad, The Shi'is of Saudi Arabia (London: Saqi Books, 2006). Al-Marshad, 'Abas, Dhakamat al-Turath wa wa'i al-Mufaraqa: al-Tayar al-Islami wa al-Mujtama' al-Saiasii fi al-Bahrain (The Huge Heritage and Differences Awareness: Islamic Trend and the Political Society in Bahrain), (Bahrain: Mujama' al-Bahrain al-Thaqafi lil Dirasat wa al-Buhuth, 2003).
33 Sheikh Hassan al-Saffar was born in 1957 in the city of al-Qatif in the Eastern Province of Saudi Arabia. He received his primary and middle school education in the official government schools in the Kingdom. In 1971 he went to Najaf to study religion, after the arrest made by the Iraqi authorities for the Saudi students, and after a short period he was forced to leave Najaf to Qom in Iran, where he stayed for one year. Later on he joined the Greatest Prophet School in Kuwait, which was established by Ayatollah Mohammad al-Shirazi. During his stay in Kuwait he made several visits to Muscat in the Sultanate of Oman, where he played a role in religious preaching there. Then he returned to his birthplace, the city of al-Qatif. In 1979, he left al-Qatif for political reasons to Tehran during the rule of Ayatollah Khomeini and stayed there for 10 years. In 1989, he left Tehran to Damascus until 1994, when he returned and settled in Saudi Arabia after the national reconciliation between the Shi'ite political opposition movements led by the Reform Movement, where King Fahd issued an amnesty for the opposition. Sheikh al-Saffar still exercises his religious, social, and political tasks. He has written about 60 books and booklets, such as al-Ta'adudiya wa al-Huriya fi al-Islam (Freedom and Pluralism in Islam) and al-Imam al-Mahday Amal al-Sh'ub (the Imam Mahdi the Hope of People). For more details refer to: Fandy, Mamoun, Saudi Arabia and the Politics of Dissent, (St. Martins, 1999, New York). pp.190–228.
34 Majallat al-Thawarah al-Islamia, No. 72, March 1986, p. 24.
35 Rauf, op. cit., p.260.
36 Before the IFLB was founded other underground Shi'ites groups appeared in Bahrain directly after the victory of the Islamic revolution in Iran. Those are: Harakat al-Tahreer al-Watania al-Islamiya fil Bahrain (The Islamic National Liberation Movement in Bahrain), al-Jama'a al-Islamiya (The Islamic group), Harakat al-Shabab al-Muslim al-Bahraini (The Young Muslim Movement in Bahrain), and al-Jabha al-Wataniyya al-Islamiya li Tahrir al-Bahrain (The Islamic National Front for the Liberation of Bahrain).
37 Marhun, Faisal, al-Bahrain Qadhaya al-Sulta wal Mujtama' (Bahrain: the Issues of Society and Authority), (London: Dar al-Safa li al-Nasher wa al-Tawza', 1998), p.212. Al-Jabha al-Sha'biya fil Bahrain, Tatawur al-Haraka al-Wataniya wal Mu'aradah fil Jazira al-'Arabiya wal Khalij, op. cit., p.13.
38 Majallat al-Nasr, No. 38, October 1994.
39 Al-Jabha al-Sha'biya fil Bahrain, Tatawur al-Hararka al-Wataniya wal Mu'aradha fil Jazira al-'Arabiya wal Khalij, op. cit., p.13. An interview with Marhun, 'Isa, the Chief of Information Department in the IFLB, published in the al-Thawar al-Risaliyya, No. 32, August 1985.
40 Majallta al-Shahid, 6 June 1982. An interview with Marhun, 'Isa, op. cit.
41 Ibid.
42 Ibid.
43 Memo about the GCC and the regional affairs issued by the IFLB published in

Majallat al-Thawra al-Risaliya, No. 59, December 1987. See also statements issued by the IFLB published in Khamsa Mars (5th of March), November 1979.

44 IFLB, al-Bahrain Jihad wa Istiqamah (Struggle and Integrity), undated.

45 For more information about the events of December 1981, refer to: Rashed Hamadeh, 'Asifa fawq Miyah Al-Khaleej (A Storm Above the Gulf Water), (London: al-Safa Publication, 1990). Marhun, op. cit., pp.206–7.

46 Ibid.

47 Al-Mdaires, Falah, 'Shism and Political Protest in Bahrain' Digest of Middle East Studies, Spring 2002, Vol. 11, No.1, p.33. For more information about the Constitutional Uprising in Bahrain refer to: al-Shamlan, Ahmad, al-Haraka al-Dusturiyya: Neddhal Sha'b al-Bahrain min ajil al-Dimuqratiyya (The Constitutional Movement: The Struggle of the Bahraini People for Democracy), (Beirut: Dar al-Wihda al-Wataniyya, 1997). The Bahrain Islamic Freedom Movement, 'Amal-Tahdaiyat wal Amal: Yawmiyyat al-Intifadha al-Disturiyya fil-Bahrain December 1994 – November 1995 (The Year of Hope and Sacrifices: The Diary of Constitutional Uprising in Bahrain December 1994 – November 1995), (London: The Bahrain Islamic Freedom Movement Publications, 1996). Ghassan al-Mulla, Riyah al-Taghyeer Fil Bahrain (The Winds of Change in Bahrain) (1996). Rabi'ah, 'Ali, Lajnat al-'Aridhah al-Sha'bia fi Masar al-Nedhal al-Watani fi al-Bahrain (the Committee for the Popular Petition for the National Struggle in Bahrain), (Beirut: Dar al-Konooz al-Adabia, 2007). Matveev, Konstantin, Bahrain: the Drive for Democracy, (UK: Prittle Brook Publishers, 1997).

48 Al-Hizb al-Shiu'i fi al-Su'udiya, Ahdath Moharam 1979 fi al-Saudia, (the Communist Party in Saudi, November Uprising 1979 in Saudi Arabia), (Manshurat Al-Hizb al-Shiui fi al-Su'udiya: 1980), pp.21–23. Intifadat al-Mantqh al-Sarqaih (East Province Uprising) (1981: Munadhamat al-Thawra al-Islamiya fi al-jazira al-'Arabiyya). For more information about Shi'ites social and political situation in the Kingdom of Saudi Arabia refer to: Hamza al-Hassen, al-Shi'ites fi al-Mamlaka al-'Arabiya al Saudia, (The Shi'ites in the Kingdom of Saudi Arabia), (London: Moasasat al Buqai' li Hia al-Turath, 1993). Col, Juan R. I. and Keddie, Nikki R. (eds.), Shi'ism and Social Protest (New Haven and London: Yale University Press, 1986). Fred H. Lawson, Opposition Movements and U.S. Policy towards the Arab Gulf States (New York: Council on Foreign Relations Press, 1992). David E. Long, 'The Impact of the Iranian Revolution on the Arabian Peninsula and the Gulf states, in: John L. Esposito (ed.), The Iranian Revolution its Global Impact (Florida International University Press, 1990). Joseph A. Kostiner, 'Shii Unrest in the Gulf,' in Martin Kramer (ed.), Shi'ism, Resistance, and Revolution (Boulder, Colorado: Westview Press, 1987). Dekmejian, R. Hrair Islam in Revolution: Fundamentalism in the Arab World, (Syracuse: Syracuse University Press, 1985). Mordechai Abir, Saudi Arabia: Government, Society and the Gulf Crisis, (London and New York: Routledge, 1993). Alexander Bligh, 'The Interplay between Opposition Activity in Saudi Arabia and Recent Trends in the Arab World', in Robert W. Stookey (ed.), The Arabian Peninsula: Zone of Ferment, (USA: Hoover Press, 1984).

49 Al-Hizb al-Shiu'i fi al-Su'udiya, Ahdath Moharam 1979 fi il-Saudia, op. cit., pp.21–23.

50 Al 'Amir, 'Abdulatif, al-Haraka al-Islamiya fi al-Jazera al-'Arabiya, (Islamic Movement in Arabian Peninsula) London: Munadhamat al Thawra al-Islamiya fi al-Jazira il 'Arabiya, undated, p.150.

51 Ibid., p.151.

52 Majallat al-Jazira al-'Arabiya, No. 18, 1992, p.47.

53 Al 'Amir, op. cit., p.102. Mansoer, 'Bdalnaby, al-Ahzab wa al-Harakhat al-Islamiya

fi al-Jazierh al-'Arabia (The Political Parties and Movements in Arabian Peninsula), unpublished, undated, p.95.

54 Mansoer, op. cit., p.94.

55 Al 'Amir, op. cit., p.50. Mansoer, op. cit., p.95.

56 Mansoer, op. cit., pp.95–96.

57 Al 'Amir, op. cit., pp.111–17.

58 Mansoer, op. cit., pp.94–99. For further details about al-Haraka al-Islahia, see Ibrahim, Fouad, op. cit.

59 Louer, Laurence, Transnational Shia Politics: Religious and Political Networks in the Gulf, (Columbia University Press, New York, 2008), p.146. For further details about the Islamic Front for the Liberation of Oman Refer to: al-Jabha al-Sha'biya fill Bahrain, Tatawur al-Haraka al-Wataniya wal Muaradha fil-Jazira al-'Arabiya wal-Khalij. op. cit.

60 For further details about Munadhamat al'Amal al-Islamy, refer to: Rauf, 'Adel, op. cit., pp.131–292.

61 A personal interview with Karam, Mahmood, an ex-member of al-Shirazi Group and one of its leaders and the Manager of Maktabat al-Rasul al-A'dham Kuwait, 4 April 2009. A personal interview with al-Moly, Talib, an ex-member of al-Shirazi Group, 6 June 2009. Ibrahim, op. cit., p.106.

62 Mohammad Taqi al-Mudarrisi was born in Karbala in 1945. He studied in religious schools from the age of 6. He participated in some political and religious activities and, after being chased by the Ba'athist regime in Iraq, he migrated to Kuwait to exercise his religious and political activity for five years. After the victory of the Islamic Revolution in Iran, he moved to Iran and settled in the capital city of Tehran.

63 Al-Khalidi, op. cit., pp.122–24, pp.129–57. A statement issued by Munadhamat al-'Amal al-Islamiya, 6 January 1984.

64 A statement issued by Harakat Talai' al-Mujahideen al-Resaliin (the Jihadist Missionaries Vanguards Movement), 8 October 1981. For more details about the threats made by the Islamic groups and organizations loyal to the Iranian Islamic Republic towards Kuwait, refer to: Abu Maqli, Mohammad, al-Tahadi al-Irani li al-Amn al-Qawmi al-'Arabi (in Arabic), Majallat Afaq al-'Arabia, September 1985, op. cit., p.159.

65 Assiri, op. cit., p.159.

66 Rauf, op. cit., p.253.

67 Mansoer, op. cit., p.104. Ibrahim, op. cit., p.195. Louer, op. cit., p.210.

68 Majallat Risalat al-Haramain, No. 45, October 1993. Mansoer, op. cit., p.104.

69 Ibrahim, op. cit., p.195. Mansoer, op. cit., p.104.

70 Mansoer, op. cit., p.104. Louer, op. cit., pp.210–11.

71 Mansoer, op. cit., p.104. For more information about the HPG refer to: an interview with al-Sheikhs, Hashim, published in Majallat al-Nasr, No. 25, March 1991.

72 Al-Qabas, 6 June 1996.

73 Ibid.

74 Ibid.

75 Ibid.

76 Al-Watan, 4 June 1996.

77 Majallat al-Nasr, No. 38, September 1994.

78 See Majallat al-Nasr issues.

79 Majallat al-Nasr, No. 26, April 1991.

80 An interview with Sheikh al-Sabah, Mash'aal, Jarrah, op. cit., p.10.

81 For more information refer to: A statement issued by the Iranian officials, such as the former Iranian Foreign Minister 'Ali Akbar Velayati, the former Chairman of the Iranian Parliament, Hashemi Rafsanjani, and the Iranian former Prime

Minister Hussein al-Moussaoui. Published in the newspaper al-Anba, 29 December 1986. al-Nahar, 31 December 1986.

82 Bayan Sader 'an Harakt al-Rafidain Tali'at Hizbollah in Iraq (A statement issued by the Land of the Two Rivers Movement, the Vanguard of the Party of God in Iraq), undated.

83 An interview with Sheikh al-Sabah, Mash'aal, Jarrah, op. cit., p.10.

84 A statement issued by Hizbolla-Kuwait, 9 January 1991.

85 Ibid.

86 Ibid.

87 Ibid.

88 A statement issued by Hizbolla-Kuwait, 10 September 1991.

89 Al-Mdaires, Falah, al-Harakh al-Sahi'ia fi al-Kuwait, op. cit., pp.32–33.

90 Majallat al-Nasr, No. 29, August 1991.

91 Ibid.

92 Al-Rai al-'Am, 10 November 1996.

93 Byman, Daniel, 'Should Hezbollah be Next?', Foreign Affairs, Vol. 82, No. 82, November–December 2003.

94 Ibid., p.57.

95 Ibid., p.61.

96 A statement issued by Tali'a Taqier al-Nidam (al-Jumhuria al-Kuwaitia), January 1979.

97 A statement issued by al-Munaduama al-Thawria Quwat Mohammad Rasol Allah in Kuwait, 26 January 1987. For more information about this organization refer to: the Kuwaiti News Agency, 26 January 1987.

98 Ibid.

99 The SCIRIKO was founded in 1983, due to several factors, such as the execution of Mohammad Baqer al-Sadr, the developments in the Iraq–Iran war, which resulted in favor of the Iranian forces, and a clear collapse of the Iraqi front. The Council includes personalities from the Arabs, Kurds, and Turkman. The majority of the members are Shi'ites, but there is a small percentage of Sunnis. The major parties that formed the Council are: the Islamic Da'wa Party, Islamic Action Organization, Movement of Iraqi Mujahedeen, and Hizbollah-Kurdistan. The Council is headed by Mohammad Baqir al-Hakim, son of the religious authority Muhsin al-Hakim. Its distinguished figures are: Hussein al-Sadr, Sayyed Taqi al-Mudarrisi, Dr. Ibrahim al-Ja'afari, Sayyed Mahmoud Hashemi, and others. The Council believes in armed struggle against the former regime in Iraq. At the military level, the SCIRIKO participated in the military operations during the liberation of Iraq, particularly in southern Iraq on the grounds that the Badr camp is located in southern Iran. At the political level it contributed to the establishment of the Joint Action Committee in Damascus in 1990. It also participated in the meetings of the Unified National Conference held in October 1992. The council also participated in the Salahidin Dialogue Committee. The Council is supported financially and militarily by the Islamic Republic of Iran. Shortly after the liberation of Iraq from Saddam Hussein's regime, Mohammad Baqer al-Hakim, the chairman of the SCIRIKO, was assassinated during his visit to al-Najaf at the hands of a terrorist group, and 'Abdul-A'ziz al-Hakim became its new chairman.

100 Wazarat al-'Adil, Taqrir Itiham Muqadam min Niyabat Amn al-Dawalah to Mahkamat Amn al-Dawalah fi Qadiyat al-jinaya Raqam 410/87–332/87 Salhiya 1/87 Amn al-Dawalah (Ministry of Justice, the report submitted by the state security prosecutor to the state security court in the case of crime 410/87–32/87 Salhia No. 1 / 87 State Security). Wazarat al-'Adil, Mahadher al-Tahqiqat Niyabat Amn al-Dawalah. (Ministry of Justice, records of the investigation on behalf of state security).

101 Ibid.
102 Ibid.
103 Ibid.
104 Ibid.
105 Ibid.
106 Ibid.
107 Ibid.
108 Ibid.
109 Ibid.
110 Ibid.
111 Ibid. Al-Wagayan, Najib, and Sabah al-Shimmari, op. cit., p.110.
112 Al-Qabas, 22 September 2005.
113 Al-Rai al-'Am, 11 October 2005.
114 Majallat al-'sar, 4 October 2005. Majallat al-'sar, 17 October 2005. al-Qabas, 6 October 2005.
115 Al-Qabas, 10 July 2007.
116 Al-Qabas, 30 October 2007.
117 Al-Qabas, 31 October 2007.

Bibliography

Books, articles and theses

A Revolution in the Heart of Mecca (in Arabic), Majallat al-Thawrah al-Islamiya, No. 66, October 1985.

'Abdullah, Anwar, al-'Lama wa al-'Arsh: Thunaeit al-Sulta fi al-Saudia (Clerics and the Throne: Bilateral Authority in Saudi Arabia), (Paris: Maktabat al-Sharq, 2004).

'Abdullah, Mohammad Hassan, al-Haraka al-Adabiya wa al-Fikriya fi al-Kuwait (the Literary and Theoretical Movement in Kuwait), (Kuwait: Rabitat al-Udaba,1973).

'Abdul-Majid, Hanan, Tathirat al-Tahawulat al-Ijtama'ya wa al-Qtasadya 'la-Intshar Dhahart al-U'nf al-Munadam Lada al-Shabab (The Effects of Social and Economic Transformations on the Spread of the Phenomenon of Youth Organized Violence), M.A. thesis, 'Ain Shams University 1995.

'Abdul-Rahman, Hussein, al-Qadiah al-Fqaniah (Afqani Issue), (Kuwait: 1989).

Abu Al'la, Mohammad, al'Nf al-Deeni fi Masar: Dirasa fi 'lm al-Ijtama' al-Siyasi (Religious Violence in Egypt: A Study in Political Sociology), (al-M'ady: Markaz al-Mahrousa: li al-Buhath wa Atadrib wa al-Nasher, 1988).

Abu al-Nasser, Mohammad, Hamid, Haqiqat al-Khilaf bain al-Ikhiwan wa 'Abdel Nasser Yarwiha Mohammad Hamid Abu al-Nasser, (Mohammad Hamid Abu al-Nasser: The Truth About the Dispute Between Brethrens and Nasser), (Cairo: Dar al-Tawzi' wa al-Nasher al-Islamiya, 1988).

Abu 'Azah, 'Abdullah, m'a al-Harakh al-Islamiya fi al-Duwal al-'Arabia (With the Islamic Movement in the Arab Countries), (Kuwait: Dar al-Qalam for Publishing and Distribution, 1986).

Abu Fakhr, Saqer, (al-Harakh al-Watanyya al-Falastinia mn al-Nidhal al-Msalah ila Dawlah Manzu'at al-Salah (the Palestinian National Movement: from Armed Struggle into a Demilitarized, State) (Beirut: al-Moassa al-'Arabia lil Dirasat wa al-Nasher, 2003).

Abukra', Lias, Aljazair al-Ru'b al-Moqadas (Algeria the Worshiped Terror), (Beirut: Dar al-Farabi, 2003).

Abu Maqli, Mohammad, al-Tahadi al-Irani li al-Amn al-Qawmi al-'Arabi (in Arabic), Majallat Afaq al-'Arabia, September 1985.

Ahmad, Rif'at, Sayed, Rasail Juhayman al-'Otaibi, Qaid al–Muqtahimin li Masjid al-Haram bi Makka (The Letters of Juhayman al-'Otaibi: Leader of the Invaders of the Holy Mosque in Mecca), (Cairo: Maktabat Madbouli, 2004).

Ahmad, Rif'at, Sayyed, Quran wa Saif: Min Malafat al-Islam al-Saiyasi: Darasah Muathaqa (The Qoran and the Sword: From the Files of Political Islam: A

Documents Study for the Files of the Political Islam), (Cairo: Maktabat Madbouli, 2002).

Ahmad, Rif'at, Sayyed, al-Nabiy al-Mosallah (The Armed Prophet), (Beirut: Riyad al-Ryis Books and Publishing, 1991).

Al-'Adsani, Khalid, Private Papers, unpublished, typewritten, undated.

Al-'Adsani, Khalid, Nisf 'Am li al-Hukm al-Niyabi fi al-Kuwayt (Half a Year of Representative Rule in Kuwait), (Beirut: Matba'at al-Kashaf, 1947).

Al-'Ajami, Mohammad, al-Haraka al-'Ummaliya wa al-Nigabiya fi al-Kuwait (The Labor and Trade Movement in Kuwait), (Kuwait: al-Rubai'an for Publication and Distribution,1982).

Al-'Akri, 'Abdu-Nnabi, al-Tandhimat al-Yasariah fi al-Jazirah wa al-Khalij al-'Arabi (Leftist Organizations in the Peninsula and the Arabian Gulf), (Beirut: Dar al-Konooz al-Adabiya, 2003).

Al-'Amir, 'Abdul-Latif, al-Haraka al-Islamiya fi al-Jazera al-'Arabiya (Islamic Movement in the Arabian Peninsula), (London: Munadhamat al Thawra al-Islamiya fi al-jazira il 'Arabiya, undated).

Al-Amir, Yahia, Akhraju al-Watan min Jazyret al-'Arab: Ayam al-Irhab fi al-S'udia (They Expelled Homeland from the Arabian Peninsula: Days of Terrorism in Saudi Arabia), (Beirut: al-Markaz al-Thaqafi al-'Arabi, 2007).

Al-'Aqail, 'Abdullah, Men 'Alam al-Da'wa wa al-Haraka al-Slamiya al-Moa'sarh (A Prominent Advocacy and Contemporary Islamic Movement), (Cairo, 2006).

Al-'Atiqi, 'Abdullah, al-Manhaj Atarbawi Lil Haraka al-Islamiya al-Mo'asarah wa Atharah Labuniat al-Muajtam' al-Kuwaiti (Educational Methodology of the Islamic Contemporary Movement and its Impact on the Kuwaiti Society), (Kuwait: Maktabat al-Manar al-Islmaia, 2006).

Al-Baghli, Mohammad, al-Harakah al-Salafiah al-'Almia (Salafiah Scientific Movement), unpublished research, undated.

Al-Banna, Hassan, Muthakirat al-Da'wa wal Da'iyya (Memoirs of the Mission and Missionary), undated.

Al-Di'aij, 'Abdu-Latif, Ma'ark Kalam (Battles of Writing), (Kuwait: Dar Qurtas 1996).

Al-Gharib, 'Awataf, 'Al-Taqirat Alty Tarat 'ala 'laqat al-Sulta al-Siayassiah fi al-Kuwait bi al-Shi'aih Mabain 'Amain 1980–90 (The Developments in the Relationship Between the Political Authority and Shi'ites in Kuwait between 1980–90), unpublished paper, 1992.

Al-Haji, Ya'coub, al-Sheikh 'Abdul-'Aziz al-Rashaid, Sirat Hayatah (Sheikh Abdul-'Aziz al-Rashaid, Biography of his Life), (Kuwait: Markaz al-Buhuth Wadirasat al-Kuwaitia, 1993).

Al-Haraka al-Dustoria al-Islamiya: Masirt Atna'sher 'Aam 1991–2003 (Islamic Constitutional Movement: The Twelfth Anniversary 1991–2003), (Kuwait: ICM, 2003).

Al-Harbi, Dibi, Man Yantakhib Man . . . wa Limatha: Wasail wa 'Wamil al-Tatheir 'Ala al-Nakhib al-Kuwaiti (Who Elects Who . . . and Why: Means that Influence Factors on the Kuwaiti Voter), (Kuwait: Dar al-Qabas Lil Tiba'ah wa al-Nasher wa al-Tawzi', 1996).

Al-Hassan, Yousuf, 'Our Attitude Towards the Religious Movements in Bahrain' (in Arabic), Majallat al-Nahj, No. 15, 1987, Cyprus.

Al-Hassen, Hamza, al-Shi'iets fi al-Mamlaka al-'Arabiya al Saudia, (The Shi'ites in the Kingdom of Saudi Arabia), (London: Moasasat al Buqai' li Hia al-Turath, 1993).

Al-Hatim, 'Abdullah, Min Huna Bada't al-Kuwait (Kuwait Started from Here), (Kuwait: Dar al-Qabas, 1980).

Al-Hizb al-Shiu'i fi al-Su'udiya, Ahdath Moharam 1979 fi al-Saudia, (The Communist Party in Saudia, November Uprising 1979 in Saudi Arabia), (Manshurat al-Hizb al-Shiu'i fi al-Su'udiya: 1980).

Al-Hsain, Ahamad, al-Bohra al-Isma'ilyah Muslmon am Kuffar (The Bohras al-Ismailis are Muslims or Infidels), (2007).

Al-Hudhaibi, Hassan, Du'at la Qudhat (Advocates not Judges), (Cairo: Dar al-Taba'a wa al-Nashir al-Islamiya, undated).

'Ali, 'Abdul-Rahim, Osama bin Laden:Hilf al-Irhab . . . Tandhim al-Qaeda min 'Abdullah 'Azzam li Ayman al-Zawahiri 1979–2003, (Osama bin Laden: Pact of Terrorism . . . al-Qaeda's Organization from 'Abdullah 'Azzam to Ayman al-Zawahiri 1979–2003), (Cairo: Maktabat Madbouli, 2004).

Al-Ibraheem, Hassan, Kuwait and the Gulf (Center for Contemporary Arab Studies, Georgetown University, 1984).

Al-Jabha al-Sha'biya fil Bahrain, Tatawur al-Haraka al-Wataniya wa Lmuarada fil Jazira al-'Arabiya wal Khalij (The Development of the Nationalists Opposition Movement in the Arabian Peninsula and the Gulf), unpublished typewritten.

Al-Jassim, Najat, al-Tatawur al-Siyasi wa al-Iqtisadi li al-Kuwait bain al Harbain, 1914–38 (Political and Economic Development in Kuwait between the Two Wars, 1914–39), (Cairo: al-Matba'a al-Fanniya al-Haditha, 1973).

Al-katib, Ahmad, al-Fikr al-Siyasi al-Wahabai: Qiraa Tahliliyya (Wahabi Political Ideology: Analytical Reading), (Dar al-Shurah lil Dirasat wa al-I'lam, 2004).

Al-Kayali, 'Abdul-Wahab, al-Moso'a al-Siasia (Political Encyclopedia), (Beirut: al-Moassah al-'Arabia lil Dirasat wa al-Nasher, 1981).

Al-Khaldi, Sami, al-Ahzab al-Islamiya fi al-Kuwait (Islamic Parties in Kuwait), (Kuwait: Dar al-Nab, 1999).

Al-Khatib, Ahmad, Muthakarati: al-Kuwait min al-Imarah il al-Dawalh (My Memoirs Kuwait from an Emirate to a State), (Beirut: al-Markaz al-Thaqafi al-'Arabi, 2007), Part I.

—— Muthakarati: al-Kuwait min al-Dawalh li al-Imarah (My Memoirs Kuwait from a State to an Emirate), (Beirut: al-Markaz al-Thaqafi al-'Arabi, 2009), Part II.

—— 'We and Iran' (in Arabic), Majallat al-Iman, No. 10. May 5, 1953.

Al-Lahi, Maso'ud, al-Islamiyon fi Mojtama' Ta'ddi: Hizbollah fi Libnan Namuthaj (The Islamists in a Multi-Society: Party of God in Lebanon as a Model), (Beirut: Markas al-Istisharat wa al-Bbuhuth, 2004).

Allen, Charles, God's Terrorists: The Wahhabi Cult and the Hidden Roots of Modern Jihad, (London: Little Brown Book Group, 2006).

Al-Maqdisi, Abu Mohammad, al-Dimuqratia wa al-Deen (Democracy and Religion).

Al-Maraa Wal'mal Al-Seyasi (Women and Political Activity), Majallat al-Forqan, No. 23, 1993.

Al-Marshad, 'Abas, Dhakamat al-Turath wa wa'i al-Mufaraqa: al-Tayar al-Islami wa al-Mujtama' al-Saiasii fi al-Bahrain (The Huge Heritage and Differences Awareness: Islamic Trend and the Political Society in Bahrain), (Bahrain: Mujama' al-Bahrain al-Thaqafi lil Dirasat wa al-Buhuth, 2003).

Al-Mdaires, Falah, 'Kuwaiti Political Groups: Post-Liberation Era' (in Arabic), al-Seyassah al-Dawillya, No. 114, October 1993.

—— Malamih Awaliyah Hawl Nash'at al-Tagamu'at wa al-Tanzimat al-Siyasiyah fi al-Kuwait (1938–75) (The Emergence of the Political Groups and Organizations in Kuwait: Initial Outline (1938–75), (Kuwait: Dar Qurtas, 1999).

—— al-Tawajuhat al-Markisiyah fi al-Kuwait (The Marxist Orientations in Kuwait), (Kuwait: Dar Qurtas, 2003).

—— al-Jam'ah al-Salafiah fi al-Kuwait: al-Nashah wa al-Fikr wa al-Tatawur (The Salafiah Group in Kuwait: Origins, Ideology and Development), (Kuwait: Dar Qurtas, 1999).

—— Jama'at al-Ikhwan al-Muslimin fi al-Kuwait (The Muslim Brotherhood in Kuwait), (Kuwait: Dar Qurtas, 1990).

—— al-Haraka al-Dustori fi al-kuwait (The Constitutional Movement in Kuwait), (Kuwait: Dar Qurtas, 2002).

—— al-Mujtama' al-Madany wa al-Harakah al-Watainya fi al-Kuwait (Civil Society and the National Movement in Kuwait), (Kuwait: Dar Qurtas, 2000).

—— al-Harkat Waltajam'at al-Seyassa fi al-Bahrain 1938–2002 (Political Movements and Groups in Bahrain 1938–2002), (Beirut: Dar al-Konooz al-Adabia, 2004).

—— al-Harakh al-Sh'ih fi al-Kuwait (Shi'ite Movement in Kuwait), (Kuwait: Dar Qurtas, 1999).

—— al-Tajammu'at al-Siyasiyah al-Kuwaytiah: Marhalat ma ba'd al-Tahrir (Kuwaiti Political Groups: Post Liberation Era), (Kuwait: al-Manar, 1996).

—— The Islamic Groups and Movements in Yemen 1929–2004, Vol. 17, May 2005, Center for Strategic Future Studies, Kuwait University.

—— 'Shi'ism and Political Protest in Bahrain' Digest of Middle East Studies, Spring 2002 Vol. 11, No. 1.

Al-Menoufi, Kamal, al-Hakwmat al-Kuwaiti (The Kuwaiti Government), (Kuwait: al-Rubay'an Advertising, 1985).

Al-Moso'a al-Falastainia (The Palestinian Encyclopedia), (Damascus: 1984).

Al-Moso'a al-Moiasarah fi al-Adian wa al-Mthahib al-Moa'sirah (Simplified Encyclopedia in Religions and Contemporary Sects), (Riyadh: Symposium Global Islamic Youth, 1972).

Al-Mulaifi, Ibrahim, Halat al-Huriya wa al-Ta'bir fi al-Kuwait 1995–2007 (The Case of Freedom and Expression in Kuwait 1995–2007), (Kuwait: Jam'iat al-Khirijeen, 2009).

Al-Mulla, Ghassan, Riyah al-Taghyeer Fil Bahrain (The Winds of Change in Bahrain), (1996).

Al-Mutairi, Hakem, 'Freedom and Identity Crisis in the Gulf and the Arabian Peninsula' (in Arabic), an unpublished study submitted to the symposium held in the Graduates Society in Kuwait, 29–30 April 2006.

—— Ahkam al-Muqawmah wa al-Shahada: Bayan Wujub Nasrat al-Muqawamah fi Falastin wa Labnan (The Rules of Resistance and Martyrdom: the Necessity of Supporting the Resistance in Lebanon and Palestine), (Kuwait, undated).

—— al-Huriyya aw al-Tawafan: Dirasah Mawdwhu'ia lilkhtab al-Siasi al-shar' wa Marahilh al-Tarikhia (Freedom or Destruction: Objective Study for the Legal Political Speech: Its Historical Stages), (Beirut: al-Muassah Al-'Arabiah Lil al-Dirasat wa al-Nasher, 2004).

Al-Muzaini Ahmad, Minhaj Gama'at Ansaar al-shura (The Approach for Consultative Supporters Group), (Kuwait: 2000).

Al-Nabhani, Taqi Eddin, al-Takatul al-Hizbi (The Party Block), undated.

—— al-Dawlah al-Islamiya (the Islamic State), (al-Qads: Liberation Party Publications,1953).

Al-Nafeesi, 'Abdullah, 'Indama Yahkum Alislam (When Islam Rules), (London: Taha Publication).

—— al-Kuwait al-Rai al-Akhar (Kuwait and the Other Opinion), (London: Taha House Publishing 1978).

—— (ed.), Al-Haraka al-Islamiya: Ruwyi Mustaqbaliyah: Awraq fi al-Naqd al-Dhati (The Islamic Movement: A Future Vision: Papers in Self-Criticism), (Kuwait: 1989).

Al-Najdi, Abu al-Bara, al-Kawashif al-Jaliyya fi Kufr al-Dawala al-Sa'udiyya (The Obvious of the Saudi State's Impiety), (London: Dar al-Qsaim, 1994).

Al-Najjar, Baqir, al-Harakat al-Dinia fi Al-Kaleej al-'Araby (The Religious Movements in the Arabian Gulf), (Beirut: Dar al-Saqi, 2007).

Al-Najjar, Ghanim, 'Parliamentary Elections in Kuwait 1992' (in Arabic), Social Affairs Journal, No. 47, Sharjah, autumn 1995.

—— Muqdma li Attawr al-Saiasi fi al-Kuwait (Introduction to the Political Development in Kuwait), (Kuwait: Dar Qurtas, 1994).

—— 'Decision-Making Process in Kuwait: the Land Acquisition Policy as a Case Study', Ph.D. thesis, University of Exeter, 1984.

Al-Nizam al-Asasi li Jam 'iyt al-Aslah al-Lijtimai (The Internal Rules of the Social Reform Society).

Al-Nogaidan, Mansour, 'The Map of the Islamists in Saudi Arabia and the Story of Excommunication' (in Arabic), Majallat al-Hejaz, No. 5, March 15, 2003.

Al-Nuri, 'Abdullah, Qissat al-Ta'lim fi al-Kuwait fi Nisf Qarn (The Story of Education in Kuwait in Half a Century), (Cairo: Matba'at al-Istiqama, undated).

Al-Qahtani, Fahd, Zilzal Juhayman fi Makka (Juhayman's Earthquake in Mecca), (London: Munadhamat al-Thawra al-Islamiya fi al-Jazira al-'Arabiya, 1987).

Al-Rashaid, 'Abdul-'Aziz, Tarikh al-Kuwait (Kuwait History), (Beirut, 1971).

—— 'The New and the Old: What Should Kuwait Follow?' (in Arabic), Majallat al-Kuwait, 1929.

Al-Rasheed, Madawi, Contesting the Saudi State: Islamic Voices from a New Generation, (London: Cambridge University Press, 2007).

—— (ed.), Kingdom without Borders: Saudi Arabia's Political, Religious, and Media Frontiers, (New York: Columbia University Press, 2008).

Al-Rumaihi, Mohammad, Asda Harb al-Kuwait: Rudud al-Fa'al al-'Arabiah 'Ala al-Qazu wa Ma Talah, (Beirut: Dar al-Saqi, 1994).

—— al-Jidhur al-Ijtma'iya Lil al-Dimuqratiya fi Mujtama'at al-Khalij al-'Arabi al-Mu'asira (The Social Roots for Democracy in the Contemporary Societies of the Arabian Gulf), (Kuwait: Kazma Publications, 1977).

—— 'The 1938 Reform Movements in Kuwait, Bahrain and Dubai' (in Arabic), Dirasat al-Khalij wa al-Jasira al-'Arabiya, Vol. no. 4, October 1975.

Al-Sa'id, Raf'at, al-Irhab al-Motaslim: Limatha Wamat Wailain? Gama'at al-IKhwan al-Mslmon (Islamic Terrorism: Why and When and Where? The Muslim Brotherhood), vol. 1 (Cairo: Dar Akhbar al-Youm, 2004).

—— al-Irhab al-Motaslm: Limatha Wamat Wailain? Hassan al-Banna al-Shkaih al-Mosalh (Islamic Terrorism: Why and When and Where: Hassan al-Banna the Armed Sheikh), (Cairo: Dar al-Akhbar al-Youm, 2004), Part II.

—— Qadat al-'Amal al-Saiasy fi Maser Ruwya 'Asryah: Hassan al-Banna Mata . . . wa Limatha? (The Political Action Leaders in Egypt Hassan al-Banna: When and Why?), (Adan: al-Hamadany Liataba'h Waalnasher,1983).

Al-S'aidi, Saleh, al-Harakah al-Salafiah (al-Salafiah Movement), (al-Qabas, April 19, 1998).

Al-Saleh, 'Abd al-Malik, Tatawur al-Ta'leem fi al-Kuwait (The Development of Education in Kuwait), (Kuwait: al-Mosam al-Thaqafy, Rabitat al-Ijtima'ian, 1968).

Al-Saqqaf, Fares, al-Yaman wa al-Irhab: Qabl Ahdath Sibtambar 11 wa ma Ba'daha (Yemen and Terrorism: Before and After the Events of September 11), Sanaa: Markas 'Abbadi li al-Dirast wa al Nashr, Markaz Dirasat al-Mustaqbal, 2003).

Al-Sawaf, Mohammad, Mahmoud Min Sejel Thekraiaty (From My Memories), (Cairo: Dar al-kalafa, 1987).

Al-Shamlan, Ahmad, al-Haraka al-Dusturiyya: Neddhal Sha'b al-Bahrain min Ajil al-Dimuqratiyya (The Constitutional Movement: The Struggle of the Bahraini People for Democracy), (Beirut: Dar al-Wihda al-Wataniyya, 1997).

Al-Shamlan, Saif Marzuq, Men Tarikh al-Kuwayt (From the History of Kuwait), (Cairo: Matba'at Nahdat Masr, 1959).

Al-Shayji, 'Abdul-Razzaq Intkhab al-Maraa Nadhra Dusturia (The Election of Women in Constitutional Vision), (Kuwait: Maktabt al-Imam al-Thahabi 1992).

Al-Shirbasi, Ahmad, Ayyam al-Kuwait (Kuwait Days), (Cairo: Dar al-Kitab al-'Arabi, 1953).

Al-Tali'a, al-Tali'a fi Ma'rakat al-Dimuqratiya (The Vanguard in the Battle for Democracy), (Kuwait: al-Tali'a Publications, 1984).

Al-Timimi, 'Abd al-Malik, al-Istatan al-Ajnaby fi al-Watan al-'Arabi (The foreign Settlement in the Arab World), (Kuwait: 1989).

Al-Wagayan, Najib, and Sabah al-Shimmari, Ashhar al-Jaraim al-Siasiya fi al-Kuwait (The Famous Political Crimes in Kuwait), (Kuwait, 1996).

Al-Zaid, Khalid Sa'ud, Udaba' al-Kuwait fi Qarnain (Kuwait Men of Letters in Two Centuries), (Kuwait: al-Matba'a al-'Asriya, 1967).

Al-Zayyat, Montasser, The Road to al-Qaeda: The Story of Bin Laden's Right-Hand Man, (London: Pluto Press, 2004).

Assiri, Abdul-Reda, Kuwait's Foreign Policy: City-State in World Politics (Boulder, San Francisco & London: Westview Press, 1990).

Assiri, Abdul-Reda, and al-Menoufi, Kamal, 'The Sixth Parliamentary Elections (1985) in Kuwait: Political Analysis' (in Arabic), Social Sciences Journal, Vol. 14, No. 1, Spring 1986.

'Atanay, Fida, al-Jihadiyoon fi li Bnan: from Quwat al-Fajr ila Fath al-Islam (The Strugglers in Lebanon from The Dawn Forces to Fath al-Islam), (Beirut: Dar al-Saqi, 2008).

Awraq Min Mofakert Mosharak: al-Theakrah A-Rab'ah Li-Ntalaqat Athnaniat al-Damoqratia (From Participant Private Papers: the Fourth Anniversary of the Mondays Democracy), Majallat al-Tali'a, December 8, 1993.

'Azi, Ghassan, Hizbollah men al-Hilm al-Idulji ila Waqaih al-Siasia (Party of God from Ideological Dream to Political Realism), (Kuwait: Dar Qurtas, 1998).

Baha al-Deen, Ahmed, 'a Week in Kuwait' (in Arabic), Sabah al-Khair, 25 April 1957.

Baqir, Ahmad and Sheikh al-Msbah, Nazim Lecture, 'The Political Rights of Women in Islam' (in Arabic), Majallat al-Forqan, December 1992, Kuwait.

Baqir, Ahmad, Dirasa Hawl al-Madah al-Thanya min Dastwer al-Kuwait (A Study About the Second Article of the Constitution of Kuwait), (Kuwait: al-Dar al-Salafiah, 1984).

Barnamaj al-Haraka al-Dustoria (The Constitutional Movement Program), unpublished manuscript.

Barot, Jamal and Daraj, Faisal, al-Ahzab wa al-Harakat wa al-Jama't al-Islamiay (Islamic Parties, Movements and Groups), (Damascus: Markaz al-Dirasat al-'Arabia al-Istratigiya, 1999).

Bashmi, Ibrahim, al-Kuwait al-Waq' wa al-Rawae (Kuwait Reality and Vision), (al-Sharjah: Matba'at Dar al-Kalij, 1982).

Bergen, Peter L., The Osama bin Laden I know: An Oral History of al Qaeda, (New York: Free Press, 2006).

Bill, James, 'A Resurgent Islam in the Persian Gulf', Foreign Affairs, (Fall 1984).

Bligh, Alexander, 'The Interplay between Opposition Activity in Saudi Arabia and Recent Trends in the Arab World', in Robert W. Stookey (ed.), The Arabian Peninsula: Zone of Ferment, (USA: Hoover Press, 1984).

Brisard, Jean-Charles and Martinez Damien, Zarqawi: The New Face of al-Qaeda, (New York: Other Press, 2005).

Brnamijuna: al-Bian wa al-Barnamaj al-Siasai li Hizb al-Da'wa al-Islamiya (Our Program: Statement and Political Program of the Islamic Da'wa Party), 1992.

Byman, Daniel, 'Should Hezbollah be Next?', Foreign Affairs, Vol. 82, No. 82, November–December 2003.

Col, Juan R. I. and Keddie, Nikki R. (eds.), Shi'ism and Social Protest (New Haven and London: Yale University Press, 1986).

Cordesman, Anthony H. Kuwait: Recovery and Security after the Gulf War, (USA: Westview Press, 1997).

Dekmejian, R. Hrair, Islam in Revolution: Fundamentalism in the Arab World, (Syracuse: Syracuse University Press, 1985).

Diab, Mohamed, Sayed Qutb, al-khitab wa al-Aidaljyah (Sayyed Qutb and Ideology Discourse), (Cairo: Dar al-Thaqafah al-Jadidah, 1987).

Dreyfuss, Robert, Devil's Game: How the United States Helped Unleash Fundamentalist Islam, (New York: An Owl Book, 2005).

Esposito, John L., The Oxford Dictionary of Islam, (Oxford: Oxford University Press, 2003).

—— (ed.), The Iranian Revolution: Its Global Impact (Florida: International University Press, 1990).

Fandy, Mamoun, Saudi Arabia and the Politics of Dissent, (New York: St. Martins, 1999).

Freeth, Zahra, A New Look at Kuwait, (London: George Allen and Unwin, 1972).

Gharib, Abdullah, Waja Dor al-Majus: al-Ab'ad al-Taraikhya wa al-'Aqaidiya wa al-Siasia li al-Thawrah al-Iraniya (The Role of the Magus: Historical, Ideological, Political Dimensions for the Iranian Revolution), (Cairo: Dar al-Jeel, 1981).

Gunaratna, Rohan, Inside al-Qaeda: Global Network of Terror, (New York: Columbia University Press, 2002).

Hadad, Amir, Majmu'at al-Tali'a: Mabadi-Mawaqif-Da'awat (al-Tali' Group: Principles, Attitudes, Calls), (Kuwait: al-Dar al-Slifiah, 1985).

Hanna, 'Abdullah, 'The General Features of the Movement in Syria from Renaissance to the Beginning of the Sixties' (in Arabic), Majallat Qthai Fakria, October 16, 1989, Cairo.

Harakat al-Murabitun (The Adherence Movement, Bazaq al-Fajar), (Kuwait, 1992).

Harakat al-Tawafuq al-Watani al-Islamiya, Ta'araf 'la Harakat al-Tawafuq al-Watani al-Islamiya (Be Introduced to the Islamic National Consensus Movement), (Kuwait, undated).

Harakat al-Tawafuq al-Watani al-Islamiya, Moutamer al-Quds al-Thani: Mohoer al-Istratijiat (Second Jerusalem Conference: Strategies Axis), (Kuwait: Mataba'al-Mahamid al-'Alamih, 2004).

Hegghammer, Thomas and Lacroix, Stephanie, 'Rejectionist Islamism in Saudi

Arabia: The Story of Juhayman al-'Otaibi Revisited', International Journal of Middle East Studies, Vol. 39, No. 1, 2007.

Hewins, Ralph, A Golden Dream: The Miracle of Kuwait, (London: W.H. Allen, 1963).

Hizb al-Tahrir, (Liberation Party) (Liberation Party Publications, 1985).

Hussein, 'Abdul-'Aziz, Muhadarat 'an al-Mujtama' al-'Arabi bi al-Kuwait (Lectures About the Arab Society in Kuwait), (Cairo: al-Jami'a al-'Arabiya, 1960).

Hussein, Fuad, al-Zarqawi al-Jeel al-Thani li al-Qaeda (al-Zarqawi: The Second Generation for al-Qaeda), (Beirut: Dar al-Khayal, 2005).

Husseini, Ishak Musa, The Moslem Brethren: The Greatest of Modern Islamic Movement, (Beirut: Khayats, 1956).

Ibrahim, Fouad, The Shi'is of Saudi Arabia (London: Saqi Books, 2006).

Ibrahim, Majed, al-Irhab: al-Dhahirah wa Ab'adaha al-Nafsyia (The Terrorism: Phenomenon and Psychological Dimensions), (Beirut: Dar al-Farabi, 2005).

IFLB, al-Bahrain Jihad wa Istiqamah (Struggle and Integrity), undated.

Intifadat al-Mantqh al-Sarqaih (East Province Uprising), (1981: Munadhamat al-Thawra al-Islamiya fi al-Jazira al-'Arabiya).

Isma'l, Fahad, al-Qissa al-'Arabiya fi al-Kuwait, Qira'a Naqidya (The Arab Story in Kuwait, a Critical Study), (Beirut: Dar al-'Awda, 1980).

Jam 'iyat al-Khireejin, Masierat al-Tasis Wal'ataa 1964–94 (The Graduates Association, the Establishment Pace and the Giving 1964–94).

Jerkhi, Jasem Mohammad, 'The Electoral Process in Kuwait: A Geographical Study', Ph.D. thesis, University of Exeter, 1984.

Kepel, Gilles, Beyond Terror and Martyrdom: The Future of the Middle East (USA: The Belknap Press of Harvard University Press, 2008).

—— Jihad: The Trail of Political Islam (Cambridge, Massachusetts, 2000).

Khalaf, Fadil, Dirasat Kuwaitiya (Kuwaiti Studies), (Kuwait: al-Matb'a al-'Asrya, 1968).

Khuri, Fuad, I, Tribe and State in Bahrain: The Transformation of Social and Political Authority in an Arab State (Chicago and London: the University of Chicago Press, 1980).

Kostiner, Joseph A., 'Shii Unrest in the Gulf,' in Martin Kramer (ed.), Shi'ism, Resistance, and Revolution (Boulder, Colorado: Westview Press, 1987).

Lacey, Jim (ed.), A Terrorist Call to Global Jihad: Deciphering Abu Musab al-Suri's Islamic Jihad Manifesto, (Maryland: Naval Institute Press, 2008).

Lawson, Fred H. Opposition Movements and U.S. Policy towards the Arab Gulf States (New York: Council on Foreign Relations Press, 1992).

Lia, Brynjar, The Society of Muslim Brothers in Egypt: The Rise of an Islamic Mass Movement 1928–42, (UK: Ithaca Press, 2006).

'Liberation Party a new party in Jordan' (in Arabic), Majallat al-Raid, No. 7, November–December, 1952.

Louer, Laurence, Transnational Shia Politics: Religious and Political Networks in the Gulf, (New York: Columbia University Press, 2008).

Majmu'at al-Rasaal li al-Imam al-Shahid Hassan al-Banna (Collection of Letters of the Martyr Hassan al-Banna), (Beirut: Muasasat al-Risalah: undated).

Majmu'at Rasal al-Imam al-Shahid Hassan al-Banna (A Collection of Letters for Martyr Imam Hassan al-Banna), (Beirut: al-Muasash al-Islamiya li Ataba'h, undated).

Mansoer, 'Abdul-Naby, al-Ahzab wa al-Harakhat al-Islamiya fi al-Jazierh al-'Arabia

(The Political Parties and Movements in Arabian Peninsula), unpublished, undated.

Marhun, Faisal, al-Bahrain Qadhaya al-Sulta walMugtama' (Bahrain: the Issues of Society and Authority), (London: Dar al-Safa li al-Nasher wa al-Tawza', 1998).

Masirat al-Dimaqratia fi al-Kuwait (The March of Democracy in Kuwait), (Kuwaiti News Agency, February 1981).

Matveev, Konstantin, Bahrain: The Drive for Democracy, (UK: Prittle Brook Publishers, 1997).

Middle East Contemporary Survey 1983–84, 1984–85, and 1987.

Middle East Contemporary Survey 1978–79.

Middle East International, September 1990, No. 348.

Mitchell, R.P., The Society of the Muslim Brothers (London, 1969).

Min Fkr al-Shahid Juhiman al-'Otaibi (From the Thought of Martyr Juhiman al-'Otaibi), Majallat al-Thawrah al-Islamiya, No. 39, July 1982.

Minutes of meetings of the National Assembly's No. 33, November 23, 1963, and No. 42, June 4, 1964.

Mohadin, Mwafaq, al-Ahzab wa al-Qwah al-Saiasia fi al-Ordun 1927–87 (The Political Parties and Forces in Jordan 1927–87), (Beirut: Dar al-Sadaqah, 1988).

Mohammad, Suleiman, 'Jordanian Jihadi Current . . . Harvesting the Clashes' (in Arabic), Majallat al'Aser, January 10, 2004.

Mordechai, Abir, Saudi Arabia: Government, Society and the Gulf Crisis, (London and New York: Routledge, 1993).

Mubarak, Hisham, al-Irhabiyon Qadimun: Dirasa Muqaranah bain al-Ikhwan al-Mosulmon wa Jama'at al-Jihad min Qadhiat al-'Onf (1938–94) (The Terrorists are Coming: A Comparative Study Between the Muslim Brotherhood and Jihad Groups Towards the Issue of Violence (1938–94), (Cairo: al-Mahroasa li al-Nasher wa Khadamat al-Sahafiah, 1995).

Munadhamat al-Thawra al-Islamiya fi al-Jazira al-'Arabiya, Dima fi al-Ka'bah: Haqaiq 'an Ahdath al-Masjid al-Haram 1979 (Bloodshed in Ka'bah: Facts about the Holy Mosque Events 1979), (London: Munadhamat al-Thawra al-Islamiya fi al-Jazira al-'Arabiya, 1986).

Mustafa, Hala, al-Islam al-Siyasi fi Masar: men Harakat al-Islah ila Jama'at al-'Naf (Political Islam in Egypt: From the Reform Movement to the Violent Groups), (Cairo: Markaz al-Drasat al-Saiysiah wa alistratijia, 1992).

Muthakarati ma' Jama'at al-Ikhwan al-Muslimin fi al-Kuwayt (My Memoirs with the Muslim Brotherhood in Kuwait), handwritten, unpublished, written by an anonymous former member in the MBG, undated, Kuwait.

Nanji, Azim, Dictionary of Islam, (London: Penguin Reference Library, 2008).

Nida Har ila Al'alm al-Islamiya (Strong Appeal to the Muslims World), undated.

O'Neill, Sean, and McGrory, Dauiel, The Suicide Factory: Abu Hamza and the Finsbury Park Mosque, (London: Harper Perennial, 2006).

'Othman, Mohammad, Riasat al-Duwal fi al-Fiqh al-Islami (State Presidency in Islamic jurisprudence), (Cairo: Matba'at Dar al-Ma'arif, undated).

Piscatori, James, (de.), Islamic Fundamentalisms and the Gulf Crisis, (USA: The American Academy of Arts and Sciences, 1999).

Qutub, Sayyed, Ma'alim fi al-Tareeq (Milestones), (Beirut: al-Itihad al-Islami al-'Aalami li al-Munadhamat al-Tulabi, 1978).

Rabi'ah, 'Ali, Lajnat al-'Aridhah al-Sha'bia fi Masar al-Nedhal al-Watani fi al-Bahrain

(The Committee for the Popular Petition for the National Struggle in Bahrain), (Beirut: Dar al-Konooz al-Adabia, 2007).

Rabtat 'Amom al-Shi'a fi al-Sa'dia, al-Shi'a fi al-Sa'dia: al-Waq' al-Sa'b wa al-Tatalu'at al-Mashro'h (Shi'ites in Saudi Arabia: Difficult Reality and the Legitimate Aspirations), (London, 1991).

Ramadan, 'Abdul-'Adhim, Jama'at al-Tkafir fi Masar: al-Osul al-Tarikhyah Walfikrya (Takfir Groups in Egypt: Historical and Theoretical Origins), (Cairo: al-Haya al-Masriya al-'Amah lil Kitab, 1995).

Ranstorp, Magnus, Hizb Allah in Lebanon, (New York: St. Martins Press, 1997).

Rashed Hamadeh, 'Asifa Fawq Miyah al-Khaleej (A Storm Above the Gulf Water), (London: al-Safa Publication, 1990).

Rashid, Hadi, Haal Majlas Alamh wa al-Haraka al-Dustoria fi al-kuwayt (The Dissolution of the National Assembly and the Constitutional Movement in Kuwait), (1992).

Rauf, 'Adel, al-'Amal al-lislami fi al-'Iraq Baina al-Marj'yia wa al-Hezbyia: Qara Naqdiya Iimaserat Nisf Qarn (1950–2000) (The Islamic Action in Iraq Between Authority and Partisan: A Critic Study for a Half Century Activity (1950–2000)), (Damascus: al-Markaz al-'Irqi li al'lam Wadarasat, 2000).

Ridha, Mohammad, Jawad, Ma'rakat al-Ikhtilat fi al-Kuwayt: Dirasah fi al-Thafikir al-Ijtima' al-Kuwaiti (A Battle of Segregated in Kuwait: A Study in Kuwaiti Social Thought), (Kuwait: al-Rubay'an Advertizing, 1983).

Sara, Fayez, al-Ahzab wa-al-Harakat al-Siasia fi Tunis 1932–84 (Political Parties and Movements in Tunisia 1932–84), (Damascus, 1986).

Sariya, Saleh, Risalat al-Iman (Message of Faith), (Cairo: 1977).

Schanzer, Jonathan, Al-Qaeda's Armies: Middle East Affiliate Groups & the Next Generation of Terror, (Washington, D.C.: The Washington Institute for Near East Policy, 2004).

Scheuer, Michael, Through Our Enemies' Eyes: Osama bin Laden, Radical Islam, and the Future of America, (Washington, D.C: Potomac Books, 2006).

Sfeir, Antoine (ed.), The Columbia World Dictionary of Islamism, (New York: Columbia University Press, 2007).

Shahatah, Marwan. 'Al-Qaeda Strategic in Iraq and its leader al-Zarqawi' (in Arabic), Markaz al-Mesbar li al-Darast wa al-Buhoth, No. 26, February 2009.

Shalabi, Rauf, al-Saikh Hassan al-Banna: wa Madrasat al-Kwan al-Moslmon (Sheikh Hassan al-Banna: School of the Muslim Brotherhood), (Cairo: Dar al-Ansar, 1978).

Sharaf al-Din, Raslan, Mdkal Lidirast al-Ahazab al-Siasia al-'Arabia (An Introduction to the Study of Arab Political Parties), (Beirut: Dar al-Farabi, 2006).

Sharaf al-Din, Nabil, Bin Laden: Taliban: al-Afghan al-'Arab wa al-Umaimia al-Isualiah (Bin Laden: Taliban: Arab Afghans and Global Fundamentalism), (Cairo: Maktabat Madbouli, 2002).

Sheikh'Abdul-Khaliq, 'Abdul-Rahman, al-Muslmoon wa al-'Amal al-Siyasi (The Muslims and Political Action), (Kuwait: al-Dar al-Salafiah, 1986).

—— 'The Legitimate Justifications for Participating in the Representative Councils' (in Arabic), Majallat al-Forqan, No. 27, July 1992.

—— 'The Legitimacy of participating in the Representative Councils' (in Arabic), Majallat al-Forqan, No. 36, April 1993.

—— 'The 'Ulama Opinions in Participating in the Representative Councils' (in Arabic), Majallat al-Forqan, No. 38, June 1993.

Shukri, Hassan, 'The Muslim Brotherhood in Yemen, by Linking with Religious Education 1939–75' (in Arabic), Majallat al-Tali'a al-Yamaniya, vol. 8, September–October 1984.

SIG, Fatawa fi Mu'amalat al-Kuffar (Religious Ruling in the Treatment of the Infidels), (Kuwait: SIG Publications, undated).

Sout al-Kuwait, al-Qawanin al-Qair Dastoriya (The Unconstitutional Laws), (Kuwait: Sout al-Kuwait, 2009).

SRS, Jam'yat al-Islah al-Ijtamaya fi 'Ishrin 'Aam (Social Reform Society in 20 Years), (Kuwait: undated).

Supporters of Democracy in Kuwait, al-Tamar 'ala al-Dimuqratiya fi al-Kuwait (A Conspiracy on Democracy in Kuwait), 1978.

Symposium About Terrorism held by the National Democratic Alliance, published in Majallat al-Tali'a, January 19, 2005.

Taheri, Amir, Holy Terror: The Inside story of Islamic Terrorism, (London: Sphere Books Limited, 1987).

The Bahrain Islamic Freedom Movement, 'Am al-Tahdaiyat wal Amal: Yawmiyyat al-Intifadha al-Disturiyya fil-Bahrain December 1994 – November 1995 (The Year of Hope and Sacrifices: The Diary of Constitutional Uprising in Bahrain December 1994 – November 1995), (London: The Bahrain Islamic Freedom Movement Publications, 1996).

The Constitutional Assembly, the Constitution of the State of Kuwait and the Electoral Law, (Kuwait Government, 1962).

The Executive Committee of the NUKS, Madha Yajri-fi Khalijina al-'Arabi? (What is Going on in our Arabian Gulf?), (Kuwait, 1967).

—— al-Khalij al-'Arabi aw Falastin Thaniya (The Arabian Gulf or a Second Palestine), (Beirut: Dar, 1969).

—— Nazra ila Dore Iran fi al-Khalij al-'Arabi (A Look at Iran's Role in the Arabian Gulf), (Kuwait, 1976).

The Ministry of Endowments and Islamic Affairs, the Department of Public Information.

Trofimov, Yaroslav, The Siege of Mecca: The Forgotten Uprising in Islam's Holiest Shrine and the Birth of al-Qaeda, (New York: Doubleday, 2007).

Yakan, fathi, Mushkilat Al-Da'wa wa al-Daa'ya (The Problems of Advocacy and Preacher), (Beirut: Moassat al-Rasalah, 1974).

Yasin, Sayyed, al-Taqrir al-Istratiji al-'Arabi,1990 (Arab Strategic Report 1990), (Cairo: Markaz al-Darasat al-Saiasiah wa al-Stratijiah bi al-Aharam, 1991).

Zaloom, 'Abdul-Qadim, Kayfa Hudimat Alkilafah (How the Caliphate was Demolished), (Beirut: 1962).

Interviews

Al-Di'aij, Ahmad, personal interview, March 17, 1983, Kuwait.

Al-Khatib, Ahmad, personal interview, April 26, 2009, Kuwait.

Al-Menayes, Sami, personal interview, October 1, 1993, Kuwait.

Al-Moly, Talib, personal interview, June 6, 2009, Kuwait.

Al-Mulaifi, Ibrahim, personal interview, May 31, 2009, Kuwait.

Al-Najjar, Ghanim, personal interview, February 1997, Kuwait.

Al-Sani', Faisal, personal interview, March 19, 1983, Kuwait.

al-Saqer, Jassim, Hamad, personal interview, April 2, 1983, Kuwait.

Al-Shatti, Isma'il, personal interview, March 22, 1983, Kuwait.
Al-Suba'ie, 'Abdallah, personal interview, April 20, 2009, Kuwait.
Al-Wazzan, 'Abdul-Wahab, personal interview, October 1992, Kuwait.
Al-Yasin, Mhalhal, Jasim, personal interview, May 5, 1992, Kuwait.
Baqir, Ahmad, personal interview, May 5, 1992, Kuwait.
Ghulum, Yousef, personal interview, winter 1983, London.
Karam, Mahmood, personal interview, April 4, 2009, Kuwait.

Pamphlets, statements and reports and other material

'Abdul Majid, Nashat, Al'Arab al-Afqhan. Muhawalah li Ata'rif: al-Rwa al-Fakhria
wa al-Kharitah al-Tandhimia li al-Afqhan al-'Arab (Afghan Arabs . . . An attempt
to Define: Ideological Visions and the Organizational Chart of the Afghan Arabs),
at www.Islam Online Net, October 7, 2001.
Adwa 'Ala Alma'raka (Spots on the Battle), Pamphlet No. 2, issued by the IGS, 1956.
Adwa 'Ala Alma'raka (Spots on the Battle), Pamphlet No. 1, issued by the IGS, 1956.
Al-Afqan al-'Arab wa asr al-Qaeda wa al-Mustaqbel (Arab Afqans and
Al-Qaeda and Future), http://www.islamonline.net/livedial.org/arabic. January 23,
2002.
Al-Barnamaj Alantkabi li al-Tajammau' al-Islamy al-Sha'abi (Electoral Program of
the Islamic Popular Gathering), Kuwait, 1992.
Al-Barnamaj al-Intikhati li Tajammu' al-Defa' 'An Thawabit al-Ummah (Electoral
Program for the Gathering of the Defense of the Nation).
Al-Barnamaj al-Intikhabi li Shabab al-Watani al-Dasturi (The Electoral program
for NYC), Kuwait, 1975.
al-Barnamaj al-Seaiasy li Harakt Ansar al-Hurai (Political Program for the Supporters
Freedom Movement), Kuwait, undated.
Al-Bayan Al-Khitamai li al-Moatamer al-Kuwaiti al-Sha'bi (The final statement
issued by the Popular Kuwaiti Congress), 13–15 October 1990, Jeddah.
Al-Bayan al-Taasisi Sadir 'an Hizb al-Umma (Constituent Statement issued by the
Nation Party), January 29, 2005. al-Qabes, January 30, 2005. A leaflet issued by
the NIGLL, Kuwait, 2001.
A leaflet issued by the IGPC, January 1986.
A leaflet, issued by Hayat Shabab al-Rumeitheya lil Taw'ia al-Diniya wa Liajtam'a),
No. 3, 1996.
A leaflet issued by the Kuwaiti Popular Organization as protest on the dissolution
of the National Assembly, Kuwait, 1967.
A leaflet issued by Jam'iyat al-Muhamin, Jam'iyat al-Sahafiyin, Jam 'iyat al-Khireejin,
Rabitat al-Udaba, Jam 'iyat al-Muhandisin, Itihad al-Mugawilin, al-Itihad al-'Am
li 'Umal al-Kuwait, and the NUKS.
A letter from the NP to the President of the National Assembly and the Kuwaiti
Government on the law on political parties.
Al-Nidham al-Asasi li al-Harakah al-Salafiya (The Internal Rules for the Salafiya
Movement).
Al-Nidham al-Asasi li Hizb al-Ummh (The Internal Rules for the National Party),
January 7, 2005.
Al-Nidham al-Asasy li Muatamer al-Khleej al-Sha'by li Muqawamat al-Mashruw'
al-Sahiuny(the Internal Rules for the Gulf Popular Resistance to the Zionist Project),
Kuwait, undated.

Al-Rouya al-Mustaqbalia li Benaa al-Kuwait al-Gadidah (The Future Vision to Build New Kuwait), December 12, 1991

Al-Ruyaai al-Islahia li al-Harakah al-Salafiah (Reformative Vision of the Salafiya Movement), June 29, 2003.

Al-Shabab (the Youth) Nashrah Sadrh ʿan Itahad al-Shabab al-Dimuqrati fi al-Kuwait (pamphlet issued by Federation of Democratic Youth in Kuwait), No. 51, October 1983.

Amnesty International Report, 2004.

A pamphlet issued by Harakat Tanqiat al-Sofoof al-Islamiya (Clearing the Islamic Ranks Movement), published in Majallat al-Taliʾa, July 24, 1996.

Al-Huda, A pamphlet No. 30, May 1994.

A pamphlet issued by the NP, Kuwait, February 3, 2006.

A pamphlet issued by the NP, 'on the occasion of the summit of the GCC', Kuwait, 2006.

A pamphlet issued by the NP, Kuwait, October 3, 2006.

A pamphlet issued by the NP, Kuwait, April 19, 2006.

A pamphlet issued by the NP, Kuwait, December 26, 2006.

A pamphlet issued by the NP, Kuwait, May 24, 2006.

A pamphlet issued by Tajammuʾ al-Shabab al-Kuwaiti, undated.

A pamphlet issued by Tajammuʾ al-shabab al-Kuwaiti, undated.

A pamphlet issued by the VG, Kuwait, November 15, 2006.

A pamphlet issued by al-Qaimah al-Hurah, Kuwait, March 29, 1994.

A pamphlet issued by the CSG Kuwait, February 2, 2001.

A pamphlet issued by the CSG, Kuwait, February 21, 2006.

A pamphlet issued by Shabab Masjed Ahmad bin Hambal, about Tahrim Musharakt al-Nasarah fi Munaasbat al-Kirsmas (Prohibiting Joining the Christians in Celebrating Christmas), Kuwait, undated.

A pamphlet issued by SIG, Hukum Tahnat al-Kufaar biaʾyaduhum (The Rule of congratulating the infidels on their religious occasions), al-Jahra branch, Kuwait, undated.

A petition addressed by the leaders of the MBG in Kuwait to the Emir of Kuwait Sheikh Jaber al-Ahmad al-Sabah, Kuwait, 1990.

A petition submitted by the MPs of the National Assembly dissolved on August 29, 1976, to the Emir of Kuwait, Sheikh Sabah al-Salem al-Sabah.

A proposal of penalties punishment law submitted by the MPs Walid Tabtabae and Mukhlid al-ʾAzmi to the National Assembly, June 24, 1996.

A Report about the Situation of Freedom and Expression in Kuwait 1995–2000 (in Arabic).

A statement issued by the list of al-Wast al-Damaqrati, Kuwait, October 20, 1995.

A statement issued by the SM, Kuwait, April 23, 2004.

A statement issued by the LP, Yemen, April 25, 2003.

A statement issued by the Media Office for the LP, Yemen.

A statement issued by the LP, Yemen, October 24, 2002.

A statement issued by the LP, August 6, 1990.

A statement issued by the LP, Kuwait, April 23, 2001.

A statement issued by the LP, December 21, 1998.

A statement issued by the LP, Kuwait, September 2003.

A statement issued by the LP, Kuwait, November 7, 2003.

A statement issued by the NIA, Kuwait, February 16, 2002.

A statement issued by the NIA, published in al-Qabas, October 9, 2004.

A statement issued by the DJM, Kuwait, December 11, 1998.

A statement issued by the LP, Kuwait, January 11, 2008.

A statement issued by the LP, Kuwait, October 24, 2001.

A statement issued by Hizbollah-Kuwait, September 10, 1991.

A statement issued by the University Faculty Association, Kuwait University.

A statement issued by the LP, Kuwait, October 7, 2008.

A statement issued by the LP, Kuwait, November 7, 2003.

A statement issued by al-Munaduama al-Thawria Quwat Mohammad Rasol Allah in Kuwait, January 26, 1987. For more information about this organization refer to: the Kuwaiti News Agency, January 26, 1987.

A statement issued by the National Democratic Alliance, Kuwait, September 22, 2006.

A statement issued by the Islamic Action Organization, January 6, 1984.

A statement issued by Harakat Talai' al-Mujahideen al-Resaliin, October 8, 1981.

A statement issued by the CM Qatuo' Intakhabat al-Majlis al-Watani (Boycott the National Council Elections), Kuwait, July 5, 1990.

A statement issued by Islamic Call Party, December 21, 1983.

A statement issued by IFLB published in Khamsa Mars (5th of March), November 1979.

A Statement issued by Tlai' Tagheer al-Nidham (al-Jumuhwari al-Kuwaiti), January 1979.

A statement issued by Hizbolla-Kuwait, January 9, 1991.

A statement issued by Hussein Al-Sa'idi, official spokesperson of the NP, Kuwai, December 28, 2005.

A statement issued by the NP, Kuwait, January 28, 2006.

A statement issued by the DJM, Kuwait, May 23, 1999.

A statement issued by National Democratic Gathering, Kuwait, 2005.

A statement issued by the CM Hawl Haqiqat Intakhabat al-Majlas al-Watani (The Truth About the National Council Elections), Kuwait, undated.

A statement issued by the candidates of the general elections held in Kuwait, January 25, 1967, Kuwait.

A statement issued by Political Forces, Hawl Haqiqat Jamiyat al-Islah al-Ijtima'i (Fact About the Social Reform Society), Kuwait, undated.

A statement issued by the Political Forces Hawl Haqaqat Maqwqif Jam'iyat Ihia al-Turath al-Islamiya (Fact about Islamic Heritage Revival Society), Kuwait, undated.

A statement issued by the NYC, Dhikra Istishad al-Hussein (Anniversary of al-Hussein Martyrdom), Kuwait, 1975.

A statement issued by the KNG, Kuwait, 1990.

A statement issued by the KIG, Kuwait, November 22, 1990.

A statement issued by the FKPV, undated.

A statement issued by the National Democratic Alliance, Kuwait, September 22, 2006.

A statement issued by CM Hawl Asbab Mqata't al-Majlis al-Watani (The Reasons for Boycotting the National Council), Kuwait, May 16, 1990.

A statement issued by the ISCGK, Kuwait, September 21, 2004.

A statement issued by the ISCGK, Kuwait, undated.

A statement issued by the ISCGK, Kuwait, January 25, 2005.

A statement issued by the ISCGK, Kuwait, September 10, 2002.

A statement issued by the ISCGK, Kuwait, November 21, 2003.

A statement issued by the ISCGK, Kuwait, April 10, 2006.

A statement issued by the Union for the people of the Arabian Peninsula, September 1979.

A statement issued by the SIG, April 14, 2004.

A statement issued by the SIG, September 18, 2006.

A statement issued by the SIG, the NIA, the ICM and SM, December 21, 2004.

A statement issued by 'Abdallah al-Kanderi the former Chairman of the Teachers Association, Kuwait, August 24, 2009.

A statement issued by the American Embassy on its participation in the meeting of the NP, of the Declaration, published in al-Qabas, January 31, 2005.

A statement issued by the NP on the investigation of the organization of Kataib Usood al-Jasira, Kuwait, March 12, 2005.

A statement issued by Secretary-General of the NP, information office.

A statement issued by the GDFN, Kuwait, undated.

A statement issued by the Secretary-General of the GDFN Mohammad al-Mutairi, published in al-Rai al-'Am, September 3, 2006.

A statement issued by Noerldain Jassim al-'Atar, Hawl Iqamat Masjad li al-Bohra, published in al-Qabas, October 10, 2007.

A statement issued by al-Harakah al-Salafiya al-'Almia (Salafiya Scientific Movement), November 15, 1993.

A statement issued by the ICM, calls on the government and the National Assembly to take diplomatic and economic actions against Denmark, Kuwait, January 28, 2006.

A statement issued by MP Nasser al-Sani', published in the website of the ICM.

A statement issued by Mohammad al-'Olaim spokesperson for the ICM, Kuwait, September 19, 2006.

A statement issued by the SRS, Kuwait, September 18, 2006.

A statement issued by the NDA, Kuwait, September 23, 2006.

A statement issued by SM, al-Moamarah 'al-al-Jihad al-Islamiya fi Falstin (The Conspiracy against the Islamic Jihad in Palestine), Kuwait, November 2, 1998.

A statement issued by the SM, Kuwait, September 24, 2003.

A statement issued by the SM, Itlaq Mobadarat Da'm wa Musanadat mn al-Kuwait li Harakat al-Muqawamah al-Islamiya Hamas (Launching an Initiative of Support from the State of Kuwait to Islamic Resistance Movement Hamas), Kuwait, 2006.

A statement issued by the SM, Kuwait, March 11, 2002.

A statement issued by the DNPG, Kuwait, October 30, 2006.

A statement issued by NCG, July 16, 2005.

Press conference for the NGC, Kuwait, October 22, 2005.

A statement issued by the NGC, Kuwait, April 11, 2006.

A statement issued by the NGC, Kuwait, November 5, 2006.

A statement issued by Tajammu' al-Defa' 'An Thawabit Al-Ummah, Kuwait, September 23, 2008.

A statement issued by Tajammu' Thawabit Shi'ites, Kuwait, undated.

A statement issued by Tajammu' Thawabit Shi'ites, Kuwait, January 20, 2009.

Bayan Raqam wahd Sader 'an Harakat Tanqiat al-Sofoof al-Islamiya, Hawl I'taqal Nakhbah men Shabab al-Kuwait (Statement No. 1 issued by the Clearing the Islamic Ranks Movement, about the arrest of a select group of young people of Kuwait), Kuwait, undated.

Bayan Raqam Athnian Sader 'an Harakat Tanqiat al-Sofoof al-Islamiya, Nada 'Ajal li Amier al-Balad (Statement No. 2 issued by the Clearing the Islamic Ranks Movement, about an urgent appeal to the Emir of the country), Kuwait, April 12, 1996.

Bayan Sadar 'an al-Jaan al-Sh'bia li al-Harakah al-Dusturiyah fi al-Kuwait, Nida men Ajal al-watan: Qatuo' Intakhabat al-Majlis al-Watani (A statement issued by the Popular Committee for the Constitutional Movement in Kuwait, An Appeal for our Citizens to boycott the National Council Elections), Kuwait, June 4, 1990.

Bayan Sader 'an Jam'iat Haaiat al-Tadries Hawl Da'wa li la-I'tasam (A statement issued by the University Faculty Association, Calling for Picketing), Kuwait, May 1990.

Bayan Sader 'an Kataib 'Abdul-aziz al-Maqren (A Statement issued by the Phalanges of 'Abdul-aziz al-Maqren), February 2, 2005.

Bayan Sader 'An Jaisah al-Qaede al-Islami-Wihdat al-Jazierah al-'Arabia (A statement issued by the al-Qaeda Islamic Army the Arabian Peninsula unit), September 22, 2001.

Bayan Sader 'an al-Tayarr al-Salafi Hawl al-Moqawamh fi al-Iraq (A Statement issued by Salafi Trend about the Resistance in Iraq), published in Majallat al-Hejaz', No. 25, November 15, 2004.

Bayan Sader 'an Hayat al-Hamlah al-'Alamiya li Muqawamat al-'Odwan al-Amriky (A statement issued by the Global campaign to resist the American aggression Commission), April 28, 2003.

Bayan Sader 'an al-Tahaluf al-Islami al-Watani Bimunasabt Istishad 'Imad Mughuniyeh (A statement issued by The National Islamic Alliance on the occasion of 'Imad Mughuniyeh Martyrdom), al-Shahid, February 17, 2008. al-Manar, satellite channel, 16 February 2008. Al-Watan, 16 February 2008.

Bayan Sader 'a Munadhamat al-Thawra al-Islamiya fi al-Jazira al-'Arabiya, Mad Hadath fi Makkah (What is happening in Mecca), A statement issued by Munadhamat al-Thawra al-Islamiya fi al-Jazira al-'Arabiya, 1979.

Bayan Sader 'an Ansar Qa'adt al-Jahad fi Balad Arafidan (Statement issued by the supporters of the Islamic Jihad in the Land of the Two Rivers), November 9, 2004.

Bayan Sader 'an Jam'yat Munahadhat al-Tathib Wala'takal al-T'asufy fi al-Kuwait (A statement issued by the Association Against Torture and Arbitrary Arrest in Kuwait), March 2004.

Bayan Sader 'an al-Masadah al-Jihadia (A Statement issued by al-Masadah jihadia), October 8, 2004.

Bayan Sader 'an al-Haraka al-kuwaitiah li al-Taqier (Statement issued by the Kuwaiti Movement for Change), October 10, 2002.

Bayan Sader 'an Lajnat al-diufa' 'an Huriat al-Rai Wata'beir, Hawal I'taqal Dacter Ahmad al Baghdadi (A statement issued by the defense of freedom and expression Committee about the arrest of Dr. Ahmad al Baghdadi), Kuwait.

Bayan Sader 'an Jammiat Adha Haiat al-Tadris fi Jaami'at al-Kuwait about al-Tahdaid biqtial idau Haiat al-Tadris (A statement issued by the University faculty Association-Kuwait University about the threat of the assassination of a member of the faculty), Kuwait, October 23, 1996.

Bayan Sader 'an Harakt al-Rafidain Tali'at Hizbollah in Iraq (A Statement issued by the Land of the Two Rivers Movement, the Vanguard of the Party of God in Iraq), undated.

Country Reports on Terrorism 2008, April 2009.

Dhawabt al-Aqhani (the Songs Restrictions), published in al-Qabas, May 13, 2004.

Fatwas issued by Ministry of Awqaf and Islamic Affairs regarding singing concerts, Fatwas No. (1675) and (1345).

Harakat al-Tawafuq al-Watani al-Islamiya, Ta'araf 'la Harakat al-Tawafuq al-Watani al-Islamiya (Be Introduced to the Islamic National Consensus Movement), Kuwait, undated.

Hawl Tahkeem al-Shari'ah al-Islamiya (On the Islamic Shari'a Arbitration), A statement issued by the IPG, Kuwait, undated.

Hukum Mahkamat al-Jinayat fi Qadiat al-Khalayah al-Irhabia li-Kataib Asoad al-Jaziera (Verdict of the Criminal Courts in the case of the Peninsula Phalanges Lions terrorist cell).

I'lan Sader 'an Jam'yat al-Mansuriah al-Ta'awiniya Far' al-Masbaqh (An Advertisement issued by the laundry of al-Mansuriah Cooperative Societies).

ISG, Lajnat al-Da'wa wa al-Irshad, al-Ndals branch, undated.

Li Takun Thikra Novamber Hafizan li al-Nidhal 'la Tariq al-Taqadum al-Ijtima'i (Let the memory of November to be an incentive for struggle for the Social Progress), A Statement issued by the Communist Party in Saudi Arabia, 27 November 1983.

Manshoer Sader 'an al-Hayaa al-'Amma li-al-shabab wa al-Riyadha (A pamphlet issued by the Public Authority for Youth and Sports), Markaz Shabab al-Faiha, Kuwait, undated.

Memo about the GCC and the regional Affairs issued by IFLB published in Majallat al-Thawra al-Risaliya, No. 59, December 1987.

Murafa'at al-Niabah al-'Amah fi Qadiat Kataib Asowad al-Jaziera (Defense prosecutors in the case of the Lions of Peninsula Phalanges), published in al-Qabas, September 25, 2005.

Murafa'at al-Niabah al-'Amah fi Qadiat Kataib Asowad al-Jaziera (Defense prosecutors in the case of the Lions of Peninsula Phalanges), published in Al-Qabas, September 25, 2005.

Musabaqat kaifan al-Thaqafiah (Kaifan cultural competition), held by the Youth of Sa'ad Bin Abi Waqqas Mosque, 1981.

Nadwat al-'Amal Al-Khairi al-Kuwaiti: al-Waq' wa al-Amal (Charity Activates: Reality and Hope), published in Al-Jarida, November 30, 2007.

Private diary, handwritten, unpublished, written by a member of the National Youth Bloc.

Risalah li Jassim al-'Oun: Risalat al-Nasah (Letter to Jassim Al-'On: an advice from the Muslim Brotherhood).

Risalat Tahdid li al-Sahafiy wa al-Murashaha li Intikhabat Majls al-Umah 2006 Aisha, al-Rasheed (Threatening Letter to the Journalist and the Candidate for the National Assembly Elections in 2006, Aisha, al-Rasheed), published in al-Rai al'Am, March 16, 2006.

Salha, Reem, Barnamaj Sina't al-Moat (The Death Industry Program), http://www.alarabiy.net

Saudi Arabia Backgrounder: Who are the Islamists, ICG Middle East Report No. 31, September 21, 2004.

Taqrir Hawl Nisbat al-Musharakah fi al-Intikhabat 'ber al-Majalis al-Niabiah (A Report about the Percentage of the Participation in the Parliamentary Elections), Markaz al-Qabes al-Ma'lumat wa al-Darasat, 2008.

Taqrir Sader 'an Wazart Al-Shon al-Ijtima'iah wa al-'Amal, Qata' al-Tanmia al-Ijtima'iah

2008 (A Report Issued by the Ministry of Social Affairs and Public Labour, Social Development Sector, 2008).

Text of the proposal for establishing al-Haya al-'Amh li al-Amr bi al-Ma'roof wa-al-Nahy 'N al-Munkar (The Public Authority for the Propagation of Virtue and Prevention of Vice), and submitted to the National Assembly, Kuwait, February 24, 1993.

The Arab Socialist Labour Party in the Arabian Peninsula, Intifadat al-Haram al-Sharif (The Holy Mosque Uprising), Nashrat al-Masira, No. 10, 6 June 1980.

The charter for the Consultative Council, unpublished manuscript, 4 March 1921.

The fatwa committee in the Ministry of Awqaf and Islamic Affairs dominated by groups of political Islamists issued a fatwa regarding the singing performances, which included strict regulations.

The proposal submitted to the National Assembly, February 24, 1993, regarding the draft law Petition to Sheikh 'Abdullah al-Salim al-Sabah, from the IGS about the ways of reform in Kuwait, July 1958.

US Treasury, From the Office of Public Affairs, February 15, 2005. Distributed by the Bureau of International Information Programs, US Department of State.

US Department of the Treasury, Kuwait Charity Designated for Bankrolling al-Qaida Network, June 17, 2008.

Watheqat al-Mabadi Walmuntalaqat li Tawjah Haiat Kiadam al-Mahdi (A Document of Principles and Perspectives to Guide the Committee for Serving al-Mahdi).

Watheqat al-Mabadi wa al-Nidham al-Asasy li Tajammu' 'Ulama al-Moslamin al-Shi'a in Kuwait (Islamic Shi'ite Clerics Gathering in Kuwait), Kuwait, 2005.

Wazarat al-'Adil, Taqrir Itiham Muqadam min Niyabat Amn al-Dawalah to Mahkamat Amn al-Dawalah fi Qadiyat al-jinaya Raqam 410/87–332/87 Salhiya 1/87 Amn al-Dawalah (Ministry of Justice, the report submitted by the state secur- ity prosecutor to the state security court in the case of crime 410/87–32/87 Salhia No. 1 / 87 State Security). Wazarat al-'Adil, Mahadher al-Tahqiqat Niyabat Amn al-Dawalah. (Ministry of Justice, Records of the investigation on behalf of state security).

Websites

Islamic Constitutional Movement.
Mohammad 'Abdul-Qader al-Jasem.
The Liberation Party.
The Nation Party.

Newspapers and magazines

Al-Anba.
'Alam al-Uiom.
Al-Bayan.
Al-Dar.
Al-Fajr.
Al-Haraka
Al-Jarida.
Al-Nahar.
Al-Jazeera.

Al-Qabas.
Al-Rai.
Al-Rai al-'Am.
Al-Rrouiah
Al-Seyassah
Al-Sharq al-Awsat.
Al-Wasat.
Al-Watan.
Majallat al-Azmina al-'Arabia.
Majallat al-Dira.
Majallat Ajial.
Majallat al-Irshad.
Majallat al-Jazira al-'Arabiya.
Majallat al-Kuwaiti
Majallat al-Majallah.
Majallat al-Mossawar.
Majallat al-Mujtama'.
Majallat al-Nasr.
Majallat al-Shira'
Majallat al-Watan Al-'Arabai.
Majallat Manber al-Huraia
Majallat Rasalat al-Kuwait.
Majallat Rose al-Yosif.
Newsweek
Sada al-Iaman.
Sout al-Kuwait.
The Guardian.
Time Magazine.

Satellite channels

Al-Arabiyya.
Al-Hurra.
Al-Manar.
Scope.

Index

In this index notes are indicated by n. The al- suffix is ignored for filing purposes; Therefore for example, al-Mubarakia School is sorted under M.

eBooks – at www.eBookstore.tandf.co.uk

A library at your fingertips!

eBooks are electronic versions of printed books. You can store them on your PC/laptop or browse them online.

They have advantages for anyone needing rapid access to a wide variety of published, copyright information.

eBooks can help your research by enabling you to bookmark chapters, annotate text and use instant searches to find specific words or phrases. Several eBook files would fit on even a small laptop or PDA.

NEW: Save money by eSubscribing: cheap, online access to any eBook for as long as you need it.

Annual subscription packages

We now offer special low-cost bulk subscriptions to packages of eBooks in certain subject areas. These are available to libraries or to individuals.

For more information please contact webmaster.ebooks@tandf.co.uk

We're continually developing the eBook concept, so keep up to date by visiting the website.

www.eBookstore.tandf.co.uk

Made in the USA
Middletown, DE
26 April 2023

29501928R00170